THE
JOURNALISM
OF
OUTRAGE

THE GUILFORD COMMUNICATION SERIES

Editors
Theodore L. Glasser
Department of Communication, Stanford University
Howard E. Sypher
Department of Communication Studies, University of Kansas

Advisory Board
Charles Berger   **Peter Monge**   **Michael Schudson**
James W. Carey   **Barbara O'Keefe**   **Ellen Wartella**

THE JOURNALISM OF OUTRAGE: INVESTIGATIVE REPORTING
AND AGENDA BUILDING IN AMERICA
David L. Protess, Fay Lomax Cook, Jack C. Doppelt, James S.
Ettema, Margaret T. Gordon, Donna R. Leff, and Peter Miller

MASS MEDIA AND POLITICAL TRANSITION: THE HONG KONG
PRESS IN CHINA'S ORBIT
Joseph Man Chan and Chin-Chuan Lee

STUDYING INTERPERSONAL INTERACTION
Barbara M. Montgomery and Steve Duck, *Editors*

VOICES OF CHINA: THE INTERPLAY OF POLITICS AND
JOURNALISM
Chin-Chuan Lee, *Editor*

CASE STUDIES IN ORGANIZATIONAL COMMUNICATION
Beverly Davenport Sypher, *Editor*

COMMUNICATION AND CONTROL: NETWORKS AND THE NEW
ECONOMIES OF COMMUNICATION
G. J. Mulgan

THE JOURNALISM OF OUTRAGE

Investigative Reporting and Agenda Building in America

DAVID L. PROTESS
FAY LOMAX COOK
JACK C. DOPPELT
JAMES S. ETTEMA
MARGARET T. GORDON
DONNA R. LEFF
PETER MILLER

THE GUILFORD PRESS
New York   London

To our children:

*Alexandra, Alison, Benjamin, Daniel,
David, Elizabeth, Jamie, Karen, Marni,
Sarah, Seth, and Sylvie.*

And in memory of Jaclyn.

© 1991 The Guilford Press
A Division of Guilford Publications, Inc.
72 Spring Street, New York, NY 10012

Printed in the United States of America

This book is printed on acid-free paper.

Last digit is print number: 9 8 7 6 5 4 3 2

Library of Congress Cataloging-in-Publication Data

The Journalism of outrage: investigative reporting in America /
    David L. Protess . . . [et al.].
       p. cm. — (The Guilford communication series)
    Includes bibliographical references and index.
    ISBN 0-89862-314-6   ISBN 0-89862-591-2 (pbk.)
    1. Investigative reporting—United States. 2. Journalism—
United States—Political aspects. I. Protess, David. II. Series.
PN4781.J85   1991
071'.3—dc20
                                      91-8932
                                      CIP

Foreword

One of the problems in writing about investigative reporting is: How do you define it? All good reporting is investigative, in a sense, in that it digs and digs. At the *Philadelphia Inquirer,* during the 18 years I was its editor, we usually ducked the term "investigative" and talked, instead, in terms of projects, series, and "take-outs." In this important book, the authors confront the problem right in their title by making it clear that what they are writing about is "Journalism of Outrage."

It is an apt description of a journalistic genre that can trace its American lineage to September 20, 1690, when Benjamin Harris, in the first and only issue of *Publick Occurrences,* exposed scandalous and "barbarous" treatment of French soldiers by the Indian allies of the British Army. "Over three centuries," this book says, "investigative reporters have tried to make a difference by raising public consciousness about perceived wrongdoings and by challenging policy makers to effectuate reforms." There was, of course, John Peter Zenger, who exposed corruption in the administration of William Cosby, the royal governor of New York; and Philip Freneau, who in the *National Gazette* in 1793 accused Alexander Hamilton and other Federalist officials of abuses and irregularities in the sale of government bonds; and *The New York Times* investigation in 1870 of "Boss" Tweed and Tammany Hall corruption; and the "muckrakers" of the early twentieth century who, at their best, turned investigative journalism into an art form.

But it is the post-Watergate era of investigative journalism that occupies most of the pages of *The Journalism of Outrage.* The authors examine the genesis, investigation, writing, editing, and ultimate impact of six modern-day investigative projects. In the process they illuminate the investigative process in a manner that makes the book mandatory reading for students and practitioners of the kind of investigative journalism that pricks at the public's capacity for outrage.

Whatever its faults and imperfections, and the authors find some, investigative reporting has stubbornly persisted and endured in America as a way of seeking reform within the system. It is one of democracy's safety valves. Without it, journalism can become sterile and barren. Without it, a newspaper can become uncaring and bloodless. Without it, it becomes easier for government and our society to develop hardening of the arteries and the heart.

One of the most colorful and skillful of American journalists, the late Edwin Lahey, of the *Chicago Daily News* and Knight Newspapers, used to say that it was tempting to throw in the towel on American newspapers when they pinched pennies to the point of savaging news hole and staff and drastically curbing the newspaper's ability to consistently inform the public. But then when things looked darkest, he said, a story would find its way into his newspaper that would right a wrong or set the record straight, and then, despite the aggravation and exasperation, he would find himself asking: Where else could he find work with such potential?

Will investigative journalism survive what seems to be an inexorable trend toward concentrated corporate ownership of American newspapers? It is often, though not always, one of the more expensive forms of journalism and, thus, especially vulnerable to the kind of corporate management that exalts the current quarter's profit goals above the long-range health of a newspaper and the community it serves. Let us hope the urge to right a wrong is too ingrained in the character of American newspapers and American society to be obliterated.

It is comforting, too, to contemplate that the urge may lie not only in the American grain, but in the human grain. Much of the reform wave that broke upon Tiananmen Square in China was stirred by Liu Binyan and other investigative journalists. And before Gabriel García Márquez shook the literary world with his remarkable novel *One Hundred Years of Solitude,* he shook newspaper readers in his native Colombia with a remarkable investigative series, "The Story of a Shipwrecked Sailor," that probed corruption and venality in the Colombian Navy.

One of the many fascinating insights in *The Journalism of Outrage* comes from a poll the authors conducted in 1989 among 987 members of the Investigative Reporters and Editors, America's leading organization of investigative journalists. The authors wanted to know what really motivates investigative reporters. The hope for larger salaries? Journalism awards? The desire for increased freedom in their assignments? Personal recognition? Or because doing an investigative story "satisfied" a need to improve and reform?

The winner was the satisfaction received from bringing about improvements and reforms. Nothing else was even close.

It gives one hope.

EUGENE L. ROBERTS, JR.
Professor of Journalism
University of Maryland
College Park, MD

About the Authors

David L. Protess, Ph.D., is an associate professor of journalism and urban affairs at Northwestern University. He teaches at the Medill School of Journalism and is a member of the research faculty at the Center for Urban Affairs and Policy Research. He is also director of Medill's Gannett Urban Journalism Center.

Before he joined the Northwestern faculty, Protess was research director of Chicago's Better Government Association, a civic organization that collaborates with the media on investigative reporting projects. He continues to write freelance investigative stories for various publications, and in 1989 he received the Peter Lisagor Award for Exemplary Journalism. His scholarly articles have appeared in *Public Opinion Quarterly, Social Service Review, Critical Studies in Mass Communication,* and *Polity.* He is coauthor of the book *Setting the Agenda: Readings in Media, Public Opinion, and Policymaking* (1991) with Maxwell E. McCombs.

Fay Lomax Cook, Ph.D., is an associate professor at Northwestern University in the School of Education and Social Policy and is a member of the research faculty at the Center for Urban Affairs and Policy Research. At Northwestern, she chairs the graduate program in human development and social policy. She is the author of the book *Who Should Be Helped? Public Support for Social Services* and numerous articles that have appeared in *Public Opinion Quarterly,* the *Social Service Review,* the *Gerontologist, Legislative Studies Quarterly,* and *Government and Policy.*

Cook was recently elected to membership in the National Academy of Social Insurance. In addition, she serves on the editorial board of the *Gerontologist* and as chair of the Gerontological Society of America's Public Policy Committee which holds congressional briefings each year on research findings that can inform policy decisions.

Jack C. Doppelt, J.D., is an associate professor at Northwestern University's Medill School of Journalism. A graduate of the University of Chicago Law School, Doppelt clerked for Illinois Supreme Court Justice Thomas J. Moran before becoming an investigative reporter and news producer. As an investigative journalist for the Better Government Association and WBBM-Newsradio in Chicago, he broke stories on court corruption, housing dangers, and governmental conflicts of interest. His expertise is media law and the reporting of legal affairs. He has published articles on libel, the media's influence on the criminal justice system, and the interactions among lawyers, judges, and journalists.

James S. Ettema, Ph.D., is an associate professor and director of graduate studies in the Department of Communication Studies, Northwestern University. He teaches and conducts research on the social organization and impact of mass communication and telecommunications. His research activities have included a study of media coverage of racially sensitive events, a project sponsored by the Chicago Community Trust Human Relations Foundation; a study of investigative journalism sponsored by the Gannett Foundation; and a project on the business and consumer applications of electronic publishing with a grant from the National Science Foundation. Before joining the Northwestern faculty, Ettema taught in the School of Journalism and Mass Communication at the University of Minnesota.

Margaret T. Gordon, Ph.D., is dean and professor at the Graduate School of Public Affairs at the University of Washington. Before assuming the deanship in 1988, she was director of the Center for Urban Affairs and Policy Research and Professor of Journalism and Sociology at Northwestern University.

In 1989 Dean Gordon coauthored *The Female Fear* with her colleague Stephanie Riger. The book, which focuses attention on the role of society's institutions in women's fear as it relates to rape, was selected by the American Library Association as one of the most important books of 1989. It will be published in 1991 as *The Female Fear: The Social Costs of Rape.*

Dean Gordon was a Senior Fellow at the Gannett Center for Media Studies at Columbia University in 1985 before attending Harvard University's Institute for Educational Management. She chaired the National Advisory Committee on Prevention and Control of Rape, and coedited *Urban Affairs Quarterly.* She is a member of the Ford Foundation's National Selection Committee on Innovations in State and Local Government, the National Academy of Sciences National Urban Policy Committee, and the Governing Board of Common Cause. She serves on the executive council of the National Association of Schools of Public Affairs and Administration and on the boards of several foundations and nonprofit agencies.

Donna R. Leff, Ph.D., teaches journalism at Northwestern University. As an investigative reporter for the Ypsilanti (Mich.) Press, she exposed the murder of patients at the Ann Arbor Veterans Administration Hospital and received several awards for her reporting. She worked as a reporter and editor at *Chicago Today* and the *Chicago Tribune* newspapers. She teaches courses on media ethics, urban problems and science writing and has coauthored several articles on tuberculosis policy in metropolitan health departments.

Peter Miller, Ph.D., is an associate professor of communication studies, associate professor of journalism, and director of The Institute for Modern Communications at Northwestern University.

Miller has served on the faculties of Purdue University, the University of Illinois at Urbana-Champaign, and the University of Michigan. While at Michigan, he served as study director in the Survey Research Center of the Institute for Social Research, as well as assistant professor of communication and sociology and director of the Detroit Area Study.

Miller is past chair of the Standards Committee of the American Association for Public Opinion Research. He is currently the chair of the Faculty Advisory Committee of the Northwestern University Survey Laboratory. He is the author of publications in survey methodology and mass communication, and serves as a consultant to industry, government, and professional associations.

Preface

Investigative journalists are no strangers to controversy. By exposing abuses of power, media muckrakers have had to endure frequent legal challenges, ethical critiques, and political attacks. Yet investigative reporting has survived and even prospered in this often hostile environment.

In the late 1970s, journalism school enrollments reached record levels as young people were inspired by the perceived impact of *The Washington Post's* Watergate exposés. (Whether their role models were the *Post's* Bob Woodward and Carl Bernstein or their movie counterparts, Robert Redford and Dustin Hoffman, is not entirely clear.) A national organization of investigative reporters and editors was formed during this period, and several textbooks were published containing cookbook-type techniques for catching and frying "the big fish." It seemed that investigative reporting was thriving *because* of the controversies it had generated.

In 1981, Northwestern University researchers decided to take a dispassionate look at investigative reporting. Since then, we have examined the techniques of investigative reporting and measured its impact on public opinion and government policymaking. In exploring different dimensions of investigative reporting we have tried to resolve some of the lingering controversies about its nature and effects.

Between 1981 and 1988 we studied six cases of "breaking" investigative stories:

- a nationally televised report about fraud and abuse in the government-funded home health care program
- a Chicago newspaper series that disclosed problems in the reporting and prosecution of sex crimes
- a five-part local television series about repeatedly brutal police officers

- a three-part local television series about the toxic waste disposal practices of a major Chicago university
- a network television report about international child abductions
- a Philadelphia newspaper series about unsanitary conditions and financial fraud by federally funded kidney dialysis centers

With the cooperation of the reporters, who informed us about their works in progress, we studied each of these stories from the point of their journalistic conception through their publication and societal impact. (For a description of our research methods, see appendix I.) We further attempted to put these findings in a broader context by examining the historical roots of investigative reporting, and by making comparisons with other investigative stories published in the 1970s and 1980s.

Finally, we completed survey interviews with more than 900 investigative reporters and editors from across the country. We discuss the findings from these surveys in the first and final sections of the book, and present them in appendix II. They provide a basis for generalizing from our individual case studies to broader trends in investigative reporting.

In Chapter 1, we consider various definitions of investigative reporting and discuss its societal relevance. We call investigative reporting "the journalism of outrage." According to the conventional wisdom about investigative reporting, published exposés outrage the general public, who in turn demand and often get reforms from government officials. We call this linear, democratic notion about investigative reporting the "Mobilization Model." Our research assesses the validity of this model.

Chapter 2 provides a historical survey of muckraking journalism. We attempt to pinpoint its origins, finding evidence of exposés as early as the seventeenth century. We focus on the two periods of sustained muckraking in American history: the Progressive period around 1900 and the Watergate era. We seek to identify the conditions in media and society that explain why this form of journalism has been prevalent in some periods and not others.

Chapters 3 through 8 consist of the six case studies. These chapters attempt to capture the dynamics of investigative reporting by reconstructing the roots of each story, the news-gathering practices used to develop the story, and the techniques of writing or production. They also attempt to specify each story's societal impact.

The final section of the book presents a new theory about investigative reporting, drawing upon the "agenda-building" literature in the social sciences. It pinpoints the conditions under which investigative journalists and policy makers construct their agendas. Contrary to the Mobilization Model, the theory shows how agenda building by societal interests is triggered even before an investigative story is published.

This book portrays a grand reportorial tradition. But it also reexamines conventional notions about the effects of media on society. Investigative reporting not only is an important subject in its own right, but is also relevant to understanding governance in a media age.

ACKNOWLEDGMENTS

The authors are deeply grateful to the many faculty, students, journalists, and policymakers who contributed to our research over the past decade. Several were there at the beginning, when we were a widely diverse and sometimes combative study group—housed at Northwestern University's Center for Urban Affairs and Policy Research, and held together by the belief that media research should be eclectic and multi-disciplinary. They included Stephen C. Brooks, University of Akron; Thomas D. Cook, Northwestern University; Harvey Molotch, University of California at Santa Barbara; Carl S. Smith, Northwestern University; and Tom R. Tyler, Northwestern University. Our collective efforts were nurtured by the faculty and staff at the Center for Urban Affairs and Policy Research; by Medill Deans I. W. Cole, Edward Bassett, and Michael Janeway; and by Dean David Zarefsky of the School of Speech.

Important contributions were made along the way by Thomas R. Curtin, Southern Illinois University; Doris A. Graber, University of Illinois at Chicago; Paul J. Lavrakas, Director, Northwestern University Survey Laboratory; and Maxwell E. McCombs, University of Texas at Austin. Our students at Northwestern offered insight and patience, especially those in the Medill course titled The News Media and Social Reform. Carol Ryzak typed many of our manuscripts over the years.

Earlier versions of this book were reviewed by Robert M. Entman, Northwestern University; Theodore L. Glasser, Stanford University; John W. Kingdon, University of Michigan; Richard A. Schwarzlose, Northwestern University; and Steve Weinberg, University of Missouri and Executive Director, Investigative Reporters & Editors. Their comments were invaluable.

Last, but not least, special thanks is due the investigative journalists who shared their stories and their time to allow this research to be conducted. We particularly acknowledge the support of Peter Karl and Doug Longhini, WMAQ-TV; Jan Legnitto, "60 Minutes"; the late Stephanie Meagher, NBC-TV; Matt Purdy and Jonathan Neumann, *The Philadelphia Inquirer;* Dennis Byrne and Alan Henry, *Chicago Sun-Times;* and Terry Brunner and Mike Lyons, the Better Government Association.

Contents

PART I

MEDIA MUCKRAKING: MEANING, ORIGINS, AND IMPACT

CHAPTER 1

The Quest for Reform

The notion that investigative reporting can be a powerful catalyst for change has gained widespread acceptance in post-Watergate America. For almost two decades, the public has been inundated with news stories by crusading journalists who expose alleged misconduct and right reputed wrongs. The reformist image of investigative reporters has been further reinforced and embellished by movies and books.

The folklore that surrounds investigative reporting closely resembles the American ideal of popular democracy. Vigilant journalists bring wrongdoing to public attention. An informed citizenry responds by demanding reforms from their elected representatives. Policy makers respond in turn by taking corrective action.

This idealized perspective is partly an outgrowth of the commonly perceived effects of exposés published in the late 1960s and early 1970s. During that time, media disclosures of Vietnam War improprieties were considered to have turned public opinion against the war, which led to changes in American foreign policy.[1] Similarly, news stories that linked top White House officials to Watergate crimes were held responsible for the public's loss of confidence in the Nixon administration, ultimately forcing the president's resignation.[2]

In the investigative frenzy that followed Watergate, few questioned the extent to which media stories actually had the impact attributed to them. Instead, the main difference of opinion about investigative reporting concerned its merit rather than its impact. To the political right, the resurgence of muckraking journalism represented a threat to legitimate corporate and public authorities.[3] To the left, investigative reporting created the false illusion that the United States was truly a democratic society whose serious ills could be addressed by merely disclosing its symptoms.[4]

Meanwhile, academicians remained uncharacteristically aloof from the

3

growing discussion about investigative reporting. Despite the proliferation of investigative stories, no systematic effort was made to study their impact. Consequently, knowledge about investigative reporting continued to be based largely on normative and anecdotal accounts of individual exposés, often written by muckrakers themselves.[5] The emphasis in these reports on "how and why I got the story" did little more than fuel existing folklore about investigative reporting.

In the pages that follow, we examine some of the myths and realities of investigative reporting. We begin by reviewing various definitions of investigative reporting, and then offer a somewhat broader notion of its meaning and purpose. Rather than simply viewing investigative reporting as a *process* of news gathering, we also explore its "agenda-building" *impact*.[6] In doing so, we test some widely held assumptions about the watchdog role of media in a democratic society.

THE JOURNALISM OF OUTRAGE

"All reporting is investigative," MacDougall states, "because newsgatherers seek facts."[7] Indeed, the digging process is supposed to be a routine part of daily journalism. From the search for stories to the selection of sources to the format of interviews, reporters and editors ideally *probe* events to find the best available version of the truth.

In reality, however, the hallmark of daily journalism is its reactiveness. Most journalists lack the time or commitment to investigate the richest dimensions of breaking news events. Consequently, investigative reporting is often viewed as journalistically distinctive—a media specialty that involves time-consuming methods and potentially high-impact results.

Most definitions of investigative journalism emphasize its unique information-gathering attributes rather than its societally relevant results. Williams states that:

> Investigative reporting is an intellectual process. It is a business of gathering and sorting ideas and facts, building patterns, analyzing options and making decisions based on logic rather than emotion—including the decision to say no at any of the several stages.[8]

Mollenhoff similarly describes investigative journalism as "a precarious profession. For the most part it is hours, days, and sometimes weeks of tedious work in combing records."[9] Hume characterizes this form of reportage as "tedious and discouraging work."[10]

For some observers, investigative reporting involves a quantitatively different approach to journalism. In MacDougall's words:

The investigative reporter is like any other kind of reporter, only more so. More inquisitive, more skeptical, more resourceful and imaginative in knowing where to look for facts, more ingenious in circumventing obstacles, more indefatigable in the pursuit of facts and able to endure drudgery and discomfort.[11]

Other observers, although still not squarely addressing the civic relevance of investigative journalism, emphasize the kind of facts that the digging process may reveal. Greene describes investigative journalism as "uncovering something somebody wants to keep secret."[12] Similarly, Anderson and Benjaminson state that "investigative reporting is simply the reporting of concealed information."[13]

Investigative Reporters and Editors (IRE), a national organization of more than 3000 journalists, further explicates the links between technique and content in this definition:

It is the reporting, through one's own work product and initiative, matters of importance which some persons or organizations wish to keep secret. The three basic elements are that the investigation be the work of the reporter, not a report of an investigation made by someone else; that the subject of the story involves something of reasonable importance to the reader or viewer; and that others are attempting to hide these matters from the public.[14]

Applying these criteria, the *Washington Post*'s relentless Watergate probe was a "classic example of investigative reporting."[15] In contrast, *The New York Times'* disclosures of Vietnam War deceit in its Pentagon Papers series "clearly was not investigative reporting" because the government-authored papers were "leaked" to the newspaper.[16] Here again, investigative reporting is typically defined by *how* journalists obtain information.

These definitions, although accurate, fail to capture the full flavor of investigative reporting. Investigative reporting is "the journalism of outrage."[17] More than a news-gathering process, the journalism of outrage is a form of storytelling that probes the boundaries of America's civic conscience. Published allegations of wrongdoing—political corruption, government inefficiency, corporate abuses—help define public morality in the United States. Journalistic exposés that trigger outrage from the public or policy makers affirm society's standards of misconduct. Societal indifference to investigative disclosures constitutes evidence of morally tolerable, if not ethically acceptable behavior.

Investigative journalists *intend* to provoke outrage in their reports of malfeasance.[18] Their work is validated when citizens respond by demanding change from their leaders. Similarly, corrective policy actions provide official legitimacy to an investigative story. Investigative reporters find personal satisfaction in doing stories that lead to civic betterment.[19]

By bringing problems to public attention, the journalists of outrage attempt to alter societal agendas. "Agenda setting"—the notion that the news media can directly influence the public's priorities—was demonstrated empirically by mass communication researchers in the early 1970s.[20] At about the same time, political scientists became interested in "agenda building," the often complicated process by which some issues become important in policy-making arenas.[21]

We use the term agenda building to describe how investigative reporters make certain issues more salient to the media, the public, and policy makers. As Lang and Lang state in their study of Watergate: "Agenda building—a more apt term than agenda setting—is a collective process in which media, government, and the citizenry reciprocally influence one another . . ."[22] A basic goal of the journalists of outrage is to *trigger* agenda-building processes in order to produce "reformist" outcomes—policy changes that promote democracy, efficiency, or social justice.

Since the lineage of investigative journalism is most directly traceable to the Progressive era at the turn of the twentieth century, it is not surprising that the president of the United States at the time was among the first to articulate its normative and political dimensions. Theodore Roosevelt called investigative reporters "muckrakers." At the ceremonial laying of the cornerstone of the new House of Representatives office building in 1906, Roosevelt spoke of the parallels between some of the leading journalists of his era and a character from Bunyon's *Pilgrim's Progress*. He referred to:

> The man with the Muck-rake, the man who could look no way but downward with the muck-rake in his hands; who was offered a celestial crown for his muck-rake, but who could neither look up nor regard the crown he was offered, but continued to rake to himself the filth of the floor . . .

The president acknowledged the need for exposés by saying that:

> There are in the body politic, economic and social, many and grave evils, and there is urgent necessity for the sternest war upon them. There should be relentless exposure of and attack upon every evil man, whether politician or businessman, every evil practice, whether in politics, in business or in social life.

But he concluded with a plea for restraint, calling upon journalists to know when enough is enough:

> The men with the muckrakes are often indispensable to the well being of society, but only if they know when to stop raking the muck, and to look upward to the celestial crown above them, to the crown of worthy endeavor. [23]

Roosevelt's speech revealed his recognition of the value-laden character of investigative journalism. The president perceived correctly that investigative reporters are committed to unearthing *wrongdoing*. In this way, they are distinctive from many other journalists, who tend to cover a broader array of events in a more reactive, restrained fashion. For investigative journalists, disclosures of morally outrageous conduct maximize the opportunity for the forces of "good" to recognize and do battle with the forces of "evil."

Roosevelt, whose meteoric political career was aided by the Progressive movement, understood the practical implications of such a struggle. His use of the term "muckraker" showed his sensitivity to the potential threat to incumbent officeholders posed by an unbridled press. Significantly, the sting of the reform-minded president's words was clearly felt by the journalists of the time. The morning after Roosevelt's speech, Lincoln Steffens, perhaps the nation's most prominent investigative reporter, called on the president and said: "Well, you have put an end to all these journalistic investigations that have made you."[24]

Despite Steffens' pessimistic assessment, investigative reporting did not end with Roosevelt's challenge in 1906. It has been practiced throughout United States history, although more often in certain eras than others.[25] In contemporary times, investigative journalism has flourished, and Roosevelt's appellation has retained its currency. Modern-day investigative reporters have been called "new muckrakers."[26]

Although it has become professionally unacceptable for today's journalists to make blatant moral appeals, the new muckrakers have maintained their role as societal watchdogs. Whether by exposing budgetary waste or by uncovering the peccadillos of presidential candidates, the new muckrakers have a mission every bit as linked to the fiber of American governance as their predecessors. Our discussion of this mission begins with an examination of the investigative narrative. In telling tales of villainy and victimization, the journalism of outrage is manifestly relevant to reform.

THE INVESTIGATIVE NARRATIVE

Dale Bakker worked hard at a meatpacking plant in Cherokee, Iowa. He was nearly crippled by oppressive working conditions. Matthew Horace was an excited Philadelphia basketball fan whose favorite team had just won a national championship. He was savagely attacked by a police dog. Kevin Parrish was a 20-year-old student arrested for a traffic offense in Maryland. Held in detention center for less than an hour, he was beaten and sexually assaulted.

Meet the victims of outrageous conduct. Mostly, they are ordinary people made known to others by the tales of investigative reporters. Sometimes their personal identities are not disclosed to protect their privacy, such as victims of street crime or child abuse. Sometimes victims are collective and anonymous, such as taxpayers or voters victimized by political corruption. But all investigative stories reveal some form of victimization with which readers or viewers can empathize.

Dale Bakker is a prototypical victim. As often is the case in the journalism of outrage, we meet him in the lead of the exposé, a 1988 *Chicago Tribune* series titled "Cutting Corners in the Slaughterhouses." Christopher Drew, a *Tribune* Washington correspondent, filed his story about Bakker from the small Iowa town where he worked:

> Knife whipping through the air, Dale Bakker, Jr. slices bones out of hams with breathtaking speed at the Wilson Foods Corp. plant on the edge of this town in northwestern Iowa.
>
> At the rate of one every 10 seconds, Bakker rips through 360 hams an hour, 2,520 a day, 12,600 a week. In the process, he says, he also has ripped up his body.
>
> Bakker, a slim 36 year old with a dark mustache, has had four operations on his fingers, wrist and shoulder to repair injuries caused by the punishment of all the bending and twisting that is his job. Yet he lives and works in nearly constant pain.
>
> His hands tingle and fall asleep on him. He cannot mow his lawn or hug his two children without feeling intense pain shooting up his arms.
>
> Company officials and doctors "all more or less are telling me to find a different job," Bakker admits.
>
> "But I told them, I say, 'Hey, I've got 13 years in packinghouses. I'm all crippled up. Where in the hell am I going to find a job?'"

Bakker's fate seems unjustifiably cruel; he has done nothing to deserve his crippling injuries. Indeed, he is selfless, working to put food on other people's tables. He is a devoted father. Bakker is portrayed as the innocent victim of a system gone awry.

A similar plight is suffered by Matthew Horace. As reported by the *Philadelphia Inquirer*'s William K. Marimow in 1984:

> It was nearly 1 o'clock in the morning last June 1 when an exuberant Matthew Horace bounded up the subway staircases on the east side of City Hall.
>
> Like thousands of others, Horace had come to Center City to celebrate the 'Sixers' sweep in the NBA Championship Series. He was looking for a good time. He never found it.
>
> As he stepped out of the stairwell, Horace saw a snarling German shepherd, followed by four or five police officers, moving rapidly toward him. Alarmed, he turned and began walking fast. It was too late. Moments later, Horace was

clinging to a traffic light and screaming as Macho, a police K-9, ripped his right sneaker off and sank his teeth repeatedly into Horace's foot.

Marimow's story goes on to say that Horace was hospitalized for a week as a result of his injuries. He is described as a "man with no criminal record, then or now . . ." Like Dale Bakker, Horace committed no offense. He is innocent.

The case of Ken Parrish is more complicated. A victim of sexual assault figuring in *Washington Post* reporter Loretta Tofani's investigation of a Maryland county jail, Parrish obviously may have done something wrong to end up in custody. Indeed, his alleged offense was drunk driving. But does this justify the assaults on Parrish and others?

Tofani writes: "The victims of these crimes are, of course, in custody at the time, but most are legally innocent citizens." Parrish was not a hardened criminal, the reader is told. In fact, he was about to be released on $50 bond (put up by his mother) when he was attacked. Parrish may not be as innocent as Bakker or Horace, but certainly he is a victim by any standard of American justice.

The victims in these three exposés are more than individuals. They are representative examples of larger patterns of wrongdoing. Drew's *Tribune* series alleges that "thousands of workers like Dale Bakker suffer painful and often crippling injuries each year" at meatpacking plants across the country. Marimow's *Inquirer* reports uncovered information that "police dog bites had grown to 358 in just over 2 1/2 years." The *Post's* Tofani found "approximately a dozen incidents of forced sex each week in jail for men and women awaiting trial or sentencing."

If scores of innocent people are being victimized in various ways, who is responsible? Enter the villains. Frequently called "targets" by investigative reporters, villains come in many forms. There are crooked politicians, uncaring bureaucrats, and greedy business people, to name a few. Invariably, they are public or private authorities who allegedly have deviated from societal standards of conduct.

The muckraking recipe sometimes contains a witch's brew of evildoers. The *Tribune* meatpacking series, for example, blames both the government and corporate sectors for the problems it reveals. It targets "the dozen or so major meatpackers that prepare nearly three-fourths of the beef and pork served on America's tables," charging they "have raised the production quotas of their workers over the last 15 years to increase profits and squeeze out smaller competitors." It also points the finger at "the Reagan administration [which] has slashed the number of safety inspectors and the power of the Federal Occupational Safety and Health Administration."

Similarly, the *Inquirer* exposé spotlights more than poorly trained or overzealous animals. It also singles out the dogs' "sadistic" police handlers and the department's unresponsive bureaucracy for blame. Reporter Marimow writes that:

> . . . a hard core of errant K-9 police officers, and their dogs, is out of control. Further, the Police Department has made no attempt to hold these men, or their colleagues, to any sort of written guidelines or standard procedures spelling out when to attack and when to hold back.

The *Post's* jail series targets a complex web of villainy. The rapists are to blame, but so are the jail administrators. Then there are the judges, who either put convicted felons back on the streets or "shut [their] mind" to the problem of prison overcrowding. In this instance, taxpayers are both villains and victims by tolerating, yet having to pay for, a woefully inadequate system.

Villains' hats are black, not gray. "Corrupt," "wasteful," "greedy," "lazy," and "scandalous" commonly pepper the investigative narrative. Just as muckrakers intend to engender empathy for victims, they mean to provoke anger against villains. Jonathan Kaufman of the *Boston Globe* readily admits that he "wants his readers to respond, 'Holy Shit!' and 'This is an outrage!' "[27] In a different context, Bob Woodward, who became a *Washington Post* editor after his Washington exposés, exhorts his reporters to come up with "holy shit stories" that are "relevant and of consequence."[28]

By juxtaposing unambiguous villainy and victimization, investigative reporting demands public attention. Through their choice of villains and victims, investigative reporters also frequently command the attention of government policy makers. After all, it is the constituents of elected officials who are being harmed, sometimes by government itself.

Investigative reporting exposes the shortcomings of American democracy and, in doing so, is policy relevant. The formula of the exposé includes a cast of characters inextricably tied to the failures of the American social system. They often include:

1. Elected officials who may be held accountable to the legal requisites of their office and the moral principles of public service.
2. Political office seekers whose public and private integrity may be challenged.
3. Government bureaucrats expected to administer programs properly and enforce regulations in their domains.
4. Business executives whose commitment to corporate responsibility may be tested.
5. An array of victims, including taxpayers and consumers, who expect their public and private services to be delivered with honesty, efficiency, and fairness.

Exposés of nursing homes, for example, commonly uncover:

- Government policy makers who receive campaign contributions from nursing home owners.
- Public administrators who fail to properly enforce their agency's regulations on quality of care.
- Private providers who put personal profit over patient care.
- Elderly people who suffer physical abuse and neglect.

Such characters have been a highly visible part of the media landscape in the post-Watergate era. We examine them in more detail in later chapters.

Despite the policy relevance of these exposés, the potential for change is not unlimited. First, investigative journalists are reformers, not revolutionaries.[29] They seek to improve the American system by pointing out its shortcomings rather than advocating its overthrow. By spotlighting specific abuses of particular policies or programs, the investigative reporter provides policy makers with the opportunity to take corrective actions without changing the distribution of power. Thus, even when muckraking journalists succeed in altering official agendas, the results may be almost imperceptible to the general public.

Second, investigative reporters may miscalculate the boundaries of civic morality. Sometimes, the public or policy makers respond with indifference to exposés of alleged wrongdoing. Perhaps the villains or victims are ill-defined, or the revelations fail to appeal to widely held societal norms, or the problem exposed is mundane or intractable. In any case, such miscalculation can be a source of frustration to media muckrakers.[30]

Finally, journalistic standards and practices may blunt the impact of the most policy-salient exposés. The tendency of contemporary muckrakers not to crusade—their unwillingness to follow up exposés by putting consistent media heat on officials—may inhibit the impetus for reform. This in turn is a function of the lack of time and resources committed to modern-day investigative reporting, and the constraints of objectivity, among other factors.

When reform occurs, however, it is cause for journalistic recognition and self-congratulation. The *Chicago Tribune,* for example, expressed pride in winning the Edgar A. Poe award for its meatpacking series by advertising its accomplishments this way:

> While workers across the Midwest responded with calls and letters, the series' real success was wrought within the industry itself:
>
> - A meatpacking industry trade group voted to spend $500,000 on research into easing the physical strain on workers.

- Federal officials levied the largest fine ever for safety violations on a
  meatpacking company.
- The nation's largest meat company adopted the plan presented in the series for
  addressing industry safety problems. . . .

The *Chicago Tribune* commends Christopher Drew on his award-winning
efforts.

Similarly, the *Philadelphia Inquirer* put the following words in bold-face
type on the front page of the reprint of its police dog series:

Within hours after reading [journalist] Marimow's report, Mayor Wilson Goode
ordered an investigation of the dogs. Within a day, the FBI began an investigation of its own. . . . Four months after the first Marimow report, police-dog
policies have been changed and 10 percent of Philadelphia's K-9 force has been
removed from duty.

Shortly thereafter, Marimow won the Pulitzer Prize for investigative reporting
for his series.

The *Washington Post's* Tofani, who also received the Pulitzer for her
series on the Maryland county detention center, expressed delight in the
changes in jail conditions that followed her reports. "The best stories," she
concludes, "are when you see situations where people are being abused or
their rights are really being trodden upon and through reporting it becomes so
clear . . . that there is the potential for bringing about results."[31]

Tofani's reaction is typical of investigative journalists. Our 1989 national survey of investigative reporters and editors shows that one of their main
motivations is to "satisfy the reformer" in them.[32] In sum, investigative
journalists seek to expose the shortcomings of American democracy in the
hope that change will result—that villains will be dealt with and victims
helped.

RALLYING PUBLIC OPINION? THE MOBILIZATION MODEL

All journalists need audiences. After all, the news media as we know them
today would cease to exist without readers or viewers. But the extent to which
journalists have an obligation to consumers of their product, and more broadly
to the public at large, is a matter of historical dispute.

In the previous century, American newspaper owners were mainly profit
seekers who believed they had limited moral responsibilities to the public. As
one nineteenth-century publisher stated:

> A newspaper is a private enterprise owing nothing whatever to the public, which grants it no franchise. It therefore is affected with no public interest. It is emphatically the property of the owner, who is selling a manufactured product at his own risk.[33]

This expression of the "libertarian theory of the press," as it has been called[34], suggests that the journalism of the time was not preoccupied with achieving societal betterment through an informed citizenry.

Today's investigative journalists reflect a different tradition—the "social responsibility theory of the press."[35] This tradition stems from late nineteenth-century changes in American society and newspaper ownership. The "socially responsible" press is committed to pursuing public enlightment and to upholding standards of civic morality. The press's duty is not just to its readers but also to the community and even to society as a whole.

Contemporary journalism invokes the social responsibility theory by citing "the public's right to know" as its calling. Professional codes of ethics, ratified as a byproduct of the movement toward social responsibility, all prominently mention the duty of modern media to fulfill this right. Thus, although journalism still has no uniform code of ethics—basically because of the heterogeneous and competitive nature of American media and the absence of government licensure—the principle of public service has come close to being a collective professional norm.

For example, the *Washington Post*'s Standards and Ethics, established shortly after its Watergate exposés, state that the newspaper "is vitally concerned with the national interest and with the community interest. We believe these interests are best served by the widest possible dissemination of information." The code pledges "an aggressive, responsible and fair pursuit of the truth without any fear of any special interest, and with favor to none."

The Code of Ethics of the Society of Professional Journalists (SPJ), the nation's largest professional society, contains similar sentiments. Adopted in 1926 and revised most recently in 1987, the Code states under the heading "Responsibility": "The public's right to know is the overriding mission of the mass media. The purpose of distributing news and enlightened opinion is to serve the general welfare." The SPJ Code concludes with a call to further link journalists with a broad public audience: "Adherence to this code is intended to preserve and strengthen the bond of mutual trust and respect between American journalists and the American people."

Similarly, "the primary purpose of gathering and distributing the news," according to the American Society of Newspaper Editors (ASNE)'s Statement of Principles, "is to serve the general welfare by informing the people and enabling them to make judgments on the issues of the time." The ASNE Code states that, to perform this function, the American press should "bring an independent scrutiny to bear on the forces of power in the society, including the conduct of official power at all levels of government."

The codification of the social responsibility theory provides a mandate for investigative reporting. By exposing villainy and victimization, the investigative reporter attempts to achieve one of the noblest aims of contemporary journalism: activating the conscience of citizens to promote the public interest. The journalism of outrage is, thereby, a vehicle for fulfilling the social obligations of modern media.

The ideal of the watchdog press receives considerable support both from working journalists and from the general public. Surveys of news organizations show a strong belief in the need for journalistic exposés. A 1982 ASNE national survey, for example, found that "readiness to expose wrongdoing" is one of the most widely shared yardsticks for evaluating the performance of media companies. Some 90 percent of publishers, 94 percent of editors, and 95 percent of staff members from more than 300 representatively chosen newsrooms rated this readiness at the highest end of a scale of important newspaper functions.[36] Thus, despite the obstacles to doing investigative reporting on a regular basis in all media markets—including cost and controversy—there appears to be a commitment to its value and importance.[37]

Gallup polls in 1981, 1986, and 1989 found substantial public convergence with journalists' beliefs on this subject.[38] The 1981 poll found that 79 percent of respondents approved of investigative reporting, and 66 percent said they would like to see more of it. The 1986 and 1989 polls showed continued strong public support for the press's watchdog role, despite eroding public confidence in the media in general.[39] The report based on the 1989 survey findings reached this conclusion:

> There is . . . a general consensus among the press, the public, and American leadership that news organizations play an important "watchdog" role, with large majorities of all groups sampled believing that press coverage of personal and ethical behavior of politicians helps weed out the kind of people who should not be in office.[40]

Of course, there may be an enormous difference between general sentiment for a vigilant media and support of press performance in specific cases. Repeated instances of alleged media invasions of privacy have generated a growing public concern.[41] Moreover, some of the news-gathering techniques of investigative journalists have received a lukewarm reception at best from the public[42] and outright criticism from journalists themselves.[43]

The public also appears to qualify its support for investigative reporting based on whether it results in corrective actions. This finding is especially important in assessing the societal relevance of investigative reporting. Some 60 percent of the public responded to a 1985 ASNE national survey by saying

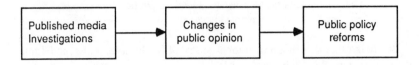

Figure 1. The Mobilization Model of investigative reporting.

that investigative reporting was "worthwhile only if something happens to correct the problem;" just 37 percent said it is "worthwhile regardless of what happens later." (Three percent said it is "never worthwhile.")[44]

These data raise the question that is central to our inquiry: what does it take for corrective action to occur? The conventional wisdom of investigative journalism holds that the general public, once mobilized, becomes a catalyst for change. The notion is that media exposés lead to public policy reforms by first changing public opinion. We call this paradigm the Mobilization Model.[45] Schematically, the process of change is highly linear (see figure 1).

For journalists, the Mobilization Model appeals to both the professional values of organizational sovereignty and social responsibility. In this paradigm, journalists remain independent of the governing process while still influencing it for the public good. The Mobilization Model, in other words, allows journalists to have their cake and eat it, too.

The Mobilization Model also is steeped in democratic tradition. It exemplifies the ideal of an informed citizenry who exerts its will on an accountable government. Clearly, media play a vital role in conventional democratic theory: " . . . the process is that the press tells the public what they need to know, the people then decide what they want, and the press helps communicate these decisions back to policy makers."[46]

There are many examples of this conventional view of American democracy. From the Progressive era, the passage of the Pure Food and Drug Act of 1906 is often cited as evidence of the Mobilization Model at work. As Regier states: "this law may justly be described as the product of muckraking, since it was the magazines which aroused the public to support a reform for which medical associations had long been pleading in vain."[47] Typically, corrective action (in this case, reform legislation) is viewed as the outcome of a three-step process in which published exposés are the original cause and an activated public the crucial intermediate link.

In contemporary times, examples of the Mobilization Model are found in scholarly as well as journalistic literature. Nelson's 1984 study of the crusade to deal with child abuse reaches this highly conventional conclusion:

> Child abuse achieved the public agenda because the interest of a few pioneering researchers crossed the bridge to mass-circulation news outlets. . . . Child abuse

remains a lively topic of media coverage. [And] the public's interest in this newly recognized social problem prompted state legislatures into action.[48]

In their otherwise unconventional study of Watergate, Lang and Lang clearly articulate the Mobilization Model at the outset of their book: "The media were there and the people approved; had the media not opened privileged political negotiations to public scrutiny, or had the polls failed to record public opinion as supportive, Congress might never have moved against Nixon."[49]

Surveys of investigative reporters and editors indicate that many muckrakers subscribe to the conventional wisdom.[50] Indeed, a recent advertisement by Scripps-Howard Newspapers reflects the pride the press takes in achieving the ideals of the Mobilization Model. "The *Albuquerque Tribune*'s investigation of the long-time alcohol problem among Indians in Gallup, N.M., is beginning to show results," the ad proclaims. It goes on to state that:

> This spring, more than 1,000 people marched on the state capitol, demanding reforms. In response to this newly awakened public conscience, the legislature tightened liquor laws and approved new taxes to fight alcoholism. And there has been a crackdown in Gallup on sales of alcohol to the intoxicated.

The ad credits the "impetus for these changes" to the *Tribune*'s six-part series: "In addition to showing how alcohol abuse was allowed, and even encouraged, the newspaper provided fresh perspective and solutions."[51]

These examples show that the social responsibility theory of the press is consonant with the Mobilization Model. In fact, some media watchers equate modern journalistic practices with conventional democratic theory. Mac-Dougall, whose view is that "all public issues are decided by public opinion," states:

> As population increases and all phases of life become more complex, "closing the gap" between governed and governors becomes a major problem in a democracy. The journalistic media have a great opportunity and responsibility to stimulate interest and participation on the part of the citizenry in governmental affairs.[52]

To this end, he proposes that journalists redouble their efforts to activate the public through investigative and interpretative reporting.

Hohenberg points to the rise of "crusading young journalists" as one of the "enormous changes" in media in the last two decades of the twentieth century.[53] He argues that this trend is decidedly relevant to modern American democracy in the following conventional way: " . . . journalism is expanding its influence in the United States. Its impact on public thinking sometimes is of so critical a nature that it has become a factor in the formulation of public policy."[54]

Similarly, Mollenhoff, a former investigative reporter, calls journalism "a profession that gives us the opportunity to be a strong voice and a strong force for good government."[55] He states that "the future of American democracy is contingent upon the performance of the American press. . . . Democracy is contingent upon an informed public with the means to learn what the government is doing."[56] The catalyst for fulfilling this statement of the Mobilization Model is a press that is "independent and aggressive in serving as a watchdog over government."[57]

Not all observers look so kindly on the modern relationship between investigative reporting and democratic institutions. Clark, in applying the logic of the Mobilization Model to international relations since World War II, complains:

> In foreign affairs, the American policy of twenty-five years has been changed or reversed because public opinion changed. It changed largely because for more than a decade, the most influential news organizations unrelentingly challenged the direct exercise of American power overseas and the motives for that exercise of power.[58]

In the corporate sector, Mobil Oil Company found muckraking exposés of business practices to be equally disturbing. Reflecting on "the journalist's power to shape the agenda," the company in a widely published 1983 advertisement attacked:

> the myth of the crusading reporter and the myth of the villainous business (which) suggest a David-vs.-Goliath scenario in which an investigative journalist goes after corruption in business. In actuality, however, the roles are much the reverse of the popular perception.[59]

Saying that the press has a "great power to shape public opinion," the ad urges journalists to adopt a broader perspective on their social responsibilities: "journalists have the responsibility to take a hard look at themselves—to ensure that they are truly open-minded."

Regardless of their point of view, many observers of contemporary journalism appear to share common assumptions about the watchdog role of media: (1) investigative journalism is capable of mobilizing public opinion; (2) the public continues to be the linchpin of American democracy; (3) an outraged public can generate government action against the abuses revealed by media muckrakers.

This view of American popular democracy is not universally shared, however. Most notably, much of modern political science rejects the idea that the general public is directly relevant to the governing process. Lippmann,[60] Key,[61] Schattschneider,[62] McConnell,[63] and Schumpeter,[64] among others, portray the public as highly passive and generally unmobilizable. Special interest groups and other elites, rather than the populace at large, are seen as the key sources of pressure on public policy makers.

"One of the main contributions of American political science," Orren states,

> was the discovery that . . . classical theory provided a simplistic and erroneous description of the democratic process. . . . Empirical research indicated that the American public had neither the knowledge nor the interest to perform the tasks assigned by classical democracy.[65]

Mass media, in this view, may be capable of changing public attitudes, but with minimal consequences. They do not activate the public to participate in civic life, although they may be important for influencing the attitudes and behavior of political elites.

Similarly, in their seminal study of Watergate, Lang and Lang dismiss the commonly held notion that investigative journalists mobilized the public to demand the downfall of the Nixon administration. Their analysis of public opinion polls indicates that the exposés of the *Washington Post* and other news organizations were not connected in time with the administration's ultimate crisis in public confidence. Further, they call the public a "bystander," not a moving force, in the politics of Watergate:

> The preferences of the mass public do not . . . translate directly into executive decisions. The bystander public is in no position to make policy, to draft a law, or even to commit a public body to follow through on a decision.[66]

Some political scientists, however, cling to more conventional notions of American democracy. Dahl[67] and Banfield[68] say that organized pressure groups can be representative of the popular will. More recently, Page and Shapiro's study of public opinion and policy data over a 44-year period found "considerable congruence between changes in (citizen) preferences and in policies."[69] The researchers conclude that "it is reasonable in most of these cases to infer that opinion change was a *cause* of policy change, or at least a proximate or intervening factor leading to government action, if not the ultimate cause."[70]

Page and Shapiro's conclusion that there is a long-term relationship among the media, the public, and policy making points out an important limitation of muckraking as a social and political force. Muckrakers' emphasis on specific instances of wrongdoing (rather than the enduring social issues monitored by Page and Shapiro) and the brief duration of exposés in print or broadcast media limit their potential to hold the public's attention and to influence its opinions. Investigative stories may be sensational, but their public life is often tightly circumscribed. Newly discovered outrages constantly appear on the media agenda and clamor for public attention. Even the most sensational exposés may become mere fragments in the explosion of media content that swirls around readers and viewers every day.

This is not to suggest, however, that investigative journalism has no impact on the public. For nearly a decade, the program of research from which this book has drawn has, in part, monitored the impact of selected exposés on the public. Thanks to the cooperation of news organizations that published these stories, we were able to assess audience effects using a pretest–posttest experimental design. That is, our awareness of forthcoming investigative stories allowed us to conduct scientific surveys of public opinion about the problems exposed in the investigative stories from *before* to *after* their publication. (See appendix I for a description of our methods.) These studies found inconsistencies in the impact of muckraking on the public's agenda of social ills.[71] As we describe in our case studies in chapters 2 through 8, at least one of the investigative stories changed both the public's attitudes and its agenda priorities. Other stories changed the public's attitudes about the problems disclosed but not its assessment of the importance of those problems. Still other exposés had no apparent impact on the public.

There are several possible explanations for these inconsistencies, and it is not yet clear which are the most tenable. However, regardless of the reasons, our findings do appear to undermine conventional notions about popular democracy. If, as suggested by the Mobilization Model, the public is a necessary link between the media and policy changes, then these studies show that link to be weak and unreliable.

Indeed, the studies show that policy making changes often occur *regardless* of the public's reaction. In addition to surveying the public, our program of research included ethnographic studies of the actions of journalists and policy makers. These additional analyses indicate that policy-making proposals may be triggered by *prepublication* transactions between journalists and policy makers.

For example, in our first study there was evidence of effects on both public opinion and policy making. "However, it was not the airing of the investigative report that created the impact," the study concluded. "Nor was it the members of the public who were so aroused over the exposé that they pressured policy makers to act. Rather, it was the active collaboration between journalists and policy makers . . . in the ongoing process of the media investigation that created the policy outcome."[72] Clearly, the Mobilization Model is not the only sort of connection between media and policy.

In chapters 3 through 8 we carefully examine the six investigative stories to capture the complexities of this relationship. Most of our account will tell a story about how these and other exposés influence public policy. It is a story that we can tell with surprisingly little mention of public opinion—at least the sort of public opinion measured by surveys.

THE POLICY PARADOXES OF INVESTIGATIVE REPORTING

On first reflection, investigative journalists and public policy makers would appear to be natural adversaries. After all, as Downie points out:

> The investigative journalist must face the fact that his stories *will* hurt people. While he was working on his story, these people were the enemy—the "targets" of his investigation. They had betrayed the public trust or wronged some individual.[73]

The journalist, in turn, "must be ready for the targets of his stories to strike back in any way possible to try to ruin his reputation, estrange his editors, or gag his sources."[74] Thus, the celebrated clashes between the *Washington Post*'s Woodward and Bernstein and Nixon administration officials during Watergate came as no surprise, given the stakes involved in that reportorial enterprise.[75]

In the post-Watergate era, adversarial relations between reporters and officials have become a recognized cultural phenomenon. Some observers disagree, however, about the desirability of adversary journalism. Journalist Tom Wicker would "encourage the developing tendency of the press to take on an adversary position toward the most powerful institutions of American life."[76] In contrast, former American Society of Newspaper Editors President Michael O'Neill says that "the press has become so adversarial in its relationship with government that it threatens the democratic process."[77]

Political scientist Ithiel de Sola Pool finds the tension between the press and politicians to be natural:

> The politician seeks to lull the people with the pleasantries of government. The journalist seeks the cold, hard facts of government. Sometimes these don't jibe, whereupon the politician reaches for the nearest microphone and assures the people that the journalist is the worst sort of skunk.[78]

Philosopher Sissela Bok is less sanguine about this issue. "Some hold that (media) vigilance must be of an adversary nature—that there can be no truce between politicians and the press," she states. "This goes on too far, since adversary relations engender so many biases (and negative consequences) of their own."[79] In fact, Lipset and Schneider attribute much of the declining public confidence in leading societal institutions since the late 1960s to the critical edge of modern media.[80]

Although the adversarial implications of post-Watergate reporting cannot be dismissed, it also is important to put them in perspective. There may be other dimensions to the journalist–policy-maker relationship. Grossman and Kumar find in their study of the press and the presidency that "it would be a mistake to view the relationship as basically antagonistic. The adversary elements of the relationship tend to be its most highly visible aspects. Cooperation and continuity are at its core."[81] The authors document how White House beat reporters rely on presidential staffers for information. They, in turn, need the press for coverage of presidential initiatives. Do similar kinds of symbiotic ties exist between muckraking journalists and policy makers?

In fact, the interactions between investigative reporters and public policy makers can be exceedingly complex. In news gathering to begin with, investigative reporters naturally are assertive and probing in their search for wrongdoing. Nevertheless, they also must depend on the constant cooperation of official sources—more often politicians and bureaucrats than whistleblowers—to obtain government records and quotes for their stories.

Consequently, investigative reporters must routinely reconcile their aggressive instincts with a pragmatic need to comply with information-keepers' rules. Confrontation has its place, but investigative journalists are more likely to court official sources, go around them, or rely on documents that can be obtained unobtrusively. Occasionally, they may misrepresent their identity to get information, a strategy that raises a paradox of its own: is it proper to lie in order to uncover truth?[82]

Journalist-policy maker transactions may, however, go far beyond the exchange of information. It is increasingly common for investigative journalists themselves to help shape the reform agenda. This may occur in several ways. Muckrakers may share their findings with policy makers whom they know to be interested in the subject matter of their exposé, even prior to its publication, in the hope that official action will be taken. They may spotlight particular programs, or policy arenas, where reform initiatives are languishing. They may point to models of "how to do it right" that have worked elsewhere.[83]

Later chapters examine specific examples of such efforts and discuss the motivations behind them. For now, it is important to emphasize that they are fraught with conflicts for investigative journalists. In choosing a course of action for dealing with policy makers, muckrakers must reconcile the conflicting demands of objectivity and advocacy. They must also decide the extent to which they are willing to cooperate—even collaborate—with officials in the interests of reform, or combat those officials by appealing to a broader audience. How these dilemmas are resolved may well determine the policy making implications of investigative stories.

A further dilemma for investigative journalists stems from conflicts inherent in the meaning of "reform." The goals of investigative reporting, and perhaps of journalism in general, do not conform to a consistent ideology. As Gans states:

> The news is not so much conservative or liberal as it is reformist; indeed, the enduring values are very much like the values of the Progressive movement of the early twentieth century. The resemblance is often uncanny, as in the common advocacy of honest, meritocratic, and anti-bureaucratic government. . . . The notion of responsible capitalism is also to be found in Progressivism, as is the dislike of bigness . . . support of individualism . . . (and) the need for morally and otherwise competent national leadership. . . . The Progressive movement is long dead, but many of its basic values and its reformist impulses have continued.[84]

Nowhere in American journalism are these "reformist impulses" more alive than in investigative journalism. But muckrakers lack a coherent agenda for change.

Investigative journalists deplore government inefficiency. Paradoxically, however, they also oppose antidemocratic practices that may be highly efficient and support widespread citizen participation, which tends to undermine efficiency.[85] They dislike bigness, but they are highly suspicious of local governments, which are small but often wasteful. Fairness is a primary virtue, but so is the system of competition (for government jobs and contracts and in the economy), which often produces inequities. They are at once civic leaders and political cynics. In sum, muckraking journalists lack a clear vision for changing the policy-making agenda they so often want to influence.

Policy makers face their own set of dilemmas. They must decide whether to release information or stonewall, collaborate with muckrakers or blame the messenger, seek solutions to the wrongdoing revealed or rationalize the problem. These dilemmas mandate reporter–official relationships that are, in practice, multifaceted and unstable, containing contrary strains of antagonism and symbiosis. De Sola Pool's metaphors are appropriate:

> The whole relationship of reporter and politician resembles a bad marriage. They cannot live without each other, nor can they live without hostility. It is also like the relationship between competing athletic teams that are part of the same league. It is conflict within a shared system.[86]

To paraphrase Diamond, reporters and officials are like professional wrestlers—competing and cooperating in the performance of their jobs, aware of each others' moves, and yet occasionally inflicting damage, one upon the other.[87]

Whereas the scope of achievements of post-Watergate muckraking is debatable—as is the question of its desirability—few dispute that investigative journalists have become players with whom policy makers must reckon. In assessing the impact of investigative reporting, we find that it may produce a variety of policy effects. We would categorize these effects in three ways: "deliberative," "individualistic," and "substantive."

Deliberative results involve official commitments to discuss policy problems and their solutions. They are evidenced when policy makers respond to media exposés by commissioning studies of the problem, by convening government hearings into the disclosures, or by promising to consider various reform initiatives. The rhetoric of reform is in the air, although nothing tangible has yet been accomplished. Change may occur later, however, as deliberative reform can be a precursor to its realization.

Individualistic results occur when policy makers apply sanctions against particular persons or enterprises. Examples include prosecutions, firings, and demotions. This type of reform is most noticeable when official "crackdowns" occur against those held responsible for the alleged wrongdoing.

Finally, substantive reforms are tangible regulatory, legislative, or administrative changes that occur after an exposé is published. When new laws or regulations are enacted, governmental units created or budgetary funding reallocated, substantive reform has occurred.

In drawing these distinctions, we do not mean to suggest that any one type of impact is more likely than another to *correct* the problem disclosed. In fact, any or all of these initiatives may fall short of remedying the wrongdoing, or may create unanticipated new problems of their own. Instead, we use these categories to describe the types of policy results that commonly have occurred in the wake of exposés we have studied.

We will show, by watching the watchdogs, that the process of American governance may be illuminated. We will also demonstrate that, popular perceptions aside, investigative journalists affect society in often exquisitely complex and paradoxical ways. Since watchdog journalism is itself a creature of different historical periods, we need to consider its roots to appreciate fully the interplay among muckrakers, citizens. and policy makers.

NOTES

1. Floyd Abrams, "The Pentagon Papers: A Decade Later," *New York Times Magazine* (June 14, 1981); and Harrison Salisbury, *Without Fear or Favor* (New York: Times Books, 1980), pp. 7–15.

2. Joan Joseph, *Political Corruption* (New York: Pocket Books, 1974), pp. 75–76; and Salisbury, ibid., p. 442.

3. For example, see Peter Braestrup, *Big Story* (2 vols., Boulder: Westview, 1977); and William P. Tavoulareas, *Fighting Back* (New York: Simon and Schuster, 1985), especially pp. 24–25. In the 1970s, the conservative group Accuracy in Media played a leading role in critiquing investigative reporting and the "adversary press." See Louis Wolf, "Accuracy In Media Rewrites News and History," *Covert Action Information Bulletin* (Spring, 1984), pp. 26–29.

4. For examples, see Edward S. Herman and Noam Chomsky, *Manufacturing Consent* (New York: Pantheon Books, 1988), especially pp. 170–175 and pp. 299–302; and Gaye Tuchman, *Making News* (New York: Free Press, 1978). FAIR, Fairness & Accuracy in Reporting, criticizes the limitations of investigative and interpretative coverage of public affairs. It has been described as a "left-liberal counterpart to the right-wing organization Accuracy in Media" (Herman and Chomsky, p. 390).

5. Carl Bernstein and Bob Woodward, *All the President's Men* (New York: Warner Books, 1974); Jack Anderson and James Boyd, *Confessions of a Muckraker* (New York: Random House, 1979); and, Zay Smith and Pam Zekman, *The Mirage* (New York: Random House, 1979).

6. The "agenda-building" (sometimes called "agenda-setting") effect of mass media—the notion that news coverage influences societal *priorities*—was first empirically demonstrated by Maxwell E. McCombs and Donald L. Shaw, "The Agenda-Setting Function of the Mass Media," *Public Opinion Quarterly*, 36 (1972), pp. 176–187. It has since preoccupied the attention of many mass communication researchers, as we discuss later in this chapter, and has been a guiding concept in our case studies on the impact of investigative reporting.

7. Curtis D. MacDougall, *Interpretative Reporting*, 8th ed. (New York: Macmillan, 1982), p. 225.

8. Paul N. Williams, *Investigative Reporting and Editing* (Englewood Cliffs, NJ: Prentice-Hall, 1978), p. 12.

9. Clark R. Mollenhoff, professor of Journalism at Washington and Lee University and former Pulitzer Prize-winning investigative reporter, quoted by MacDougall, *Interpretative Reporting*, p. 226.

10. Brit Hume, *Inside Story* (Garden City, NY: Doubleday, 1974), p. 63.

11. MacDougall, *Interpretative Reporting*, p. 227.

12. Bob Greene, "Foreword" to Clark R. Mollenhoff, *Investigative Reporting* (New York: Macmillan, 1981), p. v.

13. David Anderson and Peter Benjaminson, *Investigative Reporting* (Bloomington: Indiana University Press, 1976), p. 5.

14. Investigative Reporters and Editors, *The Reporter's Handbook* (New York: St. Martin's Press, 1983), "Foreword" by Robert W. Greene, pp. vii–viii.

15. Ibid., p. viii.

16. Ibid., p. viii.

17. This concept was developed originally by Professors James Ettema of Northwestern University and Theodore L. Glasser of Stanford University in a project entitled "The Ethics and Epistemology of Investigative Reporting." See Ettema, *The Craft of the Investigative Journalist* (Evanston, IL: Institute for Modern Communications Research Monograph, 1988), pp. 1–11; see T. L. Glasser and J. S. Ettema, "Investigative Journalism and the Moral Order," *Critical Studies in Mass Communication* (vol. 6, 1989), pp. 1–20; also see J. S. Ettema and T. L. Glasser, "Narrative Form and Moral Force: The Realization of Innocence and Guilt Through Investigative Journalism," *Journal of Communication*, 38 (1988), pp. 8–26.

18. Ettema, ibid., p. 3. Also see appendix II for supporting data from our national survey of investigative reporters and editors.

19. David L. Protess, "How Investigative Reporters See Themselves," *The IRE Journal* (Spring 1984). Also see Herbert J. Gans, *Deciding What's News* (New York: Pantheon, 1979), pp. 204–5. Also see appendix II for supporting survey data.

20. See McCombs and Shaw (*Public Opinion Quarterly* 36:176, 1972). For literature reviews of research on the agenda-setting impact of the news media on the public, see D. F. Roberts and C. M. Bachen, "Mass Communication Effects," *Annual Review of Psychology*, 32 (1981), pp. 307–356; and E. Rogers and J. Dearing, "Agenda-Setting Research: Where Has It Been, Where Is It Going?" in J. Anderson (ed.), *Communication Yearbook* 11 (Newbury Park, CA: Sage, 1988), pp. 555–594.

21. See R. W. Cobb and C. D. Elder, *Participation in American Politics: The Dynamics of Agenda-Building* (Baltimore: Johns Hopkins Press, 1972). For a discussion of the "agenda-building" process in the Watergate investigations, see G. E. Lang and K. Lang, *The Battle for Public Opinion* (New York: Columbia University Press, 1983). Many political scientists continue to use the term "agenda-setting" to describe the process by which issues become salient to policy makers. See J. Kingdon, *Agendas, Alternatives, and Public Policies* (Boston: Little, Brown, 1984); and O. H. Gandy, *Beyond Agenda-Setting: Information Subsidies and Public Policy* (Norwood, NJ: Ablex, 1982).

22. Lang and Lang, ibid., pp. 58–59. We discuss this "collective process" of agenda building in chapters 9 and 10. We also use the phrase "setting the agenda" in cases where investigative reporting is the proximate cause for moving problems onto the agendas of citizens and/or policy makers, which may or may not lead ultimately to agenda building and policy reforms.

23. Quoted by Arthur Weinberg and Lila Weinberg (eds.), *The Muckrakers* (New York: Simon & Schuster, 1961), pp. 58–65.

24. Ibid., p. 57. Steffens himself recognized the longstanding, deeply moral tradition of investigative reporting. When introduced to an audience as "the first of the muckrakers" by a history professor, he corrected the professor by saying, "I was not the original muckraker; the prophets of the Old Testament were ahead of me." Lincoln Steffens, *The Autobiography of Lincoln Steffens* (New York: Harcourt, Brace, 1931) p. 357.

25. The two eras of *sustained* muckraking occurred in the first decade of the

twentieth century, and between 1970 and the mid-1980s. We discuss the historical roots and cyclical nature of investigative reporting in chapter 2.

26. Leonard Downie, *The New Muckrakers* (Washington, DC: New Republic Books, 1976.)

27. Quoted by Ettema, *The Craft of the Investigative Journalist,* p. 7.

28. Woodward made these statements in a deposition taken in a libel suit against the *Post. Tavoulareas v. Washington Post, Media Law Reporter,* vol. 11 (Washington, DC: Bureau of National Affairs, 1986), p. 1798.

29. They tend to be "responsible capitalists" rather than Marxists. See Gans, Deciding What's News, pp. 46–48.

30. Ettema, *Craft of the Investigative Journalist,* p. 7.

31. Ibid., p. 7.

32. David L. Protess, "Investigative Reporters: Endangered Species?" *The IRE Journal* (Winter 1986). Also see appendix II for more recent survey data on this question..

33. William Peter Hamilton, former publisher of the *Wall Street Journal,* quoted by Fred Siebert, Theodore Peterson, and Wilbur Schramm, *Four Theories of the Press* (Urbana and Champaign: University of Illinois Press, 1956), pp. 73–74.

34. Ibid., see discussion on pp. 39–71.

35. Ibid., see discussion on pp. 73–103.

36. Philip Meyer, *Ethical Journalism* (New York: Longman, 1987), pp. 228–229.

37. See Gans, *Deciding What's News,* p. 118, for a discussion of the various barriers to the widespread practice of investigative reporting. Nonetheless, full-time investigative reporters are found in all media markets, although they appear to be far more numerous in larger markets. See Lawrence McGill, "Priorities in News Coverage and the Role of Beats in the Careers of U.S. Newspaper Editors" (unpublished doctoral dissertation, Northwestern University, 1987).

38. Gallup Poll, "Investigative Reporting Has Broad Public Support," *Gallup Report,* 196 (1982), pp. 31–37; Times Mirror Investigation of Public Attitudes Toward the News Media, conducted by the Gallup organization, *The People & the Press* (Times Mirror, January, 1986); *The People & and the Press, Part 5* (Times Mirror, November, 1989).

39. Times Mirror (1986), p. 41; Times Mirror (1989), p. 10.

40. Times Mirror (1989), p. 10.

41. Times Mirror (1986), p. 30; Times Mirror (1989), p. 45.

42. American Society of Newspaper Editors, *Newspaper Credibility: Building Reader Trust* (Washington, DC: ASNE, 1985). This national survey of the general public found that a minority of respondents approved "somewhat" or "very much" of six common techniques of investigative reporting. The survey showed especially limited support for using hidden cameras and not having reporters identify themselves in gathering information for a story.

43. For example, the *Chicago Sun-Times* was denied the Pulitzer Prize for its 1977 "Mirage" tavern series because prominent journalists accused the newspaper of misrepresentation and entrapment in obtaining the story (MacDougall, *Interpretative*

Reporting, p. 243. For a critique of the technique of investigative reporting by a former journalist, see Tom Goldstein, *The News at Any Cost* (New York: Simon and Schuster, 1985).

44. ASNE, *Newspaper Credibility* (1985).

45. We previously have called this paradigm the "Muckraking Model." See Harvey D. Molotch, David L. Protess, and Margaret T. Gordon, "The Media-Policy Connection: Ecologies of News," in David Paletz (ed.), *Political Communication: Theories, Cases and Assessments* (Norwood, NJ: Ablex, 1987). This model also has been called "popular mobilization" and "public advocacy" by political scientists who have studied the agenda-building process. See Roger W. Cobb and Charles D. Elder, "Communication and Public Policy," in Dan Nimmo and Keith Sanders (eds.), *Handbook of Political Communication* (Beverly Hills: Sage Publication, 1981), pp. 411–412. Cobb and Elder cite several examples in which a mobilized public produced "major policy change."

46. Martin Linsky, *Impact: How the Press Affects Federal Policymaking* (New York: W. W. Norton, 1986), p. 8.

47. C. C. Regier, *Era of the Muckrakers* (Chapel Hill: University of North Carolina Press, 1931), p. 180.

48. Barbara J. Nelson, *Making an Issue of Child Abuse* (Chicago: University of Chicago Press, 1984), pp. 74–75.

49. Gladys Engel Lang and Kurt Lang, *The Battle for Public Opinion* (New York: Columbia University Press, 1983), p. xii.

50. Protess, "How Investigative Reporters See Themselves."

51. The ad appeared, among other places, in *The Quill* magazine (June 1989).

52. MacDougall, *Interpretative Reporting,* p. 416.

53. John Hohenberg, The *Professional Journalist* (New York: Holt, Rinehart & Winston, 1978), p. 9.

54. Ibid., p. 3.

55. Clark R. Mollenhoff, "Life Line of Democracy," in Warren K. Agee (ed.), *The Press and the Public Interest* (Washington, DC: Public Affairs Press, 1968). p. 190.

56. Ibid., p. 175.

57. Ibid., p. 76.

58. Peter B. Clark, "The Opinion Machine," in Harry M. Clor (ed.), *The Mass Media and Modern Democracy* (Chicago: Rand McNally, 1974), p. 38.

59. The ad appeared, among other places, in *Washington Journalism Review* (November 1983).

60. Walter Lippmann, *Public Opinion* (New York: Harcourt, Brace, 1922).

61. V. O. Key, Jr., *Public Opinion and American Democracy* (New York: Knopf, 1964).

62. E. E. Schattschneider, *The Semi-Sovereign People* (New York: Holt, Rinehart and Winston, 1960).

63. Grant McConnell, *Private Power and American Democracy* (New York: Knopf, 1967).

64. Joseph A. Schumpeter, *Capitalism, Socialism, and Democracy* (New York: Harper & Row, 1950).

65. Linsky, *Impact*, p. 8.

66. Lang and Lang, *The Battle for Public Opinion*, p. 21.

67. Robert A. Dahl, *A Preface to Democratic Theory* (Chicago: University of Chicago Press, 1956).

68. Edward C. Banfield, *Political Influence* (New York: Free Press, 1961).

69. Benjamin I. Page and Robert Y. Shapiro, "Effects of Public Opinion on Policy" *American Political Science Review*, 77 (1983), p. 175.

70. Ibid., p. 186.

71. David L. Protess, et al., "The Impact of Investigative Reporting on Public Opinion and Policymaking: Targeting Toxic Waste," *Public Opinion Quarterly*, 51 (1987), pp. 166–185.

72. Fay L. Cook et al., p. 31.

73. Downie, *The New Muckrakers*, p. 12.

74. Ibid., p. 12.

75. Described by Downie, ibid., p. 13ff.

76. Tom Wicker, *On Press* (New York: Viking Press, 1978), p. 259.

77. Michael J. O'Neill, *The Adversary Press* (St. Petersburg, FL: Modern Media Institute, 1983), p. vii.

78. Ithiel de Sola Pool, "Newsmen and Statesmen: Adversaries or Cronies?" in William L. Rivers and Michael J. Nyhan (eds.), *Aspen Notebook on Government and the Media* (New York: Praeger, 1973), p. 48.

79. Bok, *Secrets: On the Ethics of Concealment and Revelation* (New York: Pantheon, 1984), p. 258.

80. Seymour Martin Lipset and William Schneider, *The Confidence Gap* (New York: Free Press, 1983), pp. 403–406.

81. Michael Baruch Grossman and Martha Joynt Kumar, *Portraying the President: The White House and the News Media* (Baltimore: Johns Hopkins Press, 1981), p. 1.

82. For an analysis of this question in the context of investigative reporting, see Sissela Bok, *Lying: Moral Choice in Public and Private Life* (New York: Vintage Books, 1978), pp. 127–129; and Bok, *Secrets*, pp. 259–264.

83. For documentation of these forms of interaction between muckrakers and policy makers, see Protess, "How Investigative Reporters See Themselves" (1984) and "Investigative Reporters" (1986), and Molotch, Protess and Gordon, "The Media-Policy Connection" (1987). Also see appendix II.

84. Gans, *Deciding What's News*, p. 69.

85. For a discussion of the trade-offs between "democracy" and "efficiency" in the context of urban reformism, see Theodore J. Lowi, "Gosnell's Chicago Revisited via Lindsay's New York," in Stephen M. David and Paul E. Peterson (eds.), *Urban Politics and Public Policy: The City in Crisis* (New York: Praeger, 1976), pp. 28–35.

86. De Sola Pool, "Newsmen and Statesmen," p. 15.

87. Quoted in Martin Linsky (ed.), *Television and the Presidential Elections* (Lexington, MA: Lexington Books, 1983), p. 40.

CHAPTER **2**

The Investigative Tradition

The investigative impulse has been a driving force in American journalism. The reportorial tradition of revealing misconduct was already well established by the founding of the new republic. Its practice even predates the publication of the first successful colonial newspaper in 1704. Thus, the press's watchdog role in American democracy has deep historical roots.

Investigative journalists throughout American history have shared a goal: to alter the agendas of citizens and policy makers. The methods and style of investigative reporting have evolved; however, the attempt to influence public debate about policy-related problems has remained constant. Over three centuries, investigative reporters have tried to make a difference by raising public consciousness about perceived wrongdoings and by challenging policy makers to effectuate reforms.

Until the early 1900s, however, investigative reporting was highly localized and episodic. This was a reflection of the character of early journalism, the societal preferences of the times, and the technological limits of communication. It was not until the twentieth century that a unique amalgam of forces combined to create sustained eras of national exposure.

We begin by reviewing examples of exposés published as early as the seventeenth century. Our survey of pre-1900 investigative stories reveals their rich historical tradition, their early character and their societal relevance. We subsequently examine how changing conditions at the dawn of this century spawned journalistic crusades that contributed significantly to the creation of a national reform agenda. Then, following years of relative quiescence, conditions once again became ripe for a new period of investigative reporting—the Watergate era—which resurrected the passion for change of its journalistic forebearers.

This chapter does not attempt a definitive history of investigative reporting. Rather, our primary goal is to identify the societal conditions that produce historical cycles of investigative reporting. We also spotlight notable examples of exposés from these cycles to make comparisons with our contemporary case study evidence.

EXPOSING "PUBLICK WICKEDNESS"

Historians generally credit Benjamin Harris with being the first colonial muckracker.[1] His efforts proved to be short-lived, however. On September 25, 1690, Harris published in Boston the only issue of *Publick Occurences*. In it, he exposed "barbarous" treatment of French soldiers by Native American allies of the British. He also questioned British judgment in forging an alliance with "miserable savages." Four days later, Massachusetts authorities revoked Harris' printer's license.

Publick Occurences was noteworthy in several respects, despite its limited life span. Typical of exposés that were to come, it spotlighted specific evidence of outrageous conduct. Its printer also showed a sensitivity to public opinion by leaving one of its four pages blank to invite readers' comments. Finally, it questioned established public policy, a point that obviously was not lost on colonial authorities.

Thirty-one years passed before another printer had the temerity to challenge public authority. In 1721, James Franklin launched the first newspaper crusade in his *New England Courant*. Franklin regularly attacked Puritan church leaders for sponsoring a program to inoculate Bostonians against smallpox. Documenting cases of smallpox induced by inoculations and alleging that the Puritan program would only spread disease, he prodded authorities to stop it. The eventual success of the inoculations significantly undermined Franklin's crusade. However, in the meantime he managed to generate a spirited public debate on a pressing public health problem.

In the midst of his crusade, Franklin published a defense of watchdog journalism written by two British pamphleteers under the pseudonym Cato. "Cato's Letters" mixed early social responsibility theory with a legal rationale for published criticism:

> The exposing therefore of publick Wickedness as it is a Duty which every Man owes to his country, can never be a Libel in the Nature of things. The best Way to escape the Virulence of Libels, is not to deserve them. . . . It is nothing strange that men who think themselves unaccountable, should act unaccountably.[2]

Armed with this apologia, Franklin proceeded to attack the British for failing to rid the New England coastline of pirates. He also was unwilling to put "Published by Authority" on the masthead of the *Courant,* distinguishing himself from his two Boston publishing rivals. Colonial authorities finally had enough. Franklin was jailed in 1722 for his criticism of pirate policy, and the following year the Massachusetts Assembly forbade him from publishing the *Courant.*

In New York, printer John Peter Zenger's stories about corruption in the administration of Royal Governor William Cosby received a similarly hostile response. In 1735, Cosby's attorney general jailed and tried Zenger for seditious libel. While a jury eventually acquitted Zenger, he abandoned his crusade and began printing official government notices. The message to journalists was clear. The government was willing to harass dissident printers with an array of sanctions as well as reward loyal printers with patronage. Colonial journalists proceeded more cautiously until the period of the American revolution.

Beginning in 1768, publications throughout the colonies burst forth with new challenges to British authority. Newspaper publishers and pamphleteers were instrumental in the battle for independence, both by extolling its virtues and by exposing official misconduct. As historian Thomas Leonard puts it:

> Newspaper exposés—the dramatic revelation of hidden information—show how revolutionary ideology was translated into a language ordinary citizens could use to make sense of daily events.[3]

During this period, the press regularly unearthed evidence of corruption and inequities in British rule. As armed conflicts escalated, they published tales of outrageous behavior by Royal troops. Most notably, journalist Samual Adams and the Sons of Liberty prepared a "Journal of Occurrences" that chronicled colonists' mistreatment by British soldiers. The *New York Journal* disseminated Adams' findings to other newspapers throughout the colonies.

Ultimately victorious in the battle for public opinion and political sovereignty, the colonial muckrakers redirected their efforts after the founding of the American republic. In many cases, they became officials in the new government. By the 1790s, journalists themselves had become intensely partisan. Ironically, the drive for independence produced a press co-opted by the two established political factions—Federalists and Republicans.

Nonetheless, the investigative impulse continued. In 1793, Republican newspaper editor Philip Freneau published details of a United State Treasury Department scandal in his party-financed *National Gazette.* Freneau accused Alexander Hamilton, George Washington's Secretary of the Treasury, and other Federalist officials of improprieties in the sale of government bonds.

The first exposé of the new nation had a contemporary flavor to it. Congress investigated the problem, and several officials were prosecuted. Although Hamilton was not charged, his Assistant Treasury Secretary, William Duer, was convicted of using insider knowledge of bond sales for illegal speculation schemes. The *National Gazette* ceased publication, however, when Thomas Jefferson, its leading Republican benefactor, resigned as Secretary of State at the end of 1793.

Later in the decade, newspaper criticism of Federalist foreign policy produced a harsh counterattack by the government. Eight Republican newspaper editors were convicted of violating the federal Sedition Act of 1798. Although Jefferson pardoned the editors after his election as president in 1800, a familiar message had been sent—the government was willing to try to muzzle journalistic watchdogs.

Throughout the nineteenth century, the press sporadically published exposés of various kinds of wrongdoing. Perhaps the best known of these scandals are the National Bank payoffs in the 1830s and 1840s, the Credit Mobilier affair in the administration of President Ulysses S. Grant, and the corruption of New York City's government by the Tammany Hall political machine in the 1870s. Significant reforms resulted from the publicity surrounding each of these scandals. Most notably, *The New York Times'* probe of the Tammany Hall "Tweed Ring" and Thomas Nast's sardonic cartoons of "Boss" Tweed in *Harper's Weekly* were a one-two punch that ousted many of the city's political leaders.

In general, however, the 1800s was not a century marked by sustained periods of media muckraking. What explains this? Certainly, there was no shortage of problems to expose. Nineteenth-century America was beset by repeated economic crises, domestic and foreign wars, widespread corruption, and serious social problems.

The press's unwillingness or inability to launch intensive, ongoing investigations of these problems may have resulted from a combination of factors. Some were related to the nature of the press in the 1800s. Others were caused by the limitations of nineteenth-century technology, by the conduct of the government, and by demographic factors.

In the first three decades of the nineteenth century, the partisan press generally focused its attacks on the character of the opposition party's leaders. This was sometimes an effective technique for winning public opinion to its cause. However, it distracted attention from the scrutiny of public policy abuses, the hallmark of investigative journalism. As Leonard states:

> The way to investigate a native, elected, governing class was not clear . . . shock tactics were soon tried. Hamilton, Jefferson, even Washington, found their character blackened. . . . The early press is best defined by the political information it did not offer and the questions it had not yet learned to ask.[4]

By the 1830s, the press's emphasis had shifted to covering political speeches. Traveling in packs, journalists competed mainly to provide colorful accounts of what lawmakers said. Independent and aggressive reporting of public affairs was virtually abandoned. Leonard states that "journalist and politician labored together sending speeches out to the people, convinced that this political reporting would win over a democracy."[5]

At the same time, a new form of newspaper was born that made the news of the day available to a wider segment of the populace through reduced prices and street sales. The penny press, as it was called, became the dominant media enterprise during the middle decades of the century. These newspapers often were cheap in other ways besides cost, providing sensationalized coverage of the details of crime and vice. Still, the penny press was mostly independent of partisan politics, and it showed an occasional willingness to expose government corruption and to editorialize about pressing public policy matters. In these ways, it carried on the investigative tradition and, according to Schudson, was an important forerunner of modern "public service" journalism.[6]

Toward the end of the century, newspaper publishing barons—Joseph Pulitzer, William Randolph Hearst, Adolph S. Ochs, E. W. Scripps, Joseph Medill, and others—infused new life into America's media. These men were political mavericks who were not reluctant to probe the spoils of power. Indeed, their big-city newspapers published some of the most important investigative stories of the 1870s and 1880s. Pulitzer's *St. Louis Post-Dispatch,* for example, attacked Democrats and Republicans alike, along with private gas and streetcar monopolies, gambling halls, and brothels in the early 1880s.

Until the last decade of the century, however, several important factors hindered the potential for a sustained era of exposure. First, the nineteenth-century American press was not imbued with a strong sense of social responsibility.[7] Most publications survived by appealing to narrow (but predictable) readership interests, rather than to the community as a whole. Thus, when they preached politically, it was to the converted; documenting wrongdoing to outrage the general public was not a primary component of their marketing strategy.

The highly fragmented and localized organization of nineteenth-century media further limited the potential for widespread journalistic crusades. The lack of a strong national press network—chains had not yet been established and the wire services emphasized the superficial and inoffensive—circumscribed the national marketplace of public affairs.[8] Pre-1900 exposés thereby tended to be flares, temporarily illuminating local problems without changing the priorities of the nation.

Besides the nature of newspapers, the government and the citizenry placed further inhibitions on the investigative impulse. The legal harassment of journalists common before 1800 continued unabated into the nineteenth century.[9] Libel laws, both criminal and civil, were used with impunity against journalistic critics of officialdom. (President Thomas Jefferson himself encouraged the criminal libel prosecution in 1804 of a newspaper editor who had accused the president of misconduct.[10]) Informal and military censorship were common in times of national crisis. Sometimes financially struggling publishers simply shut their presses rather than press their rights in court.

Government officials could also be benefactors to quiescent journalists. Being designated the publisher of official notices was a lucrative enterprise not shared by obstreperous newspaper editors. In fact, one explanation for why journalists ignored the corruption of New York's political machine before 1871 was that "journalism was a business with a common-sense rule: boosting paid, knocking did not."[11]

Further, the general public probably was not ready for ambitious newspaper crusades in the 1800s. At various junctures, alienation from authority was widespread, creating fertile ground for muckraking stories. However, illiteracy also was extensive until the last decades of the century, especially among social classes to whom stories about abuses of authority would have the most potential appeal.[12] Consequently, citizen disaffection with government policy often expressed itself in the form of public protest rather than published exposés.

The rise of populism in the 1890s provided an opportunity for the journalism of outrage to be practiced vigorously. But despite the populist movement's appeal to largely literate, politically aware, and alienated audiences, it failed to trigger an era of muckraking. Urban journalists, then the dominant figures in the newspaper publishing business, were not attracted by the populists' more agrarian-based message and movement.

Thus, it was not until the early 1900s that a unique combination of societal forces created America's first widespread and sustained period of investigative reporting. This is not to diminish the accomplishments of pre-1900s muckrakers. There is little question that they sometimes influenced the agendas of citizens and policy makers in the early course of American history. They also established a journalistic tradition on which their successors built. It took more than two centuries, however, for investigative reporting finally to occupy a substantial part of the journalistic landscape.

THE GOLDEN AGE OF MUCKRAKING

The dawning of the new century brought numerous changes in media and society. Conditions were ripe for an unprecedented decade of disclosure. President Theodore Roosevelt coined the term "muckraking" during this period. It would also be called the "golden period of public service journalism."[13]

In particular, two forces were present in American society that fueled the investigative impulse. First, widespread alienation from authority—government and corporate—had begun to pervade the literate middle and upper middle classes. With the industrial revolution, average Americans witnessed the rise of a burgeoning class of nouveau riche who wielded considerable influence over government and the economy.

At the other end of the economic scale, the arrival of immigrants to the cities fostered the rise of machine politics, displacing middle Americans from power at the local level. A sharp increase in inflation after 1897 added economic woes to their growing sense of political alienation. Squeezed from the top and bottom, white collar workers, professionals, and small business people sought expression for their discontent.

Their answer was the founding of the Progressive movement, of which muckraking journalism was an instrumental part. Hofstadter explains:

> The promise of social progress was not to be realized by sitting and praying, but by using the active powers—by the exposure of evils through the spreading of information and the exhortation of the citizenry. . . . It was this that "the muckrakers" thought gave special value to their voluminous and effective exposures of corruption, crime, waste, brutality, and autocracy in the dark corners of American life: they hoped that people would not read their sordid stories just for their shock value but that they would be filled with the desire to do something about corrupt bosses, sweated labor, civic decay, monopolistic extortion. If the people were sufficiently aroused, they would wrest power away from city and state bosses, millionaire senators, and the other minions of invisible government and take it back into their own hands.[14]

Herein lies the basis for the Mobilization Model discussed in chapter 1—a theoretical pronouncement of the reformist implications of investigative reporting.

Clearly, changes in the press were a prerequisite for fulfilling this mission. Indeed, the American news media were evolving significantly by the end of the nineteenth century. Between 1870 and 1900, the total number of daily newspapers increased fourfold, and their circulation jumped from 6.5 percent to 19.8 percent of the American population.[15] By 1916, there were 2,461 daily newspapers, the largest number ever to exist in American history—before or since.

Increased media competition occurred in other ways as well. The rise of newspaper chains just prior to the twentieth century produced intense rivalries between news organizations, as well as between their publishers. Magazines were also becoming a major competitive force in the publishing industry.

Their number increased from 1,200 in 1870 to 5,500 in 1900, accompanied by falling prices and a shift in content from literary works to hard news.

Significantly, a nationwide press network was emerging from these new forces in journalism. The national chains were able to publicize or reprint stories that appeared in their metropolitan dailies. The magazine explosion reached a national readership on a regular basis through a greatly expanded postal system that only recently had introduced Rural Free Delivery.[16] New publishing technologies increased the speed and lowered the cost of disseminating the news of the day, thereby further maximizing the potential to reach a mass audience. That audience—a fresh market for a revitalized media—proved to be urban Middle America.

In sum, the historical pendulum swung toward muckraking as two mutually reinforcing phenomena converged: the demand for information about societal ills from an alienated, literate population of consumers; and a fiercely competitive national media that sought to supply it. No convergence of similar forces had occurred prior to 1900, and none would occur again until the late 1960s.

Despite the uniqueness of the muckraking era, the formula of the exposé borrowed heavily from earlier times. The emphasis on abuses of authority was as old as Benjamin Harris's Publick Occurences in 1690 and as fresh as *The New York Times* and *Harper's Weekly* attacks on Tammany Hall in 1870-1871. The focus on moral disorder came straight from the penny press's spotlight on crime and vice.

Muckraking publications had the politically independent streak of Joseph Pulitzer's *St. Louis Post-Dispatch.* They used the pictorial vividness of Thomas Nast's illustrations of the Tweed Ring, the colorful cartoons of William Randolph Hearst's *New York Journal,* and the raucous editorial tone of the revolutionary war pamphleteers. Borrowing from James Franklin's *New-England Courant* and many others, they documented individual cases of abuse to crusade for systemic societal reform. Early 1900s muckraking, then, was an amalgam of past journalistic practices rolled into one sustained national movement.

Perhaps the most curiously original aspect of the golden age of muckraking, besides its scope and intensity, was its focus—or lack thereof. Muckraking villains were everywhere. Businessmen, politicians, church leaders, and even journalists themselves did not escape scrutiny. Muckrakers often shot high, and rarely missed their targets. As Edward Ross, a scholar and muckraker in his own right, said:

> Unlike the old-time villain, the latter-day malefactor does not wear a slouch hat and a comforter, breathe forth curses and an odor of gin, go about his nefarious work with clenched teeth and an evil scowl. . . . The modern high-power dealer

of woe wears immaculate linen, carries a silk hat and a lighted cigar, sins with a callous countenance and a serene soul, leagues or months from the evil he causes.[17]

Juxtaposing villainy and victimization, Ross adds that "Drunk with power . . . they boldly make their stand, ruining the innocent."[18]

First, the villains. In general, the muckrakers focused their attention on three targets: big business, power politics, and social injustice. Often, the wrongdoers were described as interconnected. In the muckraking formula, big business corrupted powerful politicians, which resulted in social injustice. But the corporate sector usually received the lion's share of the blame.

The national magazines led the attack on America's economic elite. In November 1902, *McClure's* monthly published the first installment of Ida M. Tarbell's "History of the Standard Oil Company." Tarbell traced Chairman John D. Rockefeller's rise to wealth and power, documenting how "under the combined threat and persuasion of the Standard . . . almost the entire independent oil interest of Cleveland collapsed in three months' time."[19]

Typical of muckraker's methods, Tarbell relied heavily on court records to make her case. Also typical was her goal of telling "the story of a representative monopoly"[20] to illustrate the broader problem of trusts, rather than merely targeting Rockefeller for the sake of individual exposure. In true crusading fashion, *McClure's* published 18 articles by Tarbell on the monopolistic practices of Standard Oil.

Tarbell's series opened the door for other stories about corporate improprieties. Suddenly, it seemed all big businesses had become fair game for reportorial disclosures. In 1905, *Cosmopolitan* exposed the anticompetitive practices of the International Harvester Company. In 1905–1906, *World's Work* magazine published a six-part series on corruption in the insurance industry. *McClure's* and *Collier's* targeted railroad industry payoffs in 1906. The next year, windfall profit by the banking industry was the subject of four articles in *World's Work*. In 1909, *Cosmopolitan* exposed the sugar trust's practices of false-weighting and bribing politicians, while *Hampton's* uncovered the General Electric Company's attempts to monopolize water power.

But the most widely read exposé of industry during this period was written by Upton Sinclair. Sinclair had spent 7 weeks at Chicago's meatpacking plants in 1904. He gathered information by working "undercover" at the stockyards: "He simply put on a pair of overalls, picked up a metal lunch pail, and blended in with the crowds of butcher workmen."[21] The following year, *Appeal To Reason,* a socialist weekly, began publishing Sinclair's fictionalized account of his experiences. When company officials attacked the series,

Sinclair responded with factual rebuttals in *Collier's* and *Everybody's* magazines.

It was not until Sinclair's novel, *The Jungle,* was published in early 1906 that his accounts of unsanitary meat processing and unsafe working conditions reached mass public and political audiences. The book became a best-seller and contributed to the passage of the Pure Food and Drug Act six months later. Sinclair, a socialist, was not completely satisfied with this result. "I wished to frighten the country by a picture of what its industrial masters were doing to their victims," he wrote.[22] "I aimed at the public's heart, and by accident I hit it in the stomach."[23]

Other muckrackers, whose vision was more reformist and less radical than Sinclair's, pressed the attack on governmental wrongdoing. In October 1902, *McClure's* published an exposé of the municipal spoils system entitled "Tweed Days in St. Louis." This proved to be the first of ten articles by Lincoln Steffens for *McClure's* about local government waste and corruption. Steffens drew national attention to wide-ranging abuses of power in Minneapolis, Pittsburgh, Philadelphia, Cleveland, Cincinnati, New York, and Chicago.

The muckraking tone of Steffens articles was typified by his October, 1903 description of Chicago:

> The police graft, the traffic of authority with criminals, gamblers, prostitutes, liquor dealers, all sorts of thieves, and some sorts of murderers. The evil in Chicago was obvious, general, bold.

These articles formed the basis for Steffens' influential 1904 book, *The Shame of the Cities*. The same year, Steffens was the first of the muckrakers to expose corruption in state politics, which became a popular target of newspapers and magazines for the rest of the decade.

At the federal level, Congress was the most frequent recipient of muckraking treatment. Undoubtedly the most stunning of these exposés was published in 1906 by *Cosmopolitan*. David Graham Phillips' "The Treason of the Senate," a nine-part series, began with a photograph of the wealthy and allegedly corrupt United States Senator from New York, Chauncey Depew. Depew appeared to be laughing in the reader's face. This first use of candid photography by muckrakers had a profound impact similar to Thomas Nast's illustrations of Tammany Hall's Boss Tweed three decades earlier. It led to the widespread use of visual techniques to dramatize villainy. Phillips' series also prompted President Theodore Roosevelt to coin the appellation "muckraker."[24]

The crusades against government and corporate venality were accompanied by a fight for social justice as journalistic watchdogs took up the cause of social and economic underdogs. At the turn of the century, Jacob Riis exposed the conditions of New York tenement slums in two metropolitan newspapers and later in books. In 1905, *Public Opinion* magazine's Daniel T. Pierce reported 66,000 fatal accidents and two million injuries incurred on the job by working people. The next year, Edwin Mar muckraking theme, especially in the writing of *Cosmopolitan.* Mistreatment of minorities was a common muckraking theme, especially in the writing of Ray Stannard Baker for *McClure's* and *American Magazine.*

Ida Tarbell struck a common chord among writers in describing Rhode Island textile plants for *American Magazine:*

> The laborers in the chief industry underpaid, unstable, and bent with disease, the average employers rich, self-satisfied, and as indifferent to social obligations as so many robber barons.[25]

To the muckrakers, villainy was inextricably linked to victimization and social injustice. For every greedy businessman, there was a helpless child, immigrant, minority member, or worker who suffered. For every crooked politician, there was a taxpayer whose pocket was picked.

The general population was portrayed both as victim and villain. As alienated members of the middle and upper middle classes, muckrakers harped on the theme of pervasive powerlessness, which they experienced personally.[26] But as Progressive activists, they *blamed* those in the populace who were unwilling to do something about existing conditions. They exhorted their readers to make democracy work, but they also criticized them for allowing the abuses to go on. *Cosmopolitan's* exposé of International Harvester typified this tack: "The whole presents a condition of fiscal bloodsucking; permitted by the people, who are as sheep." [27]

This somewhat unusual approach to cultivating readership apparently did not hinder the spread of muckraking publications. The circulation of the ten magazines that regularly published exposés skyrocketed between 1902 and 1912. One study estimates a readership in 20 million households in a nation with 90 million people.[28]

Moreover, the muckraking message of the popular periodicals was reinforced by the efforts of daily newspapers. In some instances, big-city dailies launched independent probes of problems in their own backyards. More commonly, they crusaded on issues that initially were disclosed by the muckraking vanguard, the national magazines. Either way, the reach of local muckrakers was broadened by an expanded press network that included newspaper chains and three national wire services established between 1900 and 1910. Because of various print media, "the great majority of American families with anything topical to read were exposed to muckraking material."[29]

But did this mean that the journalism of outrage *changed* public opinion, or that policy reforms followed? Since scientific surveys of public opinion were not available in the early 1900s, the answer to the former question is uncertain—though some historians suggest that it did.[30] Most likely, the same societal conditions that bred muckraking journalism also fueled citizen outrage, allowing journalistic practices and public alienation to feed off each other.

On the question of policy impact, the evidence is clearer. Muckraking journalism was inextricably linked to a variety of reforms. The crusades against corporate monopolies contributed to the enforcement of the Sherman Antitrust Act. The attacks on unequal distribution of wealth helped lead to the ratification of a constitutional amendment creating federal income taxes in 1909. Child labor laws were enacted in most states during this period. Workman's compensation laws were passed in 25 states by 1915, and 20 states enacted mother's pension laws between 1908 and 1913.

As has been mentioned, the Pure Food and Drug Act was passed one-half year after the publication of the *The Jungle*. *Collier's* and *Success* magazines crusaded heavily for its passage, as did the *New York World* and the *Kansas City Star*. In his 1988 *Chicago Tribune* series, "Cutting Corners in the Slaughterhouse" (see chapter 1), reporter Christopher Drew took note of the genesis of his modern-day investigative story:

> The plight of the slaughterhouse worker served as a moving force in the drive for industrial safety in the 20th century. It was working conditions at slaughterhouses in Chicago that provided the setting for Upton Sinclair's muckraking novel, "The Jungle." And it was "The Jungle" that sparked reforms and increased workplace safety through legislation and union pressure that extended into the 1970s.

On other fronts, the exposés of social injustice, antidemocratic practices, and political spoils also were connected to significant government changes. The passage of city building codes followed the published attacks on tenement conditions. An array of democratic reforms—the ratification of a constitutional amendment in 1912 to provide for the direct election of United States Senators, and changes in state election laws to allow for direct primaries, legislative referenda, and recalls of officials—were linked to exposés of political elitism. The rise of municipal reform legislation to curtail wasteful and corrupt practices paralleled the stories by Steffens and others.

"Substantive" reform, as we called this earlier, became a reality during the muckraking period. Government regulation and redistribution were the hallmarks of this "age of reform."[31] The muckrackers' contributions to changing public policy agendas cannot be overstated. Indeed, their exposés often contained specific recommendations for reforms that officials later adopted.

What is less certain, however, is the validity of the Mobilization Model for describing the *sequence* of events that generated the reforms. We already have concluded that the rise of muckraking journalism and changes in public opinion are most likely the product of mutually reinforcing conditions, rather than the latter resulting from the former. Did either or both "cause" the governmental changes we have identified?

The conventional wisdom states that the catalyst for reform is an outraged public, mobilized by journalistic disclosures. This linear notion of the workings of popular democracy may have occurred in some instances, with the passage of the Pure Food and Drug Act most often cited as the prime example. However, there also may have been other routes to reform.

At the federal level, President Theodore Roosevelt was a close collaborator of many of the muckrakers, whom he often invited to the White House to discuss the nation's reform agenda.[32] Immediately after publication of *The Jungle,* for example, the president met frequently with the socialist Sinclair to devise a strategy for change which both men promised to keep quiet.[33] "Sinclair gave advice to the President—sometimes more than once a day—on how to regulate the meat packing industry through legislation," Leonard states.[34] After the passage of the Pure Food and Drug Act, Roosevelt said to F. N. Doubleday, publisher of *The Jungle*: "Tell Sinclair to go home and let me run the country for awhile."[35]

Roosevelt also was a friend of Lincoln Steffens. The two men had known each other well since the mid-1890s, when Steffens was a police reporter for the *New York Post* and Roosevelt was a New York City police commissioner. As president, Roosevelt was willing not only to support Steffens' programs for reform but also to give Steffens considerable help in documenting his tales of government malfeasance. In 1906, Roosevelt ordered "all officials of the government" to cooperate with Steffens' investigation of federal corruption, enabling the muckraker to write ten weekly articles for a newspaper syndicate.[36]

At the state and local levels, the election of Progressive reformers to government office allowed muckraking journalists to establish similar close ties to officialdom. Although muckrakers painted political corruption with broad strokes in their exposés, they knew how to discriminate between "supportive" and "evil" politicians in their personal and professional relationships.[37] In sum, the connection between muckrakers and policy makers may have been less remote and adversarial than the conventional wisdom mandates.

Moreover, it is doubtful that the public was as active in demanding reform as the Mobilization Model suggests. Curiously, at the same time that the circulation of muckraking magazines rose, the amount of public participation in politics declined. Voting data show a precipitous drop in registration and turnout in all national elections and most state and local contests as the muckraking era advanced.[38] This may have been caused, paradoxically, by the muckrakers' attack on the legitimacy of electoral politics and governmental institutions. It also may have resulted from the declining strength of political parties, especially at the municipal level, which suffered under the weight of Progressive legislation. In either case, the notion that civic awareness and activism prompted government reforms in the wake of muckraking disclosures may be exaggerated.

The timing of reforms further calls into question the basic premises of the Mobilization Model. Roosevelt ordered the enforcement of antitrust legislation in 1902, *prior* to the start of muckraking crusades against the robber barons. In many instances, including the battle against municipal spoils and the fight for unadulterated food and drugs, reform legislation had been passed or was high on policy makers' agendas well before the publication of muckraking stories. (A Pure Food and Drug bill, for example, was awaiting action in the Congress prior to the publication of *The Jungle*.)

There is no doubt that muckraking crusades and the changing climate of public opinion significantly facilitated the enactment of reforms, but perhaps not in that order. The shifting policy agenda in the first decade of the twentieth century was the result of an unprecedented convergence of developments in media and society. So tenuous was this combination that by 1912 the muckraking era came to a virtual halt. As we shall discuss, muckraking journalism had in part become a victim of its own success.

THE RETURN TO QUIESCENCE

The golden age of muckraking, despite its intensity and impact, lasted little more than a decade. The era of exposure reached its peak in 1906 then declined somewhat in 1907–1908. The retreat from reform during the Taft presidency breathed new life into journalistic investigations, but by 1912 they were reduced to a trickle. With the onset of World War I, the muckraking era ended.

The twin forces that drove the historical pendulum toward sustained muckraking—changes in the composition of the press and the confidence of the public—combined in a different form to move media back to a lengthy period of relative quiescence. First, the competitive instabilities that marked late nineteenth-century media diminished after 1910. The dramatic growth of newspapers leveled off by the end of the first decade of the twentieth century and fell between 1910 and 1920 for the first time in American history.[39] More telling, the percentage of cities with competing daily newspapers declined from 57.1 percent to 42.6 percent between 1910 and 1920.[40]

The number of magazines also peaked in 1910, and then dropped precipitously in the next decade.[41] Significantly, this decline was attributable in part to a withdrawal of corporate advertising from muckraking publications.[42] *American Magazine* and *Everybody's* were forced into bankruptcy when hostile bankers stopped extending them credit. Some of the muckraking magazines, including *McClure's,* were purchased by large corporations and subsequently softened their content.

The diminishing media rivalry meant fewer toe-to-toe battles to out-expose the competition. It also blunted the press's interest in crusading for causes on which they had placed their mark. Clearly, one result of these changes was a reduced effort to mobilize the public. Another was to turn down the heat on policy makers.

Although coercive measures taken against the press contributed to the curbing of the investigative impulse, they do not primarily explain the change in direction after 1910. If fact, the aforementioned private pressures were not accompanied by government efforts to chill the muckraking media. There were no recorded instances of censorship or criminal libel prosecutions between 1900 and World War I. Further, there were relatively few civil libel suits against the press, and almost all were dismissed by the courts.[43]

Indeed, muckraking journalists found friends in the government. Ironically, one of the most important developments that contributed to the end of the era was the political co-optation of the muckrakers. One source of co-optation was the passage of Progressive measures for which muckrakers had long fought. The breadth of reform convinced some muckrakers that the pressing need for a crusade was gone, while it tempered the outrage of others.

The presidential election of 1912 further co-opted many muckrakers by converting them to political activists. Working against the reelection of the Republican Taft, they also worked for the election of their old ally, Progressive Party candidate Theodore Roosevelt. Others joined forces with the Democratic nominee, Woodrow Wilson. Some, including Upton Sinclair, supported Socialist Party candidate Eugene V. Debs. Journalistic competitors now became partisan rivals, fragmenting the muckraking movement.

With Wilson's victory, leading muckrakers joined the administration to press for changes from inside the government. The federal Committee on Public Information was directed by former investigative journalists who had specialized in exposing municipal corruption.[44] They created the *Official Bulletin,* the first daily newspaper published by the United States government. The *Bulletin* crusaded for military preparedness. By the time the United States finally entered World War I in 1917, muckraking had virtually disappeared.

In sum, the investigative impulse was tempered as publications declined in number and journalists left the ramparts. Those reporters who continued to cover public affairs increasingly did so in packs. They competed for official word about the president's bold domestic initiatives, or for news about the progress of the expanding war.

These changes in media were reinforced by changes in the populace. Citizen alienation from authority—a pre-condition for sustained muckraking—seemed to recede after 1910. Like the muckrakers, the outrage of the literate classes was muted by the tangible successes of the reform movement. As inflation subsided, things seemed more under control than in the previous decade. Further, the onset of war produced an added sense of public deference to established authority.[45]

The public may also have become gradually inured to the repeated and often sensational exposés of the muckraking era. As Regier succinctly puts it: "Muckraking ceased, primarily, because the American people were tired of it."[46] By 1912, having lost their audience, journalists moved on to another stage.

The end of the muckraking era did not mean the end of muckraking, however. Journalists had become imbued with a sense of social responsibility in the early 1900s. The idea that public enlightenment was an important mission of media was a lasting legacy of this period. It helped to provide a rationale for future criticisms of government, as "Cato's Letters" had for journalist James Franklin two centuries earlier.

After World War I ended, the United States entered a period of unprecedented prosperity. The public wanted "a return to normalcy," as promised by Republican Warren G. Harding in his successful 1920 presidential campaign. The media, which were becoming more concentrated and competitively stable in the 1920s, generally were willing to give the public what it wanted.

But journalists were not willing to overlook specific evidence in corruption in high places as long as they did not have to investigate to find it. In 1922, President Harding's Secretary of the Interior, Albert Fall, secretly leased the oil reserves on public land known as the Teapot Dome to the Sinc'air Consolidated Oil Corporation. In return, Fall received $260,000 in Liberty Bonds from the president of the company. When news of the scandal broke in 1924, a special prosecutor was appointed to probe the charges. Top administration officials resigned, and Fall ultimately was convicted of bribery and sentenced to one year in jail.

The press's role in covering the scandal was highly revealing of post-muckraking media. "Teapot Dome" did not come to public attention through investigative reporting but, rather, through an investigation by Montana's U.S. Senator Thomas Walsh. As Walsh's findings unfolded in Senate hearings, the story became front-page news.

Although the press played an important role in publicizing the continuing congressional revelations and court actions throughout the 1920s, it rarely did so with muckraking zeal. In fact, *The New York Times* called the official investigators "assassins of character," whereas the *New York Post* referred to them as "mud-gunners."[47] Further, the scandal tarnished the credibility of the press itself in 1924, when the publisher of the *Denver Post* was accused of accepting a million dollars in bribes for suppressing information about Teapot Dome.[48] It was not until 1927 that *St. Louis Post-Dispatch* reporter Paul Y. Anderson, working closely with U.S. Senator George W. Norris, unearthed part of the previously hidden aspects of the scandal.[49]

Journalists continued to publicize wrongdoing in the administrations that followed. However, they did not challenge authorities with independent investigations or sustained crusades. This proved to be true particularly during the twelve years of the Roosevelt presidency.

As Emery and Emery put it: "No president had more effective relationships with the press than did Franklin D. Roosevelt."[50] The president sometimes clashed with newspaper owners, editorial writers, and columnists, particularly during his first term in office. But these disputes centered on the public policy course charted by the president, rather than on the integrity of his administration. The Washington press corps, which covered the Roosevelt presidency on a daily basis, presented him with few challenges.

Roosevelt's deep popular support helped him overcome any hint of scandal.[51] The widespread public disaffection caused by the Great Depression soon was channeled into hope for success of his New Deal programs or to more radical forms of social protest than muckraking journalism. (Among the hopeful were former Progressive reformers who had become New Deal activists.) Lacking villainous industrialists or incumbent politicians to blame for the nation's economic woes, muckraking continued to flounder. In the 1920s, international conflict and postwar recovery further suppressed the investigative impulse.

By 1950, investigative journalism ebbed to its low point of the century. The early 1950s did little to revive it. The United States was entering a period of social quiescence. The only signs of rebellion came from the beginnings of the civil rights movement and the birth of rock-and-roll. The economy was sound. Politically, the country was run by former military hero Dwight D. Eisenhower, who projected a benign, grandfatherly image as President.

However, an undercurrent of insecurity pervaded 1950s American society. The Cold War was under way, and communism represented a threat to postwar stability. In this climate, Republican Senator Joseph McCarthy burst forth with a series of charges that communists had infiltrated the State Department and other agencies of government.

The press's reaction to the rise of McCarthyism reflected its evolving character since World War I. Objectivity and deference to authority had become dominant journalistic norms. This led the Senator's allegations to be dutifully disseminated, especially by the "neutral" wire services, creating the widespread impression that the charges were factual. McCarthy's understanding of journalists' deadlines and interest in colorful copy produced further imbalances in the coverage. The skewed stories contributed significantly to the Senator's overwhelming reelection in 1952.[52]

McCarthyism also presented an opportunity for the resurgence of investigative reporting. McCarthy himself was inviting scrutiny by constantly altering his figures on the extent of communist infiltration of government. He offered little proof of his allegations. Though popular, McCarthy's inflammatory rhetoric began offending members of his own party after Republicans seized control of the presidency and the Senate in 1952.

In 1953, McCarthy was criticized increasingly by prominent newspapers. He counterattacked by calling them "the left-wing press" and by threatening libel suits. The next serious challenge by the mass media to McCarthy's credibility came from a surprising source: television. From its infancy, television had been almost exclusively an entertainment medium. A notable exception was CBS's weekly "See It Now" program. A forerunner of the CBS newsmagazine "60 Minutes," the program was produced by Fred Friendly and reported by Edward R. Murrow.

On March 9, 1954, "See It Now" broadcast one of television's first investigative stories.[53] Its target was Joseph McCarthy. Friendly and Murrow used McCarthy's own words to demonstrate the Senator's "inconsistencies," "half-truths," and "distortions." Most devastating was their use of film footage of the Senator's public speeches and interrogations of witnesses before his Senate subcommittee. This visual evidence made him out to be a bully. The program closed with a call to action by Murrow:

> This is no time for men who oppose Senator McCarthy's methods to keep silent. . . . The actions of the junior senator from Wisconsin have caused alarm and dismay amongst our allies abroad and given considerable comfort to our enemies. And whose fault is that?

Murrow answered his rhetorical question by quoting from Shakespeare. In a tone reminiscent of muckrakers angered with the silence of the American public, Murrow said: "The fault, dear Brutus, is not our stars but in ourselves."

Following this seminal broadcast, McCarthy's support plummeted.[54] Within 24 hours, CBS and its affiliates received over 10,000 phone calls and telegrams overwhelmingly favoring Murrow. Eventually, the public response would be "the greatest reaction to any single program in the network's history."[55]

Just two days after Murrow's report, the United States Army filed charges with the Senate alleging that McCarthy had obtained preferential treatment for a former aide. For weeks, the nation's news media intensively covered the Senate hearings into the charges. Many of the sessions were covered live on network television. The hearings substantiated the Army's allegations and reinforced Murrow's venal portrait of McCarthy. Later that same year, McCarthy was censured by the full Senate. He died in 1957.

Journalists found encouragement in Murrow's boldness and the developments that followed. In 1958, the news media were instrumental in disclosing misconduct by Sherman Adams, a top assistant to President Eisenhower. Muckraking columnist Drew Pearson was first to reveal that Adams had been accepting gifts from a New England industrialist for whom he had intervened with several regulatory agencies.[56] By year's end, Adams resigned after a barrage of media and governmental scrutiny.

In 1960, CBS broadcast Edward R. Murrow's "Harvest of Shame" documentary on the substandard living conditions of migrant farm workers. Murrow concluded the broadcast with an appeal similar to the one that closed his report about McCarthy: "The people you have seen have the strength to harvest your fruit and vegetables. They do not have the strength to influence legislation. Maybe we do." Several major policy initiatives followed, culminating in the passage of the Economic Opportunity Act of 1964.

However, investigative reporting still was uncharacteristic of the media of this period. Until the late 1960s, the most persistent muckraking was done by independent publications, such as *I.F. Stone's Weekly*,[57] and by free-lance investigative reporters such as Jessica Mitford.[58] Conditions were not yet ripe for vigorous muckraking by mainstream media. With the popularity of the Kennedy presidency and the landslide victory of Lyndon Johnson in 1964, national political legitimacy remained high.[59] Locally, machine politics and the spoils system had been significantly curtailed. The economy, although less sound than in the 1950s, was fundamentally healthy.

Moreover, media competition remained stable for most of the 1960s. In marked contrast to the turn of the twentieth century, newspaper circulation stagnated, and the number of papers declined between 1960 and 1970. Objective reporting and pack journalism were the news media's dominant features. Broadcast media continued to deemphasize news coverage, notwithstanding Murrow's efforts. Thus, it was not until the end of the decade that major changes in media and society paved the way to the first sustained period of investigative reporting since the early 1900s.

REDISCOVERING SCANDAL: THE RESURGENCE OF INVESTIGATIVE REPORTING IN MODERN TIMES

Seymour Hersh was hard at work on a book about the Defense Department in October 1969 when he received a startling tip. A reliable source told

the former Associated Press reporter that the United States Army was secretly
court-martialing a young lieutenant for allegedly massacring scores of Vietnamese civilians the previous year. Hersh, who had become a free-lance
writer and anti-Vietnam War activist, recalls his reaction to the tip:

> I instinctively knew that I was not the first reporter to hear about the charge
> against the lieutenant, whoever he was. But I also knew that I was probably one
> of the few who would believe it. So I simply stopped all other work and began
> chasing down the story.[60]

Hersh's instincts proved correct. Despite a September 1969 Associated
Press report of the Army's formal charges against the officer, Lieutenant
William L. Calley, Jr., journalists were not pursuing the story. Hersh aggressively investigated the allegations and found that Calley indeed was responsible for the deliberate murder of at least 109 Vietnamese civilians in the hamlet
of My Lai.

In November 1969, he filed his first story about the My Lai massacre
with the Dispatch News Service, a marketing service for free-lance writers.
Thirty-six newspapers agreed to purchase the story at one hundred dollars
each. Some of them published it the next day. However, except for a brief
foray by *The New York Times,* only Hersh continued to investigate the
killings.

Although the tumultuous 1960s were ending when Hersh began his
probe, the revival of investigative reporting by mainstream media was just
beginning.[61] This does not mean that journalists were particularly hesitant to
criticize public officials during this period. The escalation of the Vietnam War
in the second half of the decade prompted many columnists and opinion
writers to question the Johnson administration's policies in Southeast Asia.
Occasionally, eyewitness reports by correspondents in Vietnam disputed
official versions of the war effort.[62] However, as in the coverage of Franklin
Roosevelt's presidency, journalists in the 1960s were far more prone to
challenge editorially a policy course than to investigate and expose wrongdoing in its implementation.

Several factors explain the general lack of investigative reporting during
this controversial period in American history. First, the norm of objectivity,
which had become "by the 1960s . . . the emblem of American journalism,"[63]
relegated most attacks on officialdom to the editorial pages of the nation's
newspapers. Further, in wartime a relatively higher burden of proof was
required to publish allegations of misconduct, even in an undeclared war that
was widely unpopular. Journalists risked being called unpatriotic if they
attempted to discredit the government's accounts of the war, and they often
faced insurmountable official barriers to substantiate rumors of impropriety.

Moreover, widespread public alienation from government and other societal institutions was not manifested until later in the decade. The "crisis in confidence" in America's leadership was found initially in public opinion polls taken in 1966.[64] It continued steadily into the early 1970s, but did not peak until 1975.[65]

Growing antiwar sentiment was only one source of the mounting disaffection. Gradually every sphere of American life was subjected to intense public re-examination. Challenges to social values came from the civil rights, feminist, and youth countercultural movements. Corporate practices were critiqued by Ralph Nader's consumer organizations. Concerns about environmental hazards were on the rise. These movements ultimately converged to raise serious questions about the legitimacy of the American system of governance.

For journalists, the growing sense of public alienation provided fertile ground for a new era of investigative reporting. But, as had been the case in the late 1890s, there was a brief time lag between the interest in news that challenged the status quo and its supply. Mainstream media were slow to adopt to the changing conditions, preferring to cover reactively the overt turmoil rather than risking to uncover its hidden dimensions.

In the context, it was free-lancer Hersh who took the lead in exposing Vietnam War atrocities. Hersh found that the killings at My Lai had been far more extensive than he originally reported, and they had initially been "covered up" by the army. He also revealed a similar mass killing of civilians at another Vietnamese village near My Lai. In 1970, Hersh won the Pulitzer Prize for international reporting. That a free-lancer would win journalism's highest honor for exposés about the Vietnam War did not escape the attention of reporters everywhere.

In March 1971, *New York Times* reporter Neil Sheehan obtained classified Defense Department documents on the history of the Vietnam War. In June, after weeks of analyzing the documents and debating the propriety of publishing "top secret" information, the *Times* began its Pentagon Papers series. The series revealed that top government officials had repeatedly lied to the American public in explaining the intervention in Southeast Asia. Sheehan had reported villainy in the design of American foreign policy, complementing Hersh's disclosures of victimization in its implementation.

After the *Times* published the third installment of its series, the Nixon administration struck back. The government obtained court orders temporarily preventing the *Times,* and later the *Washington Post* (which belatedly had begun its own series based on the documents), from continuing to publish the Pentagon Papers. In late June, the United States Supreme Court lifted the gag orders on the newspapers. Sheehan and *The New York Times* won the Pulitzer Prize for their efforts in 1972.

Meanwhile, Nixon administration officials, appalled by the high court's decision, decided to take action against the media's sources of information.

The Justice Department initiated criminal proceedings against Daniel Ellsberg, a Defense Department consultant who originally had disseminated the Pentagon Papers to the press. In addition, the President himself established a White House surveillance team—the "plumber's unit"—to plug leaks of classified information.[66]

In September 1971, the "plumbers" burglarized the office of Daniel Ellsberg's psychiatrist in search of incriminating information about the newspapers' source. This move ultimately led the courts to dismiss the government's criminal case against Ellsberg. The group also planned a subsequently aborted mission to firebomb the Brookings Institute in Washington, D.C., under the mistaken belief that it possessed an unpublished volume of the Pentagon Papers.

Undaunted, in June 1972, "plumbers" broke into the headquarters of the Democratic National Committee, located in the Watergate apartment complex. Five men were apprehended by police as they attempted to plant listening devices in the office of the Democratic Party chairman. The following day, the *Washington Post* published a story that linked one of the burglars to the United States Central Intelligence Agency. The Watergate exposés had begun.

Between June and October 1972, the *Post*'s Bob Woodward and Carl Bernstein and reporters for *The New York Times* competed to unearth further connections between the Watergate burglary and the government. They exposed other forms of political espionage and the improper use of campaign funds by officials of the Committee to Reelect the President. The Federal Bureau of Investigation, Department of Justice, and General Accounting Office conducted investigations, but only the Watergate burglars and two heads of the "plumbers unit" were convicted of charges stemming from the original break-in. As the November presidential election approached, the Watergate story stalled.

Although an increasingly cynical public was receptive to disclosures of wrongdoing in high places, the second prerequisite for a sustained muckraking era—competitive instabilities in the news media—was not yet fully present. Many American newspapers were struggling for survival in the early 1970s. Afternoon dailies were folding, while other papers were merging operations under the guidelines of the 1970 Newspaper Preservation Act. Most newspapers lacked the resources or the will for extensive, time-consuming investigative reporting.

Further, probing possible political corruption in an election year seemed unwise, especially when Democrats were attempting to make Watergate a campaign issue. Significantly, these constraints on Watergate coverage were reflected in the October 1972 Gallup poll. The poll showed that only 52 percent of Americans recognized the word Watergate.[67]

Nonetheless, the groundwork was being laid for a new form of media competition that ultimately helped to advance the Watergate story and other investigative reports that would follow. The growth of television as a news medium in the late 1960s was, ironically, one of the reasons for newspapers' financial woes. By the end of the decade, all three networks had half-hour evening news programs for the first time, drawing readers away from the afternoon dailies.

In 1970, CBS's fledgling news magazine program, "60 Minutes," demonstrated its willingness to do investigative reporting by exposing presidential deception in escalating the Vietnam War, three months before *The New York Times* published the Pentagon Papers.[68] In 1971, CBS's "Selling of the Pentagon" documentary uncovered dubious and costly public relations efforts by the Defense Department. Following the Watergate break-in the next year, the networks tracked the incipient scandal with news stories and special reports, although their preelection coverage of Watergate was largely circumscribed.[69]

Then, in 1973, broadcast media played a major role in reviving the Watergate story as new evidence of White House misdeeds became public. Much of this evidence was disclosed in public testimony before the courts and the Congress. Most notably, one of the Watergate burglars charged in a letter read in open court that he and other defendants were paid by higher-ups to keep silent about Watergate-related activities. Senate hearings further revealed tape-recorded White House conversations about the Watergate cover-up, as well as a campaign of political sabotage against Democratic Party rivals of the president.

News of these sensational developments reached the public through a variety of media, but studies show that it was live television coverage of the Senate hearings that finally made Watergate a widely credible public issue by the middle of the year.[70] The agenda-building role of television news increasingly made it a medium to be taken seriously by professional journalists, just as it no longer could be ignored by circulation-conscious newspaper publishers. The competition escalated to get the "real" story behind the Watergate affair.

The *Washington Post*'s Woodward and Bernstein, who won the Pulitzer Prize in 1973 for their early Watergate exposés, increasingly shared the task of advancing the Watergate story with newspaper and television reporters from across the country. Among them was Seymour Hersh, who was hired by *The New York Times* and put on the Watergate "beat" in 1973. The competition between the *Post* and *The Times* for recognition as the nation's premier newspaper—another new form of media rivalry—fueled the drive for Watergate scoops. Similar struggles among the television networks for national news viewership helped intensify the search for news about the widening scandal. In 1974, snowed under by an avalanche of media and government-generated evidence of his complicity in covering up the Watergate burglary, and besieged by the convictions of his top aides for Watergate crimes, Richard Nixon became the first American President to resign from office.

Was the President's resignation the direct result of investigative reporting? Undoubtedly not. In terms of the Mobilization Model, it would be incorrect to suggest that investigative reporters unearthed sufficient evidence of presidential misconduct to so outrage the public that the administration's downfall inevitably followed. In fact, the President was reelected by a landslide in 1972, following months of significant media disclosures.

Watergate only penetrated the public consciousness after it received widespread attention in 1973 by various media in different forms—spot news stories, government leaks, opinion pieces, as well as independent exposés. This saturation coverage did not occur until legislative and judicial forums yielded conclusive evidence of misconduct by high-ranking members of the administration. Much of the media coverage in 1973 and 1974 focused on these official actions. Even then, however, the public was not mobilized to demand reforms from their elected representatives. The evidence shows that the public instead played a "bystander" role: passively observing, with increasing cynicism, the developing scandal in Washington.[71]

The role of investigative reporting in Watergate was to bring the scandal to light in its infancy, to occasionally disclose fresh information in 1973 and 1974 for policy makers to investigate further, and to help frame the issue as one of wrongdoing at the highest levels of government; that is, to target "all the President's men." These indeed were vital contributions. But the impact of media muckraking on public opinion was at most indirect, and its connection to the President's ultimate resignation was even more tangential. As Lang and Lang put it:

> The press was a prime mover in the controversy only in its early phase, when the Woodward and Bernstein tandem first linked the Watergate burglars to the Nixon campaign committee and, during the campaign, uncovered other stories that hinted at the politically explosive potential of the "bugging" incident. But with Nixon's decisive electoral victory, the press came close to abandoning Watergate. Then, as the issue revived and conflict over the scope of the investigation intensified, the press mainly lived off information insiders were happy to furnish it. . . . That so many of the struggles between Nixon and his opponents should have had such wide publicity, and even been played out on television, accounts for the impression that the news media and an aroused public opinion forced the downfall of Richard Nixon.[72]

Nonetheless, the Watergate disclosures were felt throughout American society for years to come. Perhaps their most profound long-term impact was on journalism itself. The resurgence of investigative reporting, which began at the end of the 1960s, was in full force by the mid-1970s. In 1974, four Pulitzer Prizes were awarded for investigative stories, prompting *Time* magazine to declare it "a Year of the Muckrakers."[73] Multimedia competition for moral disorder news intensified at the same time that public alienation from authority was peaking. Television helped to spark this competition as a fresh journalistic force, just as magazines had done at the turn of the twentieth century.

Further, the perceived power of the press to uncover truth and right societal wrongs—the "social responsibility theory" of media—had become the conventional wisdom of modern-day journalism. Whether the Mobilization Model actually was valid had become academic. Modern muckrakers *believed* in its premises, as had their twentieth-century predecessors. To a new generation of journalists, investigative reporting could turn the tide of public opinion. It could help to end wars and topple presidents. It also could lead to fame and honor for the muckrakers themselves.

The decade following the resignation of President Nixon produced an investigative frenzy that was rivaled only by the golden age of muckraking. Newspapers and television stations across the country established investigative units to expose wide-ranging abuses of authority. Weekly news magazine programs on all three networks featured regular segments about public and private wrongdoing. Muckraking spread to popular periodicals (although not with the intensity of the early 1900s magazines) and generated new publications like the *Washington Monthly* and *Mother Jones* that specialized in investigative journalism. Investigative reporting groups were established to provide resources for media muckraking.[74]

Who are these new muckrakers? Investigative journalists in the post-Watergate era are strikingly similar to their forebears. Our national survey of investigative reporters and editors and other data show they predominantly are male, Caucasian, and work in large cities.[75] Though less active politically than the Progressives, many were educated during the Vietnam War era and are motivated by reformist goals.[76]

The formula of contemporary investigative stories also borrows heavily from past muckraking traditions. As discussed in chapter 1, the journalism of outrage is its central tenet. Individual cases of venality and victimization are woven together to reveal a broad fabric of abuse. By exposing villanous conduct—typically by authorities—new muckraking contains a moral tone that is relevant to reform.

Yet modern-day investigative reporting has developed a distinctive style, in part because of the evolution of journalistic norms. In contrast to the early 1900s, today's muckraking allegations normally are attributed to various sources of information rather than being flatly asserted. Moreover, the blatant advocacy of earlier exposés has given way to more subtle appeals to societal values and to a diminished willingness to crusade for change. Calls for reforms normally appear in separate editorials or are presented discreetly in the story by persons other than the reporters themselves; e.g., in quotes by "good government" spokespersons.

Another important trend in the post-Watergate era is the emphasis on spotlighting governmental wrongdoing. Unlike muckrakers in the early 1900s, contemporary investigative reporters tend not to target corporate venality, or when they do so, include it as part of a larger story about political malfeasance. This may partly be the result of advertising pressures and the growing corporate composition of modern media.[77] It also may be a result of changing libel laws that have given journalists broader latitude to target public officials since 1964,[78] as well as expanded legal rights of access to government information granted after Watergate.[79] Further, the seminal stories of My Lai, the Pentagon Papers, and Watergate were exposés of *government* misconduct. They set the standard for the era that followed.

Similarly, new muckraking typically does not address the problems of social inequities, except where they are a blatant consequence of governmental improprieties. One reason for this may be the personal isolation of most investigative reporters from the nation's social problems and from sources of information about those problems. Another explanation lies in the growth of organizations and spokespersons for social equality, which has led to more routine coverage of the manifestations of injustice. In any case, contemporary muckrakers are more closely aligned with the public policy concerns of Lincoln Steffens than with the social and economic targets of Ida Tarbell and Ray Stannard Baker.

These trends have made new muckraking somewhat more circumscribed in focus and commitment than old muckraking. However, its concentration on problems that have a governmental nexus may make contemporary investigative reporting more directly relevant to public policy agendas. Further, the technology of modern media has allowed contemporary exposés to reach far broader audiences than the early muckrakers, thereby potentially enhancing their societal salience.

Under what conditions and in what ways have investigative stories influenced the agenda priorities of our nation or its communities? Historical conditions seem to play an important role in determining their impact, but other factors may be influential as well, including the nature of the investigative stories themselves. In the chapters that follow, we address this question by examining evidence from six case studies of investigative stories and other relevant data. In studying the life courses of different investigative reports—from conception to birth to their societal impact—we attempt to identify the conditions under which muckraking matters.

NOTES

1. Edwin Emery and Michael Emery, *The Press and America: An Interpretative History of the Mass Media* (Englewood Cliffs, NJ: Prentice-Hall, 1984), pp. 28–29.

2. Quoted by Thomas C. Leonard, *The Power of the Press: The Birth of American Political Reporting* (New York: Oxford University Press, 1986), p. 29.

3. Ibid., p. 33.

4. Ibid., p. 57.

5. Ibid., p. 63.

6. Michael Schudson. *Discovering the News* (New York: Basic Books, 1978), pp. 22–23.

7. For a detailed discussion of the "libertarian theory of the press," see Fred Siebert, Theodore Peterson, and Wilbur Schramm, *Four Theories of the Press* (Urbana and Champaign: University of Illinois Press, 1956), pp. 39–71.

8. Richard A. Schwarzlose, "The Marketplace of Ideas: A Measure of Free Expression," *Journalism Monographs,* no. 118 (December 1989), pp. 20–27.

9. Margaret A. Blanchard, "Filling the Void: Speech and Press in State Courts Prior to *Gitlow,*" in *The First Amendment Reconsidered: New Perspectives on the Meaning of Freedom of Speech and the Press,* Bill F. Chamberlin and Charlene J. Brown (eds.) (New York: Longman, 1982), pp. 14–59.

10. Emery and Emery, *The Press and America,* p. 112.

11. Leonard, *The Power of the Press,* p. 109.

12. Arthur Weinberg and Lila Weinberg (eds.), *The Muckrakers* (New York: Simon and Schuster, 1961), p. xiv.

13. Curtis D. MacDougall, *Interpretative Reporting* (New York: Macmillan, 1982), p. 227.

14. Richard Hofstadter, *The Progressive Movement* (Englewood Cliffs, NJ: Prentice-Hall, 1963), p. 5.

15. Alfred McClung Lee, *The Daily Newspaper in America* (New York: Octagon Books, 1973), pp. 718–723; United States Census, *Historical Statistics of the United States, Colonial Times to 1970* (Washington, DC: Government Printing Office, 1976).

16. Rural Free Delivery was established in 1897. R.F.D. routes rapidly expanded from 28,685 miles in 1900 to 721,237 miles in 1910. The number of post roads also increased markedly between 1885 and 1910, from 365,251 miles to 447,998 miles. Lee, ibid., pp. 745–746.

17. Quoted by C. C. Regier, *The Era of the Muckrakers* (Chapel Hill: University of North Carolina Press, 1932), p. 6.

18. Ibid., p. 9.

19. Ida M. Tarbell, "History of the Standard Oil Company," *McClure's* (December 1902).

20. Regier, *The End of the Muckrakers,* p. 57.

21. James R. Barrett, "Introduction" to *The Jungle* by Upton Sinclair (Urbana and Champaign: University of Illinois Press), p. xvi.

22. Quoted by Weinberg and Weinberg, *The Muckrakers,* p. 205.

23. Upton Sinclair, "What Life Means to Me," *Cosmopolitan,* 45 (October 1906): 591–595

24. George E. Mowry, *The Era of Theodore Roosevelt* (New York: Harper & Row, 1958), p. 206.

25. Ida M. Tarbell, "The Mysteries and Cruelties of the Tariff," series, *American Magazine,* 71–72 (November 1910–October 1911).

26. Herbert J. Gans, *Deciding What's News* (New York: Pantheon, 1979), pp. 204–205.

27. Alfred Henry Lewis, "A Trust in Agricultural Implements," *Cosmopolitan,* 38 (April 1905), pp. 666–672.

28. Leonard, *The Power of the Press,* p. 216.

29. Ibid., p. 216

30. Richard Hofstadter, *The Age of Reform* (New York: Knopf, 1955), p. 196; Mowry, *The Era of Theodore Roosevelt,* p. 65.

31. Hofstadter, ibid., p. 3.

32. Leonard, *The Power of the Press,* pp. 211–212.

33. Upton Sinclair, "Introduction" to *The Jungle* (Cambridge, MA: Robert Bentley, 1946), p. vii. Sinclair writes: "*The Jungle* appeared and became a sensation overnight. . . . President Roosevelt sent for me, heard my story, and turned me over to two commissioners, whom he ordered to make an investigation of Stockyard conditions. This was supposed to be secret . . . the commission, after several weeks on the ground, turned in a report which sustained the book's charges."

34. Leonard, *The Power of the Press,* p. 211.

35. Quoted by Fred J. Cook, *The Muckrakers* (Garden City, NY: Doubleday, 1972), p. 120.

36. Regier, *The Era of the Muckrakers,* p. 109

37. Hofstadter, *The Age of Reform,* p. 195; Leonard, *The Power of the Press,* pp. 193–221.

38. Leonard, ibid., p. 194.

39. Lee, *The Daily Newspaper in America,* p. 723.

40. Emery and Emery, *The Press and America,* p. 399.

41. U.S. Census Bureau, *Historical Statistics.*

42. Regier, *The Era of the Muckrakers,* pp. 176–180.

43. Ibid., p. 211.

44. Leonard, *The Power of the Press,* p. 188.

45. Regier, *The Era of the Muckrakers,* p. 206.

46. Ibid., p. 207.

47. Quoted by Frederick Lewis Allen, *Only Yesterday* (New York: Harper & Row, 1931), p. 128. For a further analysis of the origins of the scandal and the press's role in publicizing it, see Burl Noggle, *Teapot Dome* (New York: W.W. Norton, 1962).

48. Clifford G. Christians, "Enforcing Media Codes," *Journal of Mass Media Ethics,* 1, no. 1 (Fall/Winter, 1985–86), p. 14.

49. Noggle, *Teapot Dome,* pp. 186–187.

50. Emery and Emery, *The Press and America,* p. 426.

51. Early critics of New Deal social programs called them wasteful "boondoggles," but Roosevelt largely silenced those critics in 1936 by winning a second term as president with the widest electoral margin in United States history. Roosevelt also co-opted some critics who charged that his economic policies favored wealthy corporations by proposing crackdowns on corporate trusts and securities firms. See Richard N. Current, T. Harry Williams, and Frank Freidel, *American History* (New York: Knopf, 1964), p. 727. Also see Arthur Schlesinger, Jr., *The Age of Roosevelt* (Boston: Houghton Mifflin, 1957–1960); and Graham J. White, *FDR and the Press* (Chicago: University of Chicago Press, 1979).

52. Edwin R. Bayley, *Joe McCarthy and the Press* (Madison: University of Wisconsin Press, 1981), pp. 123–24.

53. Joseph E. Persico, *Edward R. Murrow: An American Original* (New York: Dell, 1988), pp. 372–373.

54. Bayley, *Joe McCarthy and the Press,* p. 192.

55. Persico, *Edward R. Murrow,* p. 380.

56. Brit Hume, *Inside Story* (Garden City, NY: Doubleday, 1974), p. 31.

57. Andrew Patner, *I. F. Stone: A Portrait* (New York: Anchor, 1988); I. F. Stone and Arthur Miller, *The Haunted Fifties: Nineten Fifty-Three to Ninetween Sixty-Three* (New York: Little, Brown, 1989).

58. Jessica Mitford, *Poison Penmanship: The Gentle Art of Muckraking* (New York: Nonday Press, 1988); Jessica Mitford, *The American Way of Death* (New York: Simon and Schuster, 1963).

59. Between 1958 and 1964, public opinion surveys indicated that "trust in government" remained consistently high. See Seymour Martin Lipset and William Schneider, *The Confidence Gap: Business, Labor, and Government in the Public Mind* (New York: Free Press, 1983), p. 16.

60. Quoted by Leonard Downie, Jr., *The New Muckrakers* (Washington, DC: New Republic Book Company, 1976), p. 66. Our discussion of Hersh's involvement in the exposé comes from Downie, pp. 50–92, and from a speech by Hersh to the national student conference of Investigative Reporters and Editors in Chicago (November, 1988).

61. Muckraking by the "alternative" or "underground" press peaked between 1968 and 1973, the time when mass circulation newspaper and television stations just were beginning to show a renewed interest in investigative reporting. See Abe Peck, *Uncovering the Sixties* (New York: Pantheon, 1985), p. xv. The metropolitan daily newspapers that showed the earliest interest in reviving investigative reporting during this period included *Newsday,* which established a team of five investigative journalists in 1967; the *Chicago Tribune,* which created an investigative task force in 1968; and the *Boston Globe,* which inaugurated its "spotlight" team in 1970. Schudson, *Discovering the News,* pp. 189–190.

62. Among the most notable of these accounts were CBS News' August 1965 report on the burning of a Vietnamese village by Marines ("This is what the war in Viet Nam is all about," correspondent Morley Safer stated as he stood in front of the burning huts) and *The New York Times'* Harrison Salisbury's series from North Viet Nam that contradicted official claims about the effectiveness of United States bombing raids. Significantly, official reactions to these reports were so antagonistic that Safer

almost lost his job, and Salisbury was denied a Pulitzer Prize voted him by the judging committee. See Emery and Emery, The Press and America, pp. 564–565.

63. Michael Schudson, Discovering the News, p. 9.

64. Lipset and Schneider, The Confidence Gap, p. 46.

65. Ibid., p. 50

66. Stanley I. Kutler, The Wars of Watergate (New York: Knopf, 1990), p. 111.

67. Emery and Emery, The Press and America, p. 606.

68. Don Hewitt, Executive Producer of "60 Minutes," writes that "(the exposé) should have made a big splash. It didn't, because '60 Minutes' was in a very small pond. If we had run it ten years later, when ten times as many people would have seen it, just as sure as 7:00 p.m. Sunday comes around once a week somebody would have jumped up and down demanding equal time and hollering that we were communists . . .". Don Hewitt, Minute by Minute . . . (New York: Random House, 1985), p. 49.

69. In the seven weeks prior to the November election, the networks covered Watergate in a fairly routine manner. CBS devoted 71 minutes of air time to Watergate, while NBC and ABC spent 42 and 41 minutes, respectively. Emery and Emery, The Press and America, pp. 605–606.

70. Gladys Engel Lang and Kurt Lang, The Battle for Public Opinion (New York: Columbia University Press, 1983) pp. 62–93. Also see Kurt Lang and Gladys Engel Lang, "Televised Hearings: The Impact Out There," Columbia Journalism Review (November–December 1973), pp. 52–57.

71. Lang and Lang, The Battle for Popular Opinion, pp. 10–25.

72. Ibid., pp. 302–303.

73. Downie, The New Muckrakers, p. 10

74. These groups have provided money, and sometimes manpower, to news organizations and free-lance reporters to foster investigative reporting. Examples include Chicago's Better Government Association, which will be discussed in detail in later chapters, the Center for Investigative Reporting, Investigative Reporters and Editors, and the Fund for Investigative Journalism. The last of these was instrumental in supporting Seymour Hersh in the early days of the My Lai exposé. Philip F. Lawler, The Alternative Influence (Lanham, MD: University Press of America, 1984.)

75. Ninety-eight percent of those responding to the survey were Caucasian, 68 percent were male, and 51 percent worked in markets of 500,000 or more. See appendix II. Also see David L. Protess, "How Investigative Reporters See Themselves," The IRE Journal (Spring 1984); David L. Protess, "Investigative Reporters: Endangered Species?" The IRE Journal (Winter 1986); and the profiles by Downie, The New Muckrakers for confirming data.

76. The mean age of those surveyed was 38. Fifty-six percent stated that "satisfying the reformer in (them)" was the main reward they sought in doing investigative stories. This was ranked as their highest of five possible priorities. See appendix II.

77. This argument has been made by, among others, Ben. H. Bagdikian, The Media Monopoly (Boston: Beacon Press, 1983).

78. In New York Times v. Sullivan (376 U.S. 254), the United States Supreme

Court ruled in 1964 that public officials had to prove "actual malice"—knowledge of falsehood or reckless disregard for the truth—in libel suits against journalists. The actual malice requirement made it rare for successful libel actions to be brought against investigative journalists, who often target public officials for wrongdoing. Although the Court later ruled that actual malice had to be proven involving "public figures" as well, that burden was not required of corporations or corporation executives with the same regularity as public officials. See Randall P. Bezanson, Gilbert Cranberg, and John Soloski, *Libel Law and the Press: Myth and Reality* (New York: Free Press, 1987). This study also concluded that "contrary to the popular myth that libel suits are the result of hard-hitting, investigative stories that are run on front pages of newspapers under banner headlines, only about 46 percent of the libel suits concerned stories that had appeared on the front page of newspapers. . . ." p. 20.

79. In 1974, the federal Freedom of Information Act was amended to broaden considerably the public's right of access to government information, especially information kept by Federal executive agencies. By the mid-1980s, all states had enacted public records and open meetings laws. See Investigative Reporters and Editors, *The Reporter's Handbook* (New York: St. Martin's Press, 1983).

PART **II**

CASE STUDIES OF INVESTIGATIVE REPORTING

Introduction

Chapters 3 through 8 describe the life histories of six investigative reports. These case studies were made possible by the cooperation of investigative reporters who told us about their stories prior to publication. The reporters were willing to be interviewed about their work in progress and to provide varying degrees of access to their investigative files.[1] This inside look at investigative reporting enabled us to study the life course of each story as it evolved from its earliest form to its eventual publication and impact on society.

For analytical purposes, we describe four stages in the life course of an investigative report: (1) story genesis; (2) story investigation; (3) story preparation; and (4) story impact.

In the genesis stage, the investigative reporters learn about a particular problem and decide whether to pursue it. The decision to pursue the story leads to an investigation of the incidence and prevalence of the problem. If the investigation bears fruit, the reporters next prepare the findings in a form that can be presented in the print or electronic media. In the final stage, the published report may produce continuing consequences for the media, the public, and policy makers.

In conducting research for this book, we asked different questions about developments that occurred at each of these stages. Regarding the "story genesis" stage, we asked: How does a story idea come to the attention of investigative reporters? How do reporters decide whether to pursue the possible story? To answer these questions, we interviewed the investigative reporters and others involved in each of the six cases, read in-house memos, and in some cases attended meetings in which key story decisions were made.

Regarding the "story investigation" stage, we asked: What happens during the investigative process that propels some stories to publication and causes others to be dropped? To answer this question, we interviewed the investigative reporters about how they conducted their investigations, probing in particular to understand what types of evidence they sought and what types they ignored or discarded. We also read rough notes, memos, and progress reports. Because we learned about most of these cases well before publication, we were able to follow the twists and turns that each investigation took and did not have to rely on retrospective accounts alone.

In learning about the preparation process, we asked: How do journalists transform the investigative findings into a coherent story that attempts to capture the attention of audiences? We interviewed the investigative reporters, editors, or producers about how decisions were made to winnow the often voluminous amount of information generated during the investigative stage. In several cases, we had access to drafts of stories that allowed us to understand exactly why particular items were cut.

Finally, the investigative report is published or televised. At this stage, we asked: What impact did the report have on the public and on policy making? We assessed public opinion effects by conducting surveys both before and after the news media event, a research strategy made possible by knowing in advance the expected publication date and content of the story.[2] We measured policy-making developments over time by interviewing policy makers and by conducting analyses of official actions, such as formal hearings, legislative proposals, and administrative measures.[3]

From the above description, it might appear that sharp demarcations exist between these stages. They do not. However, the four stages approximate the developments that occurred in the cases that follow, and they provide a natural way to tell the "stories" behind these stories. This approach also facilitated the development of a theory about the process and effects of investigative reporting.

The first case examines a nationally televised investigation of fraud and abuse in the federally funded home health care program. The second focuses on a *Chicago Sun-Times* series that disclosed problems in the reporting and prosecution of sex crimes. The third case involves a multi-part Chicago television report about repeatedly brutal police officers. The fourth examines an investigation by the same station of the toxic waste disposal practices of a major midwestern university. The fifth involves a "60 Minutes" investigation of international child abductions. The sixth case examines a *Philadelphia Inquirer* investigative series about kidney dialysis clinics that have become "profit machines."

These cases are a small sample of the investigative stories published in the post-Watergate era. We selected them because they (1) have many of the attributes of investigative stories that have been published during this period; (2) involve stories published in different media—print and broadcast, as well as national and local (Chicago and Philadelphia); and (3) allowed us the most extensive access to journalistic decision making in comparison with other stories we considered studying. However, we are keenly aware of the limits of inference from such a sample. Wherever possible, we also attempt to compare these stories with others and to rely on our survey interviews with more than 900 investigative reporters and editors when making generalizations from the findings.

Each of the cases that follows is presented in narrative form. In chapters 9 and 10, we discuss the consistent patterns that emerge from the case studies. These patterns, along with other data, allow us to develop a theory of how and why some investigative stories "make it" to publication. The patterns also allow us to examine the validity of the Mobilization Model for capturing the impact of investigative reporting.

NOTES

1. We were able to conduct extensive interviews with each of the journalists who worked on these investigative projects at various junctures in the preparation of their stories. However, only in the home health and toxic waste investigations (chapters 3 and 6) did we observe directly the meetings in which the story *initially* was selected. In the police brutality and toxic waste investigations (chapters 5 and 6), Northwestern University faculty and student interns became participant-observers in the investigation and production of the story. In each of the six case studies, we were able to obtain access to aspects of reporters' work products, including notes, memoranda, progress reports, drafts of story "pitches" to media managers, drafts of actual stories, and broadcast scripts and outtakes. The extent of this access varied from one case study to another. Quotes from such documents appear in the text of each of the chapters that follow. Content analyses of follow-up stories to the investigative reports were performed in each case, and they are discussed in chapter 10.

2. See the methodological appendix (appendix I) for discussion of the research designs used to measure public opinion effects in the six case studies. Each case study chapter also includes a brief description of the methods used in the section entitled "The Investigative Influence" (see chapters 3 through 8).

3. Each of the case studies employed various techniques of policy analysis. In the first four studies (chapters 3 through 6), we interviewed samples of policy makers both before and after the publication of the investigative reports. In the last two cases, we conducted only postpublication interviews with policy makers. We also conducted legislative and administrative histories of all initiatives—related to the investigative reports—that were proposed in Washington, DC (for chapters 3, 7, and 8), in Springfield, IL (for chapter 4), in Harrisburg, PA (for chapter 8), and in Chicago (for chapters 4, 5, and 6). Sponsors of relevant initiatives or their staff members were interviewed in depth, as described in each of the case studies.

CHAPTER 3

"The Home Health Hustle"

"**A** good idea almost being destroyed. Federal money to cure the sick and elderly at home instead of in hospitals. But profiteers and thieves are stealing millions from the government." In this way, host David Brinkley introduced viewers of "NBC News Magazine" to the core problem that the program's investigative journalists had uncovered in federally funded home health care. According to Brinkley, federal money had "attracted crooks, liars, thieves, and swindlers." He promised to reveal how the conduct of these villains threatened the care of helpless elderly and disabled victims and ultimately threatened the future of home health care. In the 18 minutes that followed, the magazine program reported the results of an extensive six-month investigation of fraud and abuse in the federally funded home health care program. The segment was broadcast on national television Thursday, May 7, 1981.

Home health care programs provide services in the client's home—for example, meal preparation, health care, and physical therapy. Funded in large part by the federal Medicare program, they are designed to enable patients to avoid hospitalization and to lower costs. The alleged fraud noted involved overbilling for services and charges for agencies that existed only on paper. Abuses documented included negligence and threats to patients about loss of services.

After introducing the story, Brinkley turned it over to correspondent Garrick Utley, who explained that NBC News Magazine originally had planned to do a report on only one home health care operator in Chicago but expanded the scope because "the more we investigated, the more we found examples of fraud and abuse stretching across the country and an imposing cast of characters. They have set up ingenious and at times very complex plots to deceive and even defraud the government. And at the center of it all, often unaware of what's happening, is the patient."

Utley described home health care as "an idea whose time has come" while the picture cut to a patient being cared for at home who said, "Oh! I'd much rather be home than go to a rest home or a convalescent place." But this good idea was being undermined by "profiteers"—small companies that deliver the care and pocket Medicare funds at patients' expense.

Utley then presented four cases as evidence to illustrate the fraud and abuse uncovered by investigators from NBC and the Better Government Association (BGA), a Chicago civic organization that collaborates with journalists on investigative reporting projects. First, Utley introduced Michael Morrisroe, "a textbook case of Medicare fraud." Morrisroe had set up a storefront agency called South West Home Care that provided nurse's aides to its clients. A picture showed a former employee (disguised in shadows) who reported that the aides spent much less time for visits than Morrisroe claimed, more visits than employee hours in the day. Medicare paid for the overbilling. But this was not all. Next, Morrisroe set up a company called Chicago Home Care, which charged a fee for supplying nurse's aides to South West Home Care. In fact, all Morrisroe really did was to make a nurse's aide the titular head of this company and to transfer the names of the nurse's aides already working for South West Home Care to the accounting books of Chicago Home Care. In developing a supplier for the nurse's aides, he charged the government three times more than was necessary. Said a former employee, "Mike told me that he wasn't supposed to be involved with Chicago Home Care. People shouldn't know that he is and to be careful what I said. He was. He controlled it."

But Morrisroe still was not satisfied, the viewer learned. To make even more money, he set up a management consultant firm called Northrad. Morrisroe claimed that Northrad managed his other companies, and all Northrad bills were charged to Medicare. The camera showed a letter with a Northrad title and address and then cut to an unidentified source who explained that Northrad was "just a drawer in Mike's office," just "the letterhead and Mike." Utley concluded this case by summing up, "So Mike Morrisroe was making a huge profit from doing business with himself. That is illegal under Medicare law."

"What Morrisroe did in Illinois, others are doing across the country," noted Utley as he introduced the next case, the story of Bob Deroger in California. When he knew he was in front of the camera, Deroger said that home health provided little money for the operator. However, the segment next showed him being filmed without his knowledge in a meeting with a potential partner describing methods similar to Morrisroe's to profit heavily by charging Medicare fraudulently.

The third case was that of Dr. Albert Poindexter, who owned and ran a management firm called Intermanagement. Poindexter's firm did business with three home care agencies that Poindexter also controlled. Although Utley said Poindexter would not talk to him (the film shows a man walking away from the camera), several people who had worked with Poindexter were willing to talk about his fraudulent practices. Among these was a man named Louis Paul, a physical therapist who on paper controlled Louis Paul Physical Therapy. However, in effect, Paul's agency was controlled by Poindexter and one of his management companies. The management company paid Louis Paul a salary of $20,000 but charged the government $52,000 for keeping the books for Paul, more than Paul made from what was supposed to be his own company.

But this, the viewer also learned from the Poindexter case, was not all. Misdeeds led all the way to the nation's capital. Mutual of Omaha audited the operation run by Poindexter and his partner, Lenore Stein, and informed the government official in charge of reviewing home care agencies of suspicious practices. This government official was a man named Al Fox, a friend of Poindexter's partner Stein. Fox kept Stein and Poindexter informed of the government investigation and, Utley inferred, played a role in exonerating the pair.

The fourth case involved Vic Ceraci in Mississippi, whose home health business served mainly rural areas. Ceraci pridefully stated, "We get praised a lot, yes sir." But Utley found other opinions to be quite different. The viewer met unlicensed nurses who reported they did the work of registered nurses and a doctor whose signature Ceraci forged several times to falsify orders for the treatment of patients. Even more damning for Ceraci's enterprises, Utley introduced the television viewers to elderly patients who described Ceraci's threats that they would lose their Medicare or Medicaid benefits and their government-provided equipment if they stopped using his home heath care agency. One elderly black woman with both legs amputated told viewers, "He [Ceraci] said that if I didn't stay with him, he'd have to take the bed. . . . If I didn't stay with him, I'd lose my Medicare."

With the final of the four cases presented, Utley assured viewers that "most of the operators in the home health field are honest and dedicated," but said the problem was the profiteers. He announced that the U.S. Senate would begin holding hearings the very next week on the home health business.

Finally, the camera returned to David Brinkley who, shaking his head, asked Utley, "How can they clean up this mess?"

The piece ended with Utley's response. Looking into the camera, he answered, "There are a lot of problems. What everybody agrees is that they have to start with laws that are on the books. They have to rewrite them, revise them, tighten them up. That's where it has to begin, with the law itself."

THE GENESIS OF THE PROBE

How is it that particular problems get chosen for investigative reports and not others? What makes investigative reporters attend to some subjects and not others? In the case of home health care, we find a particular concatenation of three factors. They are the participants who were active in uncovering the issue, the nature of the problems that came to their attention, and the politics in the world of the investigative reporters.[1]

The first formal discussion of a possible investigation of home health care developed from a meeting at the Better Government Association (BGA) offices in Chicago in July 1980. The BGA has been called "the oldest, best-known, and most successful organization devoted to investigative journalism."[2] Begun in 1923 when Chicago was fighting organized crime, the BGA at first concentrated on the many problems of the Capone era. In the 1960s, the BGA began to conduct joint investigations with the media to expose government waste, inefficiency , and corruption. These investigative reporting projects included dramatic undercover probes of local government corruption and stories of waste in federal government (e.g., Medicaid fraud, Pentagon contracts, the Farm Loan Program, etc.). The BGA has "story idea" meetings about twice a year. The July 1980 meeting was attended by almost all BGA staff. They discussed a list of about a dozen investigative ideas.

Immediately prior to the meeting, BGA investigator Mindy Trossman had been contacted by NBC News Magazine producer Stephanie Meagher. Meagher suggested a possible link-up between NBC and BGA and set up a meeting to talk about story ideas. Trossman, therefore, attended the story idea meeting looking for stories to consider with NBC.

The suggestion to begin investigating home health care came from four participants at the BGA story idea session. Towards the middle of the meeting, the BGA research director brought up the idea. He had been talking to his sister-in-law, a nurse for the Visiting Nurses Association in Chicago. She had related several stories of fraud by local home health operators. Another staff member, Mike Lyons, mentioned that he had heard of similar problems from his wife, a physical therapist who works for a subcontractor for home health care agencies. Also, BGA Executive Director Terry Brunner recalled a recent telephone call concerning problems with home health care. Finally, another staff member recalled that a woman who was a former worker for a home health care agency had walked into the BGA with complaints about the industry two months before the story idea meeting. This visit, documented in a BGA file, had been forgotten until the meeting.

A few days later, Trossman met with NBC News Magazine producer Stephanie Meagher, armed with the longer list of ideas from the meeting but wanting to talk with her about two major ideas. The first was the home health care issue; the other concerned high school athletic injuries. As Trossman remembered the meeting, she never even mentioned that she had a longer list because Meagher liked these two ideas.

In deciding to suggest the issue of home health care to NBC, Trossman said she had to understand something about the politics of the network program and what would fly. For example, she would not have raised the home health care proposal with ABC-TV's "20/20" news magazine program because that program had done several health-related stories recently with the BGA, and she thought they would not want anything else health-related now. She knew NBC was anxious to work with the BGA, and she thought they would like the health care angle. The television network was recovering from its ill-advised withdrawal from the BGA's "Mirage Tavern" story, which eventually was broadcast on rival CBS's "60 Minutes" program, and its news magazine show was last in the ratings when it approached the BGA. During the next few weeks while trying to get a firm commitment from NBC to pursue the home health care story, Trossman also reminded Meagher that the BGA had earlier gone to NBC with a story idea on railroad safety that the BGA thought was great but NBC refused. The BGA later convinced ABC's "20/20" to do the story, and it had proved to be an enormous success.

From the outset, NBC News Magazine's executive producer Paul Friedman liked the sports story but was concerned with the lack of a patient abuse angle in home health. The high school sports story faced some problems of its own, however. The first problem was the discovery that ABC had done a story on injuries in organized high school sports. This forced NBC to look for another angle; perhaps they could probe the virtually untouched subject of injuries in non-school-sponsored preteen sports ("kiddie sports"). Although this story was viewed by the BGA as "great TV" it was considered to be "lousy BGA" because it now had nothing to do with any governmental agency, a self-imposed requirement for all BGA investigations. Thus, BGA staff agreed it was something with which they should not become involved. Meagher and NBC decided to take the idea and work on it on their own, while the BGA continued probing home health care. This gave Meagher her story for the new season and also gave the BGA time to develop the home health care investigation. NBC staff made it clear that they still wanted to collaborate on home care eventually.

As is common at the beginning of BGA investigations, NBC provided little more than general direction as Lyons and Trossman began work. What little was known about home health care suggested that the problems were similar to nursing homes because the industry was regulated in the same way; government financial assistance for both types of care was similar, and there was evidence that nursing home providers were moving into the home health care business. All of this made it a classic BGA investigation because home health care was a regulated industry with large amounts of government funding—just the type of situation most often examined by the BGA in recent years. The investigation began with a few leads but no detailed investigative plan and with the expectation that the home health care industry was more than an elderly issue.

THE INVESTIGATIVE PROCESS

With the issue chosen, the investigative process begins in earnest. Is each investigative process unique to each issue undertaken, or do some common elements emerge? Although each investigation has its own peculiarities, all have certain elements in common—the search for solid evidence, the search for clear villains and victims, and the search for a policy maker connection and a policy linkage.

Finding "The Angle" and Confirming the Media Connection

During August 1980, Lyons began investigating home health care in earnest. His first search for evidence involved a simple cross-tabulation of those people running home health care agencies with those people known to be involved with nursing home care and Medicare. With help from others at BGA, he also contacted the people who had put the organization onto the story, including the source who had walked into the BGA office two months earlier.

At this early stage, the story began to take a new twist. First, Lyons' search for evidence of home health care owners' links with nursing homes and Medicare agencies found that there was minimal overlap. Second, almost everyone he contacted about home health care was not concerned with problems in patient care—in fact, they said that patient care usually was excellent. Their concerns were more often financial.

The cross-tabulation did provide some other interesting information. Lyons discovered that the home health care industry was the domain of a very small group of people. When all nongovernmentally related agencies (i.e., purely private) were identified, four "king pins" of the industry came through. Investigation of these four men became the focus of the research and led Lyons to Springfield, the Illinois state capitol, to look through regulatory files on these men, examining them for violations or citations of any home health care regulations. Here the investigation into fraud and abuse was really born because Lyons realized that evidence existed—that the investigation was doable. With the assistance of a top state official, Lyons obtained documents not normally available to the public that showed an unmistakable pattern of code violations. Once Lyons had this information, his confidence grew that he had enough to make a worthwhile investigation.

At the same time, Lyons' interviews also were producing contacts that were bearing fruit. A couple of contacts were people who had worked for home health care agencies in major administrative positions and had resigned, citing ethical reasons. Most important was a woman who had worked for a man named Michael Morrisroe, one of the four king pins. Lyons talked with her, returning from that meeting full of stories about the many ways Morrisroe had defrauded the government Medicare program. Morrisroe would become the main target during most of the investigation.

By late September, Meagher was finishing her sports story and expressed renewed interest in the home health care investigation. The BGA sent her a memo detailing what they were uncovering in their investigation. The memo clearly indicated that the story was not one of patient abuse but of major fraud.

It was becoming important to find out what NBC's position was going to be on the home health question: would they commit resources to the story? Sources and research in Chicago were leading BGA investigators to look beyond Illinois. One lead was from an important source in Tennessee. Other sources suggested that home health care operators in Chicago may have had connections in California and Florida. As the investigation was uncovering a national problem, costs of doing the work were increasing. Until they got a commitment from NBC, the BGA was picking up what was getting to be an expensive tab. Pressure was placed on Trossman and Lyons by BGA Director Brunner to lock NBC into the story or to take it elsewhere. (ABC traditionally paid all BGA nonsalary expenses for stories done together.)

About the same time, Brunner went to Washington, D.C., where he met with Val Halamandaris, counsel to the U.S. House Select Committee on Aging. Brunner and Halamandaris knew each other from previous BGA investigations. In the past, Halamandaris had been a good source of information and proved willing to initate reforms in response to BGA probes. Brunner now filled Halamandaris in on the details of the budding BGA/NBC investigation. Halamandaris pledged his support to the investigation and said he would be willing to arrange Senate hearings after the piece had run. When this information was relayed to Meagher, she was especially enthusiastic about gaining access to more information, and her view of the story became more positive. The policy maker connection had been made, and policy "results" (i.e., the hearing) were assured.

In mid-October, the call finally came. Meagher telephoned Lyons and Trossman saying that executive producer Friedman had said to go ahead with the investigation and had approved a trip to California for more exploration.

Although the NBC commitment provided some relief in costs and guaranteed a media partner, it produced some difficulties. First, NBC's Friedman was very cost conscious. The BGA staff thought he had a "less is more" philosophy. In keeping with the NBC News Magazine format, he liked fairly brief (10-minute) segments, which the BGA thought were not conducive to telling a detailed investigative story. He also thought 6 weeks was enough for an investigation, whereas BGA thought gathering sufficient evidence could take longer.

Most important, from the time of the commitment throughout the development of the piece, tension existed between the BGA investigators and the NBC people over the focus of the piece. The BGA was convinced that the piece had already moved from spotlighting poor or inadequate care to exposing major fraud in home health care administration. NBC, on the other hand, was still expecting the piece to show examples of patient abuse. Friedman felt it made for a compelling story to show specific victims. Lyons attempted to demonstrate the importance of the fraud angle by reporting on the results of his investigation to date. Trossman also kept reporting back that although investigators were looking for examples of patient abuse, they just weren't finding it. She was getting frustrated with what she thought was a fixation by NBC for "people." The media connection was clear. The angle of the story was a bit less clear. Was it fraud or abuse, or was it both?

The Search for Evidence Expands

With NBC as a full-fledged partner, the scope of the investigation expanded. One reason investigators enjoyed working with Meagher on this and other pieces was that once she was committed to a piece, she became part of the investigative team. Once involved, she made numerous trips to California with Lyons.

The investigative team now consisted of three persons from the BGA and two from NBC. The BGA investigation was being supervised by Trossman in Chicago. She was doing more than home health care at this time. The California investigation was being run by Lyons, who would check in with Trossman almost daily from the West Coast. The Chicago part was being conducted by BGA investigator Jennifer Ellis, who had joined the inquiry in about mid-September. At NBC, the team was headed by Meagher, who was with Lyons in California much of the time. She had an investigative assistant, Cynthia Brush, who joined in late October and was exclusively working to find a patient abuse angle (relieving the BGA investigators of having to find an angle that they did not believe was there).

Meagher made her first trip to California in late October with Lyons. Their main reason for going to California was to sniff out any Morrisroe connections there. In checking records, Lyons began to make connections with the top regional person for the Health Care Financing Administration (HCFA). This person had heard of the BGA and was happy to cooperate by making available HCFA records. The pattern was that Lyons did his work with HCFA, and Meagher followed other leads, getting together in the evenings to compare notes. The regional HCFA office was helpful, allowing Lyons access to almost everything without his having to go through Freedom of Information Act procedures. However, HCFA was giving Lyons so much information about Medicare fraud in home health care that it became apparent only selected cases could be used for a 10-minute television story. The BGA and NBC would have to pick "representative" cases on which to focus.

The California probe was providing little information about Morrisroe. Although he seemed to have some personal holdings in California, it looked as if he had no connections with the California home health care industry. Even though Morrisroe was not involved, the research uncovered what seemed to be a similar pattern of fraud in California by others. The game was the same, but the players were different.

Outside California other story developments were occurring. Early in November, NBC correspondent Garrick Utley was assigned to the story. This made the investigative team happy. He was one of the best correspondents for NBC News Magazine and had good working relationships with investigative journalists. When he read what had been happening with the investigation, he was excited about the possibilities of the story. Meagher was under increasing pressure to bring the story to a close (especially to find Morrisroe) as she made her third and fourth trips to California. The question of expenses was constantly being raised. The piece was beginning to take too much time and money, according to executive producer Friedman.

At the BGA in November, Jennifer Ellis and Trossman were providing support for Lyons' and Meagher's work in California. Because it appeared Morrisroe was not in California, Ellis needed to continue the investigation in Illinois, his home base of operations. She also was finding out that almost everyone with whom she talked had no complaints about the care that was being given at Morrisroe's agencies, just that, to jack up the costs, too many visits were being planned. One of the biggest complaints was that because of this practice, nurses were overworked. They were still giving service, but the nurses felt they could do a better job if they could make fewer, longer visits.

NBC investigator Cynthia Brush was still pursuing any leads she could find about patient abuse. This angle had been abandoned by the BGA because its investigators' sources seemed to think care being given by home health agencies was good. But Brush was being employed by NBC. BGA's attitude was if NBC's investigator found something, that was fine, but they would not have spent their money in what they saw as a waste of time.

Part of the reason for NBC's interest in the patient abuse angle was the need expressed by Meagher to "bring the piece alive" and to show clear victims. She believed that complicated financial schemes of villainy do not come across well on television because they are hard to portray visually. Also, it is difficult to depict victims concretely when they are "taxpayers" as opposed to elderly or handicapped individuals. Although BGA agreed with the need for the piece to come alive, patient abuse was not the way to bring it alive, because patient abuse did not appear to be rampant in home health care (if it existed at all).

Beyond Evidence: The Need for "Visuals"

About this time, everyone, especially Lyons and Meagher, began to think of "stunts" to make the piece visually appealing. This led them to think about ways to get Morrisroe on videotape. Because they thought he was central to the piece, they needed to have a picture of him at least. All they could find after considerable effort was his high school graduation picture. Since this was television, it was necessary to know what he looked like. When Utley came to Chicago in December to do some shooting, he said, "We've got to find him."

The problem with Morrisroe was that he was elusive. In fact, many times investigators said they almost began to wonder if he really was a person or just some made up individual. Because Lyons and Meagher were not turning up much information about Morrisroe in California but were uncovering lots of information with help from HCFA, they decided to shift the focus of their California work and pursue a Morrisroe-type character in California.

While investigating this California angle in early December, they heard about the fraudulent operations of one of the major figures in the California industry, Bob Deroger. Lyons and Meagher went to see him, posing as a couple interested in some office space that he owned. While looking at the space, Lyons turned the conversation toward moneymaking ideas.

Deroger seemed willing to talk. Lyons suggested that they (Lyons and Meagher) really did not have the money to invest in a home health agency but his brother-in-law was interested in investing some money. Lyons took Deroger's name and adddress and said that his brother-in-law would be getting in contact with him. Lyons' "brother-in-law" actually was Lee Norrgard of the BGA's Washington office. Norrgard contacted Deroger and arranged for a meeting in Las Vegas shortly after the first of the year. Las Vegas was chosen primarily because it is not a two-party consent state; i.e., a secret taping could be done without Deroger's consent. This plan had the full support of BGA Director Brunner, who agreed that the piece needed something to make it more visual.

January, 1981, began with filming the Las Vegas meeting between Deroger and the BGA's undercover investigator, Lee Norrgard. Meagher had connections with a hotel and within a few hours they had built an "Abscam"[3] room complete with a fake wall, hidden camera mikes, etc. During the taping, everything went well. In fact, Deroger was captured on tape describing how to commit home health care fraud. Everyone left Las Vegas pleased about having something exciting on tape. The fact they did not have Morrisroe was becoming less important.

The excitement did not last long; the next day Meagher got a call from New York saying the tape of the hotel meeting was "black" because of technical problems, according to the NBC tape editor. One could hear everything but could barely see anyone. The pressure then started from NBC and Meagher to do an "Abscam II." Trossman, Lyons and others from the BGA were very skeptical because what they had just done had been very difficult to accomplish, much less to replicate a week or two later. It would be difficult to get Deroger to repeat everything a second time.

A debate developed between NBC and BGA people about the advisability of trying an "Abscam II." The reason for redoing the piece had nothing to do with investigative information—it was made necessary because of a technical error and television's need for "visuals." The BGA team even suggested using the audio and just showing a still picture of the man. They thought a week after the original was too soon to approach Deroger again. They feared they could blow their cover and jeopardize the entire project.

NBC, on the other hand, was weighing different pressures. Meagher was still being told that this investigation was taking too much time. They needed to get the "program in the can," as Friedman expressed it. But without the interview, the piece still lacked something to make it exciting. One problem with doing the interview again was the expense of recreating it. To recreate the hotel room and hire camera crews was an expensive proposition. On the other hand, the cost of "Abscam I" had to be justified by producing visual results, which required attempting "Abscam II." After lengthy and sometimes heated long-distance conversations between those in California, Chicago, and New York, the investigators reluctantly decided to try again.

Lee Norrgard called Deroger and expressed some doubts and wondered if they could get together and discuss the deal again. Deroger bought the idea and agreed to fly to Las Vegas again in three or four days. Much to the investigative team's surprise, "Abscam II" came off just about as well as the first try. Although he cased out the room at one point when Norrgard had to leave, Deroger otherwise did not act particularly suspicious.

Ironically, it later turned out that the original tape had been good enough to use. It seemed that an especially "fussy" tape editor had judged it "a total waste," but when Meagher finally saw it (after Abscam II) she thought it was good enough to use. In fact, the Las Vegas segment that actually aired was an edited combination of Abscam I and II. The other major consequence of the Las Vegas filming session was that the regional HCFA office started an investigation into Deroger's activities immediately after reading the transcript of the first session.

Lyons spent most of February putting the final touches on the California investigation, part of which involved looking into the operations of a man named Poindexter whose involvement in home health care seemed to follow the fraud pattern. There was an additional angle that the BGA especially liked. It seemed that a high-level federal Department of Health and Human Services (HHS) employee named Al Fox had been tipping off Poindexter and other home health providers about government investigations of their agencies in exchange for various personal favors. BGA investigators Lyons and Meagher wanted to research this connection between home health care operators and federal government officials.

In mid-February Lyons, Meagher, Utley, and others went to Washington to videotape a convention of home health care providers and to interview several of them. At the convention, Lyons and Meagher began getting some confusing signals about following the federal government (i.e., Al Fox) connection. At the convention Utley pulled Lyons aside and told him to "Slow Meagher down; it's time to cut it. We don't want to hear any more—we have enough."

The result of this tension was a quickly prepared memo about Fox that was given to Utley with the suggestion that Fox be interviewed and given a chance to react to the charges. Utley bought the idea because here was another visual and because the "federal government connection" was included.

By mid-February, Morrisroe had still not been interviewed. Back in late December, a plan had been devised to get Morrisroe to appear on film and talk about home health care. A former Morrisroe employee who had helped in the early investigation was contacted. She had worked in a major position in a Morrisroe operation before quitting; the relationship between the two was possibly a little more than just business. It turned out that she still had Morrisroe's various telephone numbers. She would phone Morrisroe, tell him that she had taken the children and left her husband and gone to Arizona to be with her parents. Now in Arizona she would solicit his help in starting her own business. The first problem was reaching Morrisroe. She left a message with his answering services at a number of locations. Everyone waited. Finally, Morrisroe called her back. He told her that he was out of the country and was not sure when he would return, but he promised to get in touch with her when he knew more. This lifted hopes of getting Morrisroe. In February, Utley gave his approval to delay the story until they could get pictures and possibly an interview with Morrisroe.

But weeks went by and Morrisroe did not call back.. Finally, in early March as Lyons and Meagher were closing up the California investigation and deciding to use the high school picture of Morrisroe, the woman called and said that Morrisroe was at La Costa, a California resort about 45 miles south of where Lyons and Meagher were staying. Within a matter of hours, Meagher organized a film crew and got in contact with NBC. The crew plus Lyons, Meagher, and a friend of Meagher's all checked into La Costa and started to look for Morrisroe. La Costa is a large, exclusive, extremely private resort. Once at La Costa, the team began to wonder how to find Morrisroe and then what to do once they found him.

After realizing that requesting specific room numbers and other techniques used at most hotels wouldn't work, Meagher called a friend who ran a major hotel in Las Vegas and knew the industry to see if he could get Morrisroe's telephone number. Her friend explained that there was no way he could get the room number and said that La Costa had recently filed an invasion of privacy suit against a photographer who had been bothering one of its guests.

Throughout the stay at La Costa, Meagher was in contact with NBC in New York; Lyons stayed in contact with Trossman in Chicago. Some of the discussion between Meagher and New York was to guarantee that everything they were doing was legal. The BGA relied on the advice of NBC's attorneys, although by this time they were willing to do almost anything to reach Morrisroe.

The final strategy used to find Morrisroe's room was to deliver something to it. Lyons went to a shopping area outside of La Costa and ordered a bowl of fruit made up. He then positioned Meagher and her friend in the lobby. Lyons gave the basket to the doorman saying it was "for a friend's birthday" and asked him to deliver the basket. After taking a tip, the doorman obliged while Meagher and her friend never lost sight of the basket until it went to Morrisroe's room.

The plans for subsequently taping Morrisroe included devising an escape route for the film crew (getting the tape out of La Costa before it could be confiscated), checking everyone out of the hotel as the interview was being held and working on interview questions. The first set of questions developed by Meagher and Lyons were lengthy and intricate. In discussing the questions with Trossman, Lyons and Trossman decided they needed to be shortened and go directly to the meat of the subject. The first question was to be something like, "How do you respond to allegations that your home health care agencies are defrauding the government by . . . ." Meagher was concerned with the rewrites because she thought it essential to cover the point of the story but agreed to the shortened questions in part because Lyons was the one who would be asking them.

They were ready when Morrisroe emerged from his room the next morning. Almost everything went as planned. As Morrisroe came out, Lyons walked across the grass in front of his room and called out, "Mike. Mike Morrisroe." The interview lasted for about ten minutes with Morrisroe remaining surprisingly calm and relaxed while the cameras rolled. During the interview Morrisroe suggested that maybe they could talk about this in a different setting. Lyons said that NBC would contact him. (NBC did contact him later, but he refused a follow-up interview.)

Because the investigative team had been checked out of their rooms before the filming, no one could be held or possessions confiscated by security forces alerted by Morrisroe. Lyons and Meagher were elated by this success and returned home excited about their piece.

The Search for Victims Continues

Toward the end of February, when Lyons and Meagher were still working in California, more disagreement about the importance of patient abuse in the story surfaced. NBC continued to emphasize the need to show "the victims." NBC's researcher, Cynthia Brush, followed a lead on patient abuse to Mississippi where she said she found some cases of abuse. Trossman was dubious. She hadn't seen any evidence of abuse thus far, and thought that Brush might be overly anxious to identify abuse victims to appease her superiors. Therefore, Trossman had investigator Larry Yellin from the BGA's Washington office sent to Mississippi to work with Brush to provide an independent judgment.

One aspect of the problem was defining patient abuse. Lyons believed a difference existed between patient abuse and patient intimidation. Threatening to take away someone's bed or social security checks is not abuse—it is intimidation, he thought. He and others at the BGA felt that it would be unfair to call such things patient abuse or even to show them. They saw these practices as examples of the extent to which some people in the industry would go for money, and that the money was small time compared with the financial schemes of Morrisroe and the California leaders. Besides, the BGA believed that if you have to go all the way to Mississippi after six months of investigation to find one example, it is obvious that such intimidation is not a major problem.

NBC's perspective was different. First of all, Mississippi added another state and region of the country, thus making the network TV program more national in its appeal. Also, from the very first Meagher and others at NBC had seen this piece as needing concrete victims—at least a little old lady crying somewhere. Finally, Brush had been investing four or five months of her time and NBC's money in finding patient abuse. It was in her best interest to have some of her work appear in the piece. NBC's case won. The decision was made to include the home health care "victims" from Mississippi.

PREPARING THE INVESTIGATIVE REPORT

Finally, the investigative process must end, and production of the report must begin. Usually, there is no dramatic point at which the investigative reporters say, "Voila! This investigation is absolutely finished." Amost always, more tips can be explored, hunches acted on, and records probed. However, investigative journalism is expensive in time, energy, and money, and at some point the investigation must end, ready or not. In the case of home health care, NBC executive producer Friedman was the prod, pressuring Meagher to "get this one in the can. It's gone too long already."

The production phase of a televised report involves the task of organizing into a coherent story piles of notes and many reels of film. Crucial decisions must get made—about the exact focus of the story, about the tradeoff between choice of visuals and choice of content, and about the portrayals of the "villains" and the "victims." We see all of these elements in this case.

For Friedman, the home health piece had tied up one of his top producers, Meagher, for seven months and had cost $137,000. He hoped it was worth it. He was looking for a "hard news" piece to air on Thursday, April 23, 1981. Before that date, the show's time slot was Friday at 9 p.m. where it was up against the then number-one rated CBS program "Dallas." Friedman recently had convinced network officials to change the show from that disadvantageous slot to Thursday at 7 p.m., and April 23 was the Thursday premier.

Meagher realized that Friedman's request would be impossible to meet for practical reasons. She had more than 60 hours of tape to edit. The earliest she could make it would be April 30, but May 7 was a more realistic possibility. Friedman had little choice. He unhappily agreed to wait for May 7 but insisted that it go no longer. Meagher and the BGA realized that any plans for further investigation or tying together loose ends were gone; they entered the final production phase.

The final editing and production process began during the last week of April. At that point, a somewhat new and different set of actors began to mold the piece. Each day, Meagher would work in the editing room with technicians and a tape editor. She was joined occasionally by Utley and, more regularly, Dennis Sullivan, senior producer at NBC News Magazine. Sullivan, a former producer at ABC's "20/20," supervised Meagher's work and acted as a liaison between her and Friedman. Friedman, who did not see an edited version of the piece until April 29, was kept apprised of the developments by Sullivan, who in turn made Friedman's wishes known to Meagher. The BGA received daily reports of the production progress, and Mike Lyons joined Meagher and the others in the editing room on May 4, 5, and 6.

During the week of April 27, the piece went through sixteen permutations. Meagher conceived of the piece during this period as having three main segments. One would focus on Morrisroe in Chicago, a second on Deroger and Poindexter in California, and a third on Cerasi in Mississippi. She saw the segments as having approximately equal length, with the Morrisroe fraud scheme laid out in detail at the beginning as a case study of Medicare fraud. Sullivan did not discourage this perspective, and the editing proceeded for the first few days.

Most of the actual work during this period centered around choosing the visual shots and interview bites to be included. Meagher was highly attentive to the views of Sullivan and her tape editor during this period. The tape editor became particularly influential in selecting material for the piece because of NBC's "Report System," in which tape editors are asked to complete evaluation forms on the competency of producers. Meagher, who certainly did not want to alienate her tape editor, frequently deferred to his judgment in the editing process. This often meant that tape was selected for inclusion in the piece because of its visual value as much as its content.

For example, an interview with BGA legislative counsel Peter Manikas by Utley was not used because of a distortion on the videotape. On the day of the interview, everyone had agreed that Manikas had made the most intelligent and thoughtful statements of anyone about the governmental problems in regulating home health care. However, according to Meagher, "the distortion showed up in the editing room and we had to scrap the whole interview." Similarly, an interview by Utley of a high-level federal administrator, Marty Keppart of HCFA, was not used because it was "long, dull, and boring . . . we couldn't get a good bite out of the interview." This left Meagher with an interview of Val Halamandaris, counsel to the U.S. House Select Committee on Aging, to serve as the main spokesperson about the federal government's role in preventing home health care fraud.

By Wednesday, April 29, the piece had gone through several edited versions that were not radically different from one another in terms of the overall perspective. Meagher and Sullivan agreed that the time was right to show the piece to Friedman. As executive producer of the show, he would have the final voice on how the piece would look.

From all accounts, Friedman was extremely unhappy with what he was shown. "I don't understand it. It doesn't make any sense," he told Meagher angrily. "If this is as good as you can do, it's not going on and it's $137,000 down the drain." Friedman's primary concern was with the Morrisroe segment, and the overall emphasis on Medicare fraud. "It's just too complicated. Where are the victims?" he kept asking. Meagher reported that "the only part of the piece he liked was Mississippi and an old lady from California who appreciated home health care."

Meagher later phoned the BGA to tell them that Friedman wanted to cut the entire Morrisroe segment out of the piece but she promised to fight for it because she shared the BGA's view of the importance of Morrisroe to the story. "You have to understand," Meagher told Trossman, "Friedman and Sullivan believed at the beginning that this would be a story about fraud and *patient* abuse, and they're just realizing that it's really about *program* fraud and limited abuse. They have to be brought along a bit." She expressed particular disappointment in Sullivan, however, whom she perceived as misleading her into thinking that the first few edited versions would be acceptable to Friedman.

Meagher spent the remainder of the week trying to clarify the Illinois and California fraud segments and beef up the Mississippi segment. This led to the inclusion of some visuals, and the exclusion of others. First, she cut the woman who led the team to Morrisroe out of the piece. "She gave us the best information about Morrisroe," Meagher said, "but she was very inarticulate. We couldn't even get a bite out of her interview." Next, Meagher eliminated an interview with another Morrisroe nurse, even though she talked about patient care. "We have better examples of inadequate patient care in Mississippi," Meagher said. Instead, Meagher and Sullivan developed an animated graphic of the Morrisroe scheme to substitute for the "talking heads."

Meagher also wanted to include the dramatic footage of Morrisroe at La Costa but changed her mind after a stern warning from Sullivan. On April 20, a documentary produced by WBBM-TV Chicago on the ethics of investigative reporting attacked the technique of "ambush interviews" with investigative targets. In the next few days, Sullivan cautioned every NBC producer that "if you've got any ambush interviews, be prepared to justify them." Meagher decided rather than generate additional controversy about the home health care piece, she would cut Morrisroe's dramatic confrontation from the story, leaving only his refusal to make a statement: "I would want to give a call to my lawyers just to make absolutely certain that it would be appropriate to make a statement at this time." Thus, months of work and enormous expense in trying to locate Morrisroe yielded little footage for the final product.

On the other hand, an almost purely fortuitous development during the investigation produced an interview that Meagher would use to anchor the piece. While in California, Meagher was looking for stock footage of home health care operations. Because of its good reputation, she decided to shoot the Visting Nurses Association headquarters in Los Angeles. While there, she also got the names of two home health patients for possible interviews on the merits of home health care. Now, Meagher decided to meet Friedman's demand for a more personal and emotional piece by opening and closing the show with remarks by one of those elderly women. In the opening, one said, "Oh, I'd much rather be home than go to a rest home or a convalescent place." In the closing of the show, another of the patients from California said, "I love to be home. It means a lot being here."

Meagher and Sullivan also decided to make Victor Cerasi the focal point for the expanding Mississippi segment. "He just looks so sleazy and spouts gems," Meagher explained. Though Meagher admitted that the information on Cerasi and his Mississippi operations was weaker than what they had on Morrisroe, she believed that Cerasi "made a better villain." He just looked the part of a greedy home health operator who might be willing to hurt his patients in order to "make a buck," according to Meagher. He was overweight, smoked on camera, and had an arrogant style.

In addition, Cerasi had been willing to talk freely about his home health care operations at the convention in Washington, D.C. "Let's start with my salary," he had told Utley on camera when asked about why he was in the business. Cerasi stood in marked contrast to more camera-shy home health care operators whom Utley had tried to interview at the Washington, D.C., convention. Cerasi's bold, forthcoming statements made for good television.

By the time the BGA's Mike Lyons arrived in New York on Monday, May 4, to help with the final editing, the piece had begun to take its final form. The new version of the Morrisroe segment containing the animated graphic had been given tentative approval by Friedman. As a result of diligent production work and lobbying by Meagher, as well as a gradual adjustment by Friedman to the fraud angle, Morrisroe was back in the piece. The California segment looked at that point about the same as it would at airing. The home health convention would serve as a bridge to the Mississippi segment to allow the viewer to meet Cerasi. In the end, over 8 minutes of the 18-minute segment focused on Mississippi.

In the 3 remaining working days before the air date, several issues had to be resolved. First, Lyons and Meagher had to go over the entire piece to check the accuracy of each allegation. The targets of the piece were private individuals, and *Gertz v. Welch* and other recent court decisions unfavorable to the media loomed large in the background. Lyons and Meagher realized their findings soon would have to be justified to the lawyers at NBC.

In going over their work, Lyons was able to find only one questionable allegation. Unhappily, it related to the nature of the Morrisroe scheme. After checking the facts, Lyons was compelled to suggest a change in the Morrisroe segment. The change required bringing Utley into the studio to do a new "voice over." Utley, who by this time had removed himself from the editing process, did not appreciate this intrusion into his time, and Sullivan was so angry about having to do a retake at such a late stage that he would not speak to Lyons the next day.

At the end of the day on Monday, the "finished" version of the piece was shown to Friedman. It ran more than 20 minutes, far in excess of the average piece in the NBC News Magazine show. Friedman, who believed in short, fast-moving pieces, ordered additional cutting from the Morrisroe segment and a tightening of the Mississippi segment.

By Wednesday, a second finished product running 18 minutes was ready to be viewed by an NBC attorney. In the process known as "lawyering," the attorney went over the documentation of the allegations with Meagher and Lyons, playing "devil's advocate" the entire time. Afterwards, he said that "the only one that will give you trouble is Lenore Stein [Dr. Poindexter's associate in California]. If anyone sues, it will be her."[4] After surviving legal scrutiny without change, the piece was viewed by Friedman on Wednesday evening and given final clearance to be aired on Thursday night's show.

THE INVESTIGATIVE INFLUENCE

"Home Health Hustle" aired May 7, 1981, nine months after the story idea meeting at BGA. What was its impact? The conventional model of muckraking journalism would suggest that (1) journalists work on an investigation surrounded by as much secrecy as they can muster; (2) the investigative report then appears in print or is aired on television; (3) the public is aroused by the publication of the exposé; and, therefore, (4) pressures elected officials or relevant agency personnel to correct the problem disclosed; (5) these decision makers respond to the public and work to change the relevant policies.

Did this sequence of events actually occur in this case? To find out, we interviewed a random sample of 300 members of the general public in the Chicago metropolitan area and 57 policy makers both before and after NBC News Magazine aired the segment on May 7. (See appendix I for methodological details regarding sample selection and research design.) We also examined the policy discussions and policy changes that could be attributed to the main investigation.

We asked half the respondents in the general public to watch "NBC News Magazine" and the other half to watch another news program called "PM Magazine," which aired at the same time. The purpose of this request was to provide us with a group who would see the "Home Health Hustle" and another group who would not see it in order that we could learn the extent to which watching the segment resulted in attitudinal and agenda setting changes.

We found clear changes among those who watched "Home Health Hustle." One to two weeks after watching the program, this group saw home health care as a more important program, saw government help for the program as more essential, and saw fraud and abuse as a larger problem within the program. Those who did not watch the program did not change their views in the same ways (see table 3.1).

We also interviewed samples of government policy makers and special interest group representatives active in the health care field. Of the govern-

Table 3.1
Effect of "Home Health Hustle" on General Public Sample (Mean Scores)

	All respondents ($N = 250$)				Respondents watching their assigned programs ($N = 131$)			
	Experimental group		Control group		Experimental group		Control group	
	Pre	Post	Pre	Post	Pre	Post	Pre	Post
Importance of problem								
Home health care (HHC)	3.28	3.46	3.22	3.27*	3.33	3.62	3.25	3.20*
Nursing home care (NHC)	3.48	3.58	3.55	3.47	3.47	3.72	3.59	3.32*
Combined HHC and NHC	3.39	3.52	3.38	3.36*	3.40	3.67	3.37	3.25*
Other issues	3.38	3.45	4.31	4.38	3.36	3.49	3.19	3.29
Importance of government help								
HHC	4.18	4.40	4.18	4.15*	4.17	4.45	3.98	3.95*
NHC	4.33	4.39	4.31	4.41	4.29	4.45	4.15	4.20
Combined HHC and NHC	4.26	4.39	4.25	4.28	4.24	4.44	4.07	4.08*
Other issues	4.22	4.26	4.13	4.17	4.23	4.26	4.00	4.00
Fraud as a problem								
HHC	3.17	3.37	3.19	3.15*	3.20	3.53	3.08	2.98*
NHC	3.20	3.36	3.19	3.35	3.25	3.52	3.10	3.17*
Combined HHC and NHC	3.18	3.37	3.17	3.24*	3.23	3.53	3.08	3.08*
Other issues	3.13	3.13	3.18	3.16	3.07	3.23	3.10	3.10
Government spending								
HHC	2.76	2.61	2.74	2.69	2.67	2.58	2.58	2.44
NHC	2.60	2.61	2.60	2.72	2.60	2.57	2.33	2.57
Combined HHC and NHC	2.63	2.62	2.66	2.71	2.63	2.58	2.44	2.54
Personal								
HHC	2.21	2.22	2.15	2.26	2.32	2.37	2.04	2.13
NHC	2.45	2.43	2.37	2.38	2.48	2.47	2.19	2.15
Combined HHC and NHC	2.33	2.33	2.27	2.33	2.40	2.43	2.12	2.19

[a]Significance levels are based on distributions of f ratios from analysis of covariance (ANCOVA) adjusting for initial between-group differences (Reichardt, 1979).
*$p < .05$

ment policy makers we interviewed, those who saw or heard about the "Home Health Hustle" were significantly more likely than those who did not see or hear about the program to change their views on the seriousness of fraud and abuse in home health care. They did not change their opinions about the problem of fraud and abuse in other areas such as food stamps, Medicare, Medicaid, and national defense. The lack of change in these areas lends validity to the argument that it was the NBC segment that caused their beliefs to change in the area of home health. In contrast, interest group policy members who had and had not seen or heard about the program changed their opinions very little. Probably, this is because special interest elites are already very committed to the interests of their groups and are already knowledgeable and concerned about the relevant issues (see table 3.2).

The news media segment also influenced government policy makers' beliefs that policy action was necessary. Those who saw or heard about the segment were much more likely than nonexposed policy makers to say that there should be policy action related to correcting fraud and abuse in home health care. Again, however, interest group decision makers changed their opinions very little, regardless of whether they saw or heard about the "Home Health Hustle" (see table 3.3).

Not only did exposure to the NBC segment on home health change government elites' own opinions, but it also changed their perceptions of how the general public views the importance of home health. Those who were exposed to the media report changed their views on the public's attitude regarding fraud and abuse in home health care whereas those who were not exposed did not. Again, interest group decision makers showed no significant change compared to their nonexposed counterparts in how they viewed public opinion (see table 3.2).

The discussion above describes how the opinions of both the public and government policy makers changed if they were exposed to the NBC segment on home health. When we look specifically at how the views of government policy makers compare to those of the public in their priority ranking of the problem of fraud and abuse, we find some differences. Government elites changed their assessment of the problem of fraud and abuse in home health care to a more serious one, but the problem continued to rank last as compared to the problem of fraud and abuse in other areas such as national defense, food stamps, Medicare, etc. In contrast, members of the general public who were exposed to the media presentation not only changed their assessments of the degree to which they thought fraud and abuse was a problem in home health care but also changed their priority rankings from fourth place (out of a possible five) to second place (see table 3.4).

Our survey interviews with the general public and policy makers showed both attitudinal and agenda-setting changes.[5] However, policy actions oc-

Table 3.2
Policy Elites' View of Fraud and Abuse Problems in Government Programs

| | Government policy elites (N = 27) | | | | | Interest group elites (N = 24) | | | |
| | Exposed (N = 17) | | Not exposed (N = 10) | | Sig.[a] | Exposed (N = 9) | | Not exposed (N = 15) | |
	Pre	Post	Pre	Post		Pre	Post	Pre	Post
Personal views									
Home health care (HHC)	1.706	2.177	1.500	1.375	*	1.667	2.111	1.546	2.364
Nursing health care (NHC)	2.177	2.941	2.000	2.125	*	2.222	2.444	2.857	2.571
Combined HHC and NHC	1.941	2.559	1.750	1.750	*	1.944	2.278	2.091	2.455
Other programs	2.427	2.711	3.000	3.000		2.400	2.583	2.385	2.539
Views of general public									
Home health care (HHC)	1.667	2.133	1.200	1.100	*	1.444	1.556	1.333	1.417
Nursing home care (NHC)	2.313	3.000	1.500	1.400	*	2.222	2.556	1.929	2.286
Combined HHC and NHC	2.033	2.567	1.350	1.350	*	1.833	2.056	1.667	1.833
Other programs	2.762	2.857	2.857	2.810		2.852	2.815	2.533	2.400

[a]Significance in changes from pretest to posttest in the exposed group versus the not exposed group. (We used regression analyses employing the reliability-adjusted pretest as the covariate [Reichardt, 1979].)

*p < .05.

curred independently of these changes. In fact, these policy changes were insured prior to the publication of the story. Early in the project, the investigative reporting team collaborated with policy makers in government. Several months before the story aired, members of the team began meeting with officials of the U.S. Permanent Subcommittee on Investigations to plan a series of hearings on home health care fraud. The newly elected Republican leadership of the subcommittee, headed by Senator William Roth (R—DE), wanted to use the news media report to draw public attention to the issue of fraud and abuse in governmental programs. At the same time, the investigative team wanted to obtain a governmental "reaction" to their story.

The relationship that developed between the investigations and the policy makers had a clear impact on the deliberative agenda of the U.S. Congress— that is, on the agenda of policy issues that were discussed in Congress. In fact, the NBC piece on May 7 concluded with correspondent Utley announcing forthcoming Senate hearings on the home health business and how it was being run. The day after the piece aired, the Permanent Subcommittee on Investigations issued a news release, setting the hearing dates for May 13 and 14. It began:

Table 3.3
The Impact of the News Media on Policy Elites'
Belief That Policy Action Is Necessary

	Cross-tabulation of "action" by "exposure"	
Policy action	Exposed	Not exposed
All elites[a]		
More time	84%	56%
Same time	16%	28%
Less time	0%	16%
Government elites[b]		
More time	81%	30%
Same time	19%	50%
Less time	0%	20%
Interest group elites[c]		
More time	89%	73%
Same time	11%	13%
Less time	0%	13%

[a] $N = 51$; $\chi^2 = 6.218$; $p = .0446$.
[b] $N = 27$; $\chi^2 = 7.7797$; $p = .0204$.
[c] $N = 24$; $\chi^2 = 1.394$; $p = .498$.

Table 3.4
Comparison of Attitudes Toward Fraud and Abuse in Five Areas Among Policy Elites and General Public

Elites

	Interest group elites (N = 24)				Governmental elites (N = 27)			
	Exposed (N = 9)		Not exposed (N = 15)		Exposed (N = 17)		Not exposed (N = 10)	
	Pre	Post	Pre	Post	Pre	Post	Pre	Post
National defense	(1) 3.56	(1) 3.00	(1) 3.40	(1) 3.15	(2) 2.88	(2) 3.00	(1) 3.56	(1) 3.00
Medicare/Medicaid	(2) 3.22	(2) 3.00	(2) 2.93	(2) 2.67	(1) 3.00	(1) 2.76	(2) 3.00	(2) 2.75
Food stamps	(4) 1.78	(4) 2.11	(4) 1.8	(5) 1.87	(3) 2.24	(3) 2.44	(3) 2.00	(3) 2.44
NHC	(3) 2.22	(3) 2.44	(3) 2.73	(3) 2.57	(4) 2.18	(4) 2.94	(4) 2.00	(4) 2.12
HHC	(5) 1.67	(5) 2.11	(5) 1.53	(4) 2.37	(5) 1.71	(5) 2.18	(5) 1.78	(5) 1.38

Public

	All respondents (N = 250)				Respondents who watched (N = 131)			
	Treatment group		Control group		Treatment group		Control group	
	Pre	Post	Pre	Post	Pre	Post	Pre	Post
Medicare/Medicaid	3.32	(1) 3.40	3.44	(3) 3.33	3.21	(4) 3.40	3.44	(1) 3.39
Food stamps	3.26	(4) 3.31	3.42	(1) 3.41	3.25	(3) 3.41	3.32	(2) 3.39
NHC	3.19	(3) 3.34	3.19	(2) 3.36	3.24	(2) 3.52	3.11	(3) 3.17
HHC	3.16	(2) 3.37	3.19	(4) 3.15	3.19	(1) 3.53	3.08	(5) 2.98
National defense	3.15	(5) 3.03	3.06	(5) 3.13	3.07	(5) 3.10	2.94	(4) 3.15

Senator Bill Roth (R—DE) announced today that the Permanent Subcommittee on Investigations will hold hearings on May 13 and 14 on abuses in the Federal Home Health Care Program administered by the Department of Health and Human Services. "Insufficient attention has been paid to the ease with which some nonprofit health care agencies are able to defraud the Medicare program by establishing less-than-arms-length relationships with sub-contractors," Senator Roth said.

The news release went on to cite the work of the journalists and investigators specifically. Early in the release, Senator Roth is quoted as saying, "Evidence put together by the Subcommittee staff and the Chicago-based Better Government Association (BGA) will clearly show that this program is not operating as Congress intended. Elimination of these kinds of abuses will go a long way toward bringing the budget under control and restoring confidence in government's ability to spend the taxpayers' money."

In a later paragraph, the news release said that the BGA investigators would testify at the hearings about the problems they uncovered during the investigation they conducted with NBC. The news release concluded by saying the hearing would also address "the need for legislative change to correct the inadequacies of the Home Health Care system." In addition to testimony and recommendations for change from representatives of such federal agencies as the General Accounting Office (GAO) and the Health Care Financing Administration (HCFA), and such nonprofit organizations as the American Federation of Home Health Agencies and the National Association of Home Health Agencies, the BGA investigators would give testimony suggesting possible legislative changes. Thus, not only did the investigative journalists bring the issue to the attention of the Senate Permanent Subcommittee on Investigations, but also they testified on both the problems they uncovered and on possible solutions to those problems at the committee hearings.

The Senate Permanent Subcommittee on Investigations hearings opened on May 13 with Senator Roth vowing that the purpose of the hearings was "not designed to condemn the concept of home health care" but rather to expose "the various mechanisms by which one individual or small organization can control all aspects of the delivery of home health care services through a tax-exempt, nonprofit agency while reaping profits involving hundreds of thousands of dollars." The first witness was Charles Morley, chief investigator of the Permanent Subcommittee on Investigations, who discussed audits of home health agencies, but most of the rest of the first day was concentrated on a dissection of Michael Morrisroe's system of not-for-profit home health agencies in the Chicago area and how "a tangled web of self-dealing (was) designed to defraud the government."[6]

Day 2 of the hearings on May 14 was devoted to discussion of ways to "fix" the home health program to prevent the kinds of abuses detailed the day before in the Chicago case. Witnesses included the director of the U.S. General Acounting Office Human Resources Division, the President of the National Association of Home Health Agencies, the President of the American Federation of Home Health Agencies, the Deputy Administrator of the U.S. Health Care Financing Administration, and the legislative counsel of the BGA. All the testimonies involved somewhat intricate analyses of exactly why fraud was being commited in home health care provision and of ways government oversight of the program could be tightened up.

No simple solution appeared to be immediately available to solve the problems uncovered. The frustration of the senators who listened to the testimonies was apparent. Senator Cohen (R—ME) asked angrily, " So where in this whole system are there incentives for controlling costs? Where are they?" Later, he pleaded for simplicity, "Is there some point in time where we can come back to the simplicty of the issue, some limitation on what a home health agency can legitmately contract out?"

Despite their frustration with the problem and the potential solutions, several senators during the hearings credited NBC and the investigative team for their contributions. Senator Charles Percy (R—IL), a member of the subcommittee, concluded his testimony by expressing "fullest confidence" in the investigative team, and added, "I applaud Senator Roth's initiative in securing their (i.e., the investigative team's) findings."

NBC's "Home Health Hustle" did not generate much media attention outside Chicago, but the Congressional hearings attracted attention across the country. United Press International (UPI) and the Associated Press (AP) wire services carried stories about the hearings that were picked up by papers in many cities including the *Denver Post*, the *Atlanta Constitution, The New Orleans Times-Picayune/The States-Item*, the *Dallas Morning News*, the *Indianapolis Star*, the *Salt Lake City Tribune*, and the *Chicago Tribune*. Substantively the stories were similar. A typical lead paragraph began this way: "Some providers of home health care have used Medicare to defraud ailing senior citizens—and all taxpayers—as a 'get rich quick scheme,' a Senate panel was told Wednesday" (AP story from the *Dallas Morning News*, May 14, 1981). Most of the stories then quoted from the testimony of Mike Lyons, one of the BGA investigators who conducted the investigation. The operations of Morrisroe were described in some depth, and reference was made to similar practices in Chicago, Mississippi, and California, thus giving the problem a national scope. Some articles, such as the one in the *Washington Star* (May 14, 1981), quoted a subcommittee official as saying that fraud and abuse in the home health program "is becoming a nationwide phenomenon." None of the stories, however, appeared on the front pages of these newspapers.

The most dramatic follow-up coverage of the home health probe appeared in *The New Republic* magazine of June 6, 1981. The magazine published a four-page article by the *Washington Star's* Howie Kurtz headlined "Home Care Ripoff" with the over-line "There's a Hole in the Program." The story was written in a narrative style beginning with Morrisroe's first developments of his home care business "using an initial investment of just of $41,000" and tracing him to date: "Five years later Senate investigators and a federal grand jury are trying to retrace the flow of illicit cash in Morrisroe's many repositories" (p. 11). Kurtz sustained a detailed story into which he wove an analysis showing the corruptability inherent in social programs such as Medicare and Medicaid. Thus, the reader's attention was held by the specific Morrisroe story but the wider social implication—it's more than one man in Chicago—was plain. Kurtz concluded his tale by reminding the reader that the home health idea is a good one:

> The real tragedy is that home health care is one of the best ideas to come down the pike in years. It lets old folks remain in the community with family and friends instead of shutting them away in concrete institutions. . . . The only way to persuade moderate senators like Roth and Cohen to press ahead with this new program is to redesign the crazy system that allows people like Michael Morrisroe to play three-card monte with the taxpayers' money (p. 14).

After the hearings and the subsequent media coverage, what policy changes took place? The Senate Permanent Investigation Subcommittee urged new laws to curb abuse in the federally funded Home Health Care program, including recommendations that (1) not-for-profit home health agencies should be required to subcontract only through competitive bidding and (2) a better system of audits of home health agencies by the federal government should be established (U.S. Senate, 1981). However, no bill was ever introduced. Thus, the "Home Health Hustle" affected the Congressional *deliberative* agenda in that the topics for discussion changed but it did not affect the Congressional *action* agenda in that no actual legislative actions were taken.

Our analysis shows that the "Home Health Hustle" is not consistent with the paths to reform predicted by the linear Mobilization Model. It was not the *airing* of the investigative report that created the impact on the deliberative agenda. Nor was it the *members of the public* who were so aroused over the exposé that they pressured their representatives to act. Rather it was the *active collaboration* between journalists and policy makers (i.e., high-level subcommittee staff members) in the process of the media investigation that created the policy outcome, a collaboration set in motion during the investigative phase of the life course of this issue.

NOTES

1. This is very similar to the model described by Kingdon in John W. Kingdon, *Agendas, Alternatives, and Public Policies* (Boston: Little, Brown, 1984), pp. 20–21.

2. Philip F. Lawler, *The Alternative Influence: The Impact of Investigative Reporting Groups on America's Media* (Washington, DC: University Press of America, 1984), p. 6.

3. Abscam refers to a well-known FBI undercover sting operation that occurred in 1980, the year before the home health care investigation.

4. In fact, no suits have been filed. However, Lenore Stein was the only subject to respond to the piece, writing a letter to NBC that demanded a retraction. NBC refused her request.

5. Fay Lomax Cook, Tom R. Tyler, Edward G. Goetz, Margaret T. Gordon, David Protess, Donna R. Leff, and Harvey L. Molotch, "Media and Agenda Setting: Effects on the Public, Interest Group Leaders, Policy Makers, and Policy," *Public Opinion Quarterly,* 47 (1983), pp. 16–35.

6. Michael Lyons, Testimony on Home Health Care Fraud and Abuse, Hearings Before the Permanent Subcommittee on Investigations, Committee on Governmental Affairs, U. S. Senate (Washington, DC: U.S. Government Printing Office, 1981).

CHAPTER 4

"Rape: Every Woman's Nightmare"

"Rape Epidemic: 'No Woman Immune.'" The banner headline greeted Chicago Sunday *Sun-Times* readers on July 25, 1982. "Last year," the story began,

an estimated one of every 34 females in Chicago—from children under 5 to women over 80—were victims of sex crimes, ranging from rape to fondling. . . .

Now a three-month, computer-assisted investigation by the Sun-Times of sex crimes in the Chicago area reveals the serious threat of sexual violence faced by all women in both the city and the suburbs. . . .

Rape is a serious enough problem in the Chicago area as a whole. But it is a plague in the black neighborhoods where, police statistics show, reported rape rates can be 40 times higher than some other city neighborhoods.

Inside the paper a large box dominated an entire page. It featured a chart/map headlined, "Sex Crimes in Chicago's Community Areas, 1981: Rape and Sex Crime Rates Computed on the Basis of Number of Incidents for 10,000 Female Population." Each of Chicago's 77 community areas was identified and left white if the rape rate was 0–4.99 (per 10,000 women), tinted gray if the rate was 5–19.99 per 10,000 women, and tinted black if the rate was 20 per 10,000 women or higher. Community areas were numbered and listed according to their "rank by rape rate." Also listed were total rapes, rape rates, total sex crimes, and sex crime rates for each of the 77 areas.

A large box across the entire bottom of the page contained pictures of the series reporters and a story about the nature and scope of the series. The *Sun-Times* claimed the computer-based series had produced new data on rapes, data even the police didn't have.

A sidebar story told the tragedy of two rapes of a 27-year-old black mother living in public housing. The first rape occurred when she was followed home by a man who had stripped and raped her and then urinated on her before leaving her sobbing in a stairwell. She was raped again six years later by another man from the neighborhood. Accompanying the sidebar was a large drawing that portrayed a black woman, looking down, her hand over her mouth as if to stifle sobs. As is usual in most rape stories, this account did not mention the victim's name.

A story on the op-ed page claimed that the Chicago police threw out half the rapes reported to them in 1981, a figure the story quoted feminists as saying is much too high.

These first-day stories and graphics were accompanied by an editorial, "Sex crime: social epidemic." The editorial stressed that the series was based on a three-month computer-aided study and promised that it would "document a social disgrace—an epidemic of sexual violence that our society, for all its progress, seems unable to cure."

During the next four days, the *Sun-Times* used a barrage of statistics, graphs, charts, drawings, and tales of victims to inform readers that:

- Women are more likely to be raped in 16 of Chicago's suburbs than in the city itself, and when a rapist strikes in the suburbs he is less likely to be apprehended.
- Suburban police are reluctant to disclose rapes because they want to portray their communities as safe.
- One of every three adults charged with rape or attempted rape never faces trial on those charges, and juveniles often never even get charged.
- Despite the work of feminists, aid for victims, particularly for blacks, is sorely lacking, and victims say police make them feel guilty.
- Illinois is doing virtually nothing to rehabilitate sex offenders, although experts say that an untreated rapist will rape again.

The series also educated careful readers about feminist views of the relevance of what victims are wearing when attacked, the treatment of victims by police, emotional consequences of victimization, and appropriate self-defense tactics.

On the third day of the series, the *Sun-Times* suggested that there were already some policy impacts from the series: "The Illinois House Rape Study Committee will hold public hearings to further explore the problems *spotlighted by the Sun-Times series* [emphasis ours] on rape, committee chairman Representative Aaron Jaffe (D—Skokie) said Monday." The story quoted Representative Jaffe as saying, "The series was right on the button."

Another story discussed a policy reversal by Illinois Governor James Thompson:

Legislation that would have funded hotlines and victim assistance centers and provided training for counselors and police to aid all violent crime victims was vetoed last year by Governor Thompson.

HOWEVER, UNDER PRESSURE [emphasis in original] from feminists, Thompson restored a $450,000 state appropriation for emergency treatment of sexual assault victims.

And on Tuesday [the third day of the *Sun-Times* series], Thompson approved legislation lengthening prison terms for defendants convicted of gang rape and providing additional coverage for medical expenses for sexual assault victims.

On the fifth and last day of the series, a second editorial called for changes in attitudes, behavior, and policies about rape. It said the *Sun-Times* was gratified that Jaffe's committee had promised to probe problems spotlighted by the series. It also called for a variety of legislative initiatives and concluded with a reiteration of statements by feminist sources: "Rape is a crime of violent aggression. It's time to declare war on it." On that last day of the series, the paper also began printing letters from readers about the series.

THE GENESIS OF THE PROBE

Although the *Sun-Times* series included frequent mentions of its "three-month study," the rape series had been in the planning stages much longer. Eight or nine months before the rape series appeared, Hanke Gratteau, who covered crime in Chicago, had asked the city editor, Alan Mutter, to assign "some kind of rape story" to her. She told Mutter she had been talking to sources and suspected that rape was a pretty serious problem in Chicago and that there were some new angles. Alan P. Henry, who was also a crime reporter, had proposed to Mutter that he do an enterprise story on crime and race in Chicago. At about the same time, science reporter Dennis Byrne proposed to Mutter that he add an occasional *social* science piece to his science beat—stories on social problems and demographic trends. Byrne had an MA in urban affairs and a social science undergraduate degree and had always been interested in crime as a social problem in big cities. He also had become interested in "precision journalism" described in a book by Philip Meyer.[1] The idea was to use social science research methods to gather data and other evidence on a topic and then have reporters, writers, and editors produce copy based on the data for publication in the mass media.

But before giving the go-ahead for a substantial, time-consuming piece of investigative work, the *Sun-Times* editors required evidence that such an investment was going to be worthwhile. They required a written justification—a "pitch"—with stories, sidebars, and angles all outlined. If the pitch appealed to the city editor, he passed it up the editorial hierarchy for approval. If the city editor didn't like the idea, "it got nowhere," as Henry explained.

As Mutter considered the story ideas the reporters had proposed to him, he and other editors at the *Sun-Times* were reflecting on the impressive information that Tom Moore, a *Sun-Times* correspondent in Washington, D.C., had been able to generate through computer-based analyses of congressional voting records. Mutter expressed interest in Byrne doing "something parallel" in Chicago. Mutter thought this analytical approach was coming into vogue in many of the larger, more successful newspapers, partly in response to Watergate, but also as a way to compete with the immediacy of broadcast news. "Besides," Byrne said, "the public thinks we [reporters] lie; figures don't."

Further, the *Sun-Times* had just bought its first desk-top computer for use in the newspaper's library. Both management and reporters were interested in exploring ways in which the machine could be used in the newsroom.

Mutter put all this together, and by early in 1982 the idea for a series based on computer analyses of crime statistics had jelled. "Originally we planned to look at rape *or* murder, but I thought we should focus on rape because it's scarier," said Henry. "Our readership is young women. My bet is that they are more concerned about rape. . .And besides, the editors want a little sex and violence in each day—a weeper." When asked about his role, Byrne recalled, "They came to me to do the statistical analyses, and it all matched up." This was to be just the sort of precision journalism he had wanted to do.

The trio still didn't have the final go-ahead from Mutter. They didn't yet have enough information to write the detailed pitch, but Mutter encouraged them to investigate whether there was enough for a series.

THE INVESTIGATIVE PROCESS

Crime stories seemed to be in the air in Chicago when the *Sun-Times* journalists began their probe. Local television investigative reporters were working on stories for the spring "sweeps" period.[2] Pam Zekman at WBBM-TV was doing intensive work on what turned out to be a prize-winning series, "Killing Crime," which told viewers about the extent to which Chicago Police "unfound" (i.e., dismiss) crime reports, especially rapes. Peter Karl at WMAQ-TV was working on what was to become "Street Files" and interrupted it to begin "Beating Justice" (see chapter 5). The *Sun-Times'* major competitor, the *Chicago Tribune,* was concurrently working on a story about juvenile justice.

The *Sun-Times* team began by interviewing academics and activists about rape. "We needed them to give us a sense of the field, what the issues were," said Henry. A prime source at this stage was Martha Goddard, executive director of the Citizen's Committee for Victims' Assistance, a leader of rape victim advocate movements. "We looked at a lot of what she told us," Henry said. "For example, she said, 'Too many victims are telling me they don't report the crime to police. . . . Many victims fear nothing will be done.'"

Thus, the reporters were cautioned early on about the unreliability of the statistics on rape. "We only know the number that the police *say* were reported to them and that they didn't later unfound," said Byrne. (Police unfound a crime when they think the evidence "doesn't meet the standard.") The experts told the reporters that other sources—victimization surveys and reports from rape crisis lines—were indicating the true rates of rape are much higher than the rates shown by police data.[3] They also learned that feminist activists providing services to victims had concerns about suburban rape data, insensitive treatment of victims by police, hospital personnel, and in the courts, and the general lack of services for victims.

By early February, the team finally thought they understood the issues well enough to write the detailed pitch for Mutter. Henry drafted an outline of a nine-day series with plans for sidebars. In general, Byrne was to be responsible for the computer analyses of the crime statistics from the city and suburbs and the stories based on those data. Gratteau was to study court processes and victim services, and Henry was to concentrate on the suburbs, convicted rapists, and rehabilitation programs.

Here's exactly what the reporters pitched to their editors:

Day 1: (facts, figures, and shock day) [Byrne, Gratteau, Henry]. Rape. A numbers crunch of where it is being done, what time of day, by what kind of person (age, income, race, education, etc.), against what kind of person. Also, who is being caught, how quickly, numbers on indictments, prosecutions, sentencing, recidivism. . . . Grids of where rape is occurring. . . . Data on the pervasive fear of rape. . . . These dry figures would serve as the spin-off point from which we profile a "typical" (as defined by numbers) victim and criminal in separate sidebars. [Gratteau interviewing victim; Henry interviewing rapist] A third sidebar would be a typical 24-hour cop sheet on rapes in the city.

Day 2: (blast the burbs day). Suburban police departments, we have reason to suspect, are sometimes miscategorizing rape as assault or battery in an attempt to stave off the political repercussions that come with the crime, particularly in the more well-to-do suburbs. We would question the rape stats. . . . Also, we must give examples of the kind of haroosh that accompanies rapes. . . . Hanke [Gratteau] has access to info on this one.

Day 3: (trend day . . . how the courts and cops are dealing with rape) [all three]. The difficulty of prosecuting a rape case. . . . how far have the cops come in dealing with rape. How Vitullo kits [rape evidence collection kits used by medical personnel] have standardized physical evidence and helped prosecution. Research on identifying men who might rape. Research says that too many men get a second and third chance. Sidebar: criticism has already surfaced among some feminist lawyers that overly harsh penalties can be counterproductive, by encouraging the rapist to kill his victim. Sidebar: someone who beat the system. Sidebar: treatment of rapists. Washington State has an excellent treatment program. In Illinois, while there are 1,100 convicted sex offenders in prison, as of a month ago, only 18 were being treated. . . . Superintendent of the unit says they don't have the money to treat more.

Day 4: (big picture day . . . how Illinois and Chicago compare to other cities and states on laws and busts) [will be in main story Byrne and Henry]. Compare state rape laws with Illinois rape laws. Trace the history of Illinois rape laws and the forces that came into play to change those laws. The sexually dangerous persons act. . . . Supreme court rape decisions and their impact. [sic]

Day 5: (sensitivity day) [will be first day of Gratteau]. The impact of rape on families. How their lives have changed. Their views of the court and police systems that are supposed to deal with the problem. Where the victim can turn.

Day 6: (dump on Reagan day) [Henry and Gratteau]. Rape and the Reagan budget cuts. Funds for some rape crisis hotlines are being reduced. This could be the place for a night at a rape crisis center, keeping this hackneyed story within the context of the federal cuts . . . a night on call with an advocate—someone who goes to a hospital to be with a rape victim through the examination period. What Illinois is doing: not much. Illinois does not provide funds to groups like the National Coalition Against Sexual Assault. . . . One respected source says, "Victim services in this state are pitiful." (Will be in main story first day Henry)

Day 7: (kink rape day) [Henry]. This story, a grabber in the *Midnight Globe* tradition but backed by facts instead of fancy, would discuss the kinds of rape that have caused judges to scratch their heads and lawyers to scurry for the law libraries before passing judgment. What about rape of males by females . . . men by men (gay bar pickups for example). Are they protected under the law. Also there have been cases about men raping their wives. Where does the current body of law stand on the rights of a husband to take out his cravings on his wife. . . . What about date rape. Prison rape. Rape of children. Laws that say 12-year-olds can't be accused of rape. The recent example of the 5-year-old whom a judge said was to blame for being raped.

Day 8: (protect yourself day) [Gratteau]. Discuss the opposing views of whether to fight or let it happen. Also a study that says blacks are more prone than whites to be severely beaten and that they are also more successful in fending off the initial attack. . . . Pauline Bart's study on rape avoidance showing that if you fight back you'll have a better shot at not getting raped.

Day 9. Conclusions. Why we wrote this series. Here's hoping we have figured that out by then [all three].

On the basis of this pitch, Mutter, Ralph Otwell, editor, and eventually Jim Hoge, publisher, gave the approval for intense investigative work on the series some time in late February or early March. There were, however, many delays associated with getting the data from the Chicago police, and the reporters also had other assignments. Thus, they worked on the series intermittently over the next several months.

First, to get access to the statistical information held by the Chicago police, the reporters had to get the approval of Superintendent Richard Brzeczek. They recalled Brzeczek saying the series was "a good idea," and he pledged his complete cooperation and that of the department's data-processing unit. With Brzeczek's approval in hand, the reporters asked the data-processing personnel for a computer tape containing information about all sex crimes, but the unit "had problems" with their requests. They stalled the reporters, saying that they were asking for an old file (1981 data, actually less than a year old), which was a mess. They also claimed it was being reprogrammed, that it would be impossible to give them a useful copy.

The data processors also told the reporters that the police used the data for tracking cases, founding/unfounding decisions, and indicating final disposition of cases. Therefore, the data processing didn't routinely do the management analyses the reporters were asking for—trends, kind of weapons used in the commission of the crime, locations of rapes, numbers of victims, race of victims and offenders. The reporters speculated that the data-processing staff was resistant either because they were embarrassed that they didn't already do those kinds of analyses, since the unit leader commented, "it would be interesting to know the results." They may also have resented being *told* to cooperate with the reporters.

Next, the data processors demanded a prohibitive sum of money for analyzing all the variables on the tape. Eventually, the reporters gave up on some information they had wanted—for example, the kind of weapon, if any, used in the commission of the crime—because each piece of information added to the cost and to the delays. In frustration, the reporters specified a limited number of data items and, for a price ($300), the data processors "picked off" from the composite data tape the desired information and gave it to them on a "clean" tape.

However, the reporters didn't get the clean data tape until May. The waiting "caused us fits," said Henry. Even when they got the tape, there were problems. Some data weren't in the form the reporters wanted. For example, Byrne said, "We wanted to know where the rapes were taking place, but the computer variable called 'location' on the data tape was not where the crime occurred but the precinct the crime report came in from." The reporters also had problems with the computer variable called "status" of crimes. Each crime was labeled *unfounded, cleared, exceptionally cleared,* or *open.* The labels kept changing as new facts were available to the police. It was during their examination of the unfounded crimes that reporters discovered that

Chicago police unfound rapes at a higher rate than they unfound other crimes and that that unfounding rate is higher than in most large cities.[4,5] This discovery resulted in a first-day sidebar.

To ascertain the rape rates in the 77 community areas within the city boundaries, Byrne had to superimpose by hand the maps of the police beats or districts on the community area map. Most beats fell within one of the community areas. Then Byrne was finally in a position to do statistical analyses that would produce the information they had wanted in the first place.

The reporters and editors also wanted comparable data from the suburbs. In addition to the concerns of the activists, the reporters had other reasons to examine the statistics on the suburbs. "It didn't make sense to do only the city," Henry said. "Besides, the suburbs are where the money is. Everyone knows . . . you don't have to tell anyone in the newsroom that if we don't get more suburban readers we'll be out of jobs in ten years." Eventually, the reporters decided to rely on the FBI data for the suburbs.

At this time reporters also began to confront other aspects of the story. From the inception of the investigation, Byrne said, the series had been seen by the reporters as a story on the nature and prevalence of the dangers all women face. There was disagreement among the reporters about whether they expected to uncover official wrongdoing. "We weren't going in looking for indictable offenses," Byrne said. "We didn't have the expectation that the grand jury would meet after our series." Yet Henry reflected, "Obviously we were hoping to find the laws were lousy and the justice system was just not doing its job. I'm always hoping there will be maggots under every rock . . . I'd be lying if I said otherwise. But we didn't find them."

Race was also an issue according to Henry: "Race appeared important very early on. . . . Intuitively we knew rape was a problem in the black community. Superimposed was our perception of fear in white communities that they were being victimized by blacks. First we wanted to know how much interracial rape was going on. Police came up with hand-calculated figures but said they couldn't tell us. One said, 'We did that once . . . I must have it . . . I must have lost it. . . . It's not our fault. People misunderstand.' We think the police knew it [rape] is highly *intra*-racial because all the academic research says that. So this was one of our objectives, to get the real figures for the area."

When asked if any findings surprised them, one of the reporters responded with two things—"The huge number of victims in Chicago was even higher than we'd been led by the feminists and researchers to expect," and "the police weren't doing such a bad job." The reporters also expressed some disappointment that there was "less hard news" than they had hoped for and that the series didn't have "a right up the gut" story every day.

PREPARING THE INVESTIGATIVE REPORT

In early July, the city editor, Mutter, told the reporters he wanted to start the series the third Sunday of that month. The reporters did most of the interviews and all of the writing within the last week and a half. "When they [the editors] originally assigned three people to the series, they thought we'd be done in a couple of months, but we had to wait so long for the data," Henry explained. "We ended up working on it on and off. . . . We did most of the interviews a week before." Indeed, Henry had to postpone his vacation.

It was important to the reporters that the series get the "big picture" across to the readers. The first-day story featured many of the issues frequently discussed by feminists and rape researchers.[6] It stressed that police statistics, frightening as they are, still greatly understate the frequency of the crime and in other ways tell only part of the story. Because of the emotional and physical problems associated with rape and other sex crimes, they are notoriously underreported by victims, and even if the crimes are reported to officials, the Chicago police so often unfound rapes that many never end up in the crime statistics. The *Sun-Times* estimated that 20,000 women were victims of rape, attempted rape, and deviate sexual assaults in Chicago in 1981, nearly ten times the 2,300 reported in the police statistics for the same period. That amounts to 54 rapes per day, more than two per hour. If the statistics were to include all forms of sex crimes committed against women, the number more than doubles to 45,000. Sex crimes with child victims are even more likely to go unreported to the police, with only one in twenty being recorded.

The story also pointed out that police statistics do not indicate that for every rape there are three women who are attacked but avoid being raped. Feminists and rape researchers believe this is an important, largely untold story that would encourage women to fight their attackers more often.[7] Third, the story included analysis of data debunking the commonly held stereotype that white women are raped by black men. This stereotype is thought to fuel the fears of white women and to demean the experiences and fears of black women. Fourth, the story provided facts that many women say they want, in order to assess their own safety.[8] The story reported computer-based data on victims (half are 22–30 years old; most are unemployed or students); their attackers (most are in their 20s; most are known to the police); and the circumstances of the crimes (25% occur between 8 a.m. and 4 p.m., and 80% involve strangers).[9]

A story on the page opposite the editorial page focused on the large percentage of rape cases—half—unfounded by Chicago police. Feminists and activists quoted in the story said the figure was much too high, suggesting that the judgment of the police should be questioned. Supt. Brzeczek defended the figures, saying officers investigating a rape complaint must judge whether the crime fits the legal definition of rape—by force and against the victim's will. Officers also look at the circumstances surrounding the crime and the credibility of the victim, Brzeczek said. He said that some rapes are thrown out because police determine "consent" or when police believe married women have charged rape "to provide a cover story" to tell their husbands after voluntarily having sex with other men.

Thus, the reporters and editors, through the placement and content of the main story, sidebars, graphics, editorials, and op-ed pieces signaled to the careful reader on the first day all the themes that would be touched on during the rest of the series. They also alerted activists and policy makers who hadn't already been contacted as sources that rape and its consequences were issues that were going to be getting a lot of press attention during the following week.

The first day's articles also introduced attentive readers and policy makers to most of the villains and victims who would play roles in the series. In addition to the literal victims of rape, the series portrayed all women as victims because of the dangers all women face on a daily basis and the consequences of that for their lives. Black and suburban women were seen as especially victimized. Other victims were the feminist activists and the organizations they represented, which were endeavoring to provide aid to women who had been raped. Finally, society itself was portrayed as a victim.

It also was clear that first day that there were many villains in this series—from the rapists themselves to important institutions in society. There were stories about adolescent rapists who were getting away with their crimes, and mature, repeat rapists with unflattering—some would say sick—perceptions of women. There were stories of policemen who were suppressing true figures about rape to make their communities look safer than the city. There were stories of policemen who threw out half the rapes reported to them by women, policemen who lost or failed to care for evidence (thus weakening cases of victims), and policemen who made victims feel guilty in the midst of their ordeals. There were stories about how the police fail to apprehend and prosecute many rapists. The prisons were painted as villainous because they failed to give priority to programs that try to rehabilitate rapists. The state legislature was villainous because it was slow to realize the need for reforming the rape laws, and the governor allowed corrective measures to languish unsigned on his desk for months. President Reagan appeared a villain because his budget cut social programs that could have provided for rehabilitation efforts.

Some believe the newspaper itself proved to be a villain by playing on people's fears and by unrelievedly deepening the disquiet of women through its continuous messages about both the dangers for women and the failures of institutions to deal with this serious problem faced by half the nation's population.

One theme in several of the series stories was that rape victims often are treated badly by police. For example, the Monday story said, "While suburban police departments said they are becoming more sensitive to problems of rape and its victims, victim advocates say police in many communities have a long way to go, and that they have horror stories to prove it." Then the story recounted the trauma of a pregnant victim who lost her case in court because the police failed to gather and adequately care for the evidence. "It was a problem that the police didn't take this crime seriously," Kate Dawes, Lake County assistant state's attorney, is quoted as saying.

A Monday sidebar, which focused on a victim who said the police made her feel guilty and defensive, picked up the theme of poor police treatment. The victim is quoted as saying,

> They asked me to take a polygraph test, and the chief . . . thought it would be advisable for me to undergo hypnosis. . . . They asked me if I manufactured the story so I could move in with my fiance [which she did the day after the rape]. They asked: "Were you going through a crisis where you needed to attract attention to yourself?" . . . I was being discounted as a typical female. . . . A friend told me to drop the whole thing because if I took the polygraph and showed the least sign of wavering, the police could try to get me for filing a false police report. . . . So that's what I did. I dropped the case.

The theme of poor treatment by police was once a much greater concern of feminists and other persons providing aid to rape victims. But, in large measure because of the pressures of the activists, the situation has improved[10] in most large cities. In fact, one such activist, Pam Odde,[11] said many victims now say "the police couldn't have treated them any nicer." But Henry had wanted to make the point in the series that the police treat victims badly. Odde said her organization, Northwest Action Against Rape, had been contacted by Henry, who said he was doing an article on "how suburban police departments had mistreated rape victims." When he was told that "this was not our experience," he contacted Odde, who emphasized again that they had had good experiences with the police. In fact, she had suggested Henry write instead about what she regarded as a bigger problem at the time—that the state's attorney's office was not prosecuting men accused of rape. She said Henry called her back later and wanted to set up an interview with someone who had specifically been treated unfairly by police. She told him she would tell victims and that they would call him if they wanted to. A few days later he called back to say no one had called and again later to say he'd found three victims through another agency. He added that "it was a criteria set by the editor that the victims had to have been treated poorly by the police."

Another theme emphasized again and again in the series was the fact it was based on computer analyses. The tone often was quite self-congratulatory. For example, on the second day, as on the first, there was a box at the bottom of the first page containing a story headlined,

> Computer study breaks new ground. . . . The series is the result of one of the most extensive uses ever of computers by a newspaper to analyze a complex issue such as sex crimes. The computer analyses for the first time revealed information not even in the hands of the Chicago Police Department or city, such as sex crime rates by community areas, information which had been long sought by some community groups. . . . The computer analyses also for the first time shed light on the relationship between the victim and the offender by race and other factors, and yielded information on how well Chicago and suburban law enforcement agencies as well as the courts deal with of [sic] sex crimes.

Then, in a manner unusual for a mass media story—as opposed to a scholarly article—came explanations of the statistical methods used in generating the data for this story:

> A measuring tool known as "regression analysis," which predicts the statistical relationships between [sic] several factors such as rape and race, produced a more complete picture. Statistically, the size of the black population in determining a community's rape rate is almost twice as important as income level and far more significant than the size of the Hispanic population, the population of the community or its distance from Chicago.
>
> Each factor—race, income, Hispanic population, population size and distance from Chicago—was analyzed separately by the computer, using regression analysis, and then collectively in all possible combinations with each other, such as race, with income and size of the Hispanic population. Even after this "multiple regression analysis," race stood out as the single most influential factor. . . . Analysis of rape statistics clearly indicates that poor black communities have rape rates more than triple those of poor white communities.

On the third day there were stories indicating that public officials and legislators were paying attention to the series and already taking some related action. For example, there was a quote from Representative Jaffe praising the series as "right on the button" and announcing community hearings "to further explore the problems spotlighted by the *Sun-Times* series on rape." He said his committee would investigate (1) "how to get suburban police departments to cooperate more fully [in rape investigations] than they have been and how to get some suburban law enforcement officials not to play games with statistics," and (2) "whether police need more training to improve their sensitivity toward victims and whether such courses should be mandatory in some cases." Both issues had been emphasized in the stories on Sunday and Monday.

The fourth day (Wednesday) story also indicated reaction to the series from another important public official, Governor James Thompson. Although the reporters said they had not contacted him in the course of doing any part of the series, he appeared to have taken the opportunity presented by the series to hold a Tuesday press conference during which he signed into law a bill that had been awaiting his signature for several weeks. It called for lengthening prison terms of gang rapists and for aid to cover medical expenses of victims.

On Thursday the *Sun-Times* began printing letters to the editor. One reader indicated she regarded the series as fear-provoking: "The *Sun-Times* series on the high incidence of rape in Chicago and the suburbs is frightening. The callousness shown rape victims and the leniency toward rapists reflects a debasing attitude toward women. . . ." A second letter quarreled with the statistical analyses, arguing that there were important variables left out of the regressions that, if included, may have produced different results. The author concluded, "It is annoying to see statistics used as a tool to mislead people in regard to important issues such as rape."

A final editorial restated some of the series findings and indicated "gratification" that Jaffe's committee had promised to probe issues spotlighted by the series. It also called for making deviate sexual assault a Class X felony, urged statewide evidence collection efforts, and asked for increased victim assistance, reform of the rape laws, and administrative changes in public and private agencies around the state.

As it turned out, the newspaper's call to make deviate sexual assault a Class X felony was unnecessary. It already was classified that way under Illinois law. That portion of the editorial was based on an important development that occurred during the final week of working on the series. Reporter Henry had recontacted Francine Stein in Representative Jaffe's office to discuss the state representative's legislative agenda, including whether Jaffe planned to introduce legislation that would make deviate sexual assault a Class X felony. According to Stein, Henry was confused by one of her answers.[12] Stein said she told Henry about the Class X status of rape and deviate sexual assault. "What we were pushing," said Stein, "was adding to the law that it would also be a Class X felony if a guy used a foreign object—like a bottle or broom handle—to commit the rape." This emphasis never appeared in print.

Many investigative or enterprise reporters use public officials as sources in their stories, thus providing them with platforms for announcements of new programs. In the final stages of producing a series, reporters may contact them for responses to specific points or revelations to be made in the exposé. As Henry said, "Their reaction legitimizes a story." All three of the rape series reporters contacted or re-contacted several relevant public officials and activists during the final ten days, in effect alerting them the series would soon reach the public. However, none of the reporters contacted Governor Thompson, despite the fact that new rape legislation was awaiting his signature. And when, in the middle of the series, the governor signed the legislation, the *Sun-Times* did not take any credit. Neither did anyone on the reportorial team contact Chicago Mayor Jane Byrne.

In response to specific questions about whether they had pushed public officials for reactions, Henry said, "Zekman talks to reactors ahead of time [to guarantee reforms]. We didn't do that. Could be Zekman's better. We should do it. We just didn't do it." Byrne wondered aloud whether it would have been proper to contact officials to guarantee reactions ahead of time, and then said, "I never do that, but I'm not trained as an investigative reporter."

Although Henry said the reporters stuck with the original series outline and wrote the stories in the order they were sketched out, the final series ran for only five days. The detailed pitch had plans for a nine-day series. Henry said, "they ran 65–75 percent of what we turned in," but declined to say what the editors cut. A comparison of the actual series with the pitch indicates that most of the elements were included, spread over fewer days than originally planned. However, there wasn't a "kink" rape day, and there wasn't a "conclusions" piece except for the final day editorial.

As in the case of most exposés or enterprise stories, the reporters knew much more than appeared in print. For example, Byrne said,

"One thing still bugs me. . . . I know in my gut that NU [Northwestern University] is covering up [rapes on campus] and the U of C [University of Chicago] is too. . . . The [Hyde Park] *Herald* had a story. . . . There's a pattern rapist. This guy breaks a window. Then he goes to the door and offers to fix it. He leaves out the putty and then goes back and rapes the woman. The U of C people denied it. But it was in the Herald that it was a student.

Henry also gave more details about one of the victims who was the subject in one of the sidebars. He said the police chief he interviewed about the case was "cackling" and didn't believe the woman, claimed she made it up in order to move in with her boyfriend for protection.

At one point late in the final week, the *Chicago Tribune*, the *Sun-Times'* major competitor, started running a series on Chicago's suburbs. The *Sun-Times* team feared that "they knew we were doing a story on sex crimes related to the suburbs" and had done their own story as a "spoiler" to *Sun-Times* series. "Yes, we were concerned! By this time we had invested so much in this series," said Byrne. The reporters considered doing a "spoiler to the *Tribune* spoiler" but they decided, based on the content of the early *Tribune* stories, that the *Tribune's* effort was coincidental, and they never wrote the counterspoiler.

The reporting team gave the editorial writers advance copies of most of the stories in the series on Wednesday or Thursday before the Sunday it was scheduled to begin. The team said they did not write the editorials or try to tell the editorial writers what they thought should be in them. Rather they met with the editorial writers, talked over the ideas, and fed them information.

A few days before the series began, the publicity department got involved, and "hyped" the series on a couple of local radio shows, but according to one of the reporters, there was no real marketing strategy for the series.

In this account of the "career" of the *Sun-Times* rape series, we see several journalistic traditions at work as well as journalists and organizations attempting to adapt to the mores of a changing society.

Reporters and editors are always looking for new angles, and the *Sun-Times* staffers were no different. They were looking for a new angle for an old, tried-and-true story. That is, rape and its devastating consequences is a story that has been told over and over again for many years by the *Sun-Times* and countless other newspapers through the accounts of individual women's victimizations. Daily, in any large U.S. city, there are too many rapes to report, and the typical rape is no longer news. Even the bizarre and unusual ones seem less newsworthy than they once did. Yet, from the beginning of the popular mass media in the U.S., rape stories have always been good for circulation—"They want a little sex and violence every day, a weeper," said Henry. Computer analyses of sexual assault statistics, allowing the *Sun-Times* to take a "big picture" look at the topic, was a new angle. It would also be new to shatter the stereotypes that the suburbs are safer than the city and that white women are raped by black men.

But this new angle required different methods and approaches for the reporters. With the shift to computer analyses, the standards of social science became influential in guiding the reporters' thinking about the quality of their evidence. Community activists and rape crisis counselors—instead of being tipsters exposing wrongdoing by fraudulent officials—became educators of the journalists, teaching them the "politically correct" conceptualizations of this particular social problem and about the roles of relevant social institutions. It was important to the journalists that the activists and advocates thought the series "got it right" and that it provided them with a new platform for reformist action.

In addition to the rapists, society's major institutions and their employees all became villains in this series, and all women were their victims. And, in the end, the newspaper itself was seen by some as one among the villains.

THE INVESTIGATIVE INFLUENCE

Asked about intended effects on readers, Gratteau said, "The series was meant to be informative, but it also scared people." She said she thought it was likely that more women would *not* report an acquaintance rape after the series, a sentiment she herself shared. She also thought the series might prompt suburban women to be more careful than they might have been. Gratteau added, "We also wanted to give women 'pointers,' tips on what they could do to protect themselves."

In terms of intended policy consequences, Henry said,

> We had hoped for government reaction, and some policy making to result from it, but it's not the kind of thing when someone is caught with his hand in the till. The kind of policy we're looking for is probably incremental improvements in the attitudes of policemen on the beat, improved efforts of hospitals' use of evidence kits, improved pruning of the law and statutes to make prosecution a little more sensible.

In a systematic approach to assessing the impacts of the rape series, the Northwestern University research team studied effects on the general public, policy makers, policy making, and the press.[13] As in our other case studies, we had access before publication to enough details about what would appear in the rape series to design and conduct random sample telephone surveys of the general public and policy makers both before and after the publication of the series. To assess possible impacts on policy, the team also examined proceedings of legislative hearings, bills, statutes, budgets, and news releases and interviewed relevant political actors. In order to assess the impact on the press, the research team analyzed the *Sun-Times* and *Tribune* coverage of rape three months before the series and three months afterwards.

The preseries survey of the general public indicated that many of the issues discussed in the series were already quite important to them, and the series did not appear to *increase* the salience of those issues to them (see table 4.1). That is, the general public did not think "lenient treatment" of people accused of rape or assault was any more important a social problem after the series than they had thought it was before. Similarly, providing aid for rape crisis centers appeared to be no more important after the series; people were no more likely to "strongly agree" that "rape and assaults against women are more prevalent in the suburbs than in Chicago"; people were no more likely to rate law enforcement agencies dealing with rape and sexual assault as "highly ineffective"; and they were no more likely to think rape occurred "more often" than the police statistics indicate. All of these points were made emphatically and repeatedly throughout the series.

Table 4.1
Effect of Rape Series on General Public Sample[a] (Mean Scores)

	Readers/nonreaders				Series aware/notaware			
	Treatment (readers) ($N = 85$)		Control (nonreaders) ($N = 87$)		Treatment (aware) ($N = 125$)		Control (not aware) ($N = 55$)	
	Pre	Post	Pre	Post	Pre	Post	Pre	Post
Two most critical problems (1 = crime as one, 2 = crime not mentioned)	1.59	1.40[b]	1.59	1.48	1.57	1.40[b]	1.66	1.55
Importance of problem								
Lenient treatment of rape	1.21	1.19	1.22	1.18	1.24	1.22	1.14	1.11
Inadequate day care	1.88	1.75	1.98	1.98	1.97	1.86	1.84	1.86
Fraud and waste in government	1.41	1.34	1.35	1.30	1.42	1.36	1.28	1.21
Poor health regulations	1.61	1.54	1.74	1.72	1.69	1.70	1.62	1.50
Importance of government help								
Rape crisis centers	1.31	1.22	1.41	1.36	1.38	1.29	1.34	1.32
Battered wife shelters	1.55	1.46	1.41	1.36	1.66	1.54	1.58	1.37
Abused children protection	1.17	1.13	1.27	1.16[b]	1.30	1.16[b]	1.06	1.09
Theft and burglary victims	2.34	2.28	2.50	2.41	2.44	2.33	2.43	2.32
Location of incidents								
Rape more in suburbs	3.11	3.17	3.29	3.15	3.22	3.24	3.14	3.04
Property crime more in suburbs	2.85	2.85	2.94	2.87	2.93	2.89	2.83	2.83
Child abuse more in Chicago	2.26	2.20	2.40	2.48	2.31	2.28	2.37	2.57
Drug crime more in Chicago	2.53	2.21[b]	2.59	2.39	2.51	2.32	2.72	2.30[b]
Effective law enforcement programs								
Rape and sexual assault	2.94	2.97	3.20	3.08	3.05	3.03	3.06	3.02
Drug abuse	2.95	2.86	2.90	2.80	2.89	2.90	2.98	2.74
Juvenile gang control	3.12	3.17	3.20	3.08	3.05	3.05	2.96	2.94
Drunk driving	2.72	2.89	3.04	2.80[b]	2.89	2.90	2.89	2.72
Crime the same as police statistics								
Rape	1.31	1.25	1.40	1.31	1.38	1.30	1.32	1.28
Homicide	1.56	1.57	1.52	1.57	1.63	1.60	1.33	1.49
Aggravated assault	1.41	1.37	1.61	1.48	1.65	1.43[b]	1.27	1.45
Drug-related death	1.48	1.50	1.50	1.48	1.60	1.41[b]	1.25	1.73[b]

[a]Lower numbers indicate more positive responses (i.e., 1 = very important; 4 = very unimportant).
[b]Significance of change from pretest to posttest using a dependent t-test, $p < .05$.

But there were other indications that members of the general public were affected by the series. Letters from readers published during the series and afterwards indicated the stories had provoked fear. The messages of all the elements of the series were clearly disquieting ones for women. The basic messages in the headlines and stories—rape is a very frequent event; the police unfound half the rapes reported to them; it's more common in many of the suburbs than in the city, and assailants are even more unlikely to get caught there; many of those apprehended never stand trial; the prison system does little to rehabilitate offenders, who are likely to commit rape again; and there is little help available for victims—did nothing to alleviate that fear. Gratteau, herself, said working on the series increased her own fear and, afterward, she was less likely than before to report a rape, especially an acquaintance rape, to the police.

Although it is unlikely the reporters *set out* to frighten women, they knew the series would appeal to, or play on, the fears of women. They picked rape in the first place "because it's scarier," as Henry said, and because it is of more concern to a larger number of readers than other forms of sexual assault. Byrne thought the series also provoked other feelings and issues that are hard to measure statistically—alienation, powerlessness. He said, "If only we had more money, time . . . We could have gotten at some of that. The interest is up."

Were policy makers more affected by the series than the general public? The answer is, it depends. Of the 39 policy makers surveyed before the series, we were able to reinterview 37. All but one said they had read at least some of the stories in the series. They said the series had had little effect on their personal views about rape, they did not expect it to have consequences for their work routines, and it had not changed their opinions about views of the general public on rape (see table 4.2). However, they were significantly more likely to mention a crime-related issue as one of two "most critical urban problems facing us today" after the series. Further, policy makers judged law enforcement agencies assigned the responsibility for dealing with rape as significantly less effective after the series. Both points were made repeatedly in the main stories, sidebars, and editorials.

A number of policy developments were announced during and shortly after the series ran, but these had, in fact, been initiated before the investigation began. On the basis of our analyses of legislative hearings, bills, statutes, budgets, news releases, and interviews with the political actors who responded to the rape series, we found that policy reactions to the investigative series seemed to be largely "deliberative." That is, publication of the series gave politicians and activists new opportunities to draw attention to the problem of rape, thus pushing the issue back onto the policy agenda in several arenas. However, there were no budgetary or administrative changes in the immediate wake of the series that could be said to be caused by it.

Table 4.2
Effect of Rape Series on Elite Sample (N = 37)^a (Mean Score)

	Personal view		View of public	
	Pre	Post	Pre	Post
Importance of problem				
Lenient treatment of rape	1.27	1.38		
Inadequate day care	1.92	2.24^b	Not asked	
Fraud and waste in government	1.57	1.38		
Poor health regulation	1.73	1.92		
Importance of government help				
Rape crisis centers	1.54	1.49		
Battered wife shelters	1.76	1.65	Not asked	
Abused children protection	1.30	1.22		
Theft and burglary victims	2.62	2.24		
Location of incidents				
Rape more in suburbs	3.35	3.30	3.61	3.42
Property crime more in suburbs	3.00	2.91	3.35	3.08
Child abuse more in suburbs	2.67	2.31	1.58	1.50
Drug crimes more in Chicago	2.60	2.51	1.65	1.68
Effective law enforcement programs				
Rape and sexual assault	2.32	2.70^b	2.94	3.05
Drug abuse	2.54	2.51	3.32	3.11
Juvenile gang control	2.70	2.73	3.27	3.38
Drunk driving	2.76	2.62	3.24	3.03
Crime the same as police statistics				
Rape	1.68	1.49		
Homicide	2.03	1.92	Not asked	
Aggravated assault	1.57	1.70		
Drug related death	1.95	1.73		

^{a}Lower numbers indicate more positive responses (i.e., 1 = very important, 1 = highly effective, etc.).
^{b}Significance of change from pretest to posttest using a dependent t-test, $p < .05$.

The series was, however, skillfully used by politicians to gain publicity for their policy initiatives. Within a week after the first story appeared, Mayor Jane Byrne announced the "creation" of a Rape Hotline and a public housing drop-in center for rape victims, although both services had been operational for months. On the third day of the series, Governor James Thompson called a press conference and signed a bill into law providing for increased criminal penalties for "gang rape." The bill, described by its sponsors as a "routine tightening of the state's criminal code," had been on the governor's desk for a month.

Monica Faith-Stewart, sponsor of the gang rape measure, said the *Sun-Times* series "definitely" affected the timing of the bill's signing. She explained, "I hadn't been able to get an answer as to when I could expect him to sign the bill until shortly after the series started. Then I was told he would be holding a press conference the next day to sign it."[14] The series did affect at least the pace of this "substantive" policy development.

Representative Jaffe's committee had planned legislative hearings all along, but the series prompted him to decide to hold community hearings in neighborhoods spotlighted in the *Sun-Times* series. It also allowed him to develop constituent interest in the issue, giving the committee greater support for getting a package to reform Illinois rape laws back on the legislative policy agenda. [The reform package passed the following year.] "It was decided to make police responses and rape in the black community an important part of the hearings," Faith-Stewart said. "We wanted to make our own investigation based on the *Sun-Times* findings." Ms. Stein added that the series had affected the timing and content of what the committee planned to do. That is, the

> committee decided to hold a series of closely spaced hearings to coincide with the appearance of the series in order to capitalize on the publicity generated by the stories and attract more public interest. . . . They can generate publicity to help the committee—and the professionals who staff it—to get their ideas across in Springfield [the capitol of Illinois].

Stein said the series was "generally solid and informative, but simplistic and misleading in places." She complained, "There was nothing brought out in this series that was not brought out in our reports. . . . The computer study was new, but it just verified what we had been reporting. There was absolutely nothing that was brand new. There's no question but sensationalism of a sort and a failure to give credit to what's already been done sells newspapers." She also said the series played on people's fears. Nonetheless, Stein and the other policy makers we interviewed said that the *Sun-Times* series served a useful function in providing information and focusing attention on rape as a political issue.

The series also had at least a minor effect on two political campaigns going on at the time. Frank Beaman, press secretary to gubernatorial candidate Adlai Stevenson, said the series had an impact on the Stevenson campaign. Beaman explained Stevenson's team was "studying the issue," and "thought it was a good issue that may expose some . . . indifference [in incumbent governor Thompson]."[15] Meanwhile, another candidate, Neil Hartigan, who was running as a Democrat for secretary of state, criticized

Thompson shortly after the series appeared "for cutting funds for rape emergencies."

Whereas there was no evidence in this case study of a formal coalition between the reporters and the policy makers designed to bring about reforms, there was evidence that the journalists' actions in contacting or recontacting some policy makers and activists just before the series began had alerted them to the publicity opportunities on the horizon. Furthermore, several policy makers who had not been contacted by the journalists took advantage in one way or another of the opportunity presented by the series. Others seeking elective office were forced to consider the issues for their campaign agenda.

The most striking change that followed the newspaper series, and the one least addressed by other agenda-setting research, is the effect on the *Sun-Times'* itself—its subsequent coverage of rape and the attitudes of staff.

The content analyses of the *Sun-Times* showed a significant change in the depth and extent of its rape coverage after publication of the investigative series, despite no change in police reports of rape. Specifically, the content analysis found:

1. An increase in the total number of stories about rape, from 32 during the three months preceding the series to 58 in the three months after the series.
2. A doubling of the space devoted to rape from 594 square inches before to 1,354 after the series.
3. An increase in the number of rape stories in the first 10 pages of the newspaper from 10 to 18.
4. An increase in the number of rape stories containing interpretation, analysis, or context (rather than reporting only the facts of an individual case) from 6 to 20.
5. An increase in coverage of official governmental activities related to rape from 19 stories to 35. All of these measures indicate greater apparent importance of rape to the *Sun-Times* editors and reporters.

In contrast, the content analysis of the *Chicago Tribune* found a minimal change in that newspaper's coverage of rape and related issues during the same period. The total number of stories about rape increased from 39 during the three months preceding the *Sun-Times* series to 41 in the three months after. The *Tribune* increased the space it allocated to these stories from 462 square inches to 588 square inches.

Both Mutter and Ralph Otwell, editor, said months after the series that it hadn't affected the paper's coverage of rape, but reporters said their editors "suggested" to them and to beat reporters who regularly cover crime that "more attention should be paid to the problem of rape." In fact, Byrne later said that the change in the *Sun-Times* coverage had been a source of satisfaction in doing the series. "I've become more attuned to them [rape stories] myself," he said. "I don't know if it's because my consciousness has been raised. And I don't see as much of what I call 'cheap rape' stories coming through [from the police reporters]. I've taken the rape rewrites [he writes rape stories based on facts phoned in from other reporters], and I see a difference."

Ironically, however, the *Sun-Times'* next investigative series was entitled, "Sex for Sale," and was marketed with suggestive advertising, lurid photographs, and sensual descriptions of the kinds of sexual exploitation that feminists and other researchers believe have the effect of condoning rape. [16]

The *Sun-Times* staff also expressed pleasure that the series "broke new ground" through extensive use of the computer. "Now we're just going to step back and think about what to do next," Byrne said. "Very definitely I've been told to keep my eyes open for computer stuff. And they are thinking about getting me my own computer!"

Henry said he thought that it was "an OK series" but that he wasn't "ecstatic" about it. "We didn't find all kinds of outrageous behavior or lack of it," he said. "A lot of victims said the cops were good, considerate. No story there."

Other satisfaction came to the staff as they talked to black community spokespersons. Fearing charges of racial overtones, the reporters were pleased at the response of Winston Moore, director of security at the Chicago Housing Authority. [17] "Many police think a black woman can't be raped," he said. "The value was that it educated people. It doesn't get grand jury indictments, but it tells victims, 'You are not alone. Come forward. We can get you help.'" He added, "I want reprints. I want to take them to block clubs."

Although newspapers often reprint investigative series for separate distribution, the *Sun-Times* did not reprint this one, a fact that surprised Byrne. Years later, he reflected, that "like so many things in this business, it was as if it [the topic of rape] dropped down a deep well." He added that the series hadn't won any awards, although Zekman's "Killing Crime," which he said "basically confirmed us" [on the topic of the Chicago Police Department's extraordinarily high unfounding rates] aired on channel 2 about six months later, and it won a prize for investigative journalism. "We just scratched our heads," said Byrne.

Although there is no evidence of "coalition journalism," neither is there evidence that the policy maker responses were in any way related to an aroused general public. We may speculate that the policy makers acted in a manner consistent with what they thought the public felt on this issue, but there is no evidence the policy makers acted because their constituents asked them to. Thus, once again, we see that the "Mobilization Model" is insufficient to explain what happened in this case. Instead, there appears to have been a "leaping effect"; that is, the general public was "leapt over," and the deliberative actions were taken without much reference to the public's responses to the series. Furthermore, the Mobilization Model cannot account for the effects on the press itself.

NOTES

1. Meyer, Philip, *Precision Journalism* (Bloomington, IN: Indiana University Press, 1973).

2. Stations often schedule relatively sensational and often expensive-to-produce exposés during these quarterly periods to attract additional viewers, because audience share is used to set advertising rates for the next several months.

3. Skogan, Wesley G. and M.G. Maxfield. *Coping with Crime: Victimization, Fear and Reactions to Crime in Three American Cities* (Beverly Hills: CA: Sage Publications, 1981).

4. In 1981, the police unfounded 50% of rapes, with the result that the final figures reported to the FBI for the Uniform Crime Report that year indicated the police believed only half the rapes reported to them by Chicago women met the standard well enough to be classified as a rape. Adding to the uncertainty about the figures is the fact that many many victims never tell the police in the first place. Some tell rape crisis counselors, and some tell victimization surveyors, but many victims tell only friends, pastrors, therapists, or no one at all.

5. Skogan, Wesley G. and Andrew C. Gordon, "Detective Division Reporting Practices: A Review of the Chicago Police Crime Classification Audit," in *Crime in Illinois,* 1982 (1983), pp. 166–182.

6. See, for example, Gordon, Margaret T. and Stephanie Riger, *The Female Fear* (New York: The Free Press, 1989); and Burgess, A.W. and L. L. Holmstrom, *Rape: Victims of Crisis* (Bowie, MD: Brady, 1974).

7. See, for example, Bart, Pauline and P. H. O'Brien. *Stopping Rape: Successful Survival Strategies* (Elmsford, NY: Pergamon Press, 1985).

8. Gordon and Riger, *The Female Fear.*

9. Data from the late 1980s indicate acquaitance rapes account for more than half the rapes reported to police.

10. Gordon and Riger, *The Female Fear.*

11. Interview with Pam Odde, August 5, 1982.

12. Interview with Francine Stein, August 1982.

13. For a detailed report of this research, see appendix I and David Protess, Donna Leff, Stephen Brooks, and Margaret T. Gordon, "Uncovering Rape: The Watchdog Press and the Limits of Agenda Setting," *Public Opinion Quarterly,* 49 (1985), pp. 19-37. The presurvey was conducted June 1–4, 1982, and tapped preseries attitudes of 347 members of the general public and 39 policy makers and activists on

major points to be made in the series. A comparison of responses on the presurvey to those obtained from 187 members of the general public and all 39 of the policy makers and activists approximately a week after publciation of the series, August 2–6, 1981, made possible an assessment of the influence of the series on their attitudes and opinions.

14. Interview with Monica Faith-Stewart, August 1982.
15. Interview with Frank Beaman, August 1982.
16. Gordon and Riger, *The Female Fear*.
17. Interview with Winston Moore, August 6, 1982.

CHAPTER 5

"Beating Justice"

February, 1983. Sweeps month in Chicago. Again. Ron Magers, the anchorman on channel 5, the local NBC affiliate, is warming up viewers of the ten o'clock news. They are told they are about to see a report "six months in the making," as reporter Peter Karl "exposes a police system which fails to deal with the cops who are beating justice."

Karl tells viewers that the Chicago Police Department is harboring some dangerous officers. He presents the disclaimer that most cops work hard but a small number have repeatedly been charged with brutality. Those officers he calls "repeaters" are the subject of this dramatic five-part series. Viewers are treated to incredibly graphic footage of bruised and bleeding victims of police brutality. The drama ranges from jolting police-wagon rides to black-hooded, voice-distorted interviews with anonymous former policemen who tell chilling tales of beating up hapless Chicagoans.

Karl describes the investigative team's methodology. At the beginning of the first report, he says that "Unit 5" investigators have reviewed every police brutality lawsuit filed in Federal Court during the past five years (1978 through 1982). The reporters identified 435 officers accused of brutality in the lawsuits and found that 107 of them were charged in two or more official complaints in the last ten years, either in court or at the police department.

Viewers hear a brief interview with Chicago's police superintendent, who points out that the people filing lawsuits typically are involved in "confrontational situations with the police" (implying but never stating that the plaintiffs aren't particularly credible witnesses). But the author of a nationwide study on police brutality offers a rebuttal, characterizing Chicago's brutality statistics as "outrageous, completely out of line . . ." with other large cities she has studied.

At the heart of Karl's series, however, are the villains—repeatedly brutal police officers—and their victims. The individual tales bring the statistics to life with raw detail that is difficult to dismiss. The stories will continue in the same vein for four more nights, each building on the carefully crafted theme of repeated police brutality.

Parts 2 through 5 continue nightly on the local ten o'clock news, and an expanded version from the previous night is repeated during a late afternoon local newscast daily. The stories follow a tight pattern, focusing on a few central themes:

- Despite promises of reform after a newspaper investigation ten years earlier, the department's system for policing itself is a dismal failure. Even officers cited repeatedly for using excessive force continue on the streets.
- Although never explicitly stated, the cameras show us that many of the victims are black; the abusive officers are white.
- Complaints of excessive force are much more likely to be adjudicated in favor of the plaintiff in Federal Court (63 percent); if brought through the department's internal Office of Professional Standards, only 6 percent of complaints are sustained. Viewers are told this is only the official version; channel 5 reporters found the actual rate of sustained complaints to be 1.6 percent. The reason: the office is filled with patronage employees.
- The investigative team used dramatic, credible stories that left no room for doubt about the seriousness of the injuries sustained. A particularly dramatic sequence involved an interview with a man who had been on probation, was drinking, got involved in an argument, and was arrested after fleeing officers who tried to stop him. He was thrown into a police wagon with his hands cuffed behind him and at the end of the ride, the once healthy 21-year-old man had become a quadraplegic.

THE GENESIS OF THE PROBE

The story of "Beating Justice" did not grow out of a reporter's mission to expose police brutality. After all, in Chicago and elsewhere, brutal cops were an old story. As with much investigative reporting, this story grew out of a routine news story that escalated into much more. Peter Karl was working on a story he called "Street Files," the term the police used for secret records of persons arrested. These records weren't available to defense attorneys, and if they were disclosed, typically they would cast doubt on the prosecution's case.

Karl had come to channel 5 from the local ABC affiliate, where he also had been an investigative reporter. Always brash, Karl good-naturedly tells the story of his departure from channel 7: "I called my boss a liar, cheat and a fraud, so they fired me." At channel 5, Karl put together an investigative group called "Unit 5," working with producers Doug Longhini and Bonnie Van Gilder. The producers and researchers, including some rotating student interns, typically spent several months working on a given story and often worked several investigations at once, trying to collect background on one story while polishing another. Management at the station expected them to produce major investigative pieces for each of the "sweeps" periods— February, May, and November—when ratings of local stations were assessed.

So it was in August 1982 that Karl began to pursue his tip on Street Files, planning to have that story come together in time for the November ratings period. He went to meet an attorney to talk about the files. During the interview, he learned that the attorney's client, charged with murdering a police officer after a "routine" traffic stop, was petitioning the court to suppress his confession on the grounds that it had been tortured out of him. Eventually, Karl obtained a secret file showing that the accused murderer had indeed been tortured. Police had used an electric cattle prod on the man's genitals and down his throat. During the police search for the defendant and his brother, also charged with the murder, black citizens and public officials complained that all young black men in the area of the murder were being harassed. Karl's interest heightened.

Not much had been written about police brutality since the *Chicago Tribune* had done a major investigation in 1973. For some time, Karl had been thinking about doing a television investigation of brutal cops, but he wanted to do more than just "throw together cases," as he put it. Both Karl and other members of his investigative unit were aware of the Tribune series and other local investigative efforts. Karl decided to keep working on Street Files but meanwhile to have the unit check through police reports of excessive force. "I found out there were some court records that weren't public, and police records were among them."

That lack of access to records became a driving force behind the investigation of "Beating Justice," almost an obsession. It occurred to Karl and his producer that allegations of police brutality often led to civil and criminal cases that they might be able to locate by searching through court records of completed cases. Working backwards, then, Karl's producer and a team of researchers went to Federal Court and looked up every single complaint filed against the police department in the five years from 1978 through 1983. This proved to be an exhaustive task.

Researchers checked cases naming as defendants the city, the mayor, or the police chief. As Van Gilder told a student researcher, "There was no tip here that gave us a lead. We developed our own story." Eventually a pattern began to emerge. Several cops were defendants in more than one case. Reporters began calling everyone named in the cases—plaintiffs, lawyers, police, investigators from the police department's internal unit. Thus, the channel 5 investigative unit collected and documented the cases that became the focus of "Beating Justice."

Even for an investigative unit, the reporting of "Beating Justice" was unusually thorough, methodical, and time consuming. The team had a producer, two assistant producers, and a group of three student researchers working full time on the story for six months. Karl also devoted much of his time to the story but did other work as well. The group used the latest technology, sparing no expense, which included the use of hidden cameras in an unmarked van and the administration of lie detector tests to persons charging the police with brutality in cases not yet resolved (to weed out untrue allegations of brutality). They carried electronic pagers during the investigation to stay in constant touch with one another. The path of the research was dictated by the information available. Federal Court records were the most accessible, and employees in the Court records rooms were extremely cooperative with the channel 5 team. They gave the researchers free access to large numbers of files at one time and gave them space to work, including access to typewriters. When the researchers went to cross-check cases against police officers named in excessive force lawsuits, however, employees in county courts made the work difficult. The process was slowed both by lack of cooperation from court clerks and by records that generally were sloppier and less complete than those maintained in Federal Court.

Thus, the team, under the direction of producer Van Gilder, spent whole days simply poring over court records, looking for civil rights charges, looking for successful lawsuits against the city and its police force. Taking names and making lists of plaintiffs or officers named in the Federal Court records, researchers cross-checked against county court lists (criminal cases in which the defendants became plaintiffs in the federal lawsuits) and eventually against limited records in the police department's investigative unit (Office of Professional Standards). The team had a passion for detail and would follow a lead until they could squeeze no more information from available documents. Van Gilder created a chart to organize the mass of cases. Eventually a 28-page table was drafted, which compiled data from more than 250 cases from Federal Court records of civil rights complaints. A researcher also began an alphabetical list of defendant police officers, thus identifying those who appeared more than once. The case list grew, and the team added open cases to the list of closed files. They spent time in the station's cafeteria, spreading the charts on tables and trying to identify the most promising cases for follow-up.

Van Gilder took the case narratives and devised a coding and tabbing system indicating the status of the cases from the Unit 5 team's perspective. Some cases would say "Ready to Shoot," or "Uncooperative Lawyer," or "Paddy Wagon." The team set up interviews with victims and talked to lawyers. They continued to pursue every lead.

For example, they were told by a source that police routinely picked up black men, charged them with disorderly conduct, and tossed them in the backs of "paddy wagons" for rough, abusive rides to police stations. So a researcher spent hours going through arrest logs counting "193s," the number assigned to disorderly conduct charges. That counting enabled Karl to say with authority that police routinely picked up young blacks on minor charges that did not lead to prosecution but that did lead to injury-inflicting rides to police stations.

By mid-September, a memo in the Unit 5 files shows the team working hard to pursue this angle. From a confidential source, identified as a public defender in a criminal court room on the city's South Side, comes information to a Unit 5 researcher:

> Police brutality is a regular, routine thing. Every day there'd be two or three cases of beating victims in the lock-up . . . something every cop and public defender knows about. Public defender's office would be a great place to take our troubles to. They see the clients while the wounds are fresh, but are really too busy to do much about the steady stream of brutality complaints, instead, concentrating mostly on the criminal case against their clients.

A constant problem was getting videotape that would dramatize the issues raised in the brutality series. The court records were of closed cases, and the stories that eventually aired were of past acts of brutality. The team spent three days staking out one police officer who had multiple brutality charges sustained against him and two days staking out another. In neither case were interviews conducted; producers merely wanted pictures of the officers to use with segments that included interviews with their victims, some of them badly maimed.

At least 15 evenings were spent with cameramen and producers hidden in vans near police stations where the repeaters were assigned. The team was hoping against long odds to catch a beater in the act. A student researcher reports that Van Gilder "whom I believe to be outraged at the violence evidenced in court files, wants that shot badly enough to have muttered 'hit him' as a cop walked an arrestee into a South Side station house as we watched from an undercover van." The team monitored the police radio as well but, in the end, failed to capture an ongoing incident of police brutality. Instead, producers created their own dramatization with the help of a cooperative police officer. Reporter Peter Karl, hands cuffed behind him, was locked in the back of a police wagon. Channel 5 videotaped Karl during the violent ride that ensued, with footage of him being tossed around the floor of the wagon by the force of the driving. The ride only increased Karl's sense of anger at the system that allowed police to amuse themselves at the expense of persons they arrested.

The whole team was affected by Karl's passion for the story. He was convinced that in the manhunt that triggered the police brutality story, police lumped all black people into a "class of nigger and cop killer." "There's a total gap between people in the city of Chicago," he told a student researcher. "People on the Gold Coast [city's wealthy Near North Side] think cops are a liaison between good and bad. In black and Latino neighborhoods they don't have those feelings at all."

Also during the research phase, Karl's reputation as a cop hater was growing. The Street Files story had been broadcast the previous year, after which Karl was shut out by many of his police sources. He was on general assignment at a summer festival when a police officer holding his child in his arms told the child to spit on Karl. The antagonism would spill over in an interview Karl would have with the police superintendent during production of "Beating Justice." Meanwhile, he was not deterred, telling a researcher, "I did what a journalist is supposed to do: follow a lead. I'm a reporter, and to do my job, I have to show what there is."

Still trying for visuals, researchers collected photographs from the court files and in some cases even had access to videotaped interviews conducted while the victims were in hospitals recovering from police beatings. Puffy eyes, swollen faces, and damaged limbs were in evidence. The most dramatic tape came from mass transit security cameras, which captured on videotape the arrest of a man for smoking on a train in violation of a city ordinance. The footage ended with the man beaten unconscious, hands still cuffed behind his back. Photos from his "booking" at the police station (part of the court record) also were obtained by the researchers. Those photos showed the man, still handcuffed, with a broken neck, two broken legs and broken ribs, bleeding profusely. Three hours later, the man was dead. (Eventually the police officer involved was convicted of manslaughter and imprisoned, but he was not a "repeater" and so did not become part of the station's five-part series. His case was broadcast in a 30-minute documentary a month after the series.)

PREPARING THE INVESTIGATIVE REPORT

The series was crafted with a specific focus. "We had a problem with this word, brutality. It doesn't mean anything to the average person who has heard the word brutality over and over again," Karl said. The investigative unit switched to focus on the repeater because it shifted the story from cop to administration, "a story of official indifference."

As Karl put it, the question became, "What are you doing about these guys? Why don't you get these guys off the street?"

By mid-December, the list of repeaters topped 30. A new source of information called "hard cards" was slipped to the Unit 5 team, showing all the complaints made to the Office of Professional Standards against a particular officer. Another source to cross-check was the city controller's judgment book, which documented all payments by the city of Chicago to complainants against it. With this focus in mind, Van Gilder outlined the story, determining that a five-part series would be possible. Night 1 would look at horrendous acts; night 2 at repeaters; night 3 the interview with a former repeater (which Karl had filmed in California); night 4 would focus on how OPS labeled most complaints unsustained, even when the city settled with large payments to victims; and night 5 would show how much these payments were costing Chicago taxpayers.

Van Gilder wrote the script for Karl's approval and revision. The production process followed the outline. Night 1 told the story of repeater Paul Sarpalius, a police officer for 13 years. Byron Thomas, a Chicago Housing Authority employee, filed one of four federal lawsuits against Sarpalius. Thomas tells his story to Karl on camera this way: Thomas, who is black, was driving between his two jobs when he stopped for a red light in Bridgeport (a predominantly white neighborhood notorious for racial incidents, especially violence and harassment against blacks). Thomas apparently fell asleep at the traffic light and was awakened by Sarpalius, who asked him if he was all right.

Thomas told the officer he was just tired.

> And so then Sarpalius said, "What are you doin' in this neighborhood, nigger?" And I don't know which I said first—"Can you spell it?" or "Your mother is one." Pulled me up and handcuffed me behind my back—threw me down on the ground—started stompin' on my head and kickin' you know. When they grabbed me and picked me up by the handcuffs and rammed my head into the back of the truck. . . .

Karl then reads a police sergeant's description of Thomas in the police wagon as photos of a battered Thomas in his hospital bed flash on the screen:

> He was bleeding from the face. Both his eyes were wide open and I picked up his head and looked at him. He was unconscious and trembling. I then observed the wire-mesh screen in the front of the wagon that was covered with blood. It looked as if the screen had been sprayed with blood.

Karl continues his literal blow-by-blow, reading from a hospital report on Thomas: "Byron had a brain concussion, a skull hemorrhage, black eyes, chipped teeth and some kidney damage. He has a loss of hearing."

Karl describes how Thomas's case was heard on three levels: in criminal court, where Thomas had to pay a $100 fine after being found guilty of a battery charge against one of the policemen; in a civil court, where Thomas was awarded $43,000 by the city to settle his lawsuit against Sarpalius; and in an official police investigation. There, an official investigator found that Sarpalius had "beat Mr. Thomas barbarically during the course of his arrest" and suspended Sarpalius for 30 days.

Karl calls the actions against the officer "just a slap on the wrist" and notes that he "went back on the street and beat up others, according to pending lawsuits."

Karl ties this officer's behavior to that of others assigned to the same district, observing that 13 of 68 officers who had excessive force complaints filed against them were named three or more times in a two-year period. He notes that official policy would have been to monitor these officers and to refer them for psychiatric counseling, neither of which occurred.

Karl concludes the first night's installment with the story of yet another victim of a repeater. But this victim, a decorated veteran and a scout master, can't tell his own story—he's dead. Again emphasizing the different levels of investigation, Karl points out that the county prosecutor declined to bring charges against the officer, but the victim's family settled a federal lawsuit against the officer involved for $100,000. In fact, Karl tells viewers, the city has spent about five million taxpayer dollars to settle brutality complaints over the five years studied.

Still according to plan, part 2 airs—but with one addition. For the second night piece, a repeater agreed at the last minute to be interviewed on camera, and this interview was added to the script. He came across much milder and less intimidating than the Unit 5 team would have liked. This had the unintended effect of softening the story, in the Unit 5 team's opinion. Van Gilder told a student researcher she thought the segment was disjointed and not strong enough. The segment was tied directly to the *Tribune's* series ten years earlier, although Karl never mentioned the newspaper by name. He did note that the police officer interviewed had been named in the newspaper series yet received no help and was still on the force. Even though the city paid one of his victims $6,000 after the newspaper series, the cop was taken off the streets only briefly in the mid-1970s and was back on patrol.

A second change during the production occurred after the third piece aired. After screening part 4, which was to run the next night, Karl and Van Gilder thought it dragged. The team worked until after midnight trimming the segment and increasing its pace.

That piece focused on the Office of Professional Standards and included an interview with Police Superintendent Richard Brzeczek. Karl recites a litany of complaints to OPS and then asks Brzeczek whether the system works. "Yes it does, and it works better than any other system, any place in the country." Karl uses the police chief's comment to segue into the case of a preschool teacher on a bicycle who was hit by a police car. When the man and his wife, who attempted to come to her husband's aid, questioned the policeman whose car hit the teacher, they are shoved, told "that'll teach you to keep your black ass off the street," and ultimately beaten by five policemen. Karl describes how their case took 573 days to wend its way through OPS, before OPS found the charges of brutality unsustained. Karl proceeds to document the charges, including on-camera interviews with three witnesses to the beatings. Karl observes that although each of the five cops had prior excessive force complaints against him, OPS failed to discipline them. But a federal jury awarded $24,900 to the injured couple.

The report concludes with a promise that Brzeczek will appear live on the station's 4:30 afternoon newscast the next day. The transcript of that interview shows an edgy and rambling chief trying to respond to Karl's specific allegations and getting tangled in equivocations about the limits of OPS's investigative power. The interview contrasts sharply with the drama of the rest of the series.

As for the timing, it was deliberate and carefully planned. When a researcher asked Karl whether his bosses cared about ratings, he was emphatic.

> They are concerned about ratings periods and so am I. I want my stories [broadcast] during ratings periods—they're [station officials] going to promote them—get people to watch them. I want people to see what I'm doing. I want to effect change in some way.

THE INVESTIGATIVE INFLUENCE

"Beating Justice" was broadcast during the height of a heated political primary in Chicago, one with intense racial overtones. Black candidate Congressman Harold Washington was able to seize the issue of police brutality and lax discipline by the department. Nielsen ratings show that 526,000 adults watched the ten o'clock newscast during the week of the exposé. Almost before the segment was off the air the first night, phones at channel 5 were ringing with viewers anxious to tell their stories of rough encounters with the police or to express outrage at the Unit 5 allegations. A student intern estimated that about 100 calls were received that night. A survey of the general public before and after the television series similarly showed that people who watched the stories increased their awareness of problems identified in the reports.[1]

Using methodology essentially the same as in the rape study described in the previous chapter, researchers found that a significant number of those interviewed increased their views on the importance of police brutality after being exposed to the series. Viewers and nonviewers were divided into quasi-experimental "treatment" and "control" groups and asked in pre- and posttest interviews about a variety of topics including police brutality.

Although persons who watched or heard about the series changed their views, they did not change their views of the issue's importance relative to other issues—that is, no agenda-setting effect could be determined. However, on seven of 12 tests for related items, views changed in the hypothesized direction, with changes being the strongest on general issue questions and weakest on statements of facts derived from the series. Exposed viewers were more likely to agree after the series with statements that victims of police brutality usually were nonwhite, that police discipline was lacking, and that brutality victims get compensation from the city. Persons who were not exposed to the police brutality series did not change their views on the issue (see table 5.1).

We also wanted to learn whether "policy elites," persons already concerned about or working in the area of law enforcement, also would be influenced by the channel 5 reports. A sample of 35 persons was interviewed, including several suburban police chiefs, state legislators, members of the city council, and members of a citizens' police advisory group. About a third had neither watched nor heard about the series and were used as a rough "control" group. All 35 were reinterviewed after the broadcast. The results have limited implications because of sample size and nonrandom selection.

Still, elites did change their views after exposure to the series (see table 5.2). The policy makers were asked a series of pretest and posttest questions that were identical to those in the survey of the general public. Additionally, however, they were asked to estimate the public's views on the issues in question. They also were asked a set of questions about their policy-making activity related to police brutality. After the series, researchers tracked policy changes that might be attributable to the channel 5 series by interviewing policy makers and by content-analyzing local media.

Researchers expected less significant changes in elite opinions in all groups because policy makers already are familiar with the issue (and were selected for this sample because of their interest in it). Thus, neither group showed a statistically significant change on the question of police brutality as a general urban problem or as a law enforcement problem. (Both aware and

Table 5.1
Effect of Police Brutality Series on General Public Sample[a] (Mean Scores)

	Channel 5 watchers (treatment) ($N = 171$)		Channel 5 nonwatchers (control) ($N = 103$)		Series aware (treatment) ($N = 163$)		Not aware (controls) ($N = 114$)	
	Pre	Post	Pre	Post	Pre	Post	Pre	Post
Importance of problem								
Police brutality	3.09	3.34^b	3.42	3.28	3.18	3.36^b	3.28	3.27
Violent crime	3.83	3.81	3.82	3.85	3.80	3.80	3.83	3.87
Welfare fraud	3.50	3.53	3.54	3.35^b	3.48	3.38^b	3.56	3.56
Unemployment	3.91	3.93	3.88	3.87	3.91	3.93	3.89	3.89
Govt. corruption	3.55	3.54	3.65	3.60	3.58	3.56	3.60	3.57
Importance of law enforcement problem								
Police brutality	3.15	3.38^b	3.34	3.29	3.22	3.41^b	3.23	3.28
Traffic safety laws	3.02	3.10a	3.01	3.10	2.95	3.06^b	3.09	3.13
Discrimination in department	2.96	3.05	3.14	2.98	3.02	3.07	3.01	3.01
Underreporting of crime	3.59	3.61	3.51	3.51	3.57	3.65	3.55	3.46
Police bribery	3.60	3.59	3.60	3.51	3.59	3.54	3.65	3.63
Fact statements								
Brutality more likely to nonwhites	2.95	2.83	3.07	3.00	3.02	3.01	2.92	2.81
Lack of police discipline	3.59	3.61	2.75	2.93	2.82	3.11^b	2.82	2.68
Brutality victims get money	2.03	2.34^b	2.09	2.09	2.05	2.28^b	2.10	2.20
Able to identify welfare fraud	2.44	2.65^b	2.51	2.79	2.49	2.65^b	2.46	2.80^b
Punishment for government corruption	2.15	2.20	2.03	2.09	1.96	2.09	2.27	2.24
Quality of service								
Police department	3.06	2.98	2.09	2.99	3.00	2.96	2.99	3.02
Garbage collection	3.28	3.35	3.15	3.07	3.25	3.29	3.16	3.18
Fire department	3.66	3.66	3.57	3.53	3.63	3.60	3.58	3.63
Street repair	1.83	2.09^b	1.85	1.87	1.86	1.98	1.81	2.00
Parks and recreation	2.82	2.79	2.79	2.72	2.71	2.77	2.91	2.76

[a]Higher numbers indicate more positive responses (4 = "very important," "agree strongly", and "very adequate").
[b]Significant change ($p < .05$) from pre- to posttest using a dependent t-test.

Table 5.2
Effect of Police Brutality Series on Elite Sample[a] (Mean Scores)

	Aware (N = 24)		Not aware (N = 11)	
	Pre	Post	Pre	Post
Personal View				
Importance of problem				
Police brutality	3.00	3.17	2.73	3.09
Violent crime	3.67	3.54	3.91	3.91
Welfare fraud	2.41	2.29	2.63	2.91
Unemployment	3.96	3.92	4.00	3.91
Govt. corruption	3.25	3.00	3.36	3.36
Importance of law enforcement problem				
Police brutality	3.04	3.25	2.73	3.18[b]
Traffic safety laws	1.78	1.91	1.91	2.09
Discrimination in department	2.82	2.45[b]	2.56	3.11[b]
Underreporting of crime	3.18	3.27	3.64	3.72
Police bribery	3.16	3.21	3.64	3.72
Fact statements				
Brutality more likely to nonwhites	2.96	3.26[b]	3.00	3.63[b]
Lack of police discipline	2.45	2.95[b]	2.55	2.91
Brutality victims get money	1.65	2.00	1.80	1.70
Able to identify welfare fraud	2.62	2.19	2.64	2.09
Punishment for govt. corruption	2.50	2.33	2.55	2.73
Public View				
Importance of problem				
Police brutality	2.64	3.36[b]	3.63	3.37[b]
Violent crime	4.00	4.00	3.74	3.87
Welfare fraud	3.09	3.27	2.65	2.74
Unemployment	4.00	4.00	3.96	3.96
Govt. corruption	3.27	3.45	2.78	3.09
Importance of law enforcement problem				
Police brutality	2.81	3.00	2.68	3.00
Traffic safety laws	2.09	2.00	1.86	1.90
Discrimination in department	2.70	3.10	2.70	2.80
Underreporting of crime	3.36	3.55	2.52	3.00[b]
Police bribery	3.36	3.45	2.86	2.86

[a]Higher numbers indicate more positive response (4 = "very important" or "agree strongly").
[b]Significant change ($p < .05$) from pre- to posttest using a dependent t-test.

nonaware groups in the posttest also increased their views of the importance of discrimination by the police department as a law enforcement problem.) Statistically significant changes were found on two of three fact questions relating to the exposé. The exposed elites increased their agreement with the statement that victims of police brutality were more likely to be nonwhite, and they increased their agreement with a statement that discipline in the police department was lax. They also found the problem of police brutality to be more important after viewing the series, although they didn't change their ranking of police brutality compared to other social problems; therefore, we could detect no agenda-setting effect of the exposé. Exposed elites also changed their views of the general public after the series, with more of them believing that the public would find police brutality an important problem.

The impact of the story might have subsided after the initial flurry but for the political campaign that changed Chicago forever. As Washington's campaign aide was to recall many years later, "We were delighted by Karl's series. We seized on it." He described two media events related to it. Each received wide press coverage. The first occurred just three days after the Unit 5 report, between parts 3 and 4. Washington stood in front of the Office of Professional Standards and, with cameras rolling, promised to abolish the office if he were elected. (He was, and he didn't—but that didn't matter in 1983.)

Calling the office a "mockery," Washington said, "The job of policing the police must be taken out of the Police Department and put into the hands of competent independent citizens . . . so that it can serve the purpose for which it was intended." Washington noted that the office was created in 1973 after citizen complaints of police brutality. Although he made no explicit reference to it, he obviously was aware of the *Tribune* series that had prompted the earlier reform. Several of the local television stations and all three daily newspapers covered Washington's police headquarters appearance, and some made reference to the Unit 5 investigation.

A week later, in what Washington's aide described as "the single most important press event of the campaign," Washington assembled fifty victims of police brutality in a downtown hotel room. He met with the group, then called in the press and introduced four plaintiffs and their attorneys who were suing the police department, alleging brutality. Again the event received extensive local media coverage.

The campaign aide credits the Unit 5 investigation with making police brutality a campaign issue. "I don't think it would have happened without Peter Karl's series," he said. "That made it a public issue, put it in the forefront of people's minds."

Other media often "pick up" snippets of an investigation, but "Beating Justice" was different because of the mayoral campaign. Stories in the *Chicago Tribune* and the *Chicago Sun-Times* focused on the money the city spent settling brutality lawsuits. They also observed editorially that the police superintendent and OPS were becoming major problems, and they linked the Unit 5 investigation, the mayoral campaign, and the police. As the *Sun-Times* of February 16, 1983, editorialized, "Brutality is widespread enough that it is a major campaign issue for one mayoral candidate. And WMAQ's investigation raised serious questions about the quality of work in the Office of Professional Standards."

The Unit 5 series also had the effect of calling renewed attention to a related problem with the city's police, one identified earlier by a different local television station's investigative unit. Both newspapers editorially raised new questions in mid-February about the way the department counted crimes. The FBI issued a report in early February affirming the television exposé's allegations—that the department systematically undercounted serious crimes in the city by labeling as "unfounded" crime complaints by citizens.

The most substantive reaction to "Beating Justice," however, came from the department itself. After spending the two weeks during and after the series defending himself and lambasting Karl, the police superintendent took action. Despite describing the Unit 5 report as "weasel journalism," Brzeczek was under increasing political pressure to implement reform. Washington had won the February 22 primary, and it looked as if he would be elected in April, an election that surely would end Brzeczek's service as police superintendent. Although Brzeczek continued to take the position that politics played no role in his actions, he clearly had to minimize the damage of the media barrage that followed the series and Washington's press conferences. Knowing his time in office was limited, the police chief wanted to leave on a higher note.

On March 8, 1983, one month after the broadcast, he issued a general order. The order established an extensive program for identifying and treating police officers exhibiting "patterns of behavior which would warrant concern," including those against whom complaints of excessive force had been filed. Two new management positions were created to implement the new program. These changes, then, were "substantive,"[2] in marked contrast to the highly symbolic responses we found in studies 2 and 3.

Washington was elected in April; Brzeczek resigned, and the reforms continued. Washington named a new director of OPS, firing the old one while making it clear that business as usual would not be tolerated. The focus of the office was to be more professional, with less tolerance for police misconduct and more emphasis on getting psychological help for police offenders. A member of Washington's transition staff called the channel 5 researchers and asked for supporting documents used in the series. A Unit 5 researcher remembers, "we had this giant notebook full of repeaters—basically just our working notebook. It was color-coded, and I had to find a copier that made color copies. I think it cost about $600, but we did it."

For the journalists, then, "Beating Justice" was a success. It influenced policy and politics, it was noticed by other media, and it was recognized with professional awards. As the investigative researcher on the story put it, "It was a success because no one had ever approached the issue of chronic repeaters and proved that it really did exist. It was unprecedented in that sense. We documented the problem." Other members of the research team also cited the embracing of the series by the Washington campaign and the changes in the police department as evidence of the impact. Although reluctant to be crass about it, the team was delighted to take at least some of the credit for "bringing down Brzeczek."

The team was sanguine, however, about the limits of its influence. As one researcher said,

> I very rarely think any of our stories make really significant changes. I want the world to fall in—and ["Beating Justice"] didn't do that—but it did make a difference. If you're a poor person on the South Side who's just been beaten by a cop, you might disagree.

The series was honored for making a difference, however, with the Robert F. Kennedy award, a national prize recognizing journalism that furthers the cause of justice. The series also received a prestigious Columbia University DuPont award, a local Emmy, and several smaller local honors.

CONCLUSION

Looking back at "Beating Justice," we are struck by its impact both on public opinion and on policy makers. Three factors seem to be working here, each a necessary but not sufficient condition for investigative reporting to have an impact.

1. The investigative report itself. "Beating Justice" is powerful television. The episodes in the series are riveting: nightsticks crack against human skulls, flesh is torn and bleeding, police wagons careen with their human cargo bouncing from wooden bench to metal siding. Court records are displayed in detail, and there's no doubt about villains and victims. Ambiguity never muddies the investigative report.

2. Media climate. "Beating Justice" seems to defy the notion that recurring stories have less impact than unique ones. Although Karl made an explicit attempt to say this was a "new" investigative topic (by stressing the "repeater" angle), what came across to the viewer was police brutality: stark, vivid, and not very different from earlier

descriptions. Yet the fact that Karl could point to an investigation that occurred 10 years earlier (the Tribune series) and that editorialists could lump other investigations of police misconduct (Street Files and underrerporting of serious crimes) enhanced rather than diminished Karl's work.

3. Political climate. The intensity of the political campaign enhanced the impact of the Unit 5 investigation. It is impossible to separate the piece from its context, and in the context of the mayoral race, police brutality received more attention than a single media series could have generated.

The series comes close to fulfilling the Mobilization Model. The villains (repeatedly brutal cops) and victims (those beaten, usually minorities) are clearly in place. The reporter has a mission: "I want to effect change in some way," Karl says of his work. "I go into my den at home and I see DuPonts and Peabodys [journalism awards]—35 awards on the wall—but they don't do anything for me as a man. The ones that matter are the human ones." He describes bringing the brutal police officers and their victims to life on the air—he intended to generate outrage.

The model is less than perfect in that candidate (later Mayor) Washington didn't wait for public outcry to be mobilized. He didn't know about the 100 telephone calls, but he didn't have to. He knew police brutality was an issue close to his constituency, and "Beating Justice" gave him the perfect campaign opportunity. He asked for and received a transcript from Karl, and the rest was history. So the model isn't linear; the impact goes straight from media to policy maker, skipping over public outrage. But if you put parentheses around the public and call that politics, the arrow goes from media to (public outrage/politics) to policy/politician, and there's no question that "Beating Justice" was a powerful piece of journalism. The muck that channel 5 raked, those brutal police officers and their slothful supervisors, remind one a great deal of the old targets, the foul slaughterhouses and the gritty sweatshops.

NOTES

1. See Donna R. Leff, David L. Protess, and Stephen C. Brooks, "Changing Public Attitudes and Policymaking Agendas: The Variable Effects of Crusading Journalism," *Public Opinion Quarterly* 50 (1986), pp. 300–314.

2. Harvey L. Molotch, David L. Protess, and Margaret T. Gordon, "The Media Policy Connection: Ecologies of News," in *Political Communication Research*, David L. Paletz (ed.), (Norwood, NJ: Ablex, 1987), pp. 26–48.

CHAPTER 6

"Wasted Time"

The University of Chicago was sitting on a toxic time-bomb. Hazardous chemical and radioactive wastes, some left behind from atomic bomb research done in the 1940s, were stored beneath several classroom buildings. The health and safety of unwitting students potentially was threatened. Yet, University officials, despite repeated internal warnings about the problem, were dragging their feet on proposals to clean it up. They were wasting time.

These were among the allegations leveled against the University by Chicago's WMAQ-TV (channel 5) in May 1984. The NBC station's investigative team, "Unit 5," had conducted a three-month probe of the problem. On May 13, in the middle of the period when television ratings are measured, Unit 5 reporter Peter Karl broadcast the first of the station's three-part series called "Wasted Time."

WMAQ-TV news anchor Deborah Norville introduced the story this way: "Channel 5 news has learned that the University of Chicago has been illegally storing hazardous and flammable chemical wastes on its campus for years." She then turned the story over to Karl, who stated that "Unit 5 has obtained copies of internal University memos that show high-ranking members of the University were aware of the dangers and hazards involved in this illegal storage." As shots of students going to class appeared, Karl alleged that "what these students don't know is below classrooms the University is storing hazardous wastes that could endanger their lives." He made his point by showing pictures of a chemical fire that had caused significant damage to a classroom laboratory ten years earlier.

The internal memos warning of the danger then were shown, along with an interview with their primary author, a University chemistry professor. The professor acknowledged writing them "to alert [his] superiors" to the problem

134

but claimed he did not have an additional obligation to report it to government authorities. "Shame on him," retorted a Fire Department spokesperson who felt the professor had not done enough in light of the University's alleged foot-dragging.

Karl concluded the segment by reporting the University's plans to construct a $100,000 building that "would wipe out the danger." But, he added, "bureaucratic and academic red tape has thwarted construction of that building to date."

The second and third parts of the series dealt with the University's radioactive wastes disposal practices. "Radioactive contamination . . . is more widespread than originally thought," the second story began. However, Karl quickly noted that "this is not a scare story about radioactive waste disposal problems at the University of Chicago." Later, he added that no questions have been raised about the reported levels of radiation in various classrooms today. . . ."

These stories instead focused on three alleged problem areas. First, they described a "possible conflict of interest" between the University and the laboratory whose studies found the lack of current radioactive contamination. Second, they charged that earlier clean-up efforts were delayed repeatedly by bureaucratic problems within the University and by an array of government regulatory agencies.

Finally, the series concluded with a private physician's claim that somewhat higher cancer rates in the area "may be linked" to the contamination. "Although [the physician] admits this is not a scientific analysis," Karl said in closing, "his findings raise a serious enough question that should be thoroughly examined."

Meanwhile, the Chicago Fire Department took action on Unit 5's initial disclosures about hazardous chemical waste. The morning after the first broadcast, fire officials descended on the University's Hyde Park Campus. WMAQ-TV cameras were present to record the inspection. The Department cited the University for 20 fire code violations and gave it 30 days to correct the problem. On the evening of May 14, WMAQ-TV characterized this action by officials as "a response to our Unit 5 investigation."

THE GENESIS OF THE PROBE

The Unit 5 exposé was not the first media story about public health and safety hazards at the University of Chicago. In fact, nine months earlier, reports about radioactive contamination on campus made the front pages of the city's newspapers. But these stories were distinctly different from the Unit 5 series.

Their focus was on "noteworthy" efforts by government and University officials to clean up the problem. No mention was made of possible chemical waste disposal problems.

On August 17, 1983, the *Chicago Tribune* reported an announcement by the U.S. Department of Energy that "Three University of Chicago buildings contaminated by radioactivity left by the World War II atomic bomb development project will be decontaminated at a cost of $300,000." The story stated that clean-up efforts were "expected to last a year."

Both the *Tribune* and the *Sun-Times* downplayed the possible dangers from the contamination. The *Sun-Times* quoted an Energy Department spokesperson claiming that the situation was safe and was necessitated only because of more stringent government standards. The *Tribune* story included this comment by University spokesperson James Yuenger: "Experts at the school told [me] that somebody would have to eat the concrete off the walls before there might be any effect."

These news reports, written by beat reporters, may have been reassuring to some people. But they became the subject of intense concern to Peter Treistman. Treistman, a resident of Hyde Park and a graduate of the University of Chicago, was working on his master's degree in journalism when the stories about the "clean-up" first appeared.

Treistman hoped to become an investigative reporter after graduation. In fact, he was working on an investigative story for a class project in the summer of 1983. Coincidentally, the story was about the questionable practices of a state environmental agency.

Shortly after the newspaper reports about the University of Chicago, Treistman was discussing his own environmental story with a friend who worked at the University. "We were just shooting the crap," Treistman said, "when my friend mentioned that there was a lot of stuff about the University's problems with radioactivity that hadn't been made public yet."

When pressed for details, Treistman's friend told him that the radioactivity problem was worse than what the University was publicly saying. He added that the storage of chemical waste below classroom buildings also was a problem. In fact, his friend said, both problems were "so serious that University people were writing concerned memos to their superiors that documented the lack of safety."

Treistman was shocked by what his friend told him. "I had a class in one of the buildings and didn't know it. Now other students were going to class there without really knowing about the danger," he said. He believed it was "morally wrong" for the University to "hide" the problem. He immediately began thinking in professional terms as well: "I wanted to tell the story. It was important, and it could be documented."

This mixture of personal outrage and professional interest led Treistman to ask his friend if he could obtain the internal memos. His friend said he could get them, but only gradually. The memos were in different places, he explained. While he could get access to them, he worried about attracting attention to himself. He asked Treistman if his identity could remain secret.

"I promised him complete confidentiality," Treistman said. "It helped that I'd known him for years. He trusted me. He knew I wouldn't screw him." Treistman said that his friend also was angry about what the University was doing and wanted the information to get out in the hope that it might correct the problem. "But he wasn't a 'whistleblower' who had plans to bring the memos to the media or to authorities," Treistman recalled. "The whole thing was serendipitous. If we hadn't been talking about environmental stories at the time, I might never have found out about the problem."

Over the next month or so, Treistman's friend, who now was also his confidential source, gave him the documentation necessary to expose the problem. "The memos came in dribs and drabs," Treistman recalled. "He would take the originals from the University's files, photocopy them, and put them back. He gave me the photocopies." Treistman said "the memos clearly showed that University officials had been repeatedly warned about the dangers from radioactive and chemical waste on campus. Yet, they were doing almost nothing—except trying to keep it a secret."

Treistman said he increasingly felt he had the makings of a solid exposé. "I saw it as a story that would bring the problem to public attention to warn everyone who was affected by it," he said. "But I also wanted to expose the contradiction between what the University was saying publicly and what they were doing privately. I wanted to reveal their hypocrisy in handling the problem." Treistman added he thought that policy makers might crack down on the problem if it received media attention, and "that would be a significant additional benefit to doing the story."

The only remaining question for Treistman was where he could publish his findings. In the fall of 1983, this question was resolved temporarily when Treistman got a part-time job at Chicago's WGN-TV (channel 9). His main responsibility was to do research for WGN commentator Joel Weisman. But he also was encouraged to work on investigative projects with the stations' news anchor and its investigative producer.

Since his primary loyalty was to Weisman, he decided to pitch the University of Chicago story to him first. Weisman was not encouraging, Treistman recalled. He told Treistman the story did not fit his commentary format. "This was a straight exposé where you had to lay out the facts in some detail, while Weisman only had a minute or so each night to do editorial perspectives on news events," Treistman said. Nonetheless, Weisman was willing to mull over Treistman's proposal.

But Weisman did not come around. So, Treistman seriously began to consider bringing his story to the station's investigative producer. Around this time, however, the producer and the news anchor for whom he produced announced their decisions to leave WGN to go to a rival station. "I certainly wasn't going to give my story to the competition at this point, so I decided to sit tight and work on Weisman," Treistman said.

Meanwhile, Treistman became absorbed in his other research for Weisman's commentaries. But as the year wore on with no progress on the University of Chicago story, Treistman increasingly was plagued by ethical concerns. "What if there was an explosion and people were hurt?" he wondered. "It would be in part be my fault for not doing something." Also, he was receiving pressure from his friend, the source of the internal memos, who wanted to know why the story had not yet aired.

"I thought about tipping the Fire Department to the problem," he recalled. "But I didn't think about that for very long. Mainly, I was being selfish. I wanted to do the story, if that were possible, to get some professional mileage out of the work I'd done." Treistman also doubted that sending the memos anonymously to the Fire Department ("I certainly couldn't bring them over as a WGN employee," he said) would have much effect. "I still felt that the best chance to force officials to act was if the story were done dramatically on television."

Treistman finally decided to raise his dilemma with a senior journalist who worked at the station. This journalist related a story about a similar incident that had happened to him earlier in his career. "He told me that he tried to convince his editor to let him do an exposé that he thought was really solid, but the editor turned him down," Treistman said. "So he decided to give the story to the competition. They ran it on the front page. He then brought the front page to his editor and said: 'See, I was right about the story!' "

"He [the senior journalist] was giving me a clear message," Treistman recalled. "I began to feel that the best way to go now was to give the story to someone else." So Treistman called a former professor for advice. After several conversations, Treistman decided to give the story to WMAQ-TV's Peter Karl, whose work Treistman admired. The professor agreed to act as a conduit between Treistman and Karl and not to disclose Treistman's identity without his permission.

In January 1984, the professor met with Karl and Unit 5 Executive Producer Doug Longhini and conveyed the package of internal University memoranda. Shortly thereafter, Treistman was hired by WGN as a news writer and investigative producer. "If it had been a while later, I might have been able to do the story myself," Treistman said. "At the time, it was just the wrong species for the set-up at WGN. I didn't have the clout or experience to do it then, but I'm glad that someone else was able to." Ironically, though, more time had been wasted along the way.

THE INVESTIGATIVE PROCESS

Reporter Peter Karl and executive producer Doug Longhini spent hours poring over the package of memos they had received. They were struck by the detailed descriptions of the University's toxic waste disposal problems and by the increasingly urgent tone of the memo writers. "We got the memos on a silver platter that had a golden lining," Karl said. "We knew we had a solid story in our hands," Longhini recalled. "You could hold the memos. They were tangible; the story was *there*."

The two journalists not only were excited by the story's "doability" but also by its subject matter. The environmental aspect of the story made it particularly attractive to Longhini. "They're stories that affect people, that affect the quality of the world around us," he said.

Longhini especially looked forward to pursuing the "historical angle" of the University of Chicago's environmental problems. "The problems went back to the creation of the bomb," he said. "When I read the memos, I was reminded of how scientists had created something great and something terrible at the same time. I felt this story would show how we were still living with the consequences of that creation a half century later."

Karl's initial reactions to the memos focused more on the specific target of the exposé. "I liked the idea of taking on the University of Chicago," he said. "It was appealing because it hadn't been done before and because of the University's power. The people who run that place are 'the Masters of the Universe.'"

Karl also was excited about exposing the "hypocrisy of the University's cover-up." "The University has a responsibility to teach young people ethics, but they weren't behaving ethically themselves," he believed. That made University administrators "perfect villains," he concluded.

Longhini agreed, but he put the problem in a more global perspective. He believed that "the University's failure to act in the face of repeated warnings says something about their bureaucracy. Wasting time in the face of a documented danger is what gets lawyers punitive damages and what gets us a great story."

Both men further recognized the presence of sympathetic victims in the investigative story. "Right away, I saw it as a problem that affected the well-being and health of young people," Karl recalled. He was concerned personally about this problem, since his oldest daughter was about to go to college. "The University was gambling with students' lives, and the students didn't even know it," he said.

Longhini similarly believed that "students were being victimized by unwittingly sitting in classrooms that were directly above toxic waste dumps." He was less certain about the extent to which they had been tangibly harmed, however. "Environmental stories usually don't have clear-cut victims," he said. "Even when you find them, you can't say for sure that the environmental hazard *caused* their problem." This aspect of the University of Chicago story somewhat troubled Longhini. He suspected that the exposé might only be able to allege "potential harm," thereby decreasing its "dramatic impact."

The memos triggered the same ethical concerns for the Unit 5 investigators that had been experienced by WGN's Peter Treistman. "We wanted to get on the story right away," Karl said, "because we were concerned that a catastrophe might occur." Longhini believed that "the longer we waited, the more we would be guilty of the same thing that the University was doing."

Despite these concerns, however, Karl and Longhini were not yet in a position to put their story on the air. First, they had to inform WMAQ-TV executives about the project. This responsibility fell to Longhini, who as the investigative unit's executive producer was the primary liaison to the station's management.

"We were last in the ratings at the time," Longhini recalled. "Management was willing to try anything. No one raised any questions about our doing the story." However, part of the agreement between Unit 5 and the station in 1984 was to broadcast its investigative stories only during ratings periods. "They were using Unit 5 to try to build an audience," Longhini said. "So management targeted the [University of Chicago] investigation for the next available sweeps period."

This decision meant that the exposé probably would not be broadcast until May. The February ratings period was at hand, and the station had already scheduled its "sweeps pieces" for the month. One of them was another Unit 5 investigation that would consume most of Karl's and Longhini's time for the remainder of January and early February.

Karl, in particular, wanted to get the toxic waste story on the air as soon as possible, but he also appreciated the value of broadcasting it during a sweeps period. "The station was willing to spend a lot of money on ads to promote the hell out of the piece, and I wanted them to do that," he said. "Like any other reporter, I want the biggest possible audience for my stories. To get change, you want to draw as much attention as you can to what you're doing."

Further, everyone agreed that the information about the University of Chicago, although quite detailed, also was highly incomplete. Karl and Longhini began to discuss the numerous loose ends to the story. What if the University memos somehow were misleading or even fabricated? Alternatively, perhaps there was even more wrongdoing to be discovered. What was the University of Chicago's point of view about the possible allegations? As a television exposé, many visuals needed to be obtained to show the problem graphically.

By mid-February, having completed their sweeps piece for the month, Karl and Longhini turned their full attention to these unresolved issues. Longhini first decided to visit the University's Hyde Park campus to see the toxic waste sites described in the memos. Of the four sites described in the memos, three housed University classrooms.

"I was appalled to actually see students walking in and out of the buildings, which had no warning signs," Longhini said. He also visited the site of the Manhattan Project, where scientists first split the atom. The site is marked with a sculpture that recognizes their accomplishment. "It once again made me feel a sense of awe about the historical event that occurred there," he said. "I made myself a mental note to dig up film of the Manhattan Project to use in the piece. I also wanted to try to find any file footage on the chemical fire (that had occurred in one of the classroom buildings) ten years ago."

Meanwhile, Karl was attempting to find out more about the memos that documented the danger. He decided to contact each of the memo writers. Most were scientists on the faculty of the University. They would be fairly easy to reach.

Karl first called the author of the most strongly worded memos, chemistry professor Norman Nachtrieb. One of Nachtrieb's memos to University administrators had warned that their chemical waste storage was "in violation of city buildings and fire codes." Another said: "The quantity of such material is continually increasing . . . and I regard it as a dangerous situation."

Karl recalled that "Nachtrieb admitted on the phone that he'd written these memos," and further agreed to allow Karl to interview him. "This was an important break, both because we knew now that the memos were authentic and because we could get him on camera explaining what had happened," Karl said. He arranged for a television crew to meet him and Nachtrieb in the professor's office.

The investigative reporter hoped that the college professor would be a whistleblower. This proved not to be the case. The two men spent several hours talking about the memos, only a small portion of which was videotaped. "Mostly, he tried to explain the technical reasons why he felt that the radioactivity problem did not represent a health hazard." To do this, Nachtrieb drew elaborate diagrams on his blackboard of the half-lives of radioactive isotopes. "He argued that there was not enough radioactivity left from the Manhattan Project to cause a problem," Karl said. He said that studies conducted for the United States Department of Energy by Argonne National Laboratory had reached the same conclusion and gave Karl a technical book to read on the subject.

Nachtrieb said that the chemical storage problem was serious, but he said that like the radioactivity problem, the University now was taking measures to eliminate it. "He told me about their plans to build a containment unit and how in the meantime they were using a service that removed some of the chemical waste on a certain day each week," Karl said.

In the videotaped portion of the interview, Karl questioned Nachtrieb about why the problems had been allowed to go on for so long. He was told that "there were delays in getting plans approved by government regulatory agencies." Then Karl asked: "Why didn't you notify the Fire Department if you thought they were in violation of the Fire Department codes?" Nachtrieb answered that he felt he discharged his responsibilities by alerting university administrators.

On his way back to the WMAQ-TV studios, Karl felt increasingly troubled by Nachtrieb's answers to his questions. He shared his concerns with Longhini. "I immediately recognized that Peter was going through his 'last person he spoke with cycle,' " Longhini said. Longhini's diagnosis was based on Karl's longstanding habit of believing the most recent argument made to him by an authoritative source. Longhini was not worried by this. "I figured Peter would put what Nachtrieb had told him in the proper perspective after he started questioning it and investigating further."

But as March wore on, Karl's concerns about the story lingered. Part of the problem was that none of the other University memo writers was willing to talk with him. Even worse, University officials had been alerted to Karl's inquiries and had launched a counteroffensive.

The University's public relations director, James Yuenger, challenged Karl's right to have the memos in the first place, both with Karl and with WMAQ-TV's communications director. (Coincidentally, the communications director of the television station previously had been the director of the office of radio and television at the University of Chicago.) Yuenger also issued a public statement announcing the University's plans to construct a facility to store the hazardous chemical wastes. No news stories resulted from the statement, however, and Karl said he "felt no pressure from the station to alter the course of the story."

Instead, Karl immersed himself in the technical materials that had been given to him by Nachtrieb. He also filed a federal Freedom of Information Act request to obtain a complete set of the studies done for the Department of Energy on the University of Chicago's problems, including the research by Argonne National Laboratory that Nachtrieb had mentioned. Then he sought the advice of independent experts who could assess the hazards.

"I wanted to learn everything about the subject that I possibly could," Karl said. "I felt that if I could comprehend it personally, then I could better explain it to viewers. I also would be in better position to assess the credibility of the University's arguments." Karl enjoyed the intellectual challenge of trying to master a complicated subject.

After reading the materials and contacting a scientist who supervised the disposal of toxic waste at Northwestern University and the University of Illinois, Karl and Longhini met several times informally in late March to discuss the story's progress. The two journalists played "devil's advocate" with each other, arguing the strengths and weaknesses of the allegations.

They could not dismiss the University's contention about the unlikely danger from radioactive contamination. However, the scientists from other schools led them to question the impartiality of the Argonne National Laboratory studies on which that contention was based. The scientists informed them that Argonne was, in fact, a part of the University of Chicago. Further, the University's own memos indicated the possible hazards from chemical waste, and showed that the University definitely had been recalcitrant and sometimes sloppy in trying to dispose of its toxic waste problems. Even if the danger was not imminent, the University's storage practices were, by its own admission, in violation of Fire Department regulations.

"We became convinced that there certainly was a potential danger to students and that the University had reacted far too slowly to the problem," Karl said. "You want the danger to be significant and current," Longhini said, "but you have to describe its reality, not your dreams about what you'd like to say." Both men still felt strongly they had an important story to tell, but it would have to contain a strong historical emphasis to be accurate. "I now saw it as a piece about what the University did and didn't do in the face of an environmental threat," Longhini said. The series' title, "Wasted Time," emerged from these meetings.

Karl and Longhini began to devise ways to bring the story to life with pictures. In early April, they sent a Unit 5 college intern to the University to take still photographs of the toxic waste sites with a 35-mm camera. After two trips, she returned with shots of students walking in physical proximity to the chemicals. As a college student herself, she was able to take pictures inside the classroom without attracting attention.

Then Karl remembered Nachtrieb's statement that the University had its chemical wastes removed only on certain days. "He [Nachtrieb] told me that to convince me that they were doing something about the problem, but we decided to see if we could get pictures of what was really going on." The Unit 5 investigators took a camera crew in an unmarked van to the campus on one of the expected clean-up days. Shooting from the back of the van, they got footage of men wearing heavy protective gear moving the chemicals as students walked nearby. These pictures "graphically illustrated both the potential safety problem and the University's lack of warnings to students," Karl said.

The story had entered a phase that Karl called "investigative photojournalism." Pictures were providing vital documentation for the exposé. To further this goal, Longhini began to search for footage of the University's chemical fire in 1973. He called free-lance cameraman Larry Schreiner, whose speciality is photographing fires for journalists and insurance companies. Schreiner indeed had taken film of the chemical fire, and he agreed to sell it to Unit 5.

Longhini also located film of the Manhattan Project. The film had been used recently for a WMAQ-TV special report on the anniversary of the building of the bomb and so was located conveniently in the station's videotape library. The footage showed University of Chicago scientist Enrico Fermi at work in his quest to split the atom. To put matters in a contemporary context, Longhini arranged for a helicopter that was leased to WMAQ-TV to fly over the University to take videotape footage of the area.

Then the decision was made to get pictures of a toxic waste site in Alabama mentioned in one of the memos. The memo stated that radioactive wastes had been mistakenly transported by the University to a chemical dump in Emelle, Alabama. When the University discovered the mistake, it had to dig up the radioactive container and move it back to Chicago. This provided further evidence of the University's carelessness. But since no one on the Unit 5 team was interested in going to a small Alabama town, they called the nearest NBC affiliate to get videotape of the site.

By early May, the story was beginning to take shape. At this point, Karl began doing stand-ups at the University of Chicago. With cameras rolling and the campus in the background, Karl stated some of the main allegations of the story. He also interviewed University spokesperson James Yuenger to get his side of the story. In a rather weary and patronizing tone, Yuenger once again said that there were no problems on campus that the University was not taking care of.

The series was scheduled to begin on Sunday, May 13. But there was one remaining major task to accomplish before the journalists began producing their story. For some time, Karl and Longhini had been discussing possible ways to inform government officials about their impending exposé. They wanted officials to comment on the University's failure to report its problems to the appropriate authorities. Besides, the investigative journalists felt they had an ethical obligation to inform officials directly about their findings. They also hoped officials would react by forcing the University to correct the problem.

Since the memos mentioned violations of the city's fire code, Karl and

Longhini decided to contact Fire Department officials first. On Friday, May 11, Karl called the department and was put in touch with Deputy Chief Thomas Roche. Roche was willing to do an interview with Karl the same day at his office in Fire Department headquarters.

Karl summarized his investigative findings for Roche and showed him some of the internal University memos. "Roche clearly was alarmed by the chemical storage problems. He wanted to do something about it right away," Karl recalled. "I was glad that he wanted to act, but I was concerned that word would get out if a horde of inspectors headed for the University of Chicago." Besides fearing the loss of his exclusive, Karl did not want it to appear that the University of Chicago's problems had been solved before they even were exposed.

Consequently, Karl began negotiating with Roche for a suitable time for fire officials to conduct their inspection. "This made me uncomfortable," Karl said, "because I don't believe that journalists should orchestrate results with officials. You can lose your independence when you do that." Nonetheless, Karl was not about to let anything jeopardize the Unit 5 investigation. So he convinced Roche to delay the inspection until Monday, the day after the station broadcast the beginning of its exposé.

Roche remembered the negotiations pretty much the same way. "When a problem is reported, we try to act as soon as possible," he said. "The fact that it was reported by the media probably speeded things up." Roche was upset that his inspectors had missed the problem in the first place, but said he also "was mad at the professor [Nachtrieb] for not alerting us earlier. I said 'shame on him' on camera." But Roche doubted he would have sent inspectors to the University immediately. "Monday was fine with me. I probably couldn't have done anything before then, anyway, because it was almost the weekend and no one would have been available."

Meanwhile, Karl headed back to the studio to begin writing the scripts for the exposé that would be broadcast in two days. He had given Roche the addresses of the chemical waste sites at the University and planned to go there with a crew to videotape the inspection on Monday morning. He hoped that students would be safe over the weekend.

PREPARING THE INVESTIGATIVE REPORT

It would be a long weekend of work for Karl and Longhini. Several important tasks needed to be accomplished before the exposé could be broadcast on Sunday night. The information gathered during the investigative phase had to be organized into a coherent form. Decisions had to be made about which of the documents, interviews, still photographs, and videotape would be included in the story.

To accomplish these tasks, WMAQ-TV news writer and producer V. J. McAleer joined the marathon decision-making sessions. This would be the first Unit 5 exposé that he would produce. McAleer had been working intermittently on the investigative project since the first videotape had been shot. Until now, his main responsibility had been to review in the studio footage that Karl and Longhini had obtained in the field.

"I would log videotape for them every day or two, making notes which described the visuals," McAleer recalled. "I put stars next to the shots I liked the best. Then I would give Peter my notes so that he ultimately would be able to write a script with the visuals in mind." Now, McAleer would be responsible for the technical aspects of production—matching words and pictures to create an exposé.

Before McAleer could begin this task, Karl and Longhini had to make crucial choices about the format of the story. For some time, they had decided that the story would be told in several parts rather than in just one broadcast. "There was no way that we would get the time in a half-hour newscast to lay it all out at once," Longhini said. He also believed that "doing a series is more effective for building and holding an audience."

On Friday afternoon, Karl, Longhini, and McAleer discussed the possible parts to the series. "We agreed that since there was one target (the University of Chicago), we would do separate parts on its different toxic waste problems," Longhini said. "The chemical storage problem had the strongest findings and the best visuals, so we decided that would be the first part." The planned inspection of the University's chemical waste sites by fire officials on Monday morning further influenced this decision; it could be covered as a reaction to Sunday night's story.

Karl next wrote a draft of the chemical waste story and showed it to Longhini and McAleer. The draft included several references to radioactive waste which the three journalists decided would fit better in the second day's story. It also did not mention the 1973 chemical fire at the University until the last page. They decided to move up the discussion of this incident to near the lead of the story. "The file footage of the fire was dramatic, and it showed that people could be hurt by the storage problems," Longhini explained.

Karl's draft generated further discussion about the portrayal of fire officials. The draft stated: "Unit 5 has learned that the Chicago Fire Department is aware of the potential dangers of the hazardous chemical storage but has allowed the University to continue its present practices." This language was removed from the script in part because it was not entirely true; fire officials simply had failed to discover the problems in their recent inspections.

But rather than modify the accusation to make it accurate, the journalists decided to take it out completely. "We felt that the University was the real culprit for trying to hide the problem," Karl said. "When we went back over the evidence, we just couldn't blame the Department for anything but an oversight by one of its inspectors. And that wasn't worth mentioning since the Department was about to do another inspection on Monday," he added. "Our target was the University."

Consequently, the journalists used the footage of fire official Roche accusing the University of failing to bring the problem to the Department's attention. Roche's harshest words ("shame on him") were directed specifically at chemistry professor Norman Nachtrieb, who had acknowledged choosing not to alert authorities to problems he believed were serious. Ironically, the man who had painstakingly documented the University's chemical waste problems thereby emerged as one of the main villains of the story.

With the final draft of the script completed, McAleer began the task of producing the story. "This was *not* a highly visual story," he concluded. "I couldn't show injured students, exploding chemicals or radioactive rooms. I had to visually bring these points home in other ways." To do this, McAleer used "explode-out quotes" from the internal memos "to make the best parts of them easy for the audience to read." He also devised a chart that depicted the University's increased accumulation of toxic waste. McAleer sprinkled the undercover shots of the campus throughout the piece "to remind viewers that this was an inside look at problems that affected innocent people."

After the story was produced, the journalists showed it to WMAQ-TV News Director Paul Beavers. Normally, the story also would have been reviewed by WMAQ-TV's legal counsel. But that did not occur in this case, in part because the station was in transition between attorneys. Beavers gave approval to story, and the station began running ads over the weekend to promote it. The ads heralded "a Unit 5 exclusive. Illegal storage of hazardous waste at the University of Chicago, Sunday night at 10."

On Sunday night, viewers would be introduced to the institutional target of the exposé, the University of Chicago, which was "illegally storing hazardous and flammable chemical wastes on its campus for years." The villains included "high-ranking members of the University" who were "aware of dangers involved with this illegal storage," according to Karl. Without substantiation, Karl charged that these unnamed administrators were "more concerned with cost than safety."

Next, viewers were shown pictures of University of Chicago students going to class. Suddenly, the hidden-camera videotape of nearby waste haulers wearing respirators appeared on the screen. (McAleer called this "the most effective shot in the piece to make our point.") Karl said: "What these students don't know is below some of their classrooms, the University is storing hazardous and flammable chemicals that could endanger their lives."

The footage of the chemical explosion from ten years earlier was used to demonstrate that "the danger was real." Karl alleged that the explosion "*should* have sent out warning signals that the University had some problems with its method of storing chemical waste." But almost nothing was done. Today, "the potential for problems has increased," Karl stated over McAleer's graphic showing the growth in waste. The story went on to name the classroom buildings with the alleged problems, showing them from the air with shots taken by the WMAQ-TV helicopter.

To support the allegation that "high-ranking officials knew they were violating the law," several of Professor Nachtrieb's memos appeared on the screen with McAleer's "explode-out" quotes. The accusation by fire official Roche was inserted here: "I just can't imagine someone writing this to his administrator . . . and not notifying anyone else, such as the Fire Department." When asked by Karl why he did not inform authorities, Nachtrieb replied: "Oh, well, I'm a university professor, my procedure is to deal with my superiors here . . . I wouldn't go outside of the University to say I think something is wrong." This prompted the "shame on him" comment by Roche.

After showing other memos, Karl described the University's plans to construct the building that "would wipe out the danger." But, as more pictures appeared of students walking to class, Karl alleged that "bureaucratic and academic red tape" had prevented it from being built. The piece concluded with Karl's description of the University's announcement ("made a short time after Unit 5 started questioning the illegal chemical storage," he said) that it would submit plans to the government to construct the facility. "It could be another full year before construction begins, as the wheels of bureaucracy grind away," Karl concluded.

Sunday night's story would go as planned. First, however, a dispute arose among the journalists about the remainder of the series. On Saturday, the day before the initial broadcast, Karl's concerns resurfaced about the strength of the radioactivity allegations. He had to be convinced by Longhini and McAleer that these charges were worth making. Longhini wanted the series to have at least three parts, which typically was the minimum number of stories for a local television exposé. Karl, however, was having trouble envisioning two complete stories about the University's radioactive waste disposal problems. In part, he did not think the information they had developed was unique or strong; it did not add much to the previously published announcements about the clean-up.

After protracted discussions, the journalists agreed on a compromise. They would do the radioactivity stories but deemphasize the imminent danger from the problem. Karl's script, which he ultimately read live on Monday night, would say: "This is not a scare story of radioactive contamination at the

University of Chicago. It is a story that raises questions about a possible conflict of interest, and why it took so long to start a clean-up program once the contamination was discovered."

The 1940s film of the Manhattan Project then would be shown, giving the piece a historical flavor. The film showed scientist Enrico Fermi at work on the Project. McAleer, as it turned out, had used this footage in producing the earlier WMAQ-TV special on the anniversary of the bomb. "I had 'set-off' the bomb once or twice in that piece," he recalled, "but now we wanted shots that reflected the reality of the situation at the University today." Consequently, he used the "fairly dull footage of Fermi doing calculations" rather than the "visually sexier" film of the nuclear explosions.

McAleer then tracked Karl's voice describing the "incomplete" clean-up efforts over the still photographs of the inside of affected classroom buildings and highlighted memos warning about "potential" problems. As students were shown walking by one of the buildings, Karl described the University's studies of radioactive contamination. He said the studies "were kept under wraps" by the University and that the "actual clean-up didn't begin until almost seven years after the studies began."

Next, a close-up of University spokesperson James Yuenger was shown. He stated, "I've checked with all of the authorities around campus, and they assure me that there is just not any danger from radioactivity to anybody on this campus." Karl, in a stand-up on campus, apparently agreed: "No questions have been raised about the levels of radioactivity here at the University of Chicago," he reported.

Karl instead raised the conflict-of-interest charges. He alleged that "a scientific marriage" exists between Argonne Laboratory and the University of Chicago because "the University manages Argonne under contract with the Department of Energy." This relationship led "nuclear physicists who examined the [Argonne] safety studies for Unit 5" to question their impartiality, he stated. More highlighted internal memos showing problems with the clean-up were used by Karl to contradict the University's public claim that the removal of toxic waste was proceeding uneventfully. The final script called for Karl, live from the studio, to discuss more projected delays in the clean-up and to present the University's denials about the conflict-of-interest charges.

This second part of the exposé was not approved until Monday morning. Meanwhile, the Unit 5 team got a "break" that ensured there would be a third part to the series. Karl received a call from a Hyde Park physician who had seen the station's advertisements for its series. The physician, Dr. Sidney Bild, had been doing informal studies of cancer rates in the area. He was willing to discuss on camera the possible connection between the University's use of radioactive materials and an apparent increase in bone-marrow cancer in Hyde Park.

"Suddenly, we had the possibility of including real victims in the story," Karl recalled. "Radiation and cancer make people pay attention," Longhini said. On Monday afternoon, Karl interviewed Bild in the physician's Hyde Park office. Bild said he had become concerned when he "discovered that eight neighborhood friends and associates developed multiple myeloma," and that he had become even more "alarmed" when he received letters from 15 former Hyde Park residents with the same form of cancer. Bild called for "a study to be conducted to determine the incidence of cancer . . . in the area."

Although the evidence for a connection between the University's research practices and cancer rates was thin, the Unit 5 team agreed that Bild's statement was strong enough to lead off the third part of the series. "There's a call tonight to study the health consequences of the University of Chicago's atomic research," WMAQ-TV news anchor Ron Magers said in introducing the piece. Karl's interview with Bild followed, interspersed with shots of Hyde Park streets. University spokesperson Yuenger's denial of the problem was repeated.

But then, to undermine Yuenger's credibility, Karl told the story of the University's "mistaken" shipment of the radioactive materials to Emelle, Alabama, and their subsequent return to the University. The videotape of the Emelle site taken by the NBC affiliate was shown, followed by helicopter shots of the University of Chicago hospitals, which happened to be near the campus building to which the radioactive materials were returned.

Returning live in the studio, Karl described the University's promise to correct its toxic waste problems. In closing, he turned to the news anchors and committed himself to "following up the many leads that we've established during this investigation."

The three-part series came to a close on Tuesday night, May 15. The Unit 5 investigative journalists had generated reactions from the government and private sector even before the exposé was fully broadcast. They now wondered how the viewing audience—the general public—would react to their exposé.

THE INVESTIGATIVE INFLUENCE

In the days that followed the "Wasted Time" series, the general public responded to the Unit 5 allegations with a conspicuous silence. Approximately 501,000 adult viewers had watched WMAQ-TV during that period, according to the Nielson ratings, but only a handful of persons contacted the station about the broadcasts. One of those persons was the University of Chicago's

James Yuenger, who called to complain that the series was unfair. Other calls came from the University of Chicago student newspaper and a Hyde Park community paper, both wanting further information about the story. No letters were sent to WMAQ-TV about the series.

This disappointed, but did not particularly surprise, the Unit 5 investigative journalists. "The general public may not have felt exposed to this particular problem," said producer Longhini. "What made it a larger issue to us was the bomb, the importance of the University of Chicago as an institution, and the environmental questions raised by the storage. But there was no citywide threat for viewers." Karl concluded that "the story wasn't a blockbuster because the University was taking steps to deal with the problem, and we couldn't prove that anyone had been actually hurt in the meantime."

The lack of direct viewer response to the television station was consistent with the findings from our public opinion surveys. Before the series was broadcast, we contacted a random sample of Chicago area residents by telephone. Seventy percent agreed to be interviewed. This sample was stratified by local television viewing habits yielding 208 respondents who identified themselves as regular viewers of WMAQ-TV news and 186 who said they were viewers of some other newscast or nonviewers of television news. All respondents were interviewed about issues that were both related and unrelated to the forthcoming exposé.

After the series was broadcast, we were able to reinterview 131 of the WMAQ-TV viewers (most of whom had watched "Wasted Time") and 103 of the others. We found no statistically significant changes in the attitudes or agendas of respondents who watched the investigative series compared with those who did not (see table 6.1). Both our measurements and the assessments of the journalists who worked on the story suggest that "Wasted Time" did not influence public opinion.[1]

This did not mean, however, that public policy makers would ignore the Unit 5 series. In addition to the public opinion surveys, we interviewed forty policy makers both before and after the investigative series.[2] The policy makers were asked about the importance of toxic waste disposal in comparison to other problems, and they were questioned about their assessments of several government agencies responsible for environmental protection. In addition, they were asked about their past, present, and anticipated future policy-making activities related to toxic waste disposal problems.

Unlike the general public, policy makers significantly lowered their evaluations of the job performance of several of the government agencies that had responsibility for regulating toxic waste disposal at the University of Chicago (see table 6.2). Interestingly, there was no significant downward change in their assessment of the Fire Department, which was portrayed favorably in the series.

Table 6.1
Effect of Toxic Waste Series on General Public Sample[a] (Mean Scores)[b]

	Channel 5 viewers (N=131)		Channel 5 nonviewers (N=103)		Series-aware (N=83)		Not aware (N=146)	
	Pre	Post	Pre	Post	Pre	Post	Pre	Post
Cognitive Items								
Importance of toxic waste disposal	3.48	3.43	3.53	3.41	3.51	3.42	3.50	3.42
Fire Dept. does its job	3.67	3.52	3.67	3.53	3.69	3.50	3.68	3.55
U.S. Dept. of Energy does its job	2.66	2.72	2.40	2.53	2.48	2.58	2.57	2.64
U.S. EPA does its job	2.61	2.57	2.41	2.56	2.45	2.39	2.55	2.65
OSHA does its job	2.63	2.76	2.52	2.75	2.48	2.65	2.63	2.80
NRC does its job	2.56	2.61	2.22	2.37	2.35	2.37	2.46	2.59
Federal officials adequately enforce toxic waste disposal regulations	2.50	2.48	2.41	2.42	2.49	2.43	2.44	2.43
Fire officials regularly inspect buildings for hazards	2.44	2.55	2.48	2.63	2.43	2.57	2.47	2.59
Local universities have influence in the city	2.47	2.55	2.58	2.64	2.39	2.44	2.62	2.68
Affective items								
Worry of improper storage and disposal of chemical waste	3.36	3.23	3.27	3.13	3.44	3.21	3.27	3.17
Worry of danger from radioactive accidents	3.13	3.03	3.12	2.96	3.12	3.04	3.15	3.00
News stories frustrate me	1.77	1.73	1.73	1.72	1.74	1.76	1.76	1.69
New stories confuse me	1.54	1.60	1.58	1.59	1.57	1.69	1.56	1.56
News stories make me feel helpless	1.61	1.70	1.63	1.68	1.67	1.78	1.59	1.65
News stories anger me	1.74	1.73	1.75	1.75	1.78	1.77	1.73	1.74
News stories make me feel indifferent	1.29	1.32	1.31	1.40	1.28	1.35	1.32	1.36
Shrug off or don't remember stories	1.52	1.18	1.26	1.25	1.12	1.16	1.25	1.23
Behavioral items								
Have you acted to solve problems on the report?	1.38	1.36	1.29	1.29	1.39	1.35	1.30	1.31
Have you acted to avoid risks?	1.54	1.56	1.55	1.55	1.55	1.62	1.55	1.52

[a]High numbers indicate more positive responses (4 = "very important," "agree strongly," or "very adequate").
[b]All differences are nonsignificant at $p < .05$.

Table 6.2
Effect of Toxic Waste Series on Elite Sample[a] (Mean Scores)

	Exposed (N = 23)		Unexposed (N = 8)	
	Pre	Post	Pre	Post
Agency evaluations				
Chicago Fire Department	3.42	2.79	2.71	2.71
U.S. Dept. of Energy	2.50	2.05	2.71	3.00
U.S. Environmental Protection Agency	2.91	2.27[b]	3.13	3.13
Occupational Safety and Health Administration	2.33	2.00[b]	3.13	3.25
Dept. of Streets and Sanitation	2.83	2.72	3.00	3.00
Bureau of Inspectional Services	2.20	2.07	2.75	2.75
Police Department	2.84	2.84	3.57	3.57
Park District	2.60	2.55	3.20	3.20
U.S. Social Security Commission	2.56	2.50[b]	3.00	3.50
U.S. Dept. of Immigration	2.29	2.21	3.00	3.17
U.S. Dept. of Health & Human Services	2.45	2.40	3.17	3.17
Agenda setting				
Importance of toxic waste disposal	3.52	3.61	2.63	2.63
Importance of environmental pollutants	3.09	3.27[b]	2.63	2.25
Importance of violent crime	3.48	3.39	3.38	3.50
Importance of unemployment	3.74	3.61	3.75	3.75
Importance of police brutality	2.76	2.67	2.00	2.00
Importance of child abuse	3.32	3.18	3.50	3.17
Behavioral				
Past time spent on toxic waste problems	2.39	2.57	2.38	2.38
Ideal time spent on toxic waste problems	2.64	2.73	2.50	2.63
Expected future time spent on toxic waste problems	2.50	3.05[b]	2.50	2.25

[a]High numbers indicate more positive responses (4 = "very important" or does job "very well").
[b]Significant change ($p < .05$) levels are based on distributions of F ratios from analyses of covariance adjusting for initial between-group differences.

Furthermore, significant change occured on one of the questions designed to measure the behavior of policy makers. When asked, "In the coming
months, how much of your time do you think will be spent on toxic waste
disposal problems?" policy makers exposed to the broadcast were significantly more likely to answer "more time."

These findings are consistent with the actual policy-making impact of the
Unit 5 investigation. As Fire Department Deputy Chief Thomas Roche had
promised, the morning after WMAQ-TV broadcast the first part of its investigative series, a team of three fire officials inspected the buildings where
the University stored chemical waste. The officials cited the University for
failing to comply with 20 of the city's safety regulations. They gave the
University 30 days to comply and threatened to initiate criminal prosecution if
it failed to do so.

The Fire Department's "crackdown," to be sure, did not occur in a political
vacuum. The previous year, Chicago mayoral candidate Harold Washington had
been elected on a reform platform. Many of the city's administrative aides,
including Thomas Roche, were holdovers from previous regimes. Roche explained that "we wanted to impress the new leadership by getting credit from the
media for dealing with the problem [at the University of Chicago]. We also
wanted to avoid potential embarrassment for not doing our job." These political
and bureaucratic interests provided additional motivation, besides protecting
public safety, for the Fire Department's swift action.

The University of Chicago, for its part, took immediate steps to correct
the problem. The University first established a new policy requiring the swift
disposal of any chemical that could not be kept in University laboratories
(usually for lack of space). No longer could those chemicals be stored
temporarily underneath University buildings. Further, plans for a permanent
facility to handle chemical wastes were submitted to government regulatory
agencies and approved on an expedited basis. That facility was built the
following year—at a final cost of approximately $120,000—thereby eliminat-
ing the problem.

Meanwhile, under the watchful eye of the U.S. Department of Energy,
the University continued its clean-up of radioactivity that it had begun in
1983. Floors, walls, and plumbing were removed in three campus buildings.
Several months after the WMAQ-TV broadcast, the federal agency found that
the University was in compliance with its radiation protection standards.

These actions, however, were not accompanied by any basic changes in
public policy making. No legislative, regulatory, or budgetary proposals were
made to address the larger questions of toxic waste disposal, either on college
campuses or elsewhere in U.S. society. As discussed in chapter 1, we call the
official actions "individualistic"—rather than "substantive"—reforms.

Despite its circumscribed nature, the government "crackdown" at the

University of Chicago was effective for dealing with the problems disclosed by the WMAQ-TV investigative series. It also drew a considerable amount of media attention to the issue. Just hours after the fire officials conducted their inspection, WMAQ-TV led off its Monday evening newscast by covering their actions, stating they were "taken in response to our Unit 5 investigation. . . . ." In the third part of the investigative series on Tuesday night, Peter Karl reported that "just yesterday, inspectors from the Fire Department cited the University again for storing flammable chemicals in an unsuitable area. . . ."

Both of Chicago's daily newspapers on Tuesday had stories about the inspection. "City faults U. of C. on fire safety," the *Tribune*'s headline proclaimed. "U. of C. is cited as fire violator," read the *Sun-Times'* headline. The stories credited channel 5 for its role in the crackdown. The *Tribune* report stated that "The fire department issued the citations after WMAQ-TV reported Sunday night that the university stores 'hazardous and flammable chemical waste' in the building." The *Sun-Times* quoted fire official Roche saying that his inspectors took action "following a WMAQ-TV (channel 5) investigation [that] aired Sunday night. . . ."

There were no follow-up stories by the television station or daily newspapers after the University took steps to correct its problems. However, the University's actions were tracked in the weekly community newspaper, the *Hyde Park Herald*. The *Herald*'s stories laid out the University's case in some detail. Indeed, the lead paragraph of the first *Herald* story after the Unit 5 series stated reassuringly: "Two University of Chicago spokesmen said last week that the university will correct as quickly as possible the fire violations found on Monday, May 14, at two campus chemical waste storage sites."

Not surprisingly, rival television stations did not cover the findings or aftermath of the WMAQ-TV "exclusive." However, WGN-TV's Peter Triestman silently watched and applauded the developments. For Treistman, "the story was important because it exposed deceit and got results. It was great that they pushed officials to fix the problem for public safety reasons and to get recognition for their work. That's what makes a routine investigative story successful."

Karl and Longhini were pleased with the policy-making impact of their series. "The whole idea is to bring about change," Karl said. For similar reasons, the exposé represented a professional turning point for producer A. J. McAleer. "I really liked doing a story that got results," he said of his first experience as a producer for Unit 5. "I wanted to do more stories about outrageous things like this. It brought out the 'goo-goo' [good government] in me."

McAleer would get many additional opportunities to work on investigative projects, as would Karl, Longhini, and Treistman. Meanwhile, environmental problems were rising quickly on other journalists' agendas.

Content analyses of media coverage of the environment showed that stories about toxic waste problems, especially chemical waste, had become the hottest local news topic of the first half of 1984.[3] "Wasted Time" had made a further contribution to the growing dialogue about environmental safety.

The general public, however, was not an active participant in this dialogue. Rather, the actions taken at the University of Chicago occurred independently of any manifested changes in public opinion. They resulted primarily, instead, from an ad hoc coalition between investigative reporters and public officials.[4] In the case of "Wasted Time," a crucial step in the linear Mobilization Model appears to have been skipped.

NOTES

1. See David L. Protess et al., "The Impact of Investigative Reporting on Public Opinion and Policymaking: Targeting Toxic Waste," *Public Opinion Quarterly,* 51 (1987), pp. 166–185.

2. Ibid. Those surveyed were influential in environmental policy making, including administrators of state and federal environmental protection agencies, state legislators, members of the Chicago City Council, University officials, and lobbyists from public interest groups and private waste disposal companies.

3. Jeffrey J. Hallett, "Issues Management Letter," (Washington, DC: Conference on Issues and Media, August 1, 1984), p. 6.

4. We have called this "coalition journalism." See Harvey L. Molotch, David L. Protess, and Margaret T. Gordon, "The Media–Policy Connection: Ecologies of News," in David L. Paletz (ed.), *Political Communication Research* (Norwood, NJ: Ablex, 1987), pp. 26–48.

CHAPTER 7

"Missing?"

"Whether you think of these children as missing depends on whether you're their Norwegian mother or their American father," began "60 Minutes" correspondent Diane Sawyer. Over her shoulder was a picture of two children and the title of the segment, "Missing?" Sawyer continued:

> The children are caught in a kind of legal no-man's land between Norway and the United States. That may seem surprising since Norway is America's old friend and NATO ally—not, you'd think, the kind of country that would help its citizens defy American law, which is exactly what we thought too until the Better Government Association and WBBM radio in Chicago told us about a man who went to Norway and learned the truth, the hard way.

Next, viewers saw a beautiful landscape and handsome people. "It's a dream country, Norway, picturesque and tranquil," Sawyer told her 38 million viewers. "And that's what an American named Larry Risk expected when he came here on sabbatical in 1983 with his wife and two children. But instead, Larry Risk ended up living a nightmare." The story began when Risk's Norwegian-born wife decided to stay in Norway. Against his wife's wishes, Risk brought the children back to California where a court awarded the parents joint custody under the condition that the children, both American born, remain in the United States. One day, however, Risk came home to find his children gone.

This was not just another custody battle, said Sawyer, because "the Norwegian government was behind it all." Based on documents first obtained by a reporter for the *Norway Times,* an English-language newspaper published in Brooklyn, Sawyer reported that officials of the Norwegian government paid for airline tickets and issued documents to the children as, incredi-

157

bly, Norwegian commercial seamen. Risk pursued his family to Norway only to find that authorities there helped to conceal his children from him. "I had no idea," he told Sawyer ruefully, "that the Norwegian government was in the kidnapping business."

Next, Risk and Sawyer were off to Norway, where they—along with a hidden camera—went unannounced to his daughter's school. School personnel refused to talk to them, and Sawyer concluded that the school must have been "under some kind of orders." Before leaving, Risk showed other children a picture of his daughter and asked them to tell her that he had been looking for her. The *Norway Times* reporter was then called on to explain why Norwegian officials had obstructed Risk's attempt to see his children. "I believe if you took a poll of the Norwegian population," the reporter said, "the people would say this beyond anything, 'This is without a doubt the finest country in the world in which a child could grow up.' " Nevertheless, concluded Sawyer, Risk's situation and other, similar cases have caused "a firestorm of controversy in Norway."

Another such case was that of Harald Johnstad, whose story was remarkably similar to Risk's. An Illinois court gave temporary custody of the couple's son to the mother on the condition she not leave the state. Johnstad received custody of a daughter whom, viewers were told, the mother did not want. But even before these custody arrangements were complete, the Norwegian government had sent telexes to its Chicago consulate asking if child abduction was illegal in Illinois and instructing officials to assist the mother. The words of the daughter then brought this story to its inevitable conclusion. "I tried to stay awake because I had heard my mother and her lawyer talking about passports and traveling," she recalled of her last night with her brother. It seems the children were so afraid of being taken that they tied themselves together. "I eventually fell asleep but then when I woke up the next morning, he was gone. . . ."

Next Sawyer was shown in Norway, again trying to find the child and to confront the villains. She did neither. The child remained concealed. Government officials refused to be interviewed, although their treachery and deceit were visually symbolized by their office doors, which remained closed to Sawyer and her crew. Sawyer could only report to her viewers that the U.S. State Department said it could do nothing and that a treaty on the return of abducted children had not been approved by either Norway or the United States. "Over the past decade more than 2,000 children have been abducted to countries around the world," Sawyer reported, "and no one knows if their American parents will ever see them again."

So concluded another exercise in the rhetoric of villainy and victimization that has made "60 Minutes" the most watched news magazine program in television history.

THE GENESIS OF THE PROBE

The story of this investigation begins with the fathers. Both Risk and Johnstad had independently compiled a great deal of information and had aggressively sought media attention. Johnstad, with the help of the *Norway Times* reporter who later was interviewed by "60 Minutes," had obtained a number of documents, including the incriminating telexes, using Norwegian laws granting access to government records. Johnstad's first attempt to interest "60 Minutes" in his case had been ignored, but late in 1984 he took his information to a local radio station, WBBM in Chicago, where it was received by reporter Scott Smith. "WBBM received a package that was out of the norm," recalled Smith. "It was clear to the managing editor and the news director that the information was not only compelling but that the man had done his homework. It wasn't the usual B.S."

Smith and his editors immediately saw in Johnstad's story what the "60 Minutes" staff later would see: not only good documentation but also an unambiguous villain, sympathetic victims, and a fascinating plot line. "If the information was correct, here we had a case in which a foreign government— a friendly government—had set out to break laws that existed in the U.S.," recalled Smith. "The actual story itself almost read like a novel: how the woman got out [of the U.S.] in the middle of the night, how she was driven by a consulate official to Milwaukee with great pains [sic] to surreptitiously get her on an airplane. Not only was the information good, but the way the story played out had a good deal of audience appeal."

After reading the materials, Smith immediately met with Johnstad, who, in turn, introduced Smith to Larry Risk and to the *Norway Times* reporter, Geirr Aakhus. Within two weeks Smith had produced a three-part series using interviews with the fathers and the reporter. Each of the three segments was about three minutes long, which Smith characterized as "pretty generous" for WBBM's all-news radio format. The first segment reported Johnstad's story; the second reported Risk's story; and the third, as described by Smith, reported "what had not been done by people who might have done something." The U.S. Department of State, in particular, was faulted for failing to pursue the cases. "Both [fathers]," said Smith, "had been in contact with the State Department, asking for help and not receiving any."

Before the series aired in January 1985, Smith had been unable to get comments from Norwegian officials; but only a few days after the broadcast, he was able to interview an official in the Norwegian Ministry of Justice by telephone. "The official danced around quite a bit, but he eventually indicated that what Johnstad was alleging was, in fact, true," recalled Smith. "It was not like, 'Yes, I put the gun to the victim's head.' It was more like an acknowledgment, and then he'd swiftly move on to the next subject." That very night, Smith put together a one-hour special featuring the taped interview. Johnstad was present in the WBBM studio while Risk called in from Norway were he was searching for his children. Several others participated by phone, including the Illinois judge who had taken away the Johnstad children's passports so that, presumably, they could not leave the United States.

Smith went on to report several other international abduction cases. He also updated the Johnstad and Risk cases several times even though he found the response of other news media and the public to be "pretty much nothing." When interviewed, Smith at first characterized his interest and involvement in these stories as a "crusade" but later expressed ambivalence about that term. "Maybe 'crusade' isn't the right term," he said. "It wasn't that I personally would march to Washington carrying a sign. It was just that I felt a great deal of sympathy and empathy for the fathers." He attributed his feelings, at least in part, to a bitter experience with his own divorce and child custody case. "It really made me sensitized to this whole story, and maybe for that reason I became more involved," he said. "After seeing the kind of energy and money expended by Risk and Johnstad and their dedication to their children, I became personally involved to the extent that I felt something should be done to rectify this, if not for them, then for future fathers."

Not long after the stories aired, Smith was promoted to assistant news director, and his new responsibilities directed his attention away from the child abduction story. In January 1986, however, he had a meeting with Mike Lyons, the chief investigator for the Better Government Association (BGA), the Chicago-based organization that works with the news media on investigative reporting projects. Smith and Lyons were discussing a number of potential projects when, by chance, Smith happened to mention the child abduction cases. Lyons immediately saw in the cases what Smith had seen the year before. Smith arranged a contact between Johnstad and Lyons. At the same time, Lyons used the BGA's long relationship with CBS News to arrange a contact of his own. It was with Jan Legnitto, a producer for "60 Minutes" correspondent Diane Sawyer.

THE INVESTIGATIVE PROCESS

Two years before, Johnstad's attempt to interest "60 Minutes" in his case had gone nowhere. "We get thousands of letters," explained Jan Legnitto. "People tend to overstate their case in these letters to us; and when you start to look into them, you find that it was not the case." This time, however, "60 Minutes" was interested. As the BGA pitched the story, Legnitto could see that these cases offered a new angle on the familiar story of children abducted by a divorced parent, but she was not yet convinced that the fathers' stories would stand up. "At the time, it was difficult to believe that what these fathers accused the Norwegian government of doing had actually happened," she recalled. "So, as usual, I approached [the fathers' accusations] with a certain amount of skepticism about the documentation." At Legnitto's request, BGA investigator Susan Barnett prepared a long memo that outlined the cases, reviewed the available documentation and explained some of the legal and diplomatic issues.

Legnitto was convinced. The documentation assembled by the fathers, WBBM, and the BGA was excellent, and yet, from Legnitto's point of view, the story "hadn't been done before." Although the stories produced by WBBM, a trusted CBS-owned news operation, confirmed the "doability" of the investigation, they didn't really count since they had been aired only on local radio. Legnitto pitched the story to Diane Sawyer and, with Sawyer's go-ahead, began a research process that consumed about 20 weeks in mid-1986. Following network policy concerning authentication of interviews and documents obtained from outside the CBS News organization, Legnitto and her staff traced much of the information back to original sources. They found the cases to be solid. "These fathers had so well documented their cases that it helped us tremendously in our efforts to put together the story," said Legnitto. "Their cases were so conclusively documented that they were irrefutable."

At the same time, Legnitto and her staff, with substantial help from the BGA, searched for other cases of government-assisted abduction. From BGA research, Legnitto knew that more than 2,000 cases of international child abduction were on file with the U.S. Department of State. She was interested in documenting the magnitude of the international child abduction problem, but she was also looking for other, perhaps even more dramatic or fully documented, cases of government-assisted abduction.

Drawing again on BGA research, Legnitto and her staff collected what she characterized as "a sample of 100 to 200 cases from countries throughout the world" in which there seemed to be the possibility of government involvement. However, several months of research produced acceptable documentation for government involvement in only the two orginal cases. "There were lots of accusations in those other cases but not the credible evidence that those two cases had," recalled Legnitto. "While we looked for others—we were willing to show that the United States was doing the same thing, for instance—we couldn't prove them." Ironically, then, it was the relative openness of the Norwegian government that made the segment "doable" and, in turn, made Norway a villain. "Our choice of Norway had to do with accessibility of information," said Legnitto. "Norway may not be more guilty than the others, but we couldn't find evidence that clearly implicated anyone but Norway."

In June 1986, with research well under way, Sawyer and a camera crew accompanied Larry Risk to Norway. As Sawyer made clear in the finished segment, the goal of obtaining taped interviews with the mother and children was thwarted when the family, apparently alerted to Risk's presence, could not be found. However, Sawyer did obtain from Norwegian television an interview with the mother that had been taped when her case earlier had come to public attention in Norway. A trip with a hidden camera to the school attended by Risk's daughter yielded only a brief confrontational scene between Risk and school personnel and the poignant scene in which Risk asked other children to tell his daughter he had been looking for her.

A later attempt to locate Harald Johnstad's family came only a little closer to the goal. Johnstad's wife agreed to an off-camera interview in which she made a number of accusations against Johnstad. Substantial additional research by Legnitto and her staff could confirm none of these charges, however. The only tape of this mother was, then, a brief shot of her fleeing from the camera.

Norwegian government officials were even more elusive than the mothers—none would agree to any sort of interview.

PREPARING THE INVESTIGATIVE REPORT

"Missing?" entered the final stages of production late in 1986 and emerged as little more than a visualization of Scott Smith's radio reports from two years before. Risk and Johnstad, of course, were cast in the role of the victims just as they had been in Smith's reports. They were granted substantial screen time to tell their stories and to express their pain and frustration. "The fact that you don't see your dad doesn't mean that he's abandoned you," Risk said, recalling a conversation he once had with his children. "You must know that, that I'll be looking for you, searching for you, and I'll never give up." Additional screen time was given to shots of Risk walking the streets of Bergen, Norway where, as Sawyer said in voiceover, he had "spent a year of his life and more than $50,000 . . . searching for his children."

There were also several characters in supporting roles who had first appeared in Smith's reports. Geirr Aakhus of the *Norway Times* was on hand to explain, with rhetorical flourish, how the Norwegian government assisted the mothers' escape from the United States. "Here's your recipe," he concluded. "You need an attorney and then you need to show up in court with a straight face and then you need to set up such an apparatus that you can abscond with the whole schmeer in the middle of the night." The Illnois judge who dealt with the Johnstad case was called on to report that the mother had wanted custody of the son but not the daughter because she thought the girl would "poison" the boy against her. The daughter was also present to recall the night of her brother's abduction.

Bowing to the medium's demand for visuals, the finished segment made extensive use of family snapshots to make the lost children real for the viewers. The segment also employed such visual conventions of the television exposé as shots of incriminating documents; it included a brief sound bite from the Norwegian television interview with Risk's wife who said of the abduction (in translation), "I didn't have the right, but I had the duty to take them with me." Finally, given Sawyer's limited success in Norway, Sawyer herself is shown primarily standing outside of the doors to government offices and to a mother's apartment—doors that are kept closed to her and to the camera.

Thus, as do many other investigative stories, "60 Minutes" offered its audience vicarious participation in a drama of tragic victimization and villainy, but unlike some other of the stories we have studied, the completed segment did not offer policy makers the opportunity to step into the hero's role. Officials in the U.S. Department of State were interviewed, but, according to Legnitto, their interviews produced little information of interest and were not included in the finished segment. "Their attitude was that there was nothing they could do so why should we use that in the piece?" she said. Further, according to Legnitto, there was no one in Congress who had seized the issue. "No one was taking the ball and running with it so why should we give some congressmen credit that they didn't deserve?" There was, then, no attention in the finished segment to the legal and diplomatic issues raised by these cases beyond a brief mention of a treaty concerning abducted children that was not yet in force. "The U.S. has approved treaties on everything from arms control to fishing rights," said Sawyer, "but the treaty on the return of abducted children has not been approved by the U.S. or Norway."

Beyond the fact that Legnitto found no policy elites who were "taking the ball and running with it," the absence of such elites from the segment reflects Legnitto's distaste for the sort of press–policy maker coalition building seen in some other investigations. "I don't want to go out of my way to build in official reactions just for the sake of having them," she said. "If officials are not involved, they should not be included. That's not the appropriate role for journalists to play." Indeed, Legnitto seemed to pledge her allegiance to the traditional Mobilization Model of media effects. "My job is to inform the public and let them act on the truth if they choose to," she said. "The public must have the tools to act, though, and I try to give them the tools in the form of information." Yet, she also understood that a likely effect of the segment would be to provoke policy makers to quick—if only rhetorical—action. "Child abductions is [sic] a pull-at-the-heartstrings issue, and officials get maximum political milage from a minimum number of affected constitutents because of the emotional pull on the public at large," she argued. "We didn't have to try to make anything happen in the policy-making arena. This was an issue whose time had come. . . . We didn't have to interview any policy makers to get them to act."

Still, Legnitto maintained that she, unlike some other reporters, did not have "an agenda" or particular outcome in mind when working on her investigation. "It's always gratifying to see a piece get a strong response, but it's not our goal to get one," she said. "I don't think about what's going to happen or what should happen when I'm doing a piece." She refused to equate the success of a story with its impact on either the public or on policy makers. "My definition of a successful piece is one that tells you something you did not know before," she said. "I want editorial independence from other institutions in the culture, and I can't have that and try to manipulate them."

The finished segment, Legnitto insisted, presented a "microcosm" of a larger social issue—international child abductions—but amid the pathos of the particular cases some relevant information seems to have been lost. Of the more than 2,000 cases mentioned in the segment, Norway accounted for only about a dozen. Germany, Great Britain, Mexico, and a number of other countries are all far more common destinations for abductors. Further, the abductors are more likely to be the fathers than the mothers of the children. Finally, government participation in the abductions, although rumored in other cases, could not be documented.

Legnitto's response to the question of whether these cases typify the larger issue was to argue that her job is not really to produce documentaries about such issues. "Our focus is on the individual cases whose stories we are able to tell," she said. "We don't do the broad issues at '60 Minutes'; we do stories from which issues can emerge." Thus, the only attempt to provide a larger context for the Risk and Johnstad cases was the brief mention of three abductions—all by fathers—to Lebanon, Greece, and Iran. No mention was made of government involvement in any of these cases.

But if the Risk and Johnstad cases are not typical, they are textbook examples of stories that fit the format of "60 Minutes" and, more generally, the journalistic genre of the exposé. There is a small but compelling cast of characters. There are victims whose stories, as Legnitto said, "pull at the heartstrings." These fathers, whatever the source of their marital problems may have been, now command sympathy because their children seem lost to them for all time. And there is a villain whose presence is ironic and unexpected. The government of "America's old friend," Norway, now warrants condemnation because it has betrayed American fathers and American courts. Although the villain cannot be given a specific human face, it is represented by a beautiful landscape and handsome people as if to underscore its treachery.

THE INVESTIGATIVE INFLUENCE

Given the "60 Minutes" mastery over the rhetoric of victimization and villainy, it is hardly surprising that the primary effect of the segment on public opinion was not to increase the salience of international child abductions as a policy issue but rather to vilify Norway. When surveyed shortly after the broadcast, a sample of Americans who had seen "Missing?" attached no more importance to the problem of missing children than a sample who had not seen the segment. Both viewers and nonviewers saw this as an important social problem, however (see table 7.1).

Further, the comparison of viewers to nonviewers revealed no real difference in the ranking of missing children on a list of "problems that concern the American family." For both viewers and nonviewers, this problem was firmly entrenched at about the midpoint of a list that included drug abuse, hunger, unemployment, divorce, and inadequate day care services. Similarly, questions about the need for treaties to deal with international child abductions and about the likelihood of help from the U.S. government for Americans who have legal difficulties with citizens of other countries produced no differences between viewers and nonviewers. However, one question that dealt with what the segment was really all about—villainy—did produce a significant difference: those who had seen the segment thought that Norway had less respect for U.S. law than those who had not seen it.

Another survey conducted about three months after the broadcast produced about the same results on all of these questions (see table 7.2). This survey, however, included several additional questions concerning the villains thought to be behind the child abduction problem. Viewers were more likely to expect a mother rather than a father to abduct a child. Further, viewers ranked Norway as the second most likely destination for a child abductor from among five countries. Nonviewers, on the other hand, ranked it (quite correctly according to State Department statistics) as the least likely destination.

In sum, the analysis of audience response to "Missing?" could find no agenda-setting effect, although it did find several effects that reflected the peculiarities of the abduction cases featured in the segment. Surveys indicated that the public was sympathetic to the plight of abducted children but that it certainly was not mobilized for political action by this exposé. Thus, as with the exposés reviewed in previous chapters, we can tell the story of the policy

Table 7.1
Effect of "60 Minutes: Missing?" on General Public Attitudes
Toward "Missing" Children and International Child Abduction[a]

	Pretest		Posttest 1		Posttest 2	
	Viewers (N = 96)	Non-viewers (N = 505)	Viewers (N = 96)	Non-viewers (N = 505)	Viewers (N = 74)	Non-viewers (N = 111)
Rated importance of missing children	3.63	3.69	3.55	3.66	3.51	3.57
Rank-ordered importance of missing children	3.54	3.06	3.38	2.84	3.15	3.03
International treaties are not needed	1.99	1.95	1.81	1.94	2.03	1.86
U.S. govt. likely to help American citizens	2.88	2.82	2.70	2.83	2.62	2.83
Respect of Norway toward U.S. law	3.47	3.37	2.75^b	3.33	2.87^b	3.13

[a]Higher numbers signify higher rating of importance, agreement, etc.
[b]Comparison of viewers and nonviewers adjusting for pretest differences was statistically significant at $p < .05$.

process that followed the broadcast with little further mention of public opinion as assessed by survey research.

With its "discovery" of international child abductions, "60 Minutes" helped to reactivate a policy struggle within the federal government that, by 1987, had been under way intermittently for some time. In 1981, the Hague Convention on Civil Aspects of International Child Abduction, a treaty that would resolve subsequent abduction cases by honoring the laws of the country from which the children were taken, had been signed by the United States and a number of other Western nations. Although the treaty had not been transmitted by the State Department to the Senate for ratification until 1985, the Senate gave its consent soon thereafter. However, the treaty still did not go into effect because enabling legislation—which the State Department was expected to draft—had not been transmitted to Congress. Thus, early in 1987, when the "60 Minutes" segment aired, the next move in the treaty implementation process belonged to the State Department.

Several senators, including Paul Simon (D—IL), Alan Dixon (D—IL), and Albert Gore (D—TN), had a particular interest in the issue. Simon's

Table 7.2
Effect of "60 Minutes: Missing?" on General Public Attitudes Toward Policy Options and Perceptions of "Villains"[a]

	Posttest 2	
	Viewers ($N = 74$)	Nonviewers ($N = 111$)
Policy options		
Should U.S. do something?	3.09	2.91
Treaty to return abducted kids	4.67	4.38
Law against abducting kids to foreign countries	4.56	4.51
State Department pressure on foreign leaders	4.22	4.07
Require airlines to check kids leaving U.S.	3.84	3.91
Villain perceptions		
Father or mother more likely to abduct? (1 = father, 2 = mother)	1.23[b]	1.09
Average ranking of likely destinations for abductors (1 = most likely destination)		
Mexico	2.17[b]	1.58
Norway	2.69[b]	4.05
France	2.98	2.67
West Germany	3.24[b]	2.85
Saudi Arabia	3.70	3.78

[a]Higher numbers signify more agreement.
[b]Comparison of viewers and nonviewers statistically significant at $p < .05$ (t-test).

policy entrepreneurship on behalf of missing children went back a number of years to his sponsorship of legislation that created the National Center for Missing Children. Dixon, like Gore, had become interested in the issue when several constitutents appealed for help in retrieving abducted children. Although Harald Johnstad was one of Dixon's constituents, the senator and his staff already had put far more effort into the case of Patricia Roush, whose children had been abducted to Saudi Arabia by their father who was alleged to be mentally ill. That case was particularly tragic, but it also held the tantalizing promise of resolution because Dixon and his staff had managed to interest a member of the Saudi royal family in it. However, arrangements for a meeting between the Saudi prince and the children's father had fallen apart when the U.S. ambassador, under orders from the State Department, declined to attend. Irritated with the State Department's attempts to steer clear of this and other cases, Dixon and his staff wanted to pressure the State Department to intervene in the Roush case.

Early in 1987, just as "Missing?" was nearing completion, Senator Simon, who increasingly was preoccupied with his run for the Democratic Presidential nomination, asked his home state colleague to take responsibility for the treaty legislation. Thus, Senator Dixon wanted to move two items higher on the State Department's agenda: action on the Hague Convention and attention to current abduction cases. It was into this policy game that "60 Minutes" and other media suddenly bounded.

Ten days after the broadcast of "Missing?" Dixon was ready to take control of the situation. He did so with a news conference in Washington to announce a drive to obtain the return of abducted American children. The Johnstad case was mentioned at the conference, but the dramatic highlight was provided by Patricia Roush. With "voice breaking" (according to the *Chicago Tribune*), Roush pleaded with the State Department for help in the return of her two little girls. Dixon characterized State Department inaction as "an outrage" and called on other senators to sign a letter to the Secretary of State demanding action. On that same day, a letter signed by 24 senators calling for quick progress on both the treaty legislation and the individual abduction cases was sent to Secretary George Shultz.

Shortly thereafter, just as a constituent was forming an organization called American Children Held Hostage, Senator Gore tried to get in front of the action by calling for Senate hearings to scrutinize government regulation of the documentation required to take children out of the country. "While there is no question that this is a serious problem, it is also an elusive one," Gore wrote in a letter to Ernest Hollings, chairman of the Committee on Commerce, Science and Transportation, requesting the initiation of hearings. "A common thread in all international parental child kidnappings, however, is that at one point, people show up at international airlines with a minor child illegally taken from his or her home state." Gore concluded, "Some way must be found to offset the current powerlessness of parents—U.S. citizens— losing children in this tragic manner." Meanwhile, American Children Held Hostage, which had begun with a membership of about 25 parents, organized a letter-writing campaign in support of the treaty legislation.

Although Dixon's staff refused to acknowledge any causal relationship between the "60 Minutes" broadcast and the direction or even timing of their own actions, their work did reveal a self-aware attempt to use media attention to move the issue on the State Department and Senate agendas. Sarah Pang, a Dixon legislative aide, acknowledged that the broadcast and subsequent media coverage had helped to focus the attention of the State Department and the Senate on the treaty legislation. "This has really stepped up everything," she said a few weeks after the broadcast, predicting that the legislation would soon "sail through" the rest of the process.

Pang insisted, however, that even with the treaty in effect, the State

Department still would need to seek actively the return of the children and that Secretary Shultz should raise the issue in upcoming meetings with foreign officials. "Getting this on the State Department's agenda is crucial," Pang said. "For us, the answer is to keep the media focused on this issue. That will produce the necessary response, hopefully, from the State Department and foreign officials." Thus, Pang credited media attention with the ability both to move action on the treaty ahead in time and to move action on particular cases higher within the State Department hierarchy.

As it turned out, the legislation did not sail through as easily as Pang had expected. The State Department did transmit its draft of the legislation to the President of the Senate and the Speaker of the House early in March. However, in a break with usual procedures, State failed to notify Dixon or any other legislator that the transmittal had occurred. In a subsequent interview, Pang characterized this as "very unusual," particularly for legislation that had already received substantial publicity. She interpreted it as an attempt to "get even" by making it appear that State had done its job but Dixon had not. "We were bashing them around a lot during this time," Pang said. "[They] made us look bad. That's for sure."

It was June before the legislation was introduced in the Senate by Simon with Dixon, Gore, and others as cosponsors, and in the House by Thomas Lantos (D—CA). Even then, however, the legislation did not "sail through" because of higher priority items on the Senate agenda, including confirmation hearings on the ill-fated nomination of Robert Bork to the Supreme Court. However, as the legislation worked its way through Congress, the State Department, at last, announced the creation of an office to "handle inquiries from American parents" (as *The New York Times* phrased it). In October, Dixon marked this development with another news conference featuring Patricia Roush. Dixon claimed some progress in moving individual abduction cases higher on the State Department's agenda, but he also told the department to remember that "we mean business." He outlined legislation that he planned to introduce making international child abduction a federal crime. That legislation died in the Judiciary Committee, but early in 1988 the treaty legislation received the final approval of both houses, and in April it was signed by President Reagan. The problem of abductions to countries not party to the Hague Convention remained on the policy agenda, however, and Patricia Roush's children remained in Saudi Arabia.

Looking back over the process, Judy Wagner, legislative assistant to Senator Simon, said that media attention may have moved the legislation more quickly but that its long history and bipartisan support would have been sufficient to move it "sooner or later." Dixon's additional legislation had no such history, and the attention he was able to focus on it, apparently, was not sufficient to move it at all. But if all Dixon managed to do was to move the treaty legislation ahead in time (as well as move attention to specific cases higher in the bureaucracy), his efforts were a good, work-a-day example of how influence on the media agenda can translate into influence on the policy agenda. Indeed, the skill with which Dixon and his staff used the Roush case to gain media attention and, in turn, gain policy impact provides a textbook example of how elected officials can use constituent casework to political advantage.

Dixon and his staff, of course, were not the only influences on the media's attention to international child abductions in the months after the "60 Minutes" broadcast. Nevertheless, an examination of the media agenda during that period turns up the names "Dixon" and "Pang" as well as "Roush" with great regularity. By the time the "60 Minutes" segment aired, the *Chicago Tribune* (for which the Roush and Johnstad cases were good local stories) already had run a story reviewing the abduction of Roush's children and Dixon's efforts to retrieve them. Although the article quoted Sarah Pang, it made no mention of the policy issues raised by international child abductions. On the morning before the "60 Minutes" broadcast, the *Chicago Sun-Times* tried to take local control of the story with a feature on Johnstad that it had obtained from the Better Government Association. Two days later, the *Sun-Times* followed up with an article that tried to take some of the credit for breaking the story. "As outlined in Sunday's *Chicago Sun-Times* and in an investigation by CBS' '60 Minutes' and the Better Government Association," it said, "the problem has touched the lives of at least two Chicago-area men." The article went on to review briefly the Johnstad case and another case that had been identified in a BGA press release issued the previous day. Unlike previous articles, this one did locate the cases within a policy context thanks to Simon aide Judy Wagner, who succeeded in framing the cases as examples of the more than 2,000 international child abductions that might be solved by implementation of the Hague Convention treaty.

"The CBS Evening News with Dan Rather" also followed up the "60 Minutes" segment two days later with a report by Charles Osgood. That story began with a reference to the involvement of the Norwegian government in the abductions reported on "60 Minutes." Then it reviewed two more abduction cases. One of those cases, first reported the year before by Scott Smith of WBBM radio, was yet another abduction by a Norwegian mother. The other was an abduction by a Mexican father. Although neither of these cases documented governmental involvement, Osgood's report did have something that "60 Minutes" lacked: a parent actually reunited with abducted children. The American mother, Cynthia Vargas, traveled to Mexico with a CBS crew, found her son and daughter, and then confronted their father. In a dramatic taped moment, the Vargases argued about whether their children had been kidnapped by him or abandoned by her. The story made fleeting mention of "international agreements pending" and then closed with the image of the sobbing mother.

In Norway, where the Risk and Johnstad cases already had caused a "firestorm of controversy," there were also follow-up reports in the first few days after the "60 Minutes" broadcast. One newspaper, for example, featured a column by its American correspondent who quoted several Norwegian officials in Washington lamenting what they thought to be the destruction of Norway's image in the United States and bracing for an outpouring of negative public response. Another paper, however, featured an interview with Johan Sandvin, who had helped get the Risk children their seamen's papers. Sandvin said that Norwegian officials should be commended for helping a mother to get her children home to Norway—a mother whose children had originally been taken from Norway in violation of a court order there and whose case had come to a standstill in U.S. courts.

It was only a few days later that Dixon masterfully seized control of the media agenda with a news conference that directed attention toward his highest-priority abduction case as well as the Hague Convention. The *Sun-Times* and *Tribune* portrayed the conference as the tearful plea of a local citizen for help from her government. "My government will not help me," both papers quoted Patricia Roush as saying. "What am I supposed to do? Forget my children?" Near the end of the *Tribune's* story, much as in the *Sun-Times'* version, Dixon was quoted as calling the situation "an outrage" and urging "Secretary of State George Shultz to take specific action in the Roush case and to urge worldwide ratification of the Hague Convention."

Dixon's news conference also managed to return the issue to the national media. *The Christian Science Monitor* reprised the Roush case and accepted Dixon's framing of the issue by casting the State Department as the villain of the scenario for failure to pursue aggressively the return of the children. The story quoted a State Department spokesman who said that the Department would not take the side of one parent over another. But Dixon was given the last word. Taking sides was not the issue, the senator said, because custody of Roush's children already had been decided by an American court. The State Department could help Roush, Dixon insisted, with "a simple phone call" to the Saudi government. A few days after this story, the Monitor editorialized on behalf of "child hostages abroad" by urging the State Department to make retrieval of abducted children a priority.

Three weeks after the broadcast, the *Norway Times,* which had begun it all three years before, followed up with a story on the response of the Norwegian foreign minister to questioning by that country's national assembly. The minister, finding himself in a situation familiar, no doubt, to many others who have had a brush with "60 Minutes," explained that ministry officials declined to be interviewed for the segment because, as the newspaper translated his remarks, "selections of interviews would be used to present the story as the program producer saw fit, and this would not take the Norwegian side of the story sufficiently into account." The story noted Dixon's activities as one response to the segment, but it also cited foreign ministry officials who "largely discounted the effects of the program," at least for Norway. The article concluded with a wry comment from a Norwegian government spokesman who said the only reactions from the American public that had been detected by embassy officials were either anger with the one-sided segment or else amazement that American law does not apply in Norway.

A few months later, in March 1987, Harald Johnstad reemerged in the national media with an appearance in *People* magazine. In a cover story headlined "Kids Caught in the Middle," Johnstad was portrayed as a man betrayed neither by Norway nor the State Department but, more conventionally, by his ex-wife, who had taken his child. Johnstad was presented along with other parents whose cases were the most bizarre examples that could be gleaned from the annals of child custody disputes. These included a man whose ex-wife had married a "confessed-mobster-turned-government-informant" and had taken the man's child into hiding, as well as a couple whose adopted son was being reclaimed by the Indian tribe into which he had been born. The headline act in this tribute to parental agony, however, was "Baby M," who was said to be celebrating her first birthday by awaiting a decision on whether her father or surrogate mother would take her home.

In April, Senator Dixon's aide, Sarah Pang, began negotiations with the staff of "The Oprah Winfrey Show" for a program on international child abductions featuring Patricia Roush as the victim and the State Department as the villain. "Clearly, these abducted children are being denied their constitutionally guaranteed rights," Pang wrote in a letter to a member of Winfrey's staff. "They suffer because our government refuses to accept the responsibility to protect its children." In a follow-up letter, Pang urged the Winfrey staff to produce a show timed to coincide with the Second National Conference on Missing and Exploited Children in Chicago. "[M]edia attention will already be directed toward the plight of the abducted child," she wrote, "and the added publicity that 'The Oprah Winfrey Show' generates could be the additional spark that ignites the United States Government into action that would expedite the return of these young U.S. citizens to their rightful homes."

The program never was produced. Proposals to "Nightline" and "20/20" also failed to generate stories. But by June, Roush was back in the media spotlight. "Patricia Roush's case has come to the fore again," reported *The*

Christian Science Monitor, "this time at a congressional hearing a few days ago." In her testimony to a House Foreign Affairs subcommittee investigating alleged human rights abuse of Americans in Saudi Arabia, Roush was quoted as saying, "What am I supposed to do? Forget my children?"

In this appearance, Roush was joined by another of Dixon's constituents, Kristin Uhlman. According to *The New York Times* version of the hearings, Uhlman said she had been imprisoned when she tried to retrieve her children who had been taken to Saudi Arabia by their father. The *Monitor,* unlike the *Times,* which treated the hearings as hard news, used a variety of sources to review the cultural differences between the U.S. and Muslim societies as well as the difficulties faced by the State Department when trying to help parents like Roush and Uhlman. However, the last word went once again to Dixon, who said that Roush was "a genuinely good woman who has suffered an outrageous injustice."

A few days later the *Chicago Tribune* rehearsed the Roush case once again, this time as a local feature story headlined "Love Becomes an International Battlefield." Then, in September, the *Tribune's* widely syndicated columnist Bob Greene repackaged the Roush case with several other "vignettes" of vanished, kidnapped, or murdered children. The column, he said, was intended to correct the fact that "the subject of missing children" was receiving less media attention than in the past. Greene kept politics out of this column, but he did quote Sarah Pang, who empathized with Roush's daughters: "These little girls must be so confused and so hurt and so scared." Greene also quoted Roush, who seemed to deviate a little from previous scripts. "Right now I feel my only hope is Jesse Jackson," she said.

Meanwhile, the Chicago papers finally found a case with a happy ending. Two little boys had been retrieved by an Illinois State Police officer from Mexico, where they had been taken by their father who had been indicted for murder in Illinois. The reunification of mother and children, according to the *Sun-Times,* "fired the interest of Sen. Alan J. Dixon (D—IL), who plans legislation this fall to attack the problem of international parent [sic] abduction." Sarah Pang was on hand to report that the Hague Convention legislation would create a State Department office to deal with cases such this as well as "the ongoing ordeal of Patricia Roush."

In the fall, just as substantive action on treaty implementation finally got under way, the Chicago newspapers seemed to lose interest in the story. *The New York Times,* however, briefly noted that the State Department, "under pressure from several members of Congress," had agreed to establish a bureau to handle inquiries from American parents of children abducted to foreign countries. Although this story was essentially a report on Dixon's news conference announcing his bill to make abductions a federal crime, Patricia

Roush was quoted as saying that these developments were "signs of hope." The *Monitor* also summarized these developments in a story headlined "Climate Improving for Return of Abducted American Children."

The progress of the treaty legislation through Congress and to the White House in early 1988 went largely unnoticed. The *Tribune* devoted one paragraph to House passage in March. In June, the *Washington Post* noted the last steps of implementation with a three-paragraph editorial. But if the details of the legislative process did not hold the attention of the media, individual cases of child abduction continued to do so. In January, as the legislation was working its way though Congress, "The Phil Donahue Show" repackaged the Kristin Uhlman case as part of a xenophobic exercise emphasizing the danger to American girls of seduction by a "generous, charismatic, handsome, rich" Arab student, as Uhlman described her ex-husband.

In July, *The New York Times* found another American girl who had once been attracted to an "exotically sophisticated" Egyptian and had lost her children. The ubiquitous Sarah Pang, identified in the story as an aide to "the leading Congressional backer of legislation to help parents," was quoted as saying that the treaty was "a great first step." But the story also noted the Saudis were not signatories to the treaty. "The more you work on these," said Pang, "the more unbelievable it seems how little we can do."

Reflecting on these events, Simon aide Judy Wagner expressed grudging admiration for the skill shown by Dixon and his staff in exploiting constituent case work for maximum publicity. But she added, "I don't know a senator who wouldn't take advantage of the ability to get good press on an issue. Members will always talk about what their role was in resolving these sad situations." The performance of Dixon and Pang in this regard was masterful, however. The news organizations that paid any attention at all to policy developments made Senator Dixon *the* leader on this issue and his aide, Sarah Pang, *the* source for information.

"It's interesting," Judy Wagner continued, "that the press cared a lot about developments in the individual cases while they basically ignored our releases about the legislation." Even *The Christian Science Monitor* could not resist the tales of victimization and villainy, and, in fact, it really only paid very much attention to policy developments when Dixon created a tear-streaked pseudoevent. In the refined, Eastern Establishment pages of the *Monitor,* just as in the populist pages of *People,* there were good people who had been wronged, bureaucrats whose behavior was an outrage, and little children far, far from home.

The result of this fascination with individual cases was, of course, the fragmented and trivialized news coverage of social and political issues so often condemned by press critics. Indeed, with the issue of international child abduction, the individual cases were so indiscriminantly recycled and reframed that no coherent sense of "the story" or "the issue" can be located when surveying the corpus of press coverage. What *was* the story here? According to "60 Minutes" the children were "Missing?" but according to Bob Greene they were definitely missing. *People* knew where they were: "caught in the middle." The *Tribune* suggested that they were the casualties "when love becomes an international battlefield," but the *Monitor* thought they had been taken as "hostages." What, then, was the issue here? Sometimes it was the treachery of a foreign government, and sometimes it was the indifference of the American government. Sometimes it was the erotic dangers of foreigners, and sometimes it was the collapse of the American family. Sometimes it was a legal technicality concerning the documentation needed to take children from the country, and sometimes it was a sign of these degraded times when our children are in constant danger.

It is, then, pointless to ask about "the story" as portrayed by the media or "the issue" as formulated by the media. But, of course, the policy elites in the Senate and State Department did not need the media to formulate the problem or the action to be taken. They knew very well what was going on and what was supposed to be done. In this case, media attention did not change the substance of the policy initiatives concerning international child abductions, but the attention did help to raise the priority given those initiatives by policy makers and speed the pace of action on them. As in the other cases we have studied, this outcome was accomplished, not by creating an "effect" among the general public, but by simply being there—watching.

NOTE

1. J. S Ettema, D. L. Protess, D. R. Leff, P. V. Miller, J. Doppelt, and F. L. Cook (1991). "Agenda-setting as Politics: A Case Study of the Press–Public-Policy Connection." *Communication*, 12, pp. 1–24.

CHAPTER 8

"Dialysis: The Profit Machine"

A $2.5 billion federal program, "conceived in compassion for people who otherwise would face certain death, has fallen from grace." The program, designed to provide dialysis for the nation's victims of kidney failure, has turned into a profit machine "for a handful of corporations and a nightmare for thousands of patients." The noble government effort to save lives "is being threatened by a dangerous and sometimes deadly combination—corporate profit motive, lax control of the quality of care, and meek government regulation.

"In short, the program has spawned an industry that pits profits against patients."

Against that classic backdrop of greed and suffering, the KNT News Wire, a joint venture of Knight-Ridder Newspapers and the Tribune Company, advised its 200 subscribing newspapers in May 1988 that *The Philadelphia Inquirer* was running a four-part investigative series by staff writer Matthew Purdy entitled "Dialysis: The Profit Machine." The series broke in the *Inquirer* on Sunday, May 15 and ran in edited form in *The Washington Post* on May 17 and in *The Miami Herald* on May 25.

The *Inquirer's* first-day headline, "Kidney Patients vs. the Bottom Line," immediately introduced both victim and villain. The patients were described as "some of the most needy in America"—70 percent were unemployed, half were below the poverty line, and 30 percent were black. An italicized preface to the story read, "Thousands have been saved by federally funded kidney dialysis treatments, but uncounted others have suffered misery at the hands of profit-making clinics." The prominent front page display was accompanied by a photograph stretching four columns of a young dialysis patient taking her own pulse and "doing fine today at a nonprofit clinic in Rochester after surviving a severe scare while being treated at for-profit clinics in Virginia."

The story jumped to a full-page spread capped by a headline that reinforced the theme: "Profit Quest Imperils Kidney Patients." A series of illustrations explained how the kidney dialysis process works to clean and filter a patient's blood supply. A third full page was divided into two companion stories, known as "sidebars" to the story. One sidebar, headlined "A return to Rochester is a return to health," showcased Rochester, New York, where all five dialysis clinics operated not-for-profit. The other sidebar, headlined "Problems plagued University of Pennsylvania clinic," depicted a setting where federal inspectors were critical of water contamination, patient monitoring, and communication breakdowns. The "tagline" printed in boldface at the end of the day's main story noted, "Tomorrow: Trouble in the dialysis program: several case histories."

The following day's case histories focused on two cost-cutting measures endemic to the kidney dialysis program: the reuse of dialysis equipment and the employment of less-skilled personnel. The front page story was accompanied by two close-up photos; one of a dialyzer (blood filter) label specifying it is to be for "single use" by the patient, and the other of markings on a dialyzer, showing it "has been used 14 times." The lead case history was of a Philadelphia patient whose refusal to accept a reused dialyzer was characterized as "part of an awakening protest by kidney patients nationwide who have come to believe that high-quality care is being sacrificed for corporate profits." That day's tagline told readers, "Tomorrow: How a federal program turned into a profitable industry."

Day 3's disclosures described a program being exploited increasingly by corporations providing "Jiffy Lube dialysis." Annual profits in excess of 20 percent made dialysis clinics such a good investment, "[i]t was better than Cheerios," according to one doctor. "No company has benefited more from the opportunity to make private profit," the *Inquirer* reported, than National Medical Care, the nation's largest provider of dialysis treatment. The lead paragraphs introduced the company as part of a conglomerate that used $21 million from the kidney treatment program to "finance a deal" in which it acquired the dialysis company. The *Inquirer* reported that a federal audit concluded such use of federal money was "improper." The newspaper then said:

All of this might have been a case study for the White House commission that gave President Reagan a report on waste, fraud and fiscal abuse in federal spending.

Except for two things:

The commission that delivered the "War on Waste" report was headed by J. Peter Grace.

So was the conglomerate.

A picture of Grace was the only photograph accompanying the story, which documented how federal funds were bypassing patients.

The story was replete with references to federal sources and documents to substantiate the accuracy of the information. In all, the one day's story cited "federal records," "federal audits," and "auditors" 53 times. It also reported that although auditors had uncovered false billings, double billings, inflated equipment prices, and excessive profits, audits of the kidney program are intended not to catch misuse of public funds but to determine the flat rate it pays clinics to treat patients. "As a result," the *Inquirer* reported, "the government has made no effort to recover money from any of the 'disallowed' uses of the funds it has found at clinics across the country." The tagline leading into the final day's story read, "Tomorrow: How federal officials lost control of the program."

The headline on the last story in the series read: "Despite Abuses, Guidelines Still Lax on Kidney Program." The lead recalled that in 1972 when the program had first been approved by Congress, medical advances had made the issue no longer one of medicine but of money. In answering the call to save lives, the federal government opened the tap. By 1988, the series concluded, quality of care problems and "profiteering by corporations" had transformed the government's effort into big business. "Almost from the start, the program has demonstrated the government's inability to control its own largess." A graphic showed in adjacent charts how the number of patients and the cost of the kidney program had soared since 1974 when the program went into full operation.

The concluding story drove home its dual points of suffering and greed with two "pullout" quotations from government officials. Pennsylvania Senator John Heinz, former chairman of the Senate Committee on Aging, was quoted as saying, "It's skimping dangerously on the quality of care. If it costs the life of one, let alone 50 or 100, it's not worth it." Richard P. Kusserow, inspector general of the Department of Health and Human Services, pointed a finger at medical professionals: "Those people are like the rest of us and . . . are oftentimes challenged by avarice and greed, and they are capable of doing wrong things."

The story concluded that the government had lost control of its own program. Only half the clinics were inspected on an annual basis, and only one of the 1,665 clinics nationwide had ever been shut down. The government "sets few standards for how the money (it pays out) should be spent" and "steps lightly, claiming reverence for the sanctity of medical decisions," the story reported. The story reintroduced the reused dialyzer controversy as the best illustration of government ineffectiveness, noting that a study Congress asked to be done ten years earlier had never been completed.

The four-part series ended with an anecdote about a North Carolina doctor who two years earlier ran the state's largest dialysis clinic. He bemoaned at that time the financial evolution of the program and predicted that in ten years, "you'll see three or four suppliers of dialysis treatment." The last line to the series suggested that part of his prophesy had been fulfilled: "Last year [he] sold his clinic to National Medical Care," the company the *Inquirer* had characterized as benefiting most from the program's profit motive.

THE GENESIS OF THE PROBE

Some time in 1986, as the Senate Committee on Aging was preparing to hold hearings on kidney dialysis, Jonathan Neumann received a phone call in Philadelphia from a committee investigator with whom he had worked on stories in the past. Neumann was assistant metropolitan editor in charge of investigative projects at the *Inquirer,* a position he had held since 1982. Prior to that, he had been a reporter both at *The Washington Post* and the *Inquirer,* where he had contributed on two Pulitzer Prize-winning stories, first in 1978 for a series on patterns of police violence in Philadelphia and then in 1980 for the paper's coverage of Three Mile Island.

The investigator, whom Neumann considered a source and a friend, told him that the committee probe was yielding some dramatic findings on how kidney patients were suffering. The investigation, the source told Neumann, focused primarily on the unregulated reuse of dialyzers, a 10-inch piece of equipment used to cleanse and filter a dialysis patient's blood. The source told Neumann "he thought the information would make for a really good story in any newspaper, but he had some specific cases in Philadelphia that he thought would be of interest to us," Neumann recalled.

Neumann called his *Inquirer* colleague Matthew Purdy, who worked on the paper's national desk in the Knight-Ridder offices in Washington, D.C. Purdy had recently been transferred to the *Inquirer's* Washington bureau from its New Jersey bureau, where he had been since coming over to the *Inquirer* from the *Trenton Times* in 1982.

Purdy met with the investigator, spent a week with him culling through information, followed up some of the leads, and wrote a 2000-word front-page story that ran in the *Inquirer* on Sunday, October 19, 1986, the day the committee was to release its report publicly.

The story spotlighted the case of a Philadelphia dialysis patient who doctors suspected "was a victim of a practice that congressional investigators say is putting thousands of patients at risk of illness and death: the reuse of plastic dialysis equipment." The principal sources for the story were the report, the dialysis patient, and unnamed congressional investigators who were critical of the unregulated risks of reuse. The report accused federal health agencies of "consistently misleading" kidney patients about the risks of reuse and criticized the contradictory messages the agencies were sending.

The story quoted Pennsylvania's U.S. Senator John Heinz, as chair of the Senate Committee on Aging, calling for clinical tests to ensure the safety of reuse. "We cannot, and we must not, continue to tolerate the seemingly endless pass-the-buck actions by the responsible federal agencies," Heinz was quoted as saying. The story did not address the profit incentive other than to note that one doctor said "reuse is an economic reality" and another said that "the only reason for reuse is purely financial." Though the story was picked up by the *Detroit Free Press,* the *Charlotte Observer,* the *San Jose Mercury News,* and the *Wichita Eagle-Beacon,* among others on the KNT News Wire, neither the *Inquirer* nor other papers followed up on the story, and nothing much came of it, according to Purdy.

Neumann and Purdy knew then that there was a larger story worth pursuing. "It was my intention all along," Neumann recalled, to do a project about the whole issue of kidney dialysis in America. The angle that stood out for Neumann from the hearings focusing on the issue of reuse was profit. "It was so clear that people running clinics—in some cases doctors, and in other cases businesses—just simply chose to take millions in profits straight from federal funds when they could have been giving it to care," Neumann said later. "It was so obvious from the start that it was kind of screaming at us to do that story."

Neumann and Purdy agreed to try to have Purdy freed up for a few weeks to determine if a full-scale investigative project was worth doing. The problem, as Neumann recalled, was logistics. Purdy worked on the national desk and was one of only two *Inquirer* reporters stationed in the Washington bureau. The *Inquirer* needed to have Purdy available to cover breaking stories in the nation's capital.

As the editor in charge of investigative projects, Neumann was responsible for from six to twelve reporters working on investigative stories at any given time. He and Purdy agreed that December 1986 might be an ideal time to do some spade work because congressional recesses in December might give Purdy more available time. They were given the go-ahead from the national editor.

"That was a Tuesday morning," Purdy recalled. "About three hours later, [Attorney General] Ed Meese walked into the White House press room and said there's been this diversion of funds." That diversion of funds became the Iran–Contra scandal and diverted Purdy from the dialysis story for another four months. Neumann was transferred temporarily to Washington to help with the unfolding Iran–Contra story. Although neither would work on the dialysis story full time until the summer of 1987, they were both in Washington when NBC's "Today Show" gave national play to a television exposé that covered much of the territory their later series would cover.

The television exposé, called "Blood Money," was a three-part series done by investigative reporter Lea Thompson of NBC's WRC-TV (channel 4) in Washington, D.C. Like the later *Inquirer* series "Dialysis: The Profit Machine," WRC-TV's investigative series pitted patient care against profits and used case histories to vivify the problems in the federally funded kidney dialysis program. The series began December 8, 1986, with Thompson saying,

> People are getting sick and they're dying . . . and almost nobody cares. This story involves thousands of poor, fragile people, millions of dollars in government money and a company that is reusing old equipment just to make a buck. We are calling this series "Blood Money" because we believe that's what it is.

As in the later *Inquirer* series, WRC-TV targeted for its most exacting scrutiny J. Peter Grace and his company, National Medical Care, which was portrayed as having a "virtual monopoly in the lucrative kidney dialysis business." Thompson criticized the company's reuse policy and said "it's the company's way to cut costs and *really* boost profits" (emphasis hers).

Even more than the *Inquirer* would do, WRC-TV saved its most caustic criticism for the federal government, which was allowing the industry's unsavory practices to continue. As Thompson asked rhetorically in introducing the third part in her series, "Why isn't somebody in government doing something about this?" The report faulted the Public Health Service for misleading the public on the safety of reuse, the federal Food and Drug Administration for refusing to get involved, and HCFA (Health Care Financing Administration, the financing arm of Medicare) for reneging on its promise to cut off funds for clinics that forced patients to reuse equipment. The series concluded with Thompson saying, "the FDA and HCFA can do something about it if they want to, and they can save these people's lives, but they are turning their backs and they are turning the other way, and frankly I don't think they care."

A condensed six-minute version of Thompson's series that was carried January 19, 1987, on NBC's "Today Show" included a governmental indictment from U.S. Senator John Heinz: "For anybody at HHS [Health and Human Services] or the FDA or anyplace else to say there's no problem is to be an ostrich sticking the head in the sand about five feet deep. All that's sticking out are their fannies."

The "Today Show" version allowed Thompson to extend her findings beyond her Washington, D.C., base. Regarding the reuse controversy,

Thompson reported, "some say it's safe, some say it's dangerous. Either way the profits *are staggering* [emphasis hers]. . . . And it's not just the money. We have discovered suffering and death all across the country."

The series had immediate, but fleeting, impact. The week the series ran locally, nephrologists and dialysis specialists were holding their national convention in Washington, D.C. Government policy makers and the policy elite within the medical community were exposed first hand to the series. The convention vibrated with spontaneous postmortem debate.

A few days after the series aired locally, the first of three bomb threats to Washington area dialysis clinics was received. *Contemporary Dialysis & Nephrology,* a monthly trade magazine for nephrology professionals, quoted the medical director at one of the clinics as saying that all three bomb threats "made reference to the TV program," and on all three occasions, patients were evacuated. In its next issue, the trade magazine editorialized against the series, holding it responsible for sending "a shock wave of terror through the Washington, D.C., dialysis patient community." The editorial said "anyone but a trained observer could have been easily swayed [by the series' rhetoric]—perhaps to the point of blowing up a dialysis unit."

One week after the series ran locally, the Washington, D.C., City Council passed strict regulations on reuse. The ordinance had been introduced in the aftermath of a lawsuit filed against a dialysis clinic by a group of vocal patient activists. The regulations provided that if patients refused reused dialysis equipment, clinics must either provide them with new equipment or find them another clinic. In its only follow-up (the following week), WRC-TV characterized the regulations as the most stringent in the nation. Rick Nelson, who produced the series for WRC-TV, said, "We can't really take credit for prompting those regulations. They were already in the works when we ran the story." After that, Nelson said, he didn't hear much about the dialysis controversy until the *Philadelphia Inquirer* ran its series 15 months later.

THE INVESTIGATIVE PROCESS

The *Inquirer* won 16 Pulitzer Prizes over the 15 years from 1975 through 1989, nine for investigative reporting projects. Its kidney dialysis series, which would be a finalist for a Pulitzer in the national reporting category, proceeded as most of its investigations proceed—methodically, but with no set deadline and virtual carte blanche for Purdy and Neumann.

Once freed up to pursue the investigation, Purdy and Neumann were not called on to submit a memo, a process report, or any written updates until February 1, 1988, when Purdy completed a first draft of the series. That was nearly a year after getting the go-ahead to investigate the dialysis industry nationwide. At the same time, *Inquirer* reporters Donald Bartlett and James Steele were working, undisturbed for 15 months, on a "tax reform" investigation. Their series, "The Great Tax Giveaway," ran April 10–16, 1988, and beat out the dialysis series for the Pulitzer Prize.

Two formidable hurdles are built into any investigation into kidney dialysis—causality and confidentiality. "The angle you start out with is patient suffering," Neumann explained. "But patients suffer with almost all diseases." The first challenge, as Neumann saw it, was to document "unnecessary suffering above and beyond the disease" and to link it to "profit and greed." The specific targets were yet to be determined, but the victims (the patients) and the villains (those exploiting profit and succumbing to greed) were preconceived.

Much of the investigation involved following leads from clinic to clinic in an effort to isolate the unnecessary suffering. Purdy visited clinics in Philadelphia, Wilmington, Del., and Rochester, N.Y., and talked by phone with hundreds of sources, including Robert Rosen. As chairman of the National Kidney Patients Association headquartered in Philadelphia, Rosen was probably the most available and outspoken source in the kidney dialysis area. "I introduced him to patients in the Philadelphia area," Rosen recalled. "That's all he wanted. I got the sense he didn't want my help or influence."

Purdy would hear recurring patient complaints that seemed to be evidence of a trade-off between money being made and quality of care being compromised. He would relay information to Neumann in Philadelphia a few times a week. "We were constantly in search of individual patients whose stories were compelling and that illustrated the point," Neumann recalled.

For each case history they sought to develop, they spent weeks interviewing "the patient, the family, the doctor, the nurses, everyone involved, and then making an effort to get all the records," Neumann said. Investigative reporters expect not to receive cooperation from potential targets in a story. With dialysis, a matter of life and death, cooperation could not be assumed from potential victims either. Neumann and Purdy knew that their information-gathering efforts would be met with resistance from those whose personal privacy they respected.

Even before Purdy moved off his ongoing Iran–Contra assignment, he was filing Freedom of Information Act (FOIA) requests with government agencies responsible for keeping records of Medicare payments and clinic conditions. In all, he filed nearly 30 FOIA requests, more than on any other story he had worked. It was fortunate they had processed their written requests early, Purdy noted later, because most requests took weeks to be met. Some records were not provided until a year later. One in particular

Purdy received after the series had gone through its second draft. That record indicated that one clinic in Washington, D.C., had paid its medical director $303,456 in 1986 for working 3 percent of his time at the clinic—or $4,863 an hour, based on a 40-hour work week, as the *Inquirer* reported.

Cooperation from patients opened some doors but not others. "People who heard I was interested in [dialysis abuses] would get other people to call me," Purdy said. But much of the oral information Purdy got from patients could not be substantiated. "When you're dealing with victims in any situation, you spend a lot of time digging. A lot of them are conspiracists," Purdy said.

In trying to verify patient information through medical records, Purdy and Neumann confronted confidentiality roadblocks even when they had obtained authorization from the patient. "What we had to do, and it would take several weeks, is get a lawyer involved," Neumann recounted. "You would think, we had the patient's written permission, only it doesn't work like that. The hospitals and the doctors are very protective themselves. They talk about patient/client. Their emphasis is doctor, not patient."

Purdy and Neumann deployed more than lawyers to extract documentation. They collaborated with government officials. From the outset when a congressional investigator tipped them off to abuses in the kidney dialysis business, Purdy and Neumann found common ground with policy makers and regulators intent on reforming a system the government helped create. Neumann did not view the collaboration as a threat to journalistic autonomy or an abuse of government process but as an acceptable means to a shared end—"the public interest."

"When I say work with [congressional investigators], what I mean is we both get something out of the relationship," Neumann explained. The *Inquirer* needed the officials to obtain records that were not publicly available, yet not "violating anybody's privacy." "We don't have any direct access to get those records. The way we sometimes get them is [through] federal investigators who do have access; we talk to them and essentially tell them what we need, and they get the records," Neumann said. He noted that the *Inquirer* would not even have to wait until the documents were incorporated in the public record of a congressional hearing. "As soon as they'd get them, they'd give them to us," Neumann said.

An aide to California Congressman Fortney H. "Pete" Stark, the health subcommittee chairman of the House Ways and Means Committee, recounted that his office and Purdy would trade information, data, and horror stories. "We would get cost reports for Purdy and we would pass on letters from inspectors general about various companies," said Bill Vaughn, Stark's administrative assistant. "Often I would call Matt, and he would have the information already. I tried to help, but usually I was about a week behind."

Neumann viewed the benefit to the investigators as something more immediate than the cumulative goodwill government sources often seek with reporters. "A good hearing consists of a lot of the same material as a good newspaper story. . . . They may not hold any hearings if we don't go to them with the request. They might not have ever held a hearing. If they did, they may have had no idea about [particular] material," Neumann explained.

Reconstructing a hypothetical exchange he or Purdy might have with a government investigator, Neumann went on: "'There is this clinic in Pittsburgh, and there are these records about the clinic that are not publicly available. This is the story. It's a good story, we need the records, can we get them?' If we don't go to the investigator, they never know about the clinic in Pittsburgh."

One congressional investigator who had worked and socialized with both Purdy and Neumann in the past explained the coalitional relationship as a natural byproduct of their mutual interests. "We have outrageously limited resources to investigate, and we want the biggest bang for the buck in the public interest," said Peter Stockton, research analyst for the House Subcommittee on Oversight and Investigation. In referring to his recurring linkages with investigative reporters, Stockton said it is "one of the ways to expand our staff from time to time." Though his subcommittee was not looking into the kidney dialysis program, Stockton took a professional interest in the *Inquirer* story. He was aware of the *Inquirer* investigation before the series ran. After it ran, he nominated it for a Pulitzer Prize.

As with any investigative piece, the dialysis story had its dead ends and breakthroughs. Both Neumann and Purdy independently recalled spending weeks pursuing an angle that they had heard from numerous sources. They were told that a dozen dialysis patients had died within a few months at a clinic affiliated with the Hospital at the University of Pennsylvania. The deaths were said to have resulted from bacterial contamination in the clinic's water supply in September 1987.

"When we learned about it, it seemed like perhaps the most dramatic clinic example because it was local, it was current, it was 12 deaths," Neumann recalled. Patients at the clinic believed the deaths were linked to the contaminated water, and the rumors were spreading. Neumann and Purdy kept in regular contact with sources at the federal Centers for Disease Control. But when the series ran in May, 1988, there was no proof linking any deaths to the contaminated water.

"Obviously, we aren't going to say it was and we can't write a story that 12 people died because of poor treatment at the Hospital at the University of Pennsylvania," Neumann said. "It took me a very long time to find out it wasn't true," Purdy added.

The one breakthrough, Purdy and Neumann agree, came late in the investigative process when they learned about Rochester, N.Y. By then, the recurring theme in the case histories they were documenting of dialysis patients was the pivotal role profit played in the clinics' quality-of-care decisions. Rochester had five dialysis clinics, all operated not-for-profit.

"I had this community of doctors who were doing it this way for basically the very reasons my research was leading me to see," Purdy said. "In a way, [Rochester] really struck us as a gold mine because it proved the thesis of the story, which was that people are suffering needlessly because of greed and profit," Neumann added. "It proved that it's not just the disease. In fact, it's not the disease that's the problem, it's the treatment," he said.

For Purdy, Rochester sharpened the story's focus. But it also dulled the story's villains. "It was confirmation of my story in a positive way. It wasn't like finding out someone is the root of all evil," Purdy said. "It was finding out there was something really good going on. I think that makes the story very strong because in some ways it's a subtle story." By subtle, Purdy said, he viewed the problem he was preparing to expose as essentially one of distance—how people in the dialysis business and in government can remove themselves from the life-and-death consequences of their financial decisions.

To Neumann, that same subtlety bore a compelling force, striking directly at the venality of human suffering and greed. "I think it's about as strong as they get," Neumann felt as the story was about to break.

PREPARING THE INVESTIGATIVE REPORT

Purdy submitted a first draft of the series on February 1, 1988. He was meeting an unusual deadline. His wife was having a baby that week, and Neumann wanted to move the series into the editors' hands so Purdy could spend time with his family.

The 13,000-word draft, running 26 pages single-spaced, was written as a three-part series with one sidebar (on Rochester) to accompany the first day's story. As Purdy saw it, day 1 was about victims, day 2 about money, and day 3 about government. It opened with three case histories, each of a dialysis patient who had died, the first at the Hospital at the University of Pennsylvania. "This is the gift of life, American style," the draft then read. That metaphor would not make it into the published version.

The draft naturally reflected both Purdy's and Neumann's preference for case histories. Included were documented cases from Philadelphia, Virginia, Maryland, Louisville, Ky., Baton Rouge, La., Rochester and Queens, N.Y., Wilmington, Del., and Mayaguez, P.R. It included question marks in the text where information still needed to be checked, and it noted that responses were not yet solicited from clinic officials. The draft quoted observations from dozens of sources—patients and their families, doctors, government bureaucrats, and officials.

The patients and their families were cast as victims, not merely of a disease but of greed. "If it's not greed, I don't know what it is," one patient is quoted as saying about kidney clinics around the United States. "It used to be that we were looked on as miracles. Now we are looked on as dollar signs," a Florida patient complained. A Maryland patient is quoted as outraged about the practice of dialyzer reuse. "It was explained to us that it was a matter of economics. [The clinic] couldn't afford it," she said.

Doctors sought out as disinterested elites knowledgeable about the dialysis program added weight to the suspicions of the victims. "The concern for making a profit has overridden the concern for taking care of patients," said a former president of the nationwide Renal Physicians Association. The federal program, which allows for profit making, creates "an intolerable and undesirable conflict of interest. The doctor should be the agent for the patient," said the editor of the *New England Journal of Medicine*. "I think most of the doctors [in Rochester where the clinics are not-for-profit] sleep better at night," concluded one Rochester physician.

The government regulators, whose responsibility it was to monitor aspects of the dialysis program, personified bureaucracy—hopelessly buried in a system beyond their control. "We don't ask questions about how [clinics] parcel out that amount of money. We pay the rate. It's up to the facilities to divvy up the amount," said a federal official who oversees financing for the dialysis program. Another government regulator is quoted as telling Congress that problems found in a clinic in Queens "are likely to exist elsewhere in the country." Later in the draft, he is quoted directly: "We have built programs without proper controls, on the faith that the professionals would police themselves. That, I can assure you, is flawed judgment."

Elected officials expressed indignation at the program's failings. "I think there is no question that the government is being cheated by a large percentage of unscrupulous [dialysis clinic] operators," said Congressman Pete Stark of California, the health subcommittee chairman of the House Ways and Means Committee. Senator John Heinz of Pennsylvania, ranking Republican member on the Senate Committee on Aging, was equally outraged: "Where there is such a strong incentive to cut costs, there has to be strong monitoring by government of quality of care." Implicit in their displeasure was a commitment to do something about it.

Supporting the case histories and quoted sources in Purdy's draft was detailed documentation. Purdy and Neumann had spent more than a year gathering hard figures to substantiate the largely impressionistic thesis that the dialysis program "pits profits against patients." The draft was intended to let readers (and the editors at the *Inquirer*) know about the painstaking research without cluttering the story with document titles or divulging the sources who had made the information available.

It was replete with such references as:

- *"Records show* that some clinics reuse dialyzers dozens of times."
- "Repeatedly . . . patients' blood was being exposed to levels of bacteria as much as 40 times the recommended safe level, *according to federal records."*
- "Although *the federal report* does not blame the clinic for the patient deaths, it does indicate lax procedures. . . ."
- "The clinic went from losing money to making about an 11 percent profit, *according to the clinic's financial statement."*
- "Despite this dire description of care, *a federal audit for the year 1985* showed that all was well with the bottom line." [emphasis added throughout]

After Purdy submitted the draft on February 1, it fell into an editors' hole for more than two months. The editors who needed to review it were preoccupied with their daily assignments and other projects, including Bartlett and Steele's tax giveaway series, which broke April 10. But almost at the same time, an event beyond the *Inquirer's* control thrust the series onto the front burner—one kidney dialysis patient died and two others suffered heart attacks at a clinic in Camden, N.J., just across the river from Philadelphia.

The *Inquirer* ran the breaking news story April 7 on its front page. A technician at the clinic "apparently injected [the patients] with the wrong drug by accident," the lead read under the byline of two beat reporters. *The Philadelphia Daily News* bannered the story in its front-page headline: "Drug Error Kills Man." The competition's story included reference to the deaths of "15 dialysis patients" at a Louisiana hospital in 1982. Philadelphia radio and TV stations were giving the Camden incident prominent play, and word was circulating that channel 10 in Philadelphia was inquiring about the deaths at the Hospital at the University of Pennsylvania. Purdy's reaction was immediate and intense. "This is ridiculous," he thought, "we have to get this story out."

He was concerned first that he might get "scooped"—that someone else might do a story that would preempt or dilute his dialysis story. At the very least, he argued, the *Inquirer* could put out a "stand alone" story by the following weekend, using just the material they had on the Hospital at the University of Pennsylvania. He and Neumann also felt that had his series been out, it might have changed the course of events. "I felt if this story had run on Sunday, and I don't have any high-falutin' ideas about the power of the press, maybe those technicians would have been more careful," Purdy said.

The calming influence came from Jim Naughton, the *Inquirer's* deputy managing editor in charge of news. "I remember Matt and John flapping their wings and saying, 'Oh my God, we must, we must, we must,' to which I said, 'Relax,' " Naughton recalled. If dialysis was in the news, he reasoned, it would provide a "peg" for their investigative series. It was as if the *Inquirer* would be saying, "you thought that was bad, look at this," he said.

Though the Camden incident did not push the *Inquirer* to publish, it made the dialysis series an editing priority. Ashley Halsey, the deputy national editor, was brought into the editing process immediately. Naughton and Gene Roberts, the paper's executive editor, also commented on the first draft. As the draft was being edited, Purdy looked into the dialysis clinic in Camden.

Ironically, the incident that had spooked the *Inquirer* played a bit part in the dialysis series. The second draft included only one buried reference to the Camden incident. It was used as indicative of how dialysis, once performed by doctors and highly-trained nurses, has become "the domain of lower-paid technicians—many of them trained on the job—who perform the procedure as a routine, sometimes with devastating results." That is the way it appeared, with minor wording changes, in the published series. It wasn't given emphasis, Purdy said, because he found out the clinic in Camden was operated not-for-profit.

The most noticeable change in the second draft was to make the Hospital at the University of Pennsylvania a distinct sidebar to the first day's story. The three case histories that had topped the first draft were reduced to one—Danny Frank Falgout, a 25-year-old who was one of the 14 patients who died of bacterial infections at a Louisiana clinic in 1982.

A more subtle change was to accentuate the role of the federal government throughout the dialysis series. A sentence was added immediately following the lead paragraph to the first story. It noted that the federal government "stepped in to pay for the delicate and expensive process of kidney dialysis to keep Danny Frank Falgout alive." That sentence betrayed a recurring philosophical debate at the *Inquirer*: whether to stress a story's government angle or its impact on victims. Naughton usually argued to hold the government accountable. In the dialysis story, Neumann in particular favored case histories.

"We're not merely talking about dreadful experiences in the lives of patients, and we're not merely talking about the profit motive and the way it has affected the dialysis system," Naughton recounted. "We're talking about a government which created this system, funded this system and is now ignoring what is happening to people." Naughton argued for changing the order of the stories. He felt Purdy's day 1 on case histories should be flip-flopped with day 3 on government. "I thought the reader needed to know [the government's role] coming in, so it didn't kick him as a surprise" at the end of the series. They compromised. The order would stay the same, but the reader would be reminded throughout the series of the government's responsibility for the program.

By the third draft, the series had expanded to four parts. Nothing substantial was added. Day 1 merely was split into two days. The result, though, was to highlight coverage of the dialyzer reuse controversy. In the first two drafts, it was one of many issues attendant to the dialysis program. Now, it anchored a day's coverage. The dramatic lead to the second day read: "There could be no doubt about the directions printed on the kidney dialyzer filter—they said the filter was for 'single use only.' " The reuse debate probably was the most volatile issue relating to dialysis. It was also the most extensively covered, both in the medical journals and the media.

The third draft also drew out the irony of J. Peter Grace, President Reagan's watchdog against "waste, fraud, and fiscal abuse" and the head of a conglomerate that used federal dialysis funds to finance the acquisition of a dialysis company. The first two drafts did not mention Grace until more than halfway through the day's "money" story. At Naughton's suggestion, the third draft moved Grace to the top where the irony stood out starkly as financial hypocrisy in government.

More important, as it would turn out, was the choice of words the *Inquirer* used to describe the acquisition. In the first two drafts, the story cited a confidential audit as concluding that $35 million in interest payments used by the Grace company to effect a stock buyout was "inappropriate" because it was not a cost related to the care of patients. In the third draft, the federal audit was cited as concluding that "the use of the $35 million was improper." The published version reduced the figure to $21 million but retained the language from the third draft. It read: "A federal audit concluded that the use of money from the kidney treatment program for the deal was improper." That characterization would prompt a complaint by the Grace company and the publication of a correction by the *Inquirer* nearly two months after the series ran.

The third draft was the one "lawyered" prior to publication. At the *Inquirer,* prepublication lawyering is virtually embedded in the process. The *Inquirer's* commitment to investigative reporting has resulted in a steady stream of libel suits; more than ten are pending at any given time, according to Roberts.

Purdy had sought responses from clinic operators and bureaucrats responsible for the program. They were incorporated in the draft given to the *Inquirer's* lawyers. The lawyers suggested minor revisions. The word "profiteering" was changed to "profit" at one point in the text to avoid an unintended connotation of illegality or impropriety.

The identity of a nurse whose name appeared in a clinic memo was deleted from the story, as were the names of two Washington, D.C., medical directors and the name of a blind kidney patient. That patient's identity was further veiled by describing the location of the clinic as "near Philadelphia" when it would normally be described as near another city. Neumann attributed the edits to caution and a newspaper's vulnerability in a litigious society. "The issue is not whether we made a mistake but whether we leave ourselves open to a hit from minor characters who may claim their reputations were hurt by being in the middle of an investigative story," Neumann said.

One subtle clarification was also added. In the second sentence of the sidebar on the "problems" plaguing the University of Pennsylvania dialysis clinic, a single word was inserted to describe the clinic. That word was "nonprofit." In a series detailing the abuses of the profit motive in the dialysis program, that stood as the only reference in the series to the "nonprofit" status of a clinic where 12 deaths had occurred.

The *Inquirer* did not characterize the deaths as part of the dialysis problem, but they were not forgotten either:

> In addition, investigators for the federal Centers for Disease Control are investigating a sharp increase in the death rate at the clinic between last October and February 1988. The investigators are attempting to determine whether 12 deaths during that period were linked to water contamination.
>
> The CDC's preliminary findings have found no link between the contamination and the deaths.

Ironically, juxtaposed on the same page was the Rochester experience, which stood as a paradigm for a "return to health" because all five clinics there were not-for-profit.

THE INVESTIGATIVE INFLUENCE

"Dialysis: The Profit Machine" broke in the *Inquirer* on Sunday, May 15, 1988. Though Purdy and Neumann did not know from week to week when the series would be ready for publication, they knew that when it ran, it would begin on a Sunday. The *Inquirer's* daily circulation was about 500,000; its Sunday circulation was 950,000, mostly in the Philadelphia metropolitan area. Almost twice the readership could be exposed to an investigative series if it broke in the Sunday paper. A basic marketing strategy is also at work. If an investigative series is sufficiently compelling, readers might seek out the Monday paper and continue into the week.

The KNT News Wire offered the possibility of enhanced readership nationally. In putting its stories out over the wire, the *Inquirer* was allowing any of 200 subscribing newspapers to run the stories as is or in edited form. There was little expectation that any newspapers would carry the entire four-day, 13,000-word series, but *The Washington Post* ran an edited 2500-word story on May 17 in its health section, and *The Miami Herald* ran an edited 1500-word story on May 25. Both credited the *Inquirer* and carried Purdy's byline. Neither edited version included any reference to J. Peter Grace or the conglomerate he headed.

The Associated Press wire service also picked up a part of the *Inquirer* series. Ironically, the only part the AP carried in its 650-word account on May 17 was the angle about Grace. In attributing the allegations to the *Inquirer*, the AP reported that "W. R. Grace & Co. used $21 million in federal funds earmarked for kidney patients to finance acquisition of the nation's largest kidney dialysis company." The AP also reported that a federal audit concluded that the use of the money "was improper." The AP account included a statement from a Grace company spokesman, who called the *Inquirer* series inaccurate and criticized it for failing to understand "the mechanisms that determine the dialysis reimbursement rate."

A few weeks after its series ran, the *Inquirer* published a reprint, as it did with most of its investigative projects. About 3000 copies were run. The reprint, redesigned into tabloid format, was sent to managing editors of daily newspapers and to journalism schools and was made available on request to the public.

Roberts, the *Inquirer's* executive editor, said he felt that because the paper had succeeded in making a complicated subject "readable," the series would have impact. "I hoped that readers would read it, react and have an insight into something they wouldn't otherwise have," he said.

Neumann and Purdy hoped the series would have an impact beyond its Philadelphia readership. What Purdy meant by impact was to affect those practices and policies that engendered the needless suffering the story documented. He wanted dialysis patients to be treated better, and he hoped his series might get individuals to "be more vigilant about doing things right in these clinics." He also wanted those in government to take notice. To that end, he mailed copies of the series to sources who had helped on the story and to those in a position to affect the dialysis program.

Neumann's commitment to impact was even greater. He felt the federal government "needed to do something"—to investigate, to hold hearings, and to change the law. He was aware as the series was coming out that congressional investigators were intending to initiate a probe and hold hearings. "I think publication of the story will help force the hand of the congressman who chairs the subcommittee" and push the kidney dialysis program up the congressional agenda, Neumann said. The congressman was California

Democrat Pete Stark, whose office had collaborated with the *Inquirer* investigation and who was quoted in the series as being outraged that the government was being cheated by "unscrupulous operators."

Neumann also hoped to improve the quality of care dialysis patients received. He said he would have an idea if the story mattered if the *Inquirer* got calls from kidney patients saying "things have gotten worse because we're being punished because of the stories" or "things are getting better because they're scared of the investigations." He recalled stories the *Inquirer* did on police brutality and corrupt judges that got tangible results—someone arrested or indicted. "Sometimes you see it and sometimes you don't," he said.

With the dialysis series, they saw it almost immediately. Even before the entire series ran, Purdy received an irate call from a spokesperson with the Hospital at the University of Pennsylvania. The close-up photograph of a reused dialyzer that was prominently featured in day 2 of the series resulted in a blatant breach of patient confidentiality. The close-up that vividly depicted 14 uses also captured the patient's last name. The hospital spokesperson said the patient's daughter was livid about the unintended disclosure. A few hours after apologizing to the spokesperson for the error, Purdy received another call, this time from the daughter, who thanked him for running the story. She had not known that the dialyzer had been reused so often.

Purdy estimated one month after the series ran that he had received at least 50 calls, mostly from patients or families of patients, but also from nurses and technicians encouraging him to investigate the clinics where they worked. He investigated leads that he believed might advance the story, but none resulted in a follow-up to the series. "We felt we had told the story and that the story we told had impact on those who read it," Purdy reflected. Some of the reactions were "dream responses—you feel like you gave people with real problems a voice."

Some wrote letters. A former nurse at a dialysis clinic in Virginia wrote: "The people who are running the show are looking at the bottom line and unless there's some watchdog, they're going to keep making money at the expense of poor people." Another former nurse wrote that the series only skimmed the surface. The husband of a patient on reused filters wrote: "For the almighty dollar they will subject people to this misery." And one of the dialysis patients mentioned in the series wrote: "Today, I'm very happy."

The *Inquirer* ran seven letters to the editor in the aftermath of the series, two critical and five favorable. The negative letters were both from doctors in the dialysis field. One from a physician at the University of Pennsylvania Medical Center addressed the reuse debate and criticized the series for unfairly tarnishing the efforts of medical personnel and causing needless anxiety among patients. The other attacked the series for distorting profit figures and for offering "utterly no factual evidence" for the notion that for-profit clinics deliver cheapened, dangerous care in an effort to improve the bottom line. He, too, reopened the reuse debate by countering that reuse is beneficial to patients.

With one exception, the favorable letters to the editor were from people sensitized in one way or another to the dialysis program. One encouraged the *Inquirer* to push for legislative changes, another asked what the public could do to help Congress "get the dialysis program back under control," and a third suggested that the government resolve the reuse issue and eliminate the cost-cutting incentives by sending filters directly to patients.

The exception was a letter from someone from the National Association of Retired Federal Employees. He read the *Inquirer* series as in part a "public condemnation" of J. Peter Grace, to which he responded: "So what else is new?" The letter went on to depict Grace as knowing "about fraud first hand" and owning chemical firms that are "guilty of wholesale pollution violations in several states," while denouncing rank-and-file civil servants "for allegedly dipping a covetous hand in the federal cookie jar."

At about the time the letter appeared, representatives from the Grace company were discussing with the *Inquirer* their objections to the series. The Grace company retained Floyd Abrams, a New York attorney and First Amendment expert who regularly represents media clients. After a series of telephone exchanges between Abrams and Roberts, Abrams and other representatives from Grace met at the newspaper's offices in Philadelphia with Roberts, Purdy, Neumann, Halsey, and Samuel Klein, the *Inquirer's* attorney. Grace's representatives presented a long list in writing of complaints they had with the series. Neumann and Halsey responded point by point, conceding nothing. The meeting lasted four hours and ended with Abrams and Roberts saying they would speak again by phone. Shortly thereafter, the *Inquirer* published a correction with the caption: "Clearing the record."

It ran July 10 on page 2. In it, the *Inquirer* admitted an error that it attributed to "editing changes." The unusual seven-paragraph correction noted that a government audit found that the use of federal money was "not allowable" and "contrary to federal regulation." The correction then explained that those terms meant that "the expense was not directly related to the care of patients and therefore could not be counted in calculating how much the government should pay dialysis clinics in the future." Nothing illegal was to be inferred, and the audit finding was being appealed.

Neumann and Purdy were intensely opposed to the correction and disappointed that it ran. Roberts was equally adamant that the paper had erred and was obligated to set the record straight. Before meeting with the Grace representatives, Roberts had spoken directly with the government sources involved in the audit. He was satisfied the *Inquirer* had mischaracterized the problem. He believed the problem was not with the Grace company but with the terms by which the government allowed clinics to operate and reap profits. Roberts said later that he considered the paper's error sufficiently significant that the *Inquirer* did not nominate the series for a Pulitzer Prize.

The day after the *Inquirer* ran its correction, the AP ran one, too. That correction cited a federal auditor who said the Grace company was free to use the funds "in any manner it saw fit."

The series circulated through the dialysis community. The National Kidney Patients Association printed thousands of copies of the four-day spread. Its chairman, Robert Rosen, who was quoted in the series as a dialysis patient contaminated at the University of Pennsylvania clinic, said he mailed the series to thousands of patients, state legislators, judges, and every senator and congressman on Capitol Hill.

Dr. John Sadler, chief of nephrology at the University of Maryland Hospital in Baltimore, was quoted in the series as a proponent of the federal dialysis program but one critical of lax government oversight. He was critical also of the *Inquirer* series, describing it as "slanted" and "highly inflammatory." He felt nephrologists were disturbed by the series because the paper chose to listen to patient complaints rather than to medical experts. *Contemporary Dialysis and Nephrology,* the monthly trade journal, echoed Sadler's observations. In its August 1988 issue, the publication printed critical letters from two dialysis associations. One characterized the series as a "disservice," and the other concluded that the series created "heat and distortion which, when dissipated, may harm patient care and limit patient access" to the program.

It was apparent that people involved in the dialysis issue were reacting to the *Inquirer* series. But was the general public? Did the series alter the public's perception of the issues addressed in the series? Were they affected at all by the investigative series?

As in our previous studies, we attempted to measure public reactions by conducting telephone interviews with random samples of the public both before and after publication of the series (see table 8.1).[1] We questioned readers and nonreaders of *The Philadelphia Inquirer* about issues related and unrelated to the subject of the series. The findings indicated that only two of the problems highlighted in the *Inquirer* series had an effect on those who read it. The others did not. Those who were exposed to the series were significantly more likely than the comparison group to disapprove of cleaning and reusing medical supplies. The series, with day 2 devoted to the reuse controversy, had apparently affected the exposed public's views about the issue.

This was particularly noteworthy because Neumann, Purdy, and others involved in preparing the *Inquirer* series considered dialyzer reuse as merely

Table 8.1
Effect of "Dialysis: The Profit Machine" on General Public Sample[a] (Mean Scores)

	Not exposed (N = 218)		Some exposure (N = 113)		Read whole series (N = 22)	
	Pre	Post	Pre	Post	Pre	Post
Problem rating						
Waste in government in . . .						
AIDS screening	2.07	2.21	1.98	2.19	2.10	2.78[b]
Kidney dialysis	1.94	2.16	1.93	2.18	1.67	2.86[b]
Organ transplants	2.19	2.38	2.04	2.36	2.14	2.70
Blood transfusions	2.02	2.14	1.70	2.19	2.26	2.88[b]
Cancer x-ray treatment	2.02	2.14	1.86	2.15	2.06	2.56
Evaluation of cost-control measures						
Clean and re-use dialysis supplies	1.82	1.82	1.92	1.65[b]	1.86	1.67[b]

[a]Higher scores mean higher problem rating, more agreement.
[b]Significant ($p < .05$) analysis of variance.

symptomatic of more fundamental problems in the federal dialysis program. Purdy's original reuse story had run in the *Inquirer* 19 months earlier and had had little impact then. A principal reason the *Inquirer* committed investigative resources to an in-depth series that was ultimately called "Dialysis: The Profit Machine," was to take on the bottom line.

The only other effect we found in our surveys was that the attitudes of those who reported reading *all* the series changed significantly on the question of the magnitude of the problem of waste in government spending for kidney dialysis. In fact, the series may have had a spillover effect on readers' general attitudes about waste in government spending for health care. Those who reported reading *all* the series were also significantly more likely to regard waste in government spending for blood transfusions as a big problem.

This, too, was noteworthy. The series repeatedly reinforced the government angle, as a compromise to Naughton who argued unsuccessfully to focus day 1 on government accountability instead of on victims. He also had the series play up the profile of J. Peter Grace and his "War on Waste" for the sheer irony on the issue of waste in government spending. Those two editing adjustments may possibly account for the powerful impression left on those who reported reading all the series. However, we were unable to find increased concern, even among attentive readers, about "the profit machine" the dialysis program had spawned. Ironically, the profit angle is what inspired Purdy and Neumann to initiate the project and what preoccupied them during the investigative phase.

The impact of the series on public policy was a different matter. The weekend after the series broke, the *Inquirer* editorialized about what the series had revealed. The editorial called the federal dialysis program "an out-of-control mess." It called on J. Peter Grace to "come before a congressional committee" to explain whether the clinics his company owned are not another example of government waste. In general terms, it recommended that Congress get the dialysis program under control by "providing guidelines, establishing effective penalties and ensuring that monitoring take place."

Within two weeks, the State Board of Medicine, Pennsylvania's medical licensing body, opened an investigation of a Philadelphia clinic targeted in the series. Purdy was told of the investigation by a board official who read the series and called to inform him that the agency would investigate the paper's allegations. The investigation was still pending nearly two years later, according to Purdy.

In June, a state Senate committee in Pennsylvania approved unanimously legislation to regulate the reuse of dialyzers. As Purdy reported in a follow-up to his series, the legislation would give patients in that state a choice of whether to undergo dialysis with a new dialyzer or with one that had been cleaned. His story noted that the measure was prompted by patient complaints. It said nothing of his series the month before. By mid-1990, nothing had come of the legislation.

In October, a bill was introduced in Congress that called for close inspections of the nation's 1,350 dialysis clinics and the imposition of stiff penalties for those found to be providing inadequate care. The patient's rights bill, as it was called, was sponsored by California Congressman Pete Stark, who was quoted in the *Inquirer* series as saying there was no question that the government is being cheated. In Purdy's follow-up on the legislation, Stark is quoted again, this time saying, "While there is no clear documentation that quality of care is a problem, there has been growing uneasiness (among dialysis patients) that some facilities have reduced services and staffing in a way which could jeopardize the health and safety of patients." The story noted that hearings were to be held and the legislation reintroduced when the new Congress convened next year.

This follow-up mentioned the earlier *Inquirer* series. It also noted a related development—a study by the federal Centers for Disease Control reporting that patients treated in clinics reusing dialyzers were more likely to experience outbreaks of fever and chills than patients in clinics that do not reuse.

Before the end of the year, the *Inquirer* ran two more follow-ups, both by Purdy. One in November reported that the Pennsylvania health department had increased the number of inspectors from one to nine, and one in December reported that government auditors were about to begin "a wide-ranging review" of the federal dialysis program. The latter story also noted that an inspector general's report that "has not yet been made public" concluded many clinics in 1985 were making a profit of as much as $30 a treatment from federal money. Both of those follow-ups credited the *Inquirer* series with precipitating the government action. In fact, the *Inquirer* noted that the nationwide audit would be conducted by the Philadelphia office of one of the federal agencies and was "proposed by agents of the office after the *Inquirer* published a series of articles last May detailing problems in the kidney dialysis program."

In 1989, the Congressional initiative stalled. At about the same time that Congressman Stark reintroduced his patient's rights bill in the House, Pennsylvania Senator John Heinz introduced a dialyzer reuse bill in the Senate. Heinz's legislation was the same bill that had been pending in the Senate in October 1986 when Purdy was first tipped to the dialysis issue by an aide to Heinz's committee, whose job the aide later described as putting together "high-visibility" hearings. To a large extent, the dialysis bills were preempted on the legislative agenda by debate over catastrophic health care.

But also to some extent, the bills died because the policy-making debate splintered the dialysis community. Senator Heinz and some patients' rights groups took a hard line on dialyzer reuse. Proponents on the House side argued for quality-of-care assurances and disclosure requirements. Some groups lobbied for cost-containment measures and others for a restructuring in the reimbursement rates. Providers of home dialysis seized the opportunity to put their alternative before policy makers. The *Inquirer* series became useful to legislators, particularly to Heinz, for the legitimacy it provided in their speeches on dialysis and rising health care costs, according to Stark's aide Bill Vaughn. "The hotbed of protests on dialyzer reuse was in eastern Pennsylvania, and Heinz used the series to play to that," Vaughn said.

Dr. Louis Diamond, chairman of medicine at D.C. General Hospital in Washington and a former president of the Renal Physicians Association, regarded the impact the series had on the Congressional agenda as negative. "The stories have poisoned the debate between providers and policy makers and caused a palpable friction between patients and their providers," he said. "This kind of publication really has left the dialysis program with a bad name and has diverted attention on Capitol Hill from important issues such as quality [of care] and access [to dialysis]."

Journalism awards panels also took note of the *Inquirer* series. It was a finalist for a Pulitzer Prize in the national reporting category. Interestingly, the series was submitted to the Pulitzer committee not by the *Inquirer* but by a government policy maker who regularly collaborates with reporters on parallel investigations. Peter Stockton, a research analyst for the House Subcommittee on Oversight and Investigation, knew both Purdy and Neumann well, had worked with them on investigations, but played no role in the dialysis series. He said he nominated the series because of what it means to reporters and the incentive it provides to the newspapers to pursue investigative projects. He also said he guessed the *Inquirer* itself might not nominate the series because of the correction the paper ran on the Grace affair.

The series also received honorable mention for best investigative series in the Pennsylvania Press Association's Keystone awards and won second place in the Raymond Clapper Memorial Award, bestowed for excellence in reporting by Washington-based daily newspapers. In its submission for the Clapper award, the *Inquirer* mentioned a letter the paper received from Vance Hartke, the retired senator who sponsored the federal legislation that created the dialysis program in 1972. Hartke wrote, "Your series on the kidney problem was great. You certainly produced a wealth of information which should be valuable—if the Government has the wisdom and courage to use the material to correct the abuses."

The series had made a difference. It had gotten policy makers at the federal and state levels both to take notice and to propose initiatives to deal with some of the problems addressed in the series. This occurred even though public attitudes about the issue did not appear to have changed markedly, and the *Inquirer's* readers had not risen up over abuses in the dialysis program. Yet the *Inquirer* had tapped into the policy-making pipeline through the coalitional relationships its reporters had cultivated while investigating the story and through policy elites who seized the media moment to promote their policy alternatives. The linear Mobilization Model needs to be modified in light of the evidence from the case of "Dialysis: The Profit Machine." An outraged public was not a necessary part of the changes that came. Instead, agenda building resulted from a complex web of interconnecting media and policy actors.

NOTE

1. Five hundred and two respondents from the Philadelphia metropolitan area were selected using random digit-dialing techniques a month before the *Inquirer* series broke. The respondents were stratified by their self-reported reading habits according to whether or not they read the *Inquirer*. We wanted to compare the views of those who read the *Inquirer* at least four times a week, whom we expected to be exposed to the series, with those who said they were not *Inquirer* readers.

The sample then was recontacted two weeks after the series ended. Three hundred and fifty-four people agreed to be reinterviewed, comprising the general public sample in the study. Of those, 136 reported reading at least part of the series, and 202 reported not being aware of the series at all. The 136 were considered "exposed" to the series, and those not exposed were treated as the comparison group.

In both the preseries and postseries interviews, the respondents were asked several health-related questions. To avoid sensitizing the respondents to the subject of the *Inquirer* series, questions about kidney dialysis, the profit motive in health care, and recycled medical equipment were embedded in the questionnaire so that much of the survey pertained to unrelated issues.

For instance, respondents were asked about the importance of issues such as fighting medical epidemics, the shortage of qualified nurses, inadequate health insurance coverage, waste in federal health care programs, and the profit motive in patient care. Questions about kidney dialysis were asked along with questions about organ transplants, blood transfusions, x-ray treatments, and screening tests for AIDS. Included in a question about reusing medical supplies were such other cost-cutting measures as reducing the length of hospital stays and offering more outpatient procedures. To determine if readers came away from the series with a negative attitude toward the Hospital at the University of Pennsylvania, respondents were asked to which hospital would they likely go if they had a serious health problem.

PART III

INTERSECTING INTERESTS: AGENDA BUILDING IN MEDIA AND POLICYMAKING ARENAS

Introduction

As the case studies show, each investigative story has its own dramatic history with an evolving cast of characters. Villains and victims appear. The plot thickens as patterns of wrongdoing emerge. New characters enter, creating twists in the story line. Political actors frequently try to steal the scene or relieve the tension. And always present is the audience, ready to show its outrage, affirmation, or indifference.

The storyteller—the investigative reporter—does not simply stumble on the dramatic plot. Nor is the investigative story a product of his or her imagination. Investigative stories demand the aggressive pursuit of information. They require action from an interdependent network of reporters, researchers, producers, editors, fact checkers, and technicians.

Before an investigative story is published, media personnel perform an array of collaborative tasks. Reporters cultivate sources, find and examine documents, and check and doublecheck information. Later, editors and producers join the reporters, and their collaborative decisions shape the investigative product. Promoters lure the audience. If all goes well, the creative product generates intense discussion and ongoing consequences.

Investigative reporting involves the art of building agendas within distinctive but intersecting arenas. First, journalists must set the "investigative agenda." They must decide whether to pursue one story or another. They must listen to experts, bureaucrats, interest groups, and politicians as well as ordinary people. They must sort out the credible from the incredible. They must find and define the story they want to tell, and decide how to tell it. As a result of this often lengthy and complicated process, some stories survive to publication, whereas others falter and never make it to the public stage.

Investigative artists—the journalists of outrage—do not paint their portraits for art's sake alone. Their portrayals of villainy and victimization are created to bring about change. According to the Mobilization Model, the investigative agenda, once set, influences the priorities of the public, which in turn alter the agendas of policy makers.

However, our case study evidence suggests that agenda building does not occur in such a neat and orderly manner. Sometimes it fails to occur at all. The construction of the investigative agenda involves many fits and starts. Investigations that result in publication seldom are congruent with what journalists originally envisioned. Significantly, both interest groups and policy makers can be highly influential in shaping the content of a story prior to its publication.

Once published, some investigative stories have profound policy consequences without regard for public opinion. Other stories arouse the public without changing policy-making agendas. Still others mobilize interest groups, which then exert pressure on policy makers. But in none of the cases we examined did agenda building proceed in the straightforward manner predicted by the Mobilization Model.

In chapter 9, we examine the various factors that led to the construction of the investigative agendas in our six cases studies. In particular, we extract from the case studies a theory of what reporters do in order for an embryonic investigative story to move to publication. In chapter 10, we focus on the policy-making responses to the six investigative reports. In that chapter we attempt to refine theories about investigative reporting and public policy making.

More than 900 interviews with investigative reporters and editors enable us to place the findings in this last section of the book in a broader context. Those interviews helped us determine that the cases we studied reflected national trends in investigative reporting and societal decision making. We conclude by discussing the implications of our research for the practice of journalism, citizenship, and governance.

CHAPTER 9

Building the Investigative Agenda

In this chapter we discuss how six of our society's problems eventually became the subjects of published investigative stories. We call the process by which this occurs "investigative agenda building." Our review of the case studies identifies factors that influence whether an embryonic story advances or declines on the "investigative agenda" of reporters and their news organizations.

From the case studies we identify, for analytic purposes, five stages of investigative agenda building. The stages include "initiation" and "conceptualization," which occur during the origins of the probe; "investigation," which happens during the investigative process; "presentation," which occurs when the exposé is written or produced; and "investigative influence," which includes postpublication decision making. (We discuss the last of these stages in the final chapter.) At each stage, journalists performed a series of tasks essential to the full development of the story.

Investigative stories do not develop in a societal vacuum. In the process of building an investigative agenda, reporters' interests often converge with those of other actors. A primary goal of this chapter is to describe the initial linkages between media and societal agendas.

INITIATION: ENGAGING INVESTIGATIVE INTEREST

For investigative reporters, the universe of potential problems to expose is virtually unlimited. The sheer number of possible wrongdoings should provide a sense of security to potential targets of investigative stories. Few transgressions ever will come to the attention of muckraking journalists, and even fewer will become published exposés.

How does a potential exposé get on the investigative agenda in the first place? One popular notion is that the investigative reporter receives a hot tip (often late at night) and proceeds from there. Such exposés may be called "source-generated." An alternative version—preferred by independent-minded investigative journalists—is that stories are "journalist-generated." In this scenario, journalists conceive and plan investigations on their own. Sometimes, this involves a full-scale investigation of a reporter's suspicions. On other occasions, it involves "enterprising" a story—building on an already published story by probing some yet-unexplored angle.

The six case studies show that both tips and enterprise reporting can play a role in getting a story on a journalist's agenda. However, they typically are accompanied by other crucial developments. The convergence over time of organizational and individual interests seems vital for triggering the process of agenda building. An evolving communications network rather than a single catalyst appears to move a problem onto the investigative agenda.

In the home health investigation, the agenda of "NBC Newsmagazine" was first set by the involvement of the Better Government Association (BGA), a "linking-pin organization."[1] The BGA brought the seeds of two stories to an NBC producer, who eventually agreed to jointly probe one of them. The BGA exchanged its ideas and personpower for anticipated publicity and policy impact. Indeed, one consequence of the NBC producer's willingness to accept the BGA's "information subsidy"[2] was that the reform-minded group built the legislative priorities of policy makers into the resulting investigation.

Journalists from competing news organizations also may play an important initial agenda-building role. In the toxic waste series, a frustrated reporter caused a story that failed to achieve salience at his own station to make it onto the agenda of a competing one. In the case of "Missing?" a local newspaper and radio station played a seminal role in the creation of the "60 Minutes" report.[3]

A hybrid of source-generated and journalist-generated activities occurred in the kidney dialysis series. Here, a congressional aide tipped an editor to a partial view of the problem. This led to a published story in the *Philadelphia Inquirer* and later in other media. But it was the enterprising persistence of *Inquirer* reporters, who felt there was more to uncover, that transformed the story into a priority item on the newspaper's investigative agenda.

However it happens, once the possible story gains journalistic attention, reporters take several steps before it can become a formal part of the investigative agenda. Decisions made by investigative reporters at each step help to determine whether the embryonic story advances to the next stage, or falls off the agenda. Our analysis of the six case studies indicates that agenda building is more likely to progress (1) if the information is credible; (2) if the story appears doable; (3) if the story appears to scoop the competition; (4) if the topic is personally or professionally interesting to the journalist; and (5) if the journalist thinks the story could have impact.

Evaluating the Credibility of the Information

For an investigative story to move forward, journalists must sense that the information they have received—the basic allegations and any supporting evidence—is credible. This does not mean they must be *convinced* initially of its validity; conclusive determinations are made later in the investigative process. At first, journalists evaluate whether the information appears to be credible on its face.

At this stage, journalists may call on outside "experts" on the topic, such as university researchers and community activists in the newspaper rape investigation. More commonly, they rely on their own gut instincts about the credibility of the charges. Those instincts are honed by experience and shaped by professional norms.

Whether the allegations are accompanied by seemingly authentic documentation will greatly affect the reporters' assessments at this stage. In the toxic waste series, the memoranda bearing the seal of the University of Chicago helped to convince the journalists that a story was there. Similarly, the "60 Minutes" producer was impressed from the outset by the thoroughness of the fathers' evidence that their children had been abducted with the aid of the Norwegian government. The *Philadelphia Inquirer's* kidney dialysis investigation bore instant credibility because convincing documentation accompanied the original congressional tip.

Journalists' assessments of the credibility of sources who supply information also are a determining factor. If a source has proven reliable in the past, as was the case with the BGA in the home health case, the information will receive greater initial acceptance. Investigative journalists place a great deal of faith in information, especially documents, from official sources. They believe such information is likely to be both authentic and credible. The kidney dialysis series, for one, was prompted by a congressional aide who already had probed the problem. The aide's motivations—generating media attention for his committee's legislative agenda—did not deter the journalist from proceeding. In fact, it helped the story along by enhancing the prospects of reform.

Evaluating the Feasibility of the Story

Before a story reaches prominence on the investigative agenda, journalists must also assess its feasibility—whether the allegations can be proven. Without hard evidence, the story will never be published. Thus, journalists are expected to decide, before considerable resources are expended, whether they are likely to get a return on their investment. At this stage, journalists quickly assess the prospects of finding tangible documentation of wrongdoing.

The material fruits of Norway's freedom of information law and the University of Chicago written memoranda convinced investigative journalists that those stories were doable. In the police brutality series, the public availability of vital court records helped advance the story. Although the documents were not yet in hand, journalists could anticipate being able to obtain them.

The rape series, on the other hand, stalled for months when the police department's computer tape of crime data proved to be inaccessible to the reporters. There were other conceivable ways to document the geographic distribution of sex crimes, but the costs in time and effort would have been even more prohibitive. Until the tape became available, the story fell off the newspaper's investigative agenda.

Evaluating the Competitive Situation

Competition is an important motivating factor in the journalism profession.[4] This especially is true in investigative journalism, where the stakes are particularly high. Journalists believe that countless weeks of effort could be lost if a rival beats them to the punch. Further, media managers view investigative stories as a way to attract public attention to their news organizations. To build audiences, television exposés typically are broadcast during ratings sweeps, and newspaper series often are published when circulation is greatest.

Journalists are sensitive to these commercial realities even in the initial stage of agenda building. The producers of "NBC News Magazine" were looking for solid investigative stories to establish themselves as worthy competitors to CBS's "60 Minutes" and ABC's "20/20" newsmagazine programs. The fresh and potentially hard-hitting home health care story seemed well suited to their needs.

Competition also can affect the selection of investigative subject matter. For example, the police brutality investigation rose on WMAQ-TV's agenda after rival WBBM-TV broadcast "Killing Crime," an exposé of police misconduct in recording local crime statistics. "Killing Crime" helped to spur the WMAQ-TV investigation of the same official target—the Chicago Police Department—and also contributed to the efforts by Unit 5 reporters to find a distinctive angle to their story.

However, competition does not fully explain investigative agenda building, especially in its earliest stages. At this point, reporters find it difficult to assess what the competition really is working on. Further, some journalists appear to be pleased by the prospect of other stories appearing on the same subject even before their own report is published. A *Philadelphia Inquirer* investigative editor saw this development in the kidney dialysis story as a way to maximize the opportunity to influence societal agendas.

Nonetheless, the task of scoping out the competition normally is an important step in investigative agenda building. Journalists sometimes will put out feelers to personnel at other news organizations to try to discover their rivals' investigative agendas or ask key sources if they have been interviewed recently by competing reporters.[5] They also may review everything that has been published by other journalists on the subject of the investigation.

The "60 Minutes" producer was persuaded to proceed in part because a CBS radio station had broadcast a story similar to the one she was considering. She would not be "stealing" from the competition but rather building on the work of her own network. Such idiosyncratic factors may be as important to getting on the agenda as the doability of the story and the credibility of the information. In sum, news organizations strive to be first with a story, strive to be different, and strive to draw attention to themselves and the problem they are exposing. These competitive factors help to set the investigative agenda.

Evaluating Personal and Professional Interests

Thus far, our discussion of agenda building has focused on journalists' assessments of concretely measurable risks. In fact, a host of highly intangible and subjective factors also play a role in the initial stage of a story. One such factor is journalists' evaluation of their own interest in the story. As one journalist from our national survey (tabulated in appendix II) said, "Investigative reporters should go after stories that interest them and not just ones that will make the earth move." Another reporter who has been free-lancing investigative stories for 15 years told us she seeks out stories that expand her "personal understanding of how things really work."

Sometimes "interest" is defined in highly personal terms. WBBM radio reporter Scott Smith was interested in pursuing the story of international child abductions partly because of his own child custody battle. A BGA investigator proposed the home health care story because his wife, a nurse, shared horror stories with him about problems in the industry.

A young WGN-TV reporter did not push the toxic waste story more forcefully after his superiors showed no interest because he wanted to get a full-time job at the station. In contrast, a *Philadephia Inquirer* reporter's professional stake in the dialysis story rose after he published an initial story on the subject. A major impetus to the *Chicago Sun-Times* rape investigation was the city editor's interest in using computers to analyze social problems.

Journalists employ highly situational and subjective criteria in assessing their personal and professional interests. At times, their assessments may radically alter the life course of an investigative story. For example, the WGN-TV commentator's lack of interest in the toxic waste story because it did not fit his editorial format allowed the story to be picked up by a WMAQ-TV producer who had a professional commitment to doing environmental exposés. Clearly, serendipitous factors such as these help to determine why one news organization chooses to pursue an investigation while another does not.

Evaluating Potential Impact

Investigative journalists strive to have impact. Whether they characterize "impact" as influencing policy makers, leaving an impression on their audiences, or obtaining recognition from their peers, investigative journalists want to make a difference. This *raison d'etre* often prompts them to look down the road and assess the possible effects of a story in deciding whether to pursue it. Of course, journalists cannot predict with certainty the societal or personal consequences of a story before it is investigated.

Nonetheless, they try to sense the prospects for impact at the earliest stages of agenda building. Significantly, this "sense" may influence their willingness to undertake the story. Journalists are excited by allegations that have a high potential impact. The goal, according to one investigative journalist we surveyed from Tampa, Fla., is to "hit a nerve in the community."

The WMAQ-TV reporter relished the prospect of forcing the University of Chicago's "Masters of the Universe" to take corrective action. The same reporter viewed the Chicago Police Department as vulnerable politically to charges of brutality, thereby increasing the chances his story would produce reforms. The close links between the *Philadelphia Inquirer* and Congressional investigators, and similar ties between the home health investigative team and a Senate committee, enhanced the journalistic desirability of those stories. Even the "60 Minutes" producer who eschewed the opportunity to help build the federal policy agenda was elated by the prospect of "pull[ing] at the heartstrings" of the *public*.

Whereas impact is central to the mission of investigative reporting, its prospect is not sufficiently powerful to *set* the agenda of investigative reporters and their news organizations. As we have seen, the convergence of several factors is necessary to drive a nascent story forward. Allegations of wrongdoing tend to rise in salience when they appear to be credible, potentially provable, in sync with competitive realities, and to maximize the possibilities for personal, professional, and societal gain. Others may flounder or fall off the investigative agenda.

If the story does survive at this stage, investigative reporters still have other crucial tasks to perform before an extensive probe can begin. They must first interpret the meaning of the information they have developed in order to locate the story on their agenda of interests. They also must convince themselves and their superiors that the story is worth pursuing compared to other stories competing for their attention.

CONCEPTUALIZATION: SEEING THE STORY

Once investigative interest has been triggered, journalists begin a search for meaning: "What is this story really about?" they will ask themselves and their colleagues. This question first is posed during the origins of the probe, with the tentative answer affecting the initial agenda priority given to the story. But it also will be asked repeatedly over the life course of the investigation. Significantly, the ultimate answer—provided at the point of publication—may influence whether the story affects societal agendas.

This stage involves "conceptualizing" the story. Journalists step back from the information they have obtained and attempt to visualize the story that might emerge. In doing so, as in the inititation stage, journalists perform a variety of tasks that allow them to impose meaning on the raw facts in their possession. Unlike the initiation stage, these tasks largely are intellectual in nature. However, the tasks serve practical purposes as well.

Our analysis of the six case studies indicates that, once initiated, a story in progress will increase in salience if reporters (1) can sense the drama in a potential story; (2) can deduce a pattern of wrongdoing from what appears at first to be isolated cases; and (3) can persuade their superiors that proceeding with the investigation is a sound investment of their resources.

Sensing the Drama

Muckraking journalists are societal watchdogs. They also are storytellers who produce a product for profit-seeking organizations. In conceptualizing an investigative story, reporters struggle to incorporate both considerations into their decision-making equations.[6]

The dual nature of investigative reporting becomes clear in the initial efforts to conceptualize a story. At this point, journalists sense the presence of a story with audience appeal, but they also hope to unveil problems that eventually may right wrongs. Their interest rises in the nascent story when they see the potential to tell a compelling tale and, in doing so, command societal attention.

The first specific task in conceptualizing an investigative story is to identify the possible characters and story line. In thinking about their initial information, reporters ask: what sad stories can be told? Who are the villains? The victims? From this assessment, reporters may see the kernel of an exposé. Alternatively, the absence of a sense of personal drama may lower the salience of the story.

It was the tragic plight of two fathers that initially caught the attention of the WBBM radio reporter. The fathers were victims; the story of their suffering was easy to foretell. The larger problem of international child abductions materialized later.

Early conceptualizations of villainy and victimization occurred in most of the other case studies. The kidney dialysis story was constructed around the presence of greedy clinics and helpless patients. A remarkably similar cast of characters was foreseen in the drama that became "The Home Health Hustle." In "Beating Justice," the sense of brutal cops and brutalized citizens developed during the life course of a previous exposé; it helped the television reporter conceptualize his next story. That same reporter also had little trouble imagining a story about uncaring educators and endangered students the following year.

Only in the newspaper series about rape did the individual tragedies emerge from the larger social problem This happened because reporters initially relied on demographic data and crime statistics. But even here, reporters envisioned finding sad stories that would breathe drama into their eventual series. After all, rapes are an everyday event in most large cities. If the probe had remained at the higher level of abstraction, it would have been better suited for social science than investigative reporting.

Framing the Genre of Wrongdoing

Having sensed the specific drama, investigative reporters further conceptualize the story by placing it in a broader context. This task involves putting a "picture frame" around the early evidence of wrongdoing to identify the relevant investigative genre.[7] Is this a possible story abut "political corruption?" About "corporate rip-offs?" About government "waste and inefficiency?" A particular species of moral disorder emerges from the performance of this task.

In framing the wrongdoing, journalists begin to think inductively. Having been made aware of individual cases of abuse, they wonder if there may be others. Perhaps there are additional children who have been abducted to foreign countries, or more patients who have died in dialysis clinics. The sense of an identifiable pattern of abuse helps to move the story higher on the investigative agenda.

The framing process is relevant to investigative agenda building in other ways as well. Some reporters say their news organizations prefer certain kinds of stories over others. Defining the story genre helps them decide at an early stage whether they want to pursue the investigation. The *Philadelphia Inquirer* reporters, for example, were attracted by the complex web of government regulators, service providers, and private patients they envisioned to be at the core of their story. Intricate stories about bureaucracies gone awry are an *Inquirer* specialty.[8]

The "Home Health Hustle" represents a different extreme. Here, "NBC Newsmagazine" was interested in pursuing at all costs a simple story about "patient abuse." The BGA, its investigative partner, saw the story as one of "financial fraud." The resulting conflict ultimately led to the reconceptualization of the story as one of "fraud and abuse." Significantly, the initial definition of the story genre guides the fact-finding process that follows, and is subject to refinement based on evidence gathered during later investigative stages.

To frame the wrongdoing, reporters look backward as well as forward. They often review stories that already have been published—investigative and otherwise—to locate the moral compass of their own story. That "fraud and abuse" was a hot political issue receiving considerable media attention in 1980 influenced the conceptualization of the "Home Health Hustle." Indeed, investigative journalists are attracted especially to stories that might appeal to prevailing public attitudes or established social norms. They recognize that if the story does not "fit," its potential impact will be softened.

However, even in telling familiar stories journalists look for a fresh angle. The topic of home health care had not been extensively covered at the time, creating a sense of excitement among the investigative team that they would be exploring new territory. Similarly, a new frame of "repeat offenders" was placed on the old story of "police brutality," as was "international" child abductions a fresh angle to the familiar stories about domestic abductions and missing children.

In the course of framing, reporters look beyond individual cases to the classes of problems they represent. In the words of the "60 Minutes" producer: ". . . we do stories from which issues can merge." It is here that the characters and plot line take on a broader meaning that may be relevant to societal problem solving. Eventually, the agendas of audiences may be cued by the species of story that emerges. But first, investigative reporters have a more immediate, practical task to perform. They must convince agenda setters within their own news organizations that the freshly formulated story should be pursued.

Pitching the Story

For investigative stories to survive the agenda-building process, they need more than a watchdog's scent, a playwright's imagination, and a reformer's conscience. Investigative stories must be nurtured with resources. Without the commitment of reporters' time and news organizations' money, they will wither and die.

The task of conceptualizing a story therefore serves a purpose beyond the search for meaning. Investigative reporters must not only satisfy themselves that a story idea is worth pursuing. They also must satisfy their superiors. They must pitch their stories to media managers before embarking on a full-blown probe. Unordered bits of information will not be enough to get a green light at this point; the story must be conceptualized adequately for it to be convincingly sold.

The pitch of an investigative story may take several forms. In the WMAQ-TV investigations, the selling job was highly informal. Unit 5 has its own budget and almost no organizational hierarchy. Consequently, the reporters and producers went through a process of convincing one another more than the station's management of the stories' suitability. Nonetheless, to reach a consensus and get the final green light from the WMAQ-TV news director, there was considerable discussion about whether the genre and plot of the stories made them worth pursuing over other possible stories.

In contrast, the newspaper series about rape could not proceed without a formal written pitch. Reporters were required to prepare a lengthy memorandum to their editors to convince them of the story's desirability. The four other case studies involved hybrid examples. Although written pitches were not required, reporters and producers had to cultivate the support of editors, executives, and, in the national television stories, correspondents.

Regardless of the form it takes, the pitch rarely is a one-time effort. Indeed, in the case of the home health story, the executive producer needed constantly to be reconvinced by reporters that they should be allowed to continue moving ahead. As with the other tasks in the initial stages of agenda building, reporters find themselves performing them in different forms over the life course of the investigation.

Investigative agenda building involves spiraling cycles of decision making rather than simple linear processes. Nonetheless, there are clear points of transition, and the initial successful pitch is one of them. Once a reporter has obtained the commitment of media managers, the nascent story finally achieves priority status. But the road ahead is treacherous. For the story eventually to reach public audiences, journalists must perform an array of fact-gathering and production tasks.

INVESTIGATION: DEVELOPING THE EVIDENCE

Earlier, we described the conventional argument that "investigative reporting" is a redundancy. Quoting MacDougall: "all reporting is investigative because newsgatherers seek facts."[9] The case studies show, however, that the *investigative* reporter's search for facts involves highly distinctive processes.

One distinction is time. "Beat" reporters must find facts quickly, often within a day. In contrast, investigative reporters may need weeks or months to develop a story. Beat reporters also tend to gather facts on their own, whereas investigative reporters often work in teams.

But more important qualitative differences exist as well. The practice of daily journalism largely involves telling different and often opposing sides of a public event or controversy. This form of journalism is guided by "objectivity," a professional norm that demands relative neutrality and balance.[10] Investigative reporting, on the other hand, often involves the pursuit of facts that reveal wrongdoing, thereby invoking implicit and sometimes explicit normative appeals.

In this way, the investigative process also is different from other forms of fact-gathering. For example, the journalists of outrage do not often employ the scientific method of scholarly researchers. Hypotheses are rarely deduced and then tested to rule out alternative explanations. Rather, as we suggested in the previous section, investigative reporters typically induce conclusions from particular facts. This approach involves generalizing from "vivid cases" to systemic societal problems.[11]

The investigative process requires the performance of several tasks to accomplish these ends. Having sensed the drama, reporters now must develop the characters and the plot. Having framed the genre of wrongdoing, they also must establish patterns of abuse. Our case study evidence suggests that the story will successfully complete the investigation stage of agenda building (1) if credible information can be gathered to document wrongdoing thoroughly; and (2) if the information is dramatically compelling. Significantly, it is also in this phase that reporters often build coalitions with government officials, both to obtain information and to ensure a policy impact.

Gathering the Evidence

The core of investigative reporting involves three information-gathering tasks: cultivating sources, obtaining documents, and (sometimes) directly observing the wrongdoing. This clearly is different from beat reporting, where information gathering is based largely on sources who simply are quoted (e.g., in public forums) or briefly interviewed. Another distinction is that investigative reporters rarely will attempt to get the other side of the story until their basic fact-gathering tasks are completed.

In "sourcing" a story, investigative reporters search for sources with loaded guns. The task is to get them to discharge their ammunition at the target of the investigation. This is no easy matter. Publicly discussing damaging information may backfire on a source. Reporters' sources typically are aware of the hazards of talking, which may range from getting fired to being sued to simple embarrassment. (The last of these hazards applies especially to the victims of the story whose personal plight the reporter wishes to publicize.)

Consequently, investigative reporters often must persuade their sources to talk to them. Patience is a virtue in cultivating investigative sources. Confidentiality is another helpful tool. In each of our case studies, pledges of confidentiality were made to key sources in the investigative process. In the television exposés, sources sometimes were hidden in shadows to disguise their identities. It is doubtful that investigative agenda building would have been possible in most of the cases without the ability to make this pledge.

When sources finally are convinced to talk, they rarely sing. The investigative interview involves techniques ranging from moral appeals to browbeating.[12] In probing for quotes and sound bites, reporters have been accused of unfairly manipulating their sources.[13] They typically respond by arguing that their tactics are vital to the search for truth and are fully justified when the truth comes out.[14]

Sometimes, the role of the investigative source is to keep reporters on the right track more than to attack the targets of the story. Expert sources played this role in the rape probe. They explained to reporters what the issues were and what the fact-finding process should include. Government sources performed a similar function in the kidney dialysis investigation. Sometimes, as in the home health care investigation, private sources may help reporters determine the whereabouts of villains.

Mainly, however, sources are needed for their testimony. The investigative case is built around the number and kind of sources willing to allege wrongdoing. More is better. Best is the testimony of experts and first-hand witnesses to venality. In the "Beating Justice" series, the sources who made the story were the victims who told their lurid tales on camera.

In particular, investigative reporters spend considerable time cultivating governmental and political sources. In the case studies, the quotes of legislators, administrators, judges, and even political candidates were given considerable weight. Similarly, our national survey of investigative reporters and editors found that nearly 60 percent of those responding said they had contacted government policy makers "very frequently," and another 30 percent said they did so "somewhat frequently" in the last year or so to get background information for their stories. Ninety percent said they were in very frequent or somewhat frequent contact with policy makers to get statements or quotes about the problems revealed in their stories (see appendix II). To muckraking reporters, officialdom is a source of expertise as well as impropriety.

Official documents are another staple of investigative reporting. They augment the investigative interview by providing tangible evidence of wrongdoing. Quotes from interviews may sound self-serving. Written records, in contrast, are used as unimpeachable sources of evidence. In its dialysis series, the *Inquirer* cited "federal records," "federal audits," and "auditors" 53 times in one day's story alone. Nearly 90 percent of the investigative reporters and editors we surveyed said they contacted government policy makers "very frequently" or "somewhat frequently" to get public records that might be useful in preparing their stories.

In the home health and kidney dialysis stories, previous Congressional probes into the problems produced independent documentation of the sources' allegations. In the toxic waste and child abduction reports, journalists obtained damning evidence written by the hands of the targets themselves. The rape series similarly relied on the government's own records to identify misinformation and misconduct. The police brutality reports were based on extensive reporting of official court documents. As discussed in chapter 2, muckraker Ida Tarbell used strikingly similar techniques to document her *History of the Standard Oil Company.*

Reporters use an array of strategies in locating documents for their stories.[15] Sometimes, as in the toxic waste story, the conveyance of documents to reporters is fortuitous. More often, reporters must use federal or state freedom of information acts to obtain them. Indeed, even in the toxic waste story the reporters filed foia requests to obtain official measures of radiation hazards at the University of Chicago.

The task of obtaining documents must be planned early in the investigative process. Requests for government information typically require weeks and sometimes months of waiting for processing. There is no guarantee they will produce a fruitful response. Worse yet, the request may alert the target—or the media competition—that an investigation is under way.[16] Consequently, reporters generally make requests at the outset of a probe and sometimes disguise their interest by asking for a variety of documents in addition to the ones they really seek.

Nonetheless, the records-gathering task may prompt official action in advance of publication of an exposé. In the home health probe, for example, the request for documents from a government agency in California caused that agency to launch its own investigation of the problem. As we discuss in the next chapter, this may help or hinder either reporters or policy makers. Regardless, it illustrates another early link between journalism and officialdom.

Besides cultivating sources and obtaining documents, investigative reporters sometimes try to observe directly the problems they seek to disclose. "Undercover reporting" is the generic label given to this approach. It is perhaps the least commonly used, but most controversial, form of sleuthing.[17]

In our case studies, undercover methods were used most extensively in the home health investigation. There, a target of the probe was lured to Las Vegas and filmed without his knowledge to obtain his confession of financial fraud. Further, a private resort was infiltrated to get pictures of another investigative target. These actions were taken with great legal care but with little attention to ethical concerns. The need for dramatic visual evidence was the dominant motiviation for using undercover techniques.

Indeed, hidden cameras were used in each of the television investigations in our case studies (although investigators misrepresented their identities only in the home health case). Footage secretly was shot of allegedly brutal police officers, of the University of Chicago campus, and of Norwegian school officials. More generally, the search for visuals was a driving force in the investigative strategies used by broadcast journalists.

Undercover techniques were not a part of the two newspaper investigations we studied. Both the nature of print media and those particular stories allowed reporters to document the abuses graphically in other ways. However, some of the most sensational newspaper investigations in the recent past have been based on undercover reporting.[18] As we discussed in chapter 2, Upton Sinclair's undercover observations formed the basis for his exposés of the meatpacking industry in the early 1900s. It probably would be fair to conclude that today's print journalists would use undercover reporting to get a story if necessary but that these techniques have fallen out of fashion for both media.

The arsenal of investigative methods—sources, documents, and direct observation—is extensive. As the case builds against the targets of an investigation, reporters begin to think about performing one last major task in the information-gathering process: getting the other side of the story. This typically occurs near the end of the investigative process so that reporters can be prepared with questions to which they want responses and be prepared to handle challenges to their findings.

In the home health probe, the main targets of the investigation were ambushed by television reporters—the interrogations were a surprise. This produced some spontaneous and candid responses. Primarily, however, it created a visually dramatic conflict.

More commonly, reporters truly are interested in what their targets have to say. The information they provide may poke holes in the thesis of the story, calling for additional investigation. This occurred, for example, when the chemistry professor in the toxic waste probe told reporters about scientific studies that downplayed the radiation hazards at the University of Chicago. At the opposite extreme, targets may make damning admissions that buttress the investigative case, as did the police superintendent in the brutality investigation.

Regardless of the outcome, the interviews with targets are used later in writing or producing a story. This allows journalists to fulfill the professional requirements of fairness and balance. Meanwhile, the interviews provide an additional opportunity for journalists to assess the credibility of the information they have gathered.

Evaluating the Information

During the information-gathering process, investigative reporters repeat tasks performed earlier in the life course of their story. As more information is obtained, they reassess the credibility of the original allegations, the feasibility of the project, and their professional and personal commitment to the story. Sometimes they do not like what they see, and the story loses salience. More often than not, however, the greater the investment in the story, the greater the likelihood that it eventually will see the light of day.

As the probe proceeds, reporters also reconceptualize the story in light of new information. In the rape investigation, reporters initially thought the story would focus on the types of victims and the dangers posed for all women. As it turned out, the evidence led reporters to zero in on the sheer numbers of sex crimes, the prevalence of rape in several suburbs, the lack of aid for victims, and the lack of rehabilitation programs for offenders.

The *Philadelphia Inquirer* story line went through several permutations during the investigative process. Although reporters always expected to find a network of villainy, private providers initially were seen as being their primary target. Later, federal regulators emerged as institutional villains, responsible for a program they could not control. The reconceptualization left the dialysis series with a dual theme: patients victimized by profit-seeking clinics and taxpayers victimized by a hapless bureaucracy. Similarly, the home health care story evolved from a focus on fraud to an emphasis on abuse to an exposé of fraud and abuse.

Occasionally, a story angle will be modified substantially or dropped for lack of evidence. The rape investigators originally pursued a substory on the use of cameras in the courtrooms but dropped it when it did not pan out. The absence of proven radiation dangers at the University of Chicago led reporters to emphasize a conflict-of-interest angle instead.

Reporters do more than intellectually rethink a story while they are information gathering. They also make hard choices about the amount of additional time and resources needed to develop it further. Reporters may return to media managers for help in making these decisions.

When is an investigative story ready to go? There does not seem to be a magic formula for knowing a story is there. Reporters tend to want to continue newsgathering as long as they can, as evidenced in our case studies. But at some point, a consensus is reached that they have enough, usually after some pressure is applied by resource-conscious media managers. Alternatively, journalists may decide that the story never will be nailed down and that it is time to move on to another project.

The criteria for advancing to the next stage of agenda building—writing or production—vary among news organizations, reporters, and stories. Generally, journalists take a hard look at the evidence they have gathered and decide whether they can make a convincing case against the targets of their own story. They assess how the story will play before several audiences: the public, policy makers, and their professional peers.

They ask: How solid is the story? Thoroughness is the main criterion for making this judgment. Going beyond the traditional standard of objectivity, investigative reporters substitute "mature subjectivity"—judgments based on the convergence of independent perspectives—as an alternative.[19] Reporters will sense that a story is solid when the subjective perceptions of different sources yield a common conclusion.[20] When documents buttress the observations of sources, or undercover work provides first-hand confirmation of the wrongdoing, the story gels.

Other factors play a role in reporters' evaluation of the information they have gathered, but the thoroughly reported story usually will advance to the stage of writing or production. This sense of solidity also may trigger the final interviews with the targets of the investigation. Further, it may cause journalists to look ahead for ways to ensure policy-making reactions to their forthcoming story if they have not done so already.

Coalition Building

During an investigation, reporters establish contacts with government officials to obtain information for their story. They also may rely on interest groups with expertise in the subject matter of the probe. Often, those contacts raise the possibility of other forms of collaboration between investigative reporters and policy-making interests.

Officials and interest groups have their own agendas. When journalists request information from them, it signals that a story may be coming that could affect their bureaucratic or political priorities. They may want to use the story to their advantage.

Similarly, investigative reporters are interested in impact. The journalists of outrage typically want reforms to be instituted. In fact, the majority of the investigative reporters and editors in our national survey ranked "the reformer in [them] satisfied" as the most important reward from a successful investigative story (see appendix II). Reforms provide investigative reporters with a sense of accomplishment and validate their work. As one newspaper reporter we surveyed put it, "investigative pieces are meant not just to entertain or inform the reader but also to make the policy makers aware of what's wrong so they can change it."

Moreover, 88 percent of those surveyed believe the "impact" of an investigative story is "very important" or "somewhat important" for winning professional prizes. Prize-winning investigative stories "should not merely recognize and expose societal problems," according to one special projects director for a television station in a major market, but should "stimulate solutions and answers." Or as one newspaper editor with 20 years of experience bluntly told us, "Impact is why one does investigative work in the first place."

Consequently, investigative reporters and policy makers often discuss ways of forming coalitions even before the publication of an exposé. We discuss the policy-making ramifications of such coalitions in chapter 10. For now, it is important to examine the circumstances under which they develop.

Formal coalitions between journalists and policy makers developed during the investigative stage in four of the case studies. In the home health probe, investigators met with officials weeks before the televised report and agreed to collaborate on Senate hearings into the problem. The hearings were announced at the end of the "NBC Newsmagazine" broadcast and began four days later.

Philadelphia Inquirer reporters coordinated their fact-finding efforts with Congressional staffers from the outset. This relationship matured over time. In the *Inquirer* series, congressmen were quoted expressing outrage over the dialysis problems and promising reforms. The newspaper closely tracked the Congressional hearings and legislative proposals that followed. A Congressional source with whom the *Inquirer* had collaborated in the past nominated the series for the Pulitzer Prize.

In two other cases, coalitions formed toward the end of the investigative process. Just days before the broadcast of "Wasted Time," journalists and officials orchestrated an inspection of the University of Chicago's chemical storage facilities that took place—with much media fanfare—the day after the series began. Reporters in the rape investigation recontacted concerned legislators and interest group spokespersons shortly before the newspaper series to get information and to give them an opportunity to take actions on the forthcoming disclosures. Indeed, reform measures were announced at the outset of the series and were covered as reactions to the exposé.

In each case, journalists performed an active role in helping the policy-making process. We call such journalists "activist reformers." Journalists who play this role want to *guarantee* reactions to their stories. They may be too cynical or too impatient to wait for an official response.

Activist reformers always have been on the journalistic scene. The collaborative efforts between President Theodore Roosevelt and several muckraking journalists were documented in chapter 2. Our national survey data indicate that they are a common part of today's media despite the norm against advocacy journalism.[21] Half of the reporters and editors in our survey said that "in pursuing their stories" they contacted government policy makers "very frequently" or "somewhat frequently" to "discuss policy reforms that might result from publication of the story."

Some journalists, however, eschew this form of media-policy collaboration. The prefer to play a role we call "information messenger." Information messengers are concerned primarily with revealing previously unknown facts to the public. Like activist reformers, they see change as desirable, but they believe it should come from the public rather than from their own initiatives. Half of our survey respondents said they "somewhat infrequently" or "very infrequently" contacted policy makers to discuss policy reforms that might result from publication of their stories. As one television investigative reporter from Midland, Tex., said, "[We] put the cards in the hands of the public, and it's their deal."

The information messenger role was performed clearly in our case studies by the "60 Minutes" producer, who stated that her "goal is to inform the public. They can act on the truth if they choose to." The producer rejected several opportunities to build policy-making interests into her report. "I want to maintain independence from other institutions in the culture," she explained. Nonetheless, although she questioned whether it was proper to prompt officials to take action before a story is published, she was gratified that changes had occurred in the wake of the "60 Minutes" report. The journalists of outrage may disagree about the means to reform but not its merit.

Reporters' roles may vary somewhat with the circumstances. The reporter who played an activist reformer role in the toxic waste story assumed the role of information messenger in the police brutality story. For the same reasons articulated by the "60 Minutes" producer, he felt "uncomfortable" about his role in the toxic waste series. Nevertheless, he believed his collaboration with fire officials was justified "by the threat to students safety, which was unknown to [government] authorities."

Clearly, reporters have choices in the roles they play and the tasks they perform. The outcome of those choices affects the investigative process, and it may influence policy-making priorities. As we shall see, it also helps mold the character of the investigative story.

PRESENTATION: PREPARING THE PRODUCT

Having survived the sometimes arduous process of probing, the investigative story is waiting to be told. Here, reporters encounter a host of considerations that determine the final form of the story. Foremost among them are editing or production choices and timing and marketing strategies.

Investigative stories do not tell themselves. They are constructed.[22] The construction involves transforming available information into a compelling product that will capture the attention of outside audiences. This product will be more than the total of the accumulated evidence and less than an objective recreation of reality.

In preparing the product, investigative reporters are joined by an array of media specialists. Technical producers, graphic artists, fact checkers, and copy editors help shape the content of the story. Later, news executives will determine whether the story will be published and, if so, how it will be played. Advertising personnel will decide the ways it will be promoted.

The story by now has achieved salience on the reporters' agenda; it still must overcome production hurdles before it attains priority status on their news organization's agenda. Gradually, reporters lose control over the story that they maintained during the investigative stage. Crucial decisions about the final product must be shared with a widening circle of associates.

Our analyses of the case studies show that in this stage of agenda building, the media team must be able (1) to select evidence from the information gathered in order to construct a credible thesis and (2) to illustrate clearly and convincingly the villains and victims of the story. If this occurs, the story usually will advance to publication.

Winnowing the Information

The winnowing task is painful. Reporters invested considerable time amassing facts and sometimes footage during the investigative stage. Now, organizational and space considerations require that only a minute portion of the evidence will make it into the final product. The winnowing involves selecting what gets in and what goes out.

The criteria for determining what evidence survives vary from story to story and between different media. In our case studies, the core concerns were the validity of the evidence and its dramatic value. Sometimes tensions arose between the two.

In the home health case, "NBC Newsmagazine" was consumed by a nationwide search for victims during the investigative stage. After finally finding some in Mississippi, they made the sad stories of seriously ill and handicapped people the centerpiece of the final product. Those stories were valid, but they shifted attention from the dominant problem of financial fraud in the home health industry.

Similar decisions were made in the winnowing process of the other investigations we studied. In "Missing?" the information about scores of international child abductions was largely overshadowed by the tales of two tragic fathers. Although only twelve of 2,300 cases involved abductions to Norway, that country became the focus of the report. In the process of editing the *Philadelphia Inquirer* series, the reuse of dialyzers and the deaths at the University of Pennsylvania clinic emerged as dominant angles. Both could be linked to dramatic tragedies, but the former was a minor part of the problem of proprietary clinics, and the latter operated not-for-profit.

These stories suggest that the task of winnowing evidence triggers a new stage of investigative agenda building. In this stage, some problems rise in salience, whereas others decline. Significantly, the selection of problems has little to do with larger societal realities. Instead, the choice is based on the most vivid cases that fit the story line. Having begun their probe with specific wrongdoings and having later identified emerging classes of abuse, reporters return in the presentation stage to emphasize the most compelling cases they found along the way. Elsewhere, we have called this phenomenon "the logic of particularism."[23]

Cases that survive the winnowing rarely provide inaccurate depictions of reality. Reporters' standards of thoroughness virtually ensure that each case is internally valid. Its generalizability, or external validity, may be suspect, however.[24]

Partial exceptions to this rule occurred in the editing of the rape investigation and the production of the police brutality probe. In editing the newspaper series, journalists emphasized the geographic patterns of sex crimes and the underlying bureaucratic and sociological problems that produced them. Similarly, in "Beating Justice," reporters used a variety of graphic devices to show that the individual cases of brutality were part of a larger system of abuse.

However, the logic of particularism was evidenced even in these stories. Despite reporters' plans to include statistically representative victims in the rape series, they instead included depictions of sensational sex crimes, including a detailed profile of a woman who was raped twice. The police brutality series emphasized the sordid details of victimization by a handful of police officers. Indeed, the most brutal case reported was not committed by a repeat offender, which was the main angle of the series.

We do not mean to suggest here that journalists ignore the bigger picture in the winnowing process. Rather, it is a matter of emphasis. With the audience in mind, journalists' storytelling role once again becomes dominant.

Consequently, in the effort to appeal to readers or viewers, cases are emphasized over classes, and the most compelling cases are chosen over undramatic ones. Patterns are identified, and journalists hope consumers of their product will not miss the larger message. But it requires inductive logic—learning by example—and a discerning audience to do so.

Painting Portraits of Villainy and Victimization

Having decided on the core content of the story, journalists then must draft the drama. This task requires reporters and their assistants to bring color to the focal points of their story. Investigative targets become life-sized villains. Their accusers become innocent victims or expert witnesses.

Portraits can be painted with pictures or words. In the television stories we studied, the evidence of misconduct was largely visual, like the photographs in the early 1900s muckraking magazines described in chapter 2. Police officers looked menacing, and their victims looked pained. Beneath the facade of beautiful Norway, desperate fathers searched for their missing children. A University of Chicago professor rationalized his decision not to report the toxic waste problem to authorities as students walked past waste haulers wearing respirators. Home health operators smoked and looked evasive while their clients suffered.

In our newspaper cases, colorful language was used to show unambiguous wrongdoing. The rape series profiled a "rapist, 'expert on sex,' [who] thinks he has no problem" despite being convicted of rape four times and deviate sexual assault twice. The kidney dialysis series described "a dangerous and sometimes deadly combination—corporate profit motive, lax control of the quality of care and meek government regulation . . . the program has spawned an industry that pits profits against patients." These stories contain a similar tone to the one employed by muckraker Lincoln Steffens, who wrote that "the evil of Chicago was obvious, general, bold."[25]

In preparing the product, villainy is juxtaposed with victimization. In the real world, this juxtaposition may not have occurred in the precise manner or sequence suggested by the investigative report. Societal wrongdoing normally involves interactions that are complex and evolving. But in preparing an investigative story, the task is to suggest simple causal links allowing audiences to draw clear inferences about who is to blame for whatever followed.

There is little room for ambiguity in painting pictures of villainy and victimization. The task is to present as many examples of pure venality as time or space will allow. Loaded language is used to characterize the wrongdoing for viewers or readers, even before its manifestations are presented. "Money has attracted crooks, liars, thieves and swindlers," begins the "Home Health Hustle."

Villains typically are given their say only later in the story, after an avalanche of charges has been presented against them. Under the circumstances, they naturally appear defensive. Their replies normally sound lame, superficial, or self-serving—which they may be. But they may also sound defensive because of editing and placement decisions. More credible rebuttals usually are followed by further evidence that undermines their position. Villains rarely are given the last words, unless it is an admission of guilt.

However, the charges of villainy are not limitless. Investigative portraits, like those of other artists, have boundaries. Journalists take care to avoid overly sensationalizing a story out of concern for adverse public or peer reactions. Similarly, information about villains that is considered to be in "bad taste" may not make it into the story.

Lawyers may also play a gatekeeping role in preparing the product. Our national survey of investigative reporters and editors indicates that legal matters are an important concern to today's litigation-conscious journalists (see appendix II). In most of our case studies, the scripts or drafts of the stories were closely "lawyered" to head off potential litigation. This sometimes forced investigative rhetoric to be softened. For example, the charge of "profiteering" in the original draft of the *Philadelphia Inquirer* series was replaced by "profit" to avoid the unsupported connotation of illegality.

Nevertheless, even within these boundaries journalists have considerable leeway in portraying the characters in their plot. Just as villains are portrayed as venal, victims are portrayed as innocent. Dialysis patients were described in the *Inquirer* series as "some of the most needy in America." In the "60 Minutes" report, "an American [father] . . . ended up living a nightmare" when his "abducted" children were "caught in a kind of legal no-man's land." Our other case studies spotlighted innocent women, students, elderly and handicapped people, and brutalized citizens. They were portrayed as sufferers of an undeserved fate.

In painting portraits of villainy and victimization, journalists seek to outrage the audience. Whether this in fact occurs is another matter. In chapter 10, we attempt to explain why some stories are more or less effective in achieving this result. For now, it is sufficient to conclude that the task of character portrayal involves the use of literary devices to tell moralistic stories for broader societal purposes.

Positioning the Product

After the drama has been drafted, preparations are made to pave the way for a public showing of the product. At this stage in the agenda-building process, there is almost no turning back. It is rare for a story that survives the previous hurdles to be spiked, but it does happen.[26]

More commonly, the tasks at this point involve positioning the product—deciding when, where, and how the story will be played. First, final decisions are made about the timing of the story. The prime consideration here is audience building. Three of the television reports we studied were broadcast during quarterly ratings periods.[27] The two newspaper series began on Sundays, the day of highest circulation.

In each case, the timing of the stories meant they would be heavily promoted, further enhancing their potential audience reach. The local television series were promoted with vigor, producing significant unanticipated consequences. The advertisements for the police brutality investigation grabbed the attention of the staff members of mayoral candidate Harold Washington, prompting them to sponsor related campaign events during the week the series aired. In the toxic waste case, a local physician who saw the promotions provided information that became the lead of one of the stories.

The promotions also provided indications of where and how the stories would be played. Both newspaper series began on the front page with dramatic headlines: "Rape Epidemic: 'No Woman Immune,' " proclaimed the *Chicago Sun-Times*. The *Philadelphia Inquirer* juxtaposed victimization and villainy in its first day headline: "Kidney Patients vs. the Bottom Line." Each part of the sequentially published series was headlined on the front page, with the text jumping to the body of the newspapers. News editors made it difficult for readers to miss their stories.

The broadcast investigations received similarly prominent play. The local series began in the first segment of the nightly news and were repeated in the evening newscasts the next day. The "60 Minutes" report also was first. Although the "Home Health Hustle" was sandwiched between other reports, it was teased by the show's host at the beginning of the program and before the commercial break that preceded it.

CONCLUSION

Each story finally made it to the top of the investigative agenda. To get there, it passed through several stages, each requiring the performance of numerous tasks. The decisions made by journalists in performing those tasks moved forward the stories we studied, bypassing other story ideas along the way. But this did not happen easily. In making choices, journalists encountered frequent tensions among their obligations as professionals, citizens, and entrepreneurs. Compromises among those obligations helped shape the character of the resulting story.

In building the investigative agenda, journalists also may have triggered agenda building by other interests. In the final chapter of the book, we assess the societal impact of the published investigations. We begin by examining the efforts of journalists to keep their story on the media agenda, in the expectation that it would engender public outrage and fulfill the promise of the Mobilization Model.

NOTES

1. J. Turow, "Cultural Argumentation through the Mass Media: A Framework for Organizational Research," *Communication*, 8 (1985), pp. 139–164.

2. O. H. Gandy, *Beyond Agenda-Setting: Information Subsidies and Public Policy* (Norwood, NJ: Ablex, 1982).

3. For a discussion of the factors that contribute to the "homogeneity in news supply," see D. Graber, *Mass Media and American Politics* (Washington, DC: Congressional Quarterly, 1984), pp. 44–46.

4. For a discussion of various manifestations of media competition, see H. Gans, *Deciding What's News* (New York: Vintage Books, 1980), pp. 176–181. Gans calls competition "endemic to the profession." (p. 176). Not all media managers cherish competition. Some believe it contributes to sloppy, sensational reporting. See N. Isaacs, *Untended Gates: The Mismanaged Press* (New York: Columbia University Press, 1986).

5. See L. Downie, *The New Muckrakers* (Washington, DC: New Republic Book Company, 1976) for numerous examples of how investigative reporters "scope-out" the competition. Also see R. Whitehead, "Toe-to-toe in the Windy City," *Columbia Journalism Review* (July/August 1983).

6. For a discussion of the reciprocity and tensions between the professional and business functions of journalism, see L. Bogart, *Press and Public* (Hillsdale, NJ: Lawrence Erlbaum, 1989), p. 333ff.

7. For an analysis of "framing," see T. Gitlin, *The Whole World Is Watching* (Berkeley: University of California Press, 1980).

8. The *Inquirer* won nine Pulitzer Prizes for investigative reporting between 1975 and 1989, most of which were for stories that dealt with complicated public policy problems. For example, the dialysis series was a Pulitzer runner-up in 1988 to the *Inquirer's* "Great Tax Giveaway," a detailed analysis of changes in the federal tax code.

9. C. MacDougall, *Interpretative Reporting* (New York: Macmillan, 1982), p. 225.

10. For a discussion of the meaning and evolution of the journalistic norm of objectivity, see D. Schiller, *Objectivity and the News* (Philadelphia: University of Pennsylvania Press, 1981).

11. J.S. Ettema, D. Protess, D. Leff, P. Miller, J. Doppelt, and F. L. Cook, "Agenda-setting as Politics: A Case Study of the Press–Public-Policy Connection," *Communication*, 12 (1991), pp. 1–24.

12. For a description of the various interviewing techniques used by in-

vestigative reporters, including how they question "hostile sources," see F. Fedler, *Reporting for the Print Media* (New York: Harcourt Brace Jovanovich, 1989), pp. 509–518. See also Paul N. Williams, *Investigative Reporting and Editing* (Englewood Cliffs, NJ: Prentice-Hall, 1978), pp. 61–92.

13. These criticisms have been made by, among others, J. Malcolm, *The Journalist and the Murderer* (New York: Alfred A. Knopf, 1990); R. Adler, *Reckless Disregard* (New York: Alfred A. Knopf, 1986); and T. Goldstein, *The News at Any Cost* (New York: Simon and Schuster, 1985).

14. For a discussion of the various rationales used by journalists to pursue a story aggressively, including the use of deception, see M. Mencher, *News Reporting and Writing* (Dubuque, IA: William C. Brown, 1987), pp. 634–639. Also see S. Bok, *Lying* (New York: Vintage Books, 1978), p. 127–129.

15. For a discussion of the strategies used by reporters to locate public documents, see IRE, *Reporter's Handbook* (New York: St. Martin's Press, 1983); S. Weinberg, *Trade Secrets of Washington Journalists* (Washington, D.C.: Acropolis Books, 1981); and Williams, *Investigative Reporting and Editing*, pp. 37–60.

16. See J. S. Ettema, *The Craft of the Investigative Journalist* (Evanston, IL: Research Monograph, Institute for Modern Communications, 1988), pp. 24–25.

17. Journalists increasingly appear to recognize the perils of "masquerading" to get a story. See MacDougall, *Interpretative Reporting*, pp. 243–244; Williams, *Investigative Reporting and Editing*, pp. 96–98; Fedler, *Reporting for the Print Media*, pp. 269–271.

18. Coincidentally, two of the most controversial modern-day newspaper stories that relied extensively on undercover reporting were done by the *Chicago Sun-Times*. They were "The Mirage" in 1977 and "The Abortion Profiteers" in 1978. See Zay Smith and Pam Zekman, *The Mirage* (New York: Random House, 1979); and Clifford P. Christians, Kim B. Rotzoll and Mark Fackler (eds.), *Media Ethics* (New York: Longman, 1987), "The Abortion Profiteers" case study.

19. M. Schudson, *Discovering the News* (New York: Basic Books, 1978), p. 192.

20. This has been called "intersubjectivity." See S. Greer, *The Logic of Social Inquiry* (Chicago: Aldine, 1969), pp. 109–111.

21. Investigative reporters do not easily resolve the tension between their quest for impact and their professional "obligation" to remain disinterested and detached. Generally, they consider themselves a different breed of journalist—an active watchdog rather than a passive observer—that allows them more latitude in promoting societal change. See D. L. Protess, "How Investigative Reporters See Themselves," *The IRE Journal* (Spring 1984); and D. L. Protess, "Investigative Reporters: Endangered Species?" *The IRE Journal* (Winter 1986).

22. P. Berger and T. Luckmann, *The Social Construction of Reality* (Garden City, NY: Anchor/Doubleday), 1967.

23. J. S. Ettema, "Agenda Setting as Politics," (1991).

24. For a general discussion of threats to external validity, many of which are applicable to media stories, see T. D. Cook and D. T. Campbell, *Quasi-Experimentation: Design and Analysis Issues for Field Settings* (Boston: Houghton

Mifflin, 1979), pp. 73–80. Journalists have become increasingly aware of the need to guard against this problem and to be more cautious in drawing inferences from their findings. See P. Meyer, *Precision Journalism* (Bloomington: Indiana University Press, 1979).

25. Quoted by C. C. Regier, *Era of the Muckrakers* (Chapel Hill: University of North Carolina Press, 1932), p. 66.

26. A. Kreig, *Spiked* (Old Saybrook, CT: Peregrine Press, 1987); B. Bagdikian, *The Effete Conspiracy* (New York: Harper & Row, 1974); B. Bagdikian, *The Media Monopoly* (Boston: Beacon Press, 1987).

27. "Missing?" was not broadcast during one of the quarterly sweeps periods. "60 Minutes" has been an exception to the rule of scheduling sensational programming during these periods, partly because of its consistently high ratings and partly because of its well-established news magazine format. See D. Hewitt, *Minute by Minute* . . . (New York: Random House, 1985).

CHAPTER 10

Building Media and Policy Agendas

After weeks and often months of digging, interpreting, and packaging a story, journalists finally go public with their allegations. For most people who will read or watch the investigative story—the mass audience—the allegations will be news. This is partly because media investigations disclose previously hidden misdeeds.[1] It also will be news because the public typically discovers investigative stories the same way they learn about other news events—by reading their daily newspaper or by watching their favorite television news program.

However, the published allegations will come as no surprise to certain policy-making audiences. As the case studies show, key officials and organizations interested in the subject matter of the story are likely to have learned about the investigation in its embryonic stages. This may have occurred when journalists sought them out for quotes, documents, or expert advice. It also may have resulted from journalists' efforts to form prepublication coalitions with policymakers to enhance the impact of their story. Or, policy makers may have tipped journalists to the story in the first place. Regardless of the precise scenario, agenda building in public policy arenas may be under way by the time the investigative story becomes published news.

Journalists outside of the news organization that published the investigative story also may have obtained advance knowledge of its existence. The task of scoping out the competition, described in the previous chapter, sometimes allows rival news organizations to discover what is on one another's investigative agendas. This may lead the competition to publish spoiler stories, in which they present the main findings as their own, or knockdown stories, in which they attempt to discredit the legitimacy of the findings.[2]

Once published, some investigative stories are greeted with a conspicuous silence by other media. Others may trigger a media feeding frenzy. The investigative reporters who broke the original story may themselves choose to follow up with additional reports, or let it drop. As we shall discuss, the media course that a story takes may be important for influencing its impact on society.

This chapter examines the postpublication actions of journalists and policy makers in our six case studies. We analyze the effects of their behavior on different forms of agenda building, including public opinion formation. Our primary focus, however, is on where the main action seems to be— agenda building in media and policy-making arenas. We conclude by refining the conventional Mobilization Model and by discussing the implications for democracy of contemporary trends in investigative reporting.

BUILDING MEDIA AGENDAS: PROPRIETARY AND NONPROPRIETARY FOLLOW-UP

In chapter 9, we discussed how various problems made it onto the investigative agenda of journalists and their news organizations. Once a story is in the public domain, investigative agenda building often continues. Journalists will follow up their stories by developing new leads, exploring fresh angles, or covering various reactions. The play their news organization gives to follow-up stories reflects whether the story continues to be salient to media managers, which in turn may affect the future commitment to the story by journalists. We call the efforts by journalists and their superiors to continue working on an investigative story "proprietary follow-up."

Clearly, whether a story remains on the investigative agenda is only one factor for determining its audience reach. Another factor is whether a story makes it onto the larger media agenda. We call investigative stories that attract attention in other media "nonproprietary follow-up."

The conventional yardstick used by journalists to determine whether to pursue a story of any kind is newsworthiness.[3] If an investigative story is newsworthy, the argument goes, then it will merit continued attention by investigative reporters and other journalists. Newsworthiness is defined in different ways, but it most commonly refers to pronouncements or events that are controversial, unusual, and/or topical. The news value of the pronouncements or events is enhanced when they hold public importance or involve people who are powerful or well recognized.[4]

Of course, journalists' judgments of these attributes are both situational and subjective. Individuals and events are not intrinsically newsworthy; journalistic norms and routines shape what is news on a particular day. As Gans states, "news" is:

Information which is transmitted from sources to audiences, with journalists—who are both employees of bureaucratic commercial organizations and members of a profession—summarizing, refining and altering what becomes available to them from sources in order to make the information suitable for their audiences . . .[5]

These notions of news suggest that investigative stories should be covered widely after their publication. After all, they often reveal matters that are unusual, controversial, and topical. Further, they usually discuss matters of importance and generate public reactions by newsmakers.

Indeed, we found that each of our investigative stories resulted in continuing coverage of the problems revealed, both by the news organization that disclosed them and by other media. However, the nature and duration of the stories varied considerably from case to case. It seems that some investigative stories have more potential than others to trigger extensive postpublication coverage and that "newsworthiness" alone does not account for the patterns that emerged.

In the next section, we discuss the motivations for proprietary follow-up. We then explore the factors that explain nonproprietary coverage. Both kinds of media agenda-building processes are compared with muckraking journalism in the early 1900s, and the implications for agenda building in other arenas are discussed.

Proprietary Follow-Up

As we have seen in the case studies, investigative reporting requires a significant investment of news organizations' resources. Each story we studied occupied teams of reporters for several months. Journalists' time is a valuable commodity. Salary is one consideration. Another factor is that journalists who pursue a particular story will have little time to work on others.

Further, investigative projects may require significant out-of-pocket expenses. The photocopying of court files in the police brutality investigation cost hundreds of dollars. The trips to California and Mississippi in the home health care investigation cost even more, as did the one to Norway in the "60 Minutes" probe. The expense of analyzing the entire computer tape in the rape story was prohibitive; it forced journalists to focus only on certain crimes.

Once resources are committed to an investigative project, media managers and journalists alike want the biggest "bang for their buck." They want results. Having brought an investigative project to publication, they are unlikely to abandon it afterwards. There is a proprietary interest at this point in some form of continuing coverage of the problems they have revealed.

However, the commitment to follow up an investigative story is not open-ended. Our review of the case studies suggests that the nature and scope of the follow-up depend on several factors, including journalists' (1) need to defend the story in public, (2) ability to amplify the story, and (3) commitment to crusade.

First, investigative reporting often puts the credibility of journalists and their news organizations on the line. The targets of exposés may counterattack, as did the police superintendent in the brutality investigation, the University of Chicago in the toxic waste probe, and a private firm in the kidney dialysis series. If possible, news organizations want to respond to such counterattacks by "standing by the story."

One strategy for accomplishing this, called "legitimacy conferral,"[6] is to publish statements by sources who corroborate or otherwise support the story findings. This happened when WMAQ-TV extensively covered the political attacks on the police department in the wake of its brutality investigation. The same station used the fire department's crackdown to dispute the University of Chicago's claims about the safety of its chemical waste disposal practices. Similarly, the *Chicago Sun-Times* quoted the chairman of the Illinois House Rape Study Committee saying "the series was right on the button," and later quoted a black official who dismissed the possible racist implications of the series.

Such follow-up stories frequently focus on official reactions. Pronouncements by leaders, including promises of reform, can be justifiably covered because they are newsworthy in the conventional sense. The coverage also allows reporters to say that their investigative stories made a societal difference, which enhances their potential to win journalism awards. As one newspaper reporter we surveyed from Wilmington, Del., said: "It seems award-winning stories are honored because they fed a series of follow-ups or reactions to the original piece." Another reporter we surveyed from Bergen, N.J., cautioned that such proprietary follow-ups can manufacture newsworthiness. "We risk generating reaction to justify the research and publication," he said.

Sometimes, journalists may be forced to backtrack publicly because an angle in their story is not fully supported by fact. When the kidney dialysis series came under attack from a private health provider, the newspaper published a correction. This was an unpleasant reaction story for the journalists who worked on the series. However, it was offset considerably by the numerous congratulatory letters that the newspaper published.

News organizations do not always respond to public challenges with follow-up reports. For example, "60 Minutes" ignored the outcry from Norwegian officials and others about "Missing?" While a postpublication controversy swirled in Norwegian media, no one wrote to complain to "60

Minutes," which regularly broadcasts letters with opposing points of view. Consequently, the challenges to the story occurred outside the response format of the news magazine program and were not covered.

Another factor that influences the nature of proprietary follow-up is the opportunity to amplify an investigative story. Amplification may take several forms. There may be untold stories to be reported, old stories to be packaged in new forms, and other media to be reached.

After publication, investigative journalists ordinarily will hear about other instances of the wrongdoing they have uncovered. If the evidence is fresh, compelling, and easily obtained, they may use it to amplify the original story. This occurred in the toxic waste series when journalists were told cancer rates were high near the University of Chicago campus. The allegations created the basis for an additional part to the series.

In the kidney dialysis series, however, journalists did not pursue allegations made in a postpublication stream of calls and letters about particular clinics that were not mentioned in the series. The journalists decided this form of amplification would have been too time consuming in relation to the value of the information they expected to find.

In some cases, journalists who are not given the space or time to report all of the sad stories they want to tell will share their findings with "friendly" reporters. For example, "60 Minutes" gave information about a mother whose child was abducted to Norway to the "CBS Evening News," which aired a story about the case the day after the broadcast of "Missing?"; CBS News anchor Dan Rather introduced the report by crediting "60 Minutes" with breaking the international child abductions story.

Perhaps the most significant form of case amplification we found occurred in the wake of the rape series. Content analysis of the *Chicago Sun-Times* showed significant qualitative and quantitative changes in its coverage of rape in the months after the series was published. Journalists stated that the series raised their consciousness about the problem.

Another form of amplification occurs when investigative stories are repackaged and disseminated. This happened when the *Philadelphia Inquirer* published reprints of its dialysis series. Some 3,000 of these reprints were made available to public and policy-making audiences. Similarly, *Chicago Sun-Times* reporters sent photocopies of their series to interested persons and groups, and WMAQ-TV broadcast a documentary about its police brutality findings a month after the airing of "Beating Justice."

However, the local station did not do this with its toxic waste investigation. Journalists concluded that the findings were less compelling, especially to a citywide audience. Neither of the national television reports we studied broadcast updates to their stories. This would have required somewhat of a departure from routine; notable postpublication developments normally are treated as network news. Indeed, "60 Minutes" rebroadcast "Missing?" during its seasonal reruns without mentioning the controversy that followed its original airing.

A third form of amplification occurs when the story is disseminated directly to other media. This happened when the *Philadelphia Inquirer* put the dialysis series on its news wire. Several member news organizations republished parts of the series. This phenomenon of "feeding the wires," which originated at the turn of the twentieth century, can be an effective technique for influencing national media and policy agendas. As Cobb and Elder state:

> The development of mass media that are truly national in scope and communications technologies that allow members of the public to be reached both directly and selectively has . . . had profound effects on the agenda-building process.[7]

Finally, the commitment to crusade has traditionally been an important component of proprietary follow-up to investigative stories. As we discussed in chapter 2, early 1900s muckrakers usually dwelled on particular wrongdoings over long periods of time, both because of space constraints and because they believed this approach would facilitate change. Ida Tarbell's series on Standard Oil, for example, was serialized monthly in *McClure's* from November 1902 to October 1904. Lincoln Steffens' crusade against local political corruption covered eight cities over nearly a three-year period.

In contrast, contemporary investigative reporting appears to have virtually abandoned this form of proprietary follow-up. Our case studies suggest that reporters were reluctant to pursue their stories far beyond the boundaries of the original publication. Postpublication follow-up editorials or coverage of official developments occurred mostly within a few days; only the *Philadelphia Inquirer* published a handful of stories over the succeeding months, and even the reporter felt reluctant to milk the story.[8] Moreover, contemporary follow-up stories lack the crusading tone of earlier muckracking. They instead tend to spotlight the reactions by officials to the investigative disclosures.

There are several reasons for this important change in investigative reporting. We discuss these in detail in the final section of this book. For now, we conclude that the significant organizational expenditure needed for investigative reporting produces paradoxical consequences. On one hand it generates a commitment to postpublication coverage. On the other hand, it mandates that reporters not commit to following up one story at the expense of investigating new ones. In contemporary times, this dilemma usually is resolved by doing short-term reaction stories and leaving long-term follow-up to others.

Nonproprietary Follow-Up

Journalists generally have little interest in following up exclusive stories published in other media. However, circumstances do arise that compel them to put their own imprimatur on an investigative story. Our review of the case studies suggests that "nonproprietary" follow-up is influenced by several factors, including (1) the nature of the competitive media environment, (2) whether newsmakers react to the story, and (3) the potential to develop fresh angles to the original investigation. These factors can be mutually reinforcing.

In some cases, heated media competition can help to generate follow-up stories. For example, the aftermath of the "60 Minutes" story saw a struggle between the *Chicago Tribune* and the *Chicago Sun-Times* to cover the local ramifications of the story. There, neither newspaper saw itself as a rival of the television magazine program that broadcast the original story. The press conferences by the Better Government Association, a Chicago newsmaker, also helped draw additional attention to the story.

Conversely, the intense competition between local television stations led WMAQ-TV's rivals to ignore the crackdown by fire officials at the University of Chicago. However, both newspapers covered the department's inspection as spot news. It involved a clash between two newsmakers—a government regulator and a powerful private educational institution.

In the police brutality story, a similar blend of competitive factors and newsmakers' actions created extensive postpublication publicity. When mayoral candidates attacked the incumbent mayor and police superintendent in the aftermath of "Beating Justice," reporters on the campaign trail covered the events as news. This kind of media phenomenon has been called pack journalism.[9]

The discovery of additional victims may fuel the follow-up coverage. Most notably, candidate Harold Washington surrounded himself at a press conference by citizens who alleged that they or their family members had been beaten by Chicago police officers. This created dramatic new stories for other journalists to report.

This example suggests an additional basis for nonproprietary follow-up: the potential to develop fresh angles to the original story. Of course, most media investigations have this potential. There are virtually infinite permutations to any story about social problems. However, some stories are better catalysts than others for triggering nonproprietary follow-up.

In our case studies, the "60 Minutes" investigation of international child abductions appears to have had the best ingredients for such follow-up. The story involved a "pull at the heartstrings issue," as the "60 Minutes" producer put it. There were more than 2,300 cases to be discovered. Further, policymaking interests, including several U.S. senators and a private interest group, were willing to speak continually and colorfully about the issue and to help journalists locate victims.

In contrast, the case of toxic waste at the University of Chicago had the least potential for nonproprietary follow-up. The findings were highly focused, there were no apparent victims, and newsmakers were unwilling to crusade on the problem. Our other studies involved in-between cases. In particular, official actions and fresh information kept the home health story alive in daily newspapers and the *New Republic* magazine, whereas the kidney dialysis stories triggered a spirited debate of the problem in a monthly trade journal.

Besides the scope of nonproprietary follow-up, its content is distinctive from proprietary coverage. Specifically, the focus of the original investigation is invariably lost as the story plays itself out in different media. This phenomenon, which has been called "rethematization,"[10] was most apparent in the wake of the "60 Minutes" exposé. The tale of Norwegian villainy and paternal victimization was transformed into stories about desperate mothers, missing children, broken families, hapless bureaucracies, and cultural conflicts.

This is similar to developments in early twentieth-century America, where the follow-up stories to muckraking exposés often diffused the definition of the problem at hand. Nonetheless, in some cases this maximized the public policy consequences resulting from the coverage. For example, the extensive newspaper follow-up to *The Jungle* helped prompt the passage of an omnibus Pure Food and Drug Act. Reflecting the newspaper's diverse concerns, this legislation dealt not only with impure meat but also with other adulterated foods and medicine.

In contemporary times, the pattern of postpublication coverage also may affect society. The media's impact on public opinion, for example, has been found to be strongest when coverage of societal problems is widespread and lengthy.[11] In some cases, similar effects have occurred in policy-making arenas, as we discuss in the next section of the book. Regardless of its impact, we conclude here that media follow-up is most prevalent when investigative stories are published in competitively nonthreatening media environments in which newsmakers speak out on problems that have fresh angles to be explored.

BUILDING POLICY AGENDAS

It is no easy matter for social problems to get on policy makers' agendas and produce corrective actions. The number of problems that policy makers might address is virtually infinite. The number that actually come to their attention is circumscribed, but each of those must still vie for policy makers' interest. Policy makers must decide which problems will receive priority attention, just as journalists did in building their investigative and media agendas.

Policy agenda building is the process by which some problems "come to command the active and serious attention of government as prospective matters of public policy," Elder and Cobb state.[12] Once a problem becomes salient, some sort of ameliorative outcome often follows. Solutions, however, are not guaranteed. Some problems may languish when they get to the top of the policy agenda and may eventually fall off before corrective actions are taken.[13] Other problems may be addressed incompletely by policy makers or in ways that create new problems.[14]

Despite the hazards, policy agenda building is the ultimate mission of many investigative reporters. Our historical analysis, the evidence from the case studies, and the surveys of journalists all suggest that a primary goal of investigative reporting is fulfilled when media disclosures grab policy makers' attention and produce reforms. This is the final, and perhaps the most vital step, in the Mobilization Model.

In discussing the impact of investigative reporting on policy making, we identify three aspects of agenda building: priority, pace, and particularity. When the problem disclosed by an investigative story moves onto the policy-making agenda, we describe it as having attained relative priority status. The problem is in a position to compete with others already in the policy-making stream. Pace means the relative speed with which policy makers address the problem. Some problems produce faster policy responses than others.

By particularity, we mean the effect of investigative reporting on the particular content of the policy initiatives. Some media investigations offer prescriptions for the problems they have revealed. The prescriptions may be presented in editorials, normative story language, and even discussions between reporters and reform-minded policy makers. When these proposals are transformed into specific policy proposals, the agenda-building effect of particularity has occurred.

The selection of policy proposals may heighten or diminish the priority and pace of social problem solving. Indeed, investigative reporting may trigger various policy-making combinations. Significantly, the resulting policy-making processes may affect the eventual policy *outcomes* or "reforms." The next section examines the policy-making processes and outcomes in our six case studies. We then identify the various motives of policy makers for taking action on the investigative findings and show how the paths to reform depart from the conventional Mobilization Model.

The Realities of Reform

Once agenda-building processes have been catalyzed by investigative reporting, several kinds of policy-making results are possible. These may be more or less consistent with the reformist goals of investigative reporters. As we have suggested, the revelation of a social problem may affect the priority, pace, and particularity of agenda building without ultimately resulting in meaningful change.

In chapter 1, we described three types of possible policy-making outcomes: deliberative, individualistic, and substantive. Deliberative results occur when policy makers hold formal discussions of policy problems and their solutions, such as legislative hearings or executive commissions. Individualistic outcomes occur when policy makers apply sanctions against particular persons or entities, including prosecutions, firings, and demotions. Finally, substantive results include regulatory, legislative, and/or administrative changes.

As table 10.1 indicates, each of the media investigations we studied influenced public policy making in various ways. The rape reports, the police

Table 10.1
Summary of the Policy-making Impact of Six Media Investigative Reports

Investigative report	Agenda-building impact	Policy-making outcome
"Home Health Hustle"	Priority pace	Deliberative (U.S. Senate hearings)
"Rape: Every Woman's Nightmare"	Priority, pace, particularity	Deliberative (community hearings) Substantive (law signed)
"Beating Justice"	Priority, pace, particularity	Substantive (regulatory changes)
"Wasted Time"	Pace	Individualistic (local code enforcement)
"Missing?"	Priority, pace	Deliberative (congressional hearings) Substantive (treaty passed/agency created)
"Dialysis: The Profit Machine"	Priority, pace, particularity	Deliberative (U.S. bills/ state bills/federal audits) Individualistic (state code enforcement) Substantive (additional inspectors hired)

brutality broadcasts, and the dialysis series triggered all three types of agenda building. The rape reports made legislative changes an immediate priority and engendered community hearings that were not previously planned. The police brutality broadcasts mobilized political actors and produced swift and fundamental revisions of regulations regarding police misconduct. The dialysis series fueled a state and federal debate over the regulation of clinics and, in particular, the reuse of dialyzers. In each case, agenda building resulted in substantive reforms.

At the opposite extreme, the toxic waste series affected only the pace of bureaucratic activity at one locale. The problem of toxic waste disposal did not become more salient to policy makers, nor were measures considered to ensure that the problem was not occurring in places other than the University of Chicago. However, the swift actions taken in this case were effective for remedying the problems disclosed.

The other investigative stories involved in-between cases. The home health probe prompted the U.S. Senate to hold immediate hearings that raised significant questions about fraud and abuse in federal social programs, but no bills were introduced to address the problem. In the international child abductions case, treaty legislation that had languished for years moved higher on the State Department and Congressional agendas and passed unanimously after brief legislative hearings.

Clearly, the investigative stories that we studied significantly affected various policy-making arenas. Yet, the effects varied considerably from case to case. To develop a model that explains the impact of investigative reporting, we need to consider the factors that differentially influenced policy-making in the six cases.

In recent years, research on policy agenda building has flourished.[15] These studies have employed different methodologies to try to identify actors who might influence agenda-building processes, including political leaders, bureaucrats, interest groups, citizens, and the media. Some studies have focused on agenda-building influences in specific social problem areas, such as child abuse[16] and criminal victimization of the elderly.[17] Others have examined institutional agenda building.[18]

Regardless of the divergent paths taken by scholars, certain common agenda-building influences have been identified. For example, Cook and Skogan have demonstrated empirically a "convergent voice" model indicating that agenda building "depends upon the same issue being independently articulated by different groups inside and outside government at about the same time, within the context of a ripe issue climate."[19] This model overlaps with Kingdon's theory of agenda building, which holds that issues rise on policy agendas when separate "streams" of policies, problems, and politics join together at an opportune time.[20] Specifically, these theories of agenda building identify three factors that may be useful in for understanding the investigative case study findings: (1) the recognition by policy makers that a legitimate problem exists; (2) the availability of policy alternatives to address the problem; and (3) the presence of a ripe political climate.

The first condition for agenda building, problem recognition, was present in each of our case studies. Interviews with key policy makers indicate that they often learned about the problems in the six cases through different kinds of media disclosures—by reading or viewing the original exposé, by following the proprietary and nonproprietary coverage of the findings, or through interviews with journalists. Further, some policy makers had pre-publication knowledge of the problems, either because journalists interviewed them to obtain information or to build reactions into their stories or because they had heard about them earlier from sources other than media.

In each case, policy makers also were readily able to ascertain the legitimacy of the investigative findings. In the reports about home health care, rape, international child abductions, and dialysis, policy makers had in-dependently studied the problems and found them to be credible. In the toxic waste story, policy makers were able to confirm the series findings through a simple inspection at the University of Chicago. In the brutality reports, the police superintendent was unable to deny the problem of repeat offenders. These developments were important, since credible indicators of social prob-lems may enhance the agenda status of those problems,[21] whereas the absence of such indicators may lead a problem to fall off the policy agenda.[22]

In sum, policy makers perceived that legitimate problems were identified in all six of the cases that we studied. Further, the news media, in various ways, played an important agenda-building role by helping draw policy makers' attention to those problems. Specifically, policy makers temporarily set aside other problems they were addressing to react to the media dis-closures. Because of this, the *pace* of reform was accelerated in each of the cases, and the underlying problems became *priority* items in five of the six cases. (This proved to be unnecessary to resolve the toxic waste problems at the University of Chicago.)

Problem recognition, though, is not sufficient to explain the content of the various reforms proposed. Here, we need to consider the policy alterna-tives available to remedy the problems that were disclosed. Once again, problem-solving proposals were under consideration at the time that several of the investigative stories were published.

At the point that the rape series was published, legislation to crack down on gang rape was awaiting the governor's signature, and an Illinois House committee was formulating additional legislation to deal with the problems of sex crimes. In the international child abductions case, a relevant treaty was awaiting action by the State Department. When the *Philadelphia Inquirer* first published a brief story that was a forerunner to its eventual dialysis series, legislation was pending in the U.S. Senate regarding the reuse of dialyzers.

Consequently, policy makers were able to react readily to the investigative revelations and follow-up coverage with reforms that specifically addressed the problems disclosed. This significantly facilitated the agenda-building process in those cases. As Kingdon states:

> Items are sometimes found on a governmental agenda without a solution attached to them. . . . But normally, before a subject can attain a solid position on a decision agenda, a viable alternative is available for decision makers to consider. It is not enough that there is a problem, even quite a pressing problem. There also is generally a solution ready to go, already softened up, already worked out.[23]

This logic also applies to the toxic waste disposal case. Although policy *alternatives* were not at hand when the investigative series was broadcast, and none was proposed, the enforcement of the *existing* fire code was sufficient to ameliorate the problem.

The other two cases did not have alternatives for policy makers to seize, yet they resulted in policy change anyway. In the police brutality case, viable remedies were not available at the time of the series, nor were they in the policy pipeline. Nonetheless, substantive reforms followed the broadcast of the series. In the home health case, policy makers expressed frustration over the lack of apparent remedies. Yet, the media probe set the deliberative agenda of the U.S. Senate.

In sum, our evidence suggests that the availability of the alternatives helps affect the policies that are proposed in the wake of an investigative series. However, this factor is not sufficient to explain the policy outcomes in each of the cases. Moreover, it does not explain policy makers' motivations for offering those alternatives in the first place.

Policy makers' willingness to propose available alternatives or to innovate has been found to depend, to some extent, on the political timing of the appearance of the problem. In particular, the proximity of problem disclosure to an election is conventionally believed to affect this decision.[24] Indeed, the broadcast of the police brutality series in the middle of a hotly contested mayoral campaign may have influenced the priority, pace, and particularity of the reform measures that followed. Similarly, the hearings that followed the "Home Health Hustle" were timed to showcase the new Republican Senate majority's concern for waste in federal social programs.

However, immediate electoral or political interests do not adequately explain the developments in the other case studies. For example, the State

Department's willingness finally to submit the child abductions treaty legislation appeared to be timed mainly to get crusading politicians and the media off its bureaucratic back. In the other investigative stories we studied, political events or developments seemed entirely unrelated to the timing of policy reactions to the investigative stories.

Of course, the "ripeness" of a political climate may include more than short-term political stakes. The "national mood" and the actions of organized interests also are politicial factors that may affect the nature and scope of policy agenda building.[25] Indeed, established theories of American governance place great emphasis on the policy-making influences of the public[26] and of pressure groups.[27] At this juncture, we need to consider the validity of these conventional models for explaining the findings in our investigative case studies.

The Mobilization Model Revisited

Consistent with recent studies of policy agenda building, we have concluded that the recognition of problems, the availability of alternatives, and the immediate political climate each provide partial explanations for the policy-making processes in our six case studies of investigative reporting. However, none of these factors, nor all of them together, explains the policy-making outcomes that resulted in most of the cases.

The Mobilization Model, on the other hand, proposes a more complete explanation for our findings. The conventional wisdom of journalists and advocates of popular democracy holds that the general public, outraged at the disclosures about fraud and abuse, sex crimes, police brutality, environmental pollution, child abductions, and dialysis rip-offs, responds by demanding reform. The policy results in each of our cases, according to the conventional wisdom, may be explained by the extent of public reaction to the disclosures.

A more contemporary version of this model, offerred by pluralist political scientists, suggests that each exposé mobilizes organizations with a stake in the controversy. These groups pressure policy makers to produce changes that serve the interests of its members. Although the general public may not become actively involved in decision making, it is possible for its views to be expressed through group membership or identity. The pluralist model further suggests that where group conflict occurs over policy alternatives, policy makers attempt to facilitate compromises that reflect a broad spectrum of interests.

We find, however, that neither the conventional statement of the Mobilization Model nor its more contemporary version is useful for explaining our particular case study results. The policy developments that we found clearly occurred independently of either manifest changes in public opinion or interest group pressures. This was demonstrated in two ways. First, the policy agenda was set well before there was any overt expression of citizen preferences. Second, the rhetoric and actions of policy makers indicated they were not responding to public pressure but, rather, were seizing the initiative to promote programs in which they had a stake.

In most of the case studies, reform proposals were announced even before the original exposé had been fully published. Viewers of the "Home Health Hustle" were told toward the end of the 18-minute segment that "next week there will be Senate hearings into the home health business." In the rape reports, community hearings were announced the day after the five-part series began, and the gang rape law was signed on the third day of the series.

Between the third and fourth parts of "Beating Justice," mayoral candidate Harold Washington proposed the abolition of the police department's disciplinary review board. The fire department crackdown at the University of Chicago occurred the morning after the first broadcast. The last part of the dialysis series quoted federal officials who promised reforms, several of which were proposed shortly thereafter.

Only in the child abductions story, where the "60 Minutes" producer refused to give credit to policy makers that she believed was undeserved, did policy actions come later. But even there, officials responded only ten days after the broadcast. Clearly, these developments undermine the Mobilization Model's requisite that public outcry in the wake of an investigative story is a necessary precursor to change.

Second, the tone of policy makers appeared inconsistent with the formulation of the Moblization Model. Officials seemed neither reactive nor defensive about published allegations of wrongdoing, even when the problems were in their bailiwick. Instead, they responded to the investigative disclosures as if they provided policy *opportunities*.

The home health exposé allowed the new Republican Senate majority to showcase its concern for wasteful social welfare programs. The rape series provided a forum for a governor and a state legislative panel to flex their muscle about crime. The toxic waste reports were viewed by a fire department bureaucrat as an opportunity to impress his new reform-minded boss. The child abductions story gave several U.S. senators a chance to obtain widespread recognition for their routine casework. The dialysis series allowed two Congressional committees and other governmental agencies to spotlight their crusade against health care rip-offs.

In each case, policy makers and their spokespersons used the media disclosures to exhibit positive leadership traits. Rather than risk being portrayed as part of the problem, in the conventional terms of adversary journalism, they took steps that allowed them to be described as part of the solution. This occurred even where policy makers actually had contributed to the problems because they had allowed policy reforms to languish (for example, in the child abductions and kidney dialysis cases).

In most of the cases, exposés could be exploited as opportunities because of prepublication transactions between journalists and policy makers. In the home health, toxic waste, and dialysis stories, journalists and policy makers actively collaborated to set policy-making agendas prior to the public dissemination of the investigative findings. Specifically, coalitions were established that ensured both the nature and timing of the postpublication announcements of reforms. We have called these symbiotic alliances between journalists and officials "coalition journalism."[28] The motivations for forming such coalitions are described later.

Prepublication transactions also occurred in the rape series. There, journalists recontacted reform-minded officials to obtain information about the status of legislative initiatives just prior to the publication of the series. Unlike the other cases, however, the nature and timing of the subsequent policy initiatives were decided independently by officials. Nonetheless, the initiatives clearly were prompted by journalists' contacts with those policy makers, and the newspaper covered them as reactions to its series. Contrary to the Mobilization Model, agenda building began in all four of these cases before the public was made aware of the investigative findings.

The policy agendas in the police brutality and child abductions cases were not set by formal journalist–policy-maker coalitions. Nonetheless, similar kinds of symbiotic transactions occurred after publication in both cases. In "Beating Justice," the local television station closely covered the reactions of political candidates as part of its proprietary follow-up. Indeed, campaign aides notified investigative reporters as well as nonproprietary media before each round of public announcements. In the follow-up to "Missing?" a senator's staff helped set the nonproprietary media agenda by supplying journalists with fresh information about additional victims and updates on the status of reform proposals that they supported.

As summarized in table 10.2, we find that policy-making agendas are catalyzed by the formal transactions between journalists and officials more than by the direct influence of the public or interest groups. Further, those transactional relationships seem more important than the actual publication or broadcast of an investigative series in influencing the agenda-building process. Finally, the character of the policy outcomes—the reforms—may be affected significantly by collaboration among journalists and officials.

This is not to dismiss the role of the public or pressure groups in influencing the possibility of reform. Pressure groups, in particular, played an important agenda-building role later in the policy-making process in three cases. The rape reports, for example, provided a platform for feminist groups

Table 10.2
The Media–Opinion–Policy-making Connection

Investigative report	Journalist–policy-maker transaction	Impact on general public	Interest group pressure	Type policy result
"Home Health Hustle"	Prepublication coalition (formal)	Highly significant	No	Deliberative
"Rape: Every Woman's Nightmare"	Prepublication coalition (informal)	Not significant	Yes (supportive)	Deliberative, Substantive
"Beating Justice"	Proprietary and nonproprietary follow-up	Moderately significant	No	Substantive
"Wasted Time"	Prepublication coalition (formal)	Not significant	No	Individualistic
"Missing?"	Nonproprietary follow-up	Not significant	Yes (supportive)	Deliberative, Substantive
"Dialysis: The Profit Machine"	Prepublication coalition (formal)	Moderately significant	Yes (conflictual)	Deliberative, Individualistic, Substantive

to push for sweeping changes in the Illinois criminal code. The Illinois law was fundamentally revised the year after the newspaper series was published. Similarly, American Children Held Hostage, an organization formed one month after the "60 Minutes" report, was instrumental in keeping the problem of international child abductions on the media agenda. The group also broadened the policy-making support for legislative reforms.

Interest group activity also was important in the aftermath of the dialysis series, but with different consequences. There, patients' groups conflicted with providers' organizations over proposed reform legislation, creating at least a temporary policy stalemate. This is consistent with Kingdon's findings: "Much of interest group activity in these processes consists not of positive promotion, but rather of negative blocking," he reports.[29] Nonetheless, the dialysis case was the only one in which pressure groups approximated the conventional role assigned by pluralist political scientists. In the other cases, groups played no discernible role in agenda building, or they facilitated reforms already in the works.

The general public also is not to be dismissed entirely as an agenda-building force. To some extent, policy makers have the public in mind when they develop their collaborative media strategies. As Linsky puts it: "agenda setting (by the media) is accepted by officials because what becomes a high priority issue for the media may be a reflection of what people are thinking about."[30] In an age when the news media have become a vital link between political actors and their constituencies, getting good press on issues of concern to the public may be a prerequisite for career enhancement.[31]

In particular, establishing collaborative relationships with investigative journalists is a double-edged sword. It allows policy makers to send positive messages to the public about their problem-solving abilities, and, with Richard Nixon's mishandling of the media in Watergate fresh in their minds, to avoid negative portrayals of their performance. Indeed, our interviews with policy makers suggest they respond to investigative reporters as if they *were* the public.

Still, this is very different from the role ascribed to the press and the public by the Mobilization Model. As table 10.2 indicates, actual public preferences seem unrelated to policy makers' reactions to the investigative findings. In the rape and toxic waste cases, significant policy-making reactions occurred despite the lack of measured changes in public opinion. In the home health and dialysis cases, relevant changes in public opinion were preceded by policy-making initiatives. Following "Missing?" the public became increasingly antagonistic to the government of Norway without becoming more concerned about international child abductions, the larger problem that policy makers actually were addressing.

The conventional role of public opinion in a popular democracy was approximated only in the police brutality case. There, our surveys of the public, journalists, and policy makers suggest public opinion was catalyzed in the immediate aftermath of the investigative reports. But even here, there were significant departures from the linear Mobilization Model. Rather than a media crusade to outrage the general public, it was a mayoral candidate who used the issue of police brutality to mobilize a specific portion of the electorate. Further, the substantive reforms that followed were made without media fanfare by the incumbent administration, and only after it had been defeated at the polls.

Nonetheless, the police brutality case provides evidence that support certain premises of the Mobilization Model. In particular, this case indicates that the public mood may affect the possibility of reform. As Kingdon observes:

People in and around government sense a national mood. They are comfortable discussing its content, and believe that they know when the mood shifts. The idea goes by different names—the national mood, the climate in the country, changes in public opinion, or broad social movements . . . these changes in mood or climate have important impacts on policy agendas and policy outcomes. . . . Governmental participants sense of the national mood serves to promote some items on their policy agendas and to restrain others from rising to prominence.[32]

In Chicago, in 1983, reform was in the air. The local climate was ripe both for a general change in administrations—the election of the city's first black reform mayor—and a specific change in the regulation of its police force.

Similarly, the political mood in the country in the early 1900s and the mid-1970s was conducive to building reform agendas. In those periods, an alienated citizenry and organized public interest groups helped facilitate an array of changes in American society by challenging the status quo. The media played a significant role in bringing about those changes by relentlessly unearthing wrongdoings and crusading to right wrongs.

The cases we studied were set in the 1980s, however, where pragmatism and incrementalism dominated our country's social and political milieu. In this context, it is perhaps surprising that we found any evidence of change, much less some of the important corrective actions documented in our case studies. This is testimony to the ongoing spirit of reform, even if it often resulted from surprising coalitions that appear to defy our expectations of adversary journalism.

In the remaining section, we discuss further the societal implications of our conclusions and examine trends in investigative reporting. Both the recent and distant past demonstrate that muckraking journalists have the power to set the agendas of the public and of policy makers. Consequently, the future course of investigative reporting may have important consequences for governing practices in American society.

SUMMING UP AND LOOKING AHEAD

Old ideas die hard. The tenets of the Mobilization Model continue to be embraced, especially by the journalism community. Witness the 1989 advertising campaign by the Society of Professional Journalists, a national association with 19,000 members. The SPJ campaign, designed to promote public awareness of the value of a free press, included this advertisement about the impact of a Pittsburgh newspaper exposé of drug addiction among airline pilots:

The newspaper's story brought the problem to the attention of the public. The public was outraged. And demanded immediate reform As a result, several reforms were initated. . . . Reforms that may never have occurred if it hadn't been for a couple of reporters pursuing a story.[33]

It may have happened that way. Indeed, we have shown that new muckrakers can powerfully influence the agendas of citizens and policy makers. However, although we have no evidence to contradict the specific claims made in the SPJ advertisement, it is clear that the paths to reform commonly depart from such conventional ideals.

Muckraking is most likely to matter, it seems, when journalists form coalitions with policy makers, sometimes early in the investigative process. For journalists, the driving forces behind these alliances include the need for information, the quest for impact, and the desire to attain legitimacy and recognition for their stories and themselves. For policy makers, coalitions with journalists provide an important vehicle for image building in a media age.

Journalist-policy-maker transactions, then, are often symbiotic. Rather than the conventional notion of investigative reporting, which posits adversarial relationships as the norm, the muckraking–policy-making connection may be just the opposite. Mutually self-interested ad hoc alliances appear to be commonplace.

Some investigative reporters we surveyed perceived the coalitional relationship as an easy fix, providing an opportunity for posturing as well as for policy making. One investigative reporter from Seattle characterized the governmental reaction to investigative stories as "choreographed and shallow." An editor from Milwaukee saw the trend as one in which the results tend to be "bogus, prearranged or negotiated."

Our case study evidence suggests that symbiotic coalitions can also be effective catalysts for setting reform agendas. In some circumstances, such as the toxic waste case study, they provide a sufficient condition for corrective action. In other cases, they are necessary or helpful for triggering the deliberation of reform measures. However, such coalitions may not be enough to carry the day. The availability of policy alternatives, the role of pressure groups, and the existing political climate must converge for investigative influence to be maximized.

As figure 2 indicates, policy reforms result from complex interactive factors rather than from the simple linear progression specified by the Mobilization Model. The journalist–policy-maker connection occupies center stage in this alternative Coalition Model of agenda building. However, their dialogue does not play to an empty theater. The actors seek approbation from the public audience, which in turn is affected by what transpires on the stage.

Although the audience has no direct influence over the events that unfold before their eyes, they certainly are kept in mind by the script writers.

Further, the stage is set by a host of contextual factors, which the actors also help to arrange. The timing of the public showing is crucial for determining the effect it has on various audiences. We have found that conditions are more ripe for reform in certain eras, and for certain problems, than for others. In the 1980s, the climate in the country changed. The spirit of reform that so clearly pervaded the Progressive period and the Watergate era began to abate.

At the same time, the willingness of the journalism profession to commit resources necessary for investigative reporting was tempered by corporate ownership of the media, by court decisions, and perhaps by a sense of growing public inurement to exposés. The trend instead has been toward less confrontational and more reader-friendly journalism. This trend was be-

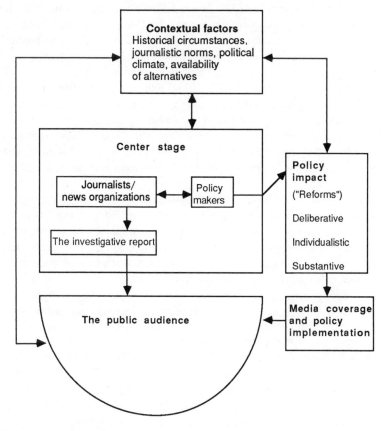

Figure 2. The Coalition Model of investigative reporting.

moaned in a March 1990 speech to the National Press Foundation by Norman Pearlstine, managing editor of the *Wall Street Journal*. Pearlstine expressed "some very real concerns" about the declining willingness of the press to do "the difficult investigative story." Such a story, he said,

> Really tries to take on major institutions, major organizations, important people in our society . . . and to expose them as thieves when it is appropriate. . . . It is very different from the kind of service journalism that all of us are engaging more in. It's not about being reader friendly. It's not about how many items you can get into a paper to appeal to as many people as possible. . . . I do question whether the kinds of large companies that are publicly held will be able to commit themselves (in the 1990s) to the kind of journalism I am talking about.

"But," he concluded, "(investigative reporting) is really fundamental to the republic and really fundamental to journalism."[34]

The *Journal's* managing editor is not the only one in recent times to fret about the future of muckraking journalism. In 1984, *Editor and Publisher* magazine reported the "death" of investigative reporting.[35] This prognostication proved to be unnecessarily gloomy. Still, cutbacks in local television "I teams" and in newspaper investigative units have been widely publicized.[36]

Our surveys of investigative reporters and editors in 1986 and 1989 suggest that investigative reporting retains a core strength, although it may be shifting directions.[37] Both surveys show that most muckrakers continue to spend as much time on investigative reporting as in the past. However, there is a trend toward doing more short-term investigative stories. This might well lead to a decline in the lengthy project stories that have been the focus of this book.

Investigative reporters also may be becoming less of an elite breed of journalist. The success of Investigative Reporters and Editors' workshops for different kinds of journalists suggests that the techniques of investigative reporting are being adapted by the professional mainstream. Thus, although separate investigative units have been disbanded, investigative practices have become more widespread. As we concluded in 1986:

> the IRE survey findings point to the institutionalization of investigative reporting. Rather than bordering on extinction, investigative journalists have merely become less visible as their efforts become more conventional. Today's muckrakers may be more akin to inveterate watchdogs than starving wolves.[38]

These apparent trends in investigative reporting may seem somewhat contradictory. However, they have certain common elements that have significant implications for future governing practices. The decline in resources for investigative reporting, especially long-term projects, probably will mean an increase in collaboration among journalists and policy makers. Journalists will more readily seek out policy partners because they will need information more quickly, and because they will not be given the time to follow up their stories to ensure impact. Similarly, the use of investigative techniques by beat reporters, for whom transactions with officials are already routine, will further facilitate Coalition journalism.

For policy makers, these trends will provide additional opportunities for image and agenda building. The institutionalization of investigative reporting creates increased potential to draw the media spotlight to their problem-solving activities. Policy makers will be able to decrease their reliance on a handful of reporters—some of whom see themselves as adversaries of officialdom—and broaden their capacity to achieve results through a diffusion of partnerships.

The implications of these developments for public policy making are significant. The expansion of the media-policy connection means journalists will play a greater direct role in helping set public policy agendas. The actual content of stories may become even less important for policy making than the kinds of alliances that form between journalists and officials.

Second, the long-term policy impact of investigative reporting may be circumscribed by the declining commitment to crusade. Media muckrakers may be able to continue to set the deliberative agenda of policy makers. However, as they move fleetingly from one story to another, the action agenda—the substance of reform—will remain under the control of established policy-making interests.

Finally, present trends suggest the general public will play even less of an active policy-making role. American popular democracy has been victimized by twentieth-century developments in media and society. Scholarly analyses have described the American people as the "phantom public," the "captive public," the "semi-sovereign people," and the "bystander public."[39] Our media age has produced, in one scholar's words, a "democracy without citizens."[40] "Manufacturing consent" is what others have called it.[41]

There is every reason to conclude that present trends in investigative reporting will exacerbate this problem in the future. Muckraker–policy-maker transactions will continue to bypass the public in the resolution of important public issues. Even where such issues are not resolved, the public will be led to *believe* they have been resolved by viewing or reading the reaction stories of reporters. Public outrage about important social problems may not have been manifested for some time; in contemporary times, outrage may prove to be irrelevant even where it does surface.

These trends are not immutable. The historical pendulum may swing back to an era of reform at some future juncture. We have concluded that conditions will be ripe for such an era when public alienation toward authority recurs, and at the same time changes in media engender fierce competition for stories about moral disorder. If and when this does happen, conventional notions about popular democracy may once again become relevant. Until that time, investigative reporting will continue to be a catalyst for policy reform without necessarily being a vehicle for mass public mobilization or enlightenment.

NOTES

1. Several texts have viewed this trait to be integral to the definition of investigative reporting. See Clark R. Mollenhoff, *Investigative Reporting* (New York: Macmillan, 1981), p. v; David Anderson and Peter Benjaminson, *Investigative Reporting* (Bloomington: University of Indiana Press, 1976), p. 5; Investigative Reporters and Editors, *The Reporter's Handbook* (New York: St. Martin's Press, 1983), pp. vii–viii.

2. See Ralph Whitehead, Jr., "Toe-to-toe in the Windy City," *Columbia Journalism Review* (March/April 1982), pp. 34–42.

3. For different explorations of the meaning of "newsworthiness," see Herbert J. Gans, *Deciding What's News* (New York: Vintage Books, 1979); Gaye Tuchman, *Making News* (New York: Free Press, 1978); Mark Fishman, *Manufacturing the News* (Austin: University of Texas Press, 1980); Edward Epstein, *News from Nowhere* (New York: Random House, 1973).

4. This observation is made especially by Bernard Roshco, *Newsmaking* (Chicago: University of Chicago Press, 1975), p. 50.

5. Gans, *Deciding What's News*, p. 80.

6. This concept was developed and applied in a somewhat different context by Fay Lomax Cook, "Crime and the Elderly: The Emergence of a Policy Issue," in Dan A. Lewis (ed.), *Reactions to Crime* (Beverly Hills: Sage, 1981).

7. Roger W. Cobb and Charles D. Elder, *Participation in American Politics: The Dynamics of Agenda-Building* (New York: Johns Hopkins University Press, 1983), p. 188.

8. Even in this case, the *Inquirer* reporter told us he ultimately dropped the story because he was "reluctant to crusade." Interview with Matthew Purdy by Jack Doppelt, March, 1990. However, in the origins of the international child abductions probe, WBBM reporter Scott Smith was an exception to this rule, as described in chapter 7.

9. See Timothy Crouse, *The Boys on the Bus* (New York: Ballantine, 1976). It also has been called the "jackal syndrome." See J. Herbert Altschull, "The Journalist and Instant History: An Example of the Jackal Syndrome," *Journalism Quarterly*, 54 (Fall 1977), pp. 389–396.

10. This concept is derived from Mark Fishman, "Crime Waves as Ideology," *Social Problems*, 25 (June 1978), pp. 531–543.

11. See Gladys Lang and Kurt Lang, *The Battle for Public Opinion* (New

York: Columbia University Press, 1983); J. P. Winter and C. H. Eyal, "Agenda Setting for Civil Rights Issue," *Public Opinion Quarterly*, 45 (1981), pp. 376–383.

12. Charles D. Elder and Roger W. Cobb, "Agenda-Building and the Politics of Aging," *Policy Studies Journal*, 13 (1984), p. 115. Borrowing from Lang and Lang, ibid., pp. 58–61, we use the term "policy agenda building" to refer to an evolving, interactive process among many actors as opposed to a one-directional influence of media on policy making. We are primarily concerned here with the effects of those interactions on the "formal" agendas of government policy makers, and secondarily with the influence on the "public" agendas of citizens. This distinction is drawn by Anthony Downs, "Up and Down with Ecology—The 'Issue-Attention Cycle,' " *The Public Interest*, 28 (Summer 1972), pp. 38–50.

13. For an example of this phenomenon, see Fay L. Cook and Wesley G. Skogan, "Agenda-Setting: Convergent and Divergent Voice Models and Rise and Fall of Policy Issues," in Maxwell E. McCombs and David L. Protess (eds.), *Agenda-Setting: Readings in Media, Public Opinion and Policymaking* (Hillsdale, NJ: Lawrence Erlbaum, 1991).

14. As we discussed in chapter 2, the regulatory reforms of the early 1900s provided a partial solution to the problems revealed by muckraking journalists. However, these "reforms" created an array of unanticipated problems. See Richard Hofstadter, *The Age of Reform* (New York: Knopf, 1955). Ironically, as our case studies show, new muckrakers often spotlight failures of the regulatory system that was created partly in response to problems revealed by old muckrakers.

15. See E. Rogers and J. Dearing, "Agenda-Setting Research: Where Has It Been Where Is It Going?" in J. Anderson (ed.), *Communication Yearbook 11* (Newbury Park, CA: Sage, 1988), pp. 555–594.

16. Barbara J. Nelson, *Making an Issue of Child Abuse* (Chicago: University of Chicago Press, 1984).

17. Cook and Skogan, "Agenda Setting."

18. See Roger W. Cobb and Charles D. Elder, "Communications and Public Policy," in Dan Nimmo and Keith Sanders (eds.), *Handbook of Political Communications* (Beverly Hills: Sage, 1981); and Roger Cobb, Jennie-Keith Ross, and Marc Howard Ross, "Agenda-Building as a Comparative Political Process," *American Political Science Review*, 70 (March 1976) p. 127.

19. Cook and Skogan, "Agenda Setting," p. 2.

20. John W. Kingdon, *Agendas, Alternatives, and Public Policies* (Boston: Little, Brown and Company, 1984). Kingdon's theory in turn draws from Michael Cohen, James March, and Johan Olsen, "A Garbage Can Model of Organizational Choice," *Administrative Science Quarterly*, 17 (March 1972), pp. 1–25.

21. For example, social science research about the seriousness of child abuse was found both to facilitate media coverage of that problem and enhance its status on policy makers' agendas. See Nelson, *Making an Issue of Child Abuse*.

22. The lack of credible evidence that the elderly were a high-risk crime population contributed significantly to the decline of that issue on policy makers' agendas. See Cook and Skogan, "Agenda Setting."

23. Kingdon, *Agendas, Alternatives, and Public Policies*, p. 150.

24. For discussions of the role of elections in agenda building and public policy making, see Anthony Downs, *An Economic Theory of Democracy* (New York: Harper & Row, 1957); Benjamin Ginsberg, "Elections and Public Policy," *American Political Science Review*, 70 (March 1976), pp. 41–49; Barbara Deckard Sinclair, "Party Realignment and the Transformation of the Political Agenda," *American Political Science Review*, 71 (September 1977), pp. 940–953.

25. Kingdon, *Agendas, Alternatives, and Public Policies*, pp. 153–160.

26. See Harold A. Lasswell, *Democracy Through Public Opinion* (Menasha, WI: Banta, 1941); Robert A. Dahl, *A Preface to Democratic Theory* (Chicago: University of Chicago Press, 1956); Benjamin I. Page and Robert Y. Shapiro, "Effects of Public Opinion on Policy," *American Political Science Review*, 77 (1983), p. 175.

27. See Grant McConnell, *Private Power and American Democracy* (New York: Knopf, 1967); E. E. Schattschneider, *The Semi-Sovereign People* (New York: Holt, Rinehart and Winston, 1960); John W. Kingdon, *Congressmen's Voting Decisions* (New York: Harper & Row, 1981).

28. Harvey D. Molotch, David L. Protess, and Margaret T. Gordon, "The Media-Policy Connection: Ecologies of News," in David Paletz (ed.), *Political Communication: Theories, Cases and Assessments* (Norwood, NJ: Ablex, 1987).

29. Kingdon, *Agendas, Alternatives, and Public Policies*, p. 52.

30. Martin Linsky, *Impact: How the Press Affects Federal Policymaking* (New York: W. W. Norton, 1986), p. 90.

31. For discussions of the news media's displacement of political parties as vehicles for linking politicians with constituencies, see Thomas E. Patterson, *The Mass Media Election* (New York: Praeger, 1980); David Broder, *The Party's Over* (New York, Harper & Row, 1972); and Robert M. Entman, *Democracy Without Citizens* (New York: Oxford, 1989).

32. Kingdon, *Agendas, Alternatives, and Public Policies*, p. 153.

33. The advertisement appeared in print media across the country. *Wednesday Journal* (October 4, 1989), B-15.

34. Speech by Norman Pearlstine to the National Press Foundation Annual Awards Dinner, March 2, 1990.

35. *Editor and Publisher*, "Is Investigative Reporting Dead?" August 25, 1984.

36. For example, see William K. Marimow, "Who Silenced the I-Team," *Philadelphia Inquirer Magazine* (April 14, 1985), pp. 22–30; Jonathan Friendly, "Investigative Journalism Is Changing Some of Its Goals and Softening Tone," *New York Times* (August 23, 1983), p. 8; Michael O'Neill, "The Ebbing of the 'Great Investigative Wave,'" *ASNE Bulletin* (September 1983), p. 26.

37. David L. Protess, "Investigative Reporters: Endangered Species?" *The Investigative Reporters and Editors Journal* (Winter 1976); also see appendix II.

38. Ibid.

39. See Walter Lippmann, *The Phantom Public* (New York: Harcourt, Brace, 1925); Benjamin Ginsberg, *The Captive Public* (New York; Basic Books, 1986); and E. E. Schattschneider, *The Semi-Sovereign People* (New York: Holt, Rinehart and

Winston, 1960). Lang and Lang, *The Battle for Public Opinion,* refer to the "bystander public," pp. 10–25.

40. This is the title of the book by Robert M. Entman (1989).

41. Edward S. Herman and Noam Chomsky, *Manufacturing Consent: The Political Economy of the Mass Media* (New York: Pantheon, 1988).

APPENDIXES

APPENDIXES

APPENDIX I

Methodological Discussion

This appendix presents an overview of the research methods employed in the six case studies (chapters 3–8). The following discussion assumes a knowledge of the fundamentals of experimental and quasi-experimental research designs. Readers may want to consult references such as Campbell and Stanley[1] and Cook and Campbell[2] for extended discussions of experimental and quasi-experimental design.

Preceding chapters have detailed the findings of the case studies and have offered a framework for understanding the impact of investigative journalism. The aim of this appendix is to describe in more detail the methods through which data on public and elite impacts of investigative stories were gathered and analyzed. We pay particular attention to the quantitative evidence of impact and consider alternative methodological explanations for the findings.

BASIC DESIGN

Public Impact

Each of the six case studies involved a quasi-experiment in which the investigative report in question served as the stimulus. Both pre- and poststimulus measurements were made on a probability sample of adults in the geographic region in which the investigative report was publicized. In each study, one part of the sample was designated as the "treatment" or "exposed" group, and the remainder of the sample constituted the "control" or "comparison" group. The various studies differed in the way respondents were assigned to the treatment or control conditions (see Exposure Measurement below). The multiple-wave (pretest–posttest) sample sizes for the studies ranged from 190 for the "Rape" investigation to 690 for the "60 Minutes" study. All of the interviews were conducted by telephone, and sampling was done either through random digit dialing or through the use of telephone directories for "seed" numbers, and replacement of the last digit in sampled numbers.[3]

Elite Impact

In addition to the public sample, most of the case studies made an assessment of the impact of the investigative report on a sample of policy-making elites—public officials, members of interest groups, etc. The first four studies involved a quantitative pretest–posttest measurement of effect, and the last two utilized only qualitative posttreatment interviews. The elite interviews in the first case study were conducted in person. Thereafter, interviews were conducted by telephone; the elite samples for most of the studies ranged in size from approximately 30 to 50.

Process and Policy Analysis

The investigative reporting process was also monitored in each case study. Some of the cases involved participant observation of reporters and editors at work, and others involved intensive interviews with media professionals (see "Introduction to the Case Studies" and chapters 3–8 for details). Most of the cases also involved postinvestigation content analysis to locate stories in various media that were related to the original report. Finally, all of the case studies examined the policy impact of the investigative reports, tracing legislation, legislative hearings, executive actions, and the like that followed publication of the reports.

ASSESSMENT OF IMPACT: METHODOLOGICAL CONSIDERATIONS

Causal Inference and Generalization

The quasi-experimental approach taken in these studies, although by no means unique, is comparatively unusual in the literature on mass media effects. Many mass media effects research studies are laboratory based, wherein sorting out matters of cause and effect is facilitated by the ability to randomize subjects to conditions, maximize exposure potential while controlling other influences, and measure change in dependent variables. The ability to discern cause and effect in the laboratory is offset by the disadvantage that study findings may not generalize beyond the laboratory setting.

Effects research outside the laboratory is largely correlational, based on one-time sample surveys. The findings of such investigations are more generalizable than those generated in the artificial laboratory environment. However, the inference of media causality is always tempered by the fact that change is not actually measured and exposure is not controlled and is confounded with factors related to self-selection. Thus, in correlational studies, we are never sure whether the relationships observed are indicative of media effects or of respondents' predispositions, or both. Inferences about media effects typically are drawn by assessing the relationship between exposure and the dependent variable while statistically controlling for factors related to self-selection (education, gender, race, and so forth). In other words, there is often some attempt—through a "selection model"—to adjust for the fact that people reporting exposure to the media stimulus are different from people who report no or less exposure.

Quasi-experiments like the case studies in this volume are hybrids of the laboratory and survey approaches. A measure of "laboratory-like" control is sought through measurements taken over time (rather than in a single cross-section survey) and, to the extent possible, through assignment to treatment and control conditions. At the same time, the quasi-experiments described here were conducted in very "real-world" contexts, involving stimuli produced by media practitioners and audiences constructed of probability samples of adults. The context of discovery is not the artificial laboratory environment but the more "natural" conditions permitted by survey investigation. The goal of the resulting quasi-experiments is to capture some of the benefits of the two types of research approaches—the laboratory's advantage in establishing cause and effect and the survey's value in generalizing the findings.

Exposure Measurement I: Request to View

The difference between "quasi-" and "true" experiments is that in the latter researchers randomly assign people to experimental conditions (treatment and control groups). The ability to randomize is important, since it allows researchers to isolate the effect of the treatment from the myriad of other factors that might produce change in the dependent variable. Without randomization—giving subjects an equal chance of being assigned to treatment or control group—the individual effect of the treatment (in our case, an investigative report) is confounded with the characteristics of people who are exposed to it. The *internal validity* of the experiment is threatened by the fact that we are not sure whether the treatment caused any observed change or whether the people exposed to the treatment have special characteristics that produced or influenced the observed change. In the ideal case, we want those exposed to the investigative report and those not exposed to it to be the *same kinds* of people across a broad range of characteristics. Randomization allows us to achieve that desired state.

But most "real-world" media effects research contexts do not allow us to randomize. Researchers have no control over whether people decide to be exposed to the media content under study, and it is reasonable to assume that those who choose to be exposed are different from those who choose otherwise. The case studies reported in this volume took different approaches to dealing with this issue.

The first study, "Home Health Hustle," attempted random assignment. At the pretest interview, respondents were requested either to watch the program containing the investigative report or to view a control program. Laboratory experiments do not normally involve actively requesting respondents to participate in experimental conditions, since investigators have control of the treatment stimulus. But, with no such control possible for the "NBC Newsmagazine" program, investigators in the "Home Health" study had to ask respondents to watch the program of interest or a control program, in order to randomly assign them. Subsequent case studies did not attempt random assignment. Rather, researchers identified treatment and control groups by obtaining self-reports of *regular exposure* to the media "vehicle" (e.g., *Chicago Sun-Times* readers and nonreaders) or retrospective self-reports of exposure to the content of particular interest in the study (e.g., viewers or nonviewers of a particular "60 Minutes" segment). In these investigations, respondents who reported exposure in one of these ways constituted the treatment group, and the remainder served as the control.

The tradeoffs between the "Home Health" and other case study designs are instructive. It is unusual to be asked to watch a particular television program, as respondents were prior to the airing of the "NBC Newsmagazine" that contained "Home Health Hustle." Requested viewing sets up conditions for watching that are unlike normal circumstances—people who cooperate may view more conscientiously than they otherwise would. In other words, requested viewing is likely to increase the impact of the investigative report being studied because those who promise to view it in advance are likely to pay more attention to it than viewers who just happen to watch. The assignment strategy used with the "Home Health" program trades off the ability to generalize about "normal" viewing (reading, listening) in favor of a more careful look at possible media effects. The "Home Health Hustle" study—the first in the series of case studies reported here—is the most like a classic laboratory experiment of any of the investigations. It attempted to randomize respondents to conditions and to control exposure to the stimulus through request to view. This study featured the strongest agenda-setting findings of the six, at least in part because of its more "laboratory-like" approach.

Though it achieved the most control over exposure of any of the six case studies, the "Home Health" study did not achieve complete control. About half of those recruited to view the "NBC Newsmagazine" or the control program did not follow through with the commitment to do so. Because there was self-selection among the eventual viewers of the program, it was necessary to compare the magnitude of the effects of the program for the *originally assigned* respondents to the size of the effects for those who *actually watched*.

Analysis of the first set of effects speaks to impact on an audience with less selection bias but some misclassification of viewing, whereas analysis of the second set of effects addresses the impact on a group in which viewing is more validly measured but self-selection exists. The more similar the pattern of findings in the two analyses, the stronger the case will be for effects of the investigative report. Indeed, both analyses showed evidence of a treatment effect, though it was somewhat larger for the self-selected audience (see table 3.1).

The requested viewing case produced the strongest evidence for agenda-setting effects of any of the five case studies whether exposure was defined by random assignment or by reported viewing. Although it is impossible to prove that the request to view played a major role in the strength of the findings in the "Home Health" study, we are inclined to believe that the procedure did contribute to the effects observed.

Exposure Measurement II: "Regular Audience" versus "Stimulus Aware"

The other studies in the series did not attempt to randomize respondents or otherwise control exposure to the investigative reports under study. These case studies traded the opportunity for enhanced scrutiny of media effects for the ability to address more "normal" exposure circumstances. This tradeoff between *internal* and *external* validity was deliberate, as there was a desire to observe agenda-setting effects, if any, outside the recruitment-to-view context.

In addition, there were other factors that argued against attempted randomization through recruitment in the subsequent case studies. First, the sorts of stimuli under investigation differed from the "Home Health" case. With the exception of the "60 Minutes" study, all of the other inquiries involved investigative *series*. Asking respondents to watch or read a *number* of newscasts or several newspaper editions, rather than just one, is a much less achievable goal. (As noted above, even in the "Home Health" study only about one-half of the respondents actually viewed their assigned program, and the desired random assignment was not achieved in practice.)

Second, whereas "Home Health Hustle" and "Missing?" were lengthy stories in three-story television newsmagazine formats, the subsequent investigative series were contained in local half-hour newscasts or in newspapers that, obviously, had many other stories. One could not be sure in asking respondents to view or read that they would be exposed to the right story unless they were directed to it in advance. This procedure would have produced an even more unusual exposure condition than in the "Home Health" study, and certainly a more unusual exposure condition than desirable. Finally, the cost of screening respondents in the hopes of arriving at a large enough number who agreed to view or read the target media vehicles was prohibitive in the other five case studies.

In these subsequent studies, pretest interviews were taken with a sample of adults, including both "regular" viewers or readers of the media vehicle that would contain the investigative report and infrequent or nonviewers or readers. Respondents were questioned as to their usual exposure to the media vehicle under study during these pretest contacts. After publication of the investigative report, posttest interviews were taken to measure agenda-setting changes. At the end of the posttest interviews, respondents were asked if they had been exposed specifically to the investigative report in question (i.e., if they were "stimulus aware").

Both the "regular viewer/reader" and the "stimulus-aware" definitions of exposure were used in analyses to define the treatment group for the five quasi-experiments that followed the "Home Health" study. Although randomized recruitment was not attempted in any of these later case studies, the template for analyzing story impact in a number of them was similar to that in the "Home Health" study. The effects of investigative reports on a more general, representative audience ("regular" readers/ viewers) were compared with effects on a more narrow, self-selected "stimulus-aware" audience. Again, the more similar the effects were on the differently defined exposure groups, the stronger was the case for effects of the investigative report.

Chapters 4–6 and tables 4.1, 5.1, and 6.1 offer evidence that, by and large, the effects of the investigative reports on the general public samples in the "Rape," "Police Brutality," and "Toxic Waste" cases were not strong by "interocular test" regardless of how exposure was measured. The strongest impacts of the three—the "Police Brutality" case described in chapter 5—suggest slightly more impact for the "series-aware" group than for the "regular viewer" group. That is, like the self-reported audience for the "Home Health Hustle," the self-selected program audience for the "Police Brutality" series showed slightly higher impact than the "regular" audience for that television news program. Chapters 7 and 8 do not directly compare the "regular viewer/reader" and "stimulus-aware" definitions of exposure. Instead, they merely compare "stimulus aware" with all other respondents. For example, in the "60 Minutes" case, table 8.1 shows effects for 96 individuals who remembered seeing the "Missing?" segment of the program versus a markedly larger group who did not recall exposure. Chapter 8 notes that the impact of the *Philadelphia Inquirer* series was strongest for those who reported exposure to *all* of the articles.

Although none of the agenda-setting effects is strong in the case studies of chapters 4–8, the evidence of impact that we have suggests that they are stronger when the audience is defined as the group in more deliberate contact with the investigative report. This pattern follows the precedent in the first case study, where respondents who reported actually viewing "Home Health Hustle" evidenced somewhat greater impact than the randomly assigned group.

Selection Models

As noted above in the section on "causal inference and generalization," self-selected exposure appears to play a role in the effects of the various investigative reports. Therefore, we must find a way to distinguish between the effects of the reports themselves and the contribution of viewers'/readers' characteristics on changes in the dependent variables. The various case studies approached this common problem in different ways. In the "Home Health" study, an analysis of covariance controlling for respondents' demographic characteristics was used to test for program effects. In the other case studies, the demographic profiles of exposed and nonexposed respondents were compared to check for differences.

In most of the case studies, the self-selection hypothesis was not strong because the agenda-setting differences observed between exposed and nonexposed groups were small. In the "Home Health" study, where observed agenda-setting effects were strong, and where there were demographic differences between the exposed and nonexposed groups, the multivariate model showed that the investigative report effects held up when controls for demographic factors were introduced.

Dependent Variables

Thus far we have examined issues of quasi-experimental design and exposure measurement that play a role in internal and external validity of the case studies. Now we want to turn to the way in which agenda setting and other sorts of effects of the investigative reports were measured.

Agenda-setting effects typically are assessed by asking people to give judgments on the importance of public problems. Following the aphorism that serves as the "theoretical framework" for agenda-setting research—that the media are less successful in telling people what to *think* than in telling them what to think *about*[4]— respondents in agenda-setting studies are asked to nominate issues or problems that they think are important or to rate the importance of problems supplied by the investigator. The importance or salience judgment is distinguished from an attitudinal change; knowledge of an issue is not the same as taking a position on it.

Measurement of effects of the various investigative reports in this volume included the usual "importance-rating" approach but went somewhat beyond it. Each case study examined possible cognitive and attitudinal effects of the investigative reports in addition to seeing if respondents rated the problem portrayed in the reports as more important after exposure. The cognitive effects examined were beliefs that might have been engendered by the reports (e.g., whether rapes were more common in Chicago suburbs than in the city, or whether Norway has respect for U.S. law). The attitudinal items focused on policy preferences and evaluations, such as whether respondents favored more spending on home health care or whether they thought that the Chicago Fire Department was doing a good job. As noted in chapters 3–8 and the accompanying tables, sometimes changes were observed in agenda-setting items and sometimes in the other kinds of dependent variables.

The measures tapping hypothesized effects of the investigative stories in each case study were embedded in a series of "irrelevant" items. For example, there might be items about the importance of the problem of "drug abuse" or "welfare fraud" in the questionnaire measuring the impact of an investigative report on police brutality. This strategy was a further control on the internal validity of the quasi-experiments. If it could be shown that changes occurred in items related to the investigative reports and not in irrelevant items, the possibility of pretest sensitization would be discounted, and the inference that exposure to the reports produced the changes would be further supported.

REFLECTIONS ON NULL FINDINGS

Measurement of "irrelevant" items, along with the other tactics employed in the case studies to increase or measure internal validity—e.g., recruitment-to-view, selection models—were employed to give more confidence in judgments that the investigative reports themselves produced observed changes in dependent variables of interest. But an overview of the case studies finds that, in most instances, there were few changes in the dependent measures. This observation leads us to consider whether there might be methodological explanations for the null findings. (We have already offered other explanations, involving the nature of the investigative reports themselves, elsewhere in this volume).

Limited Knowledge

Although foreknowledge of the investigative reports examined here was a necessary condition for studying their impact, the extent and nature of that knowledge varied from study to study. In no instance did we know precisely what the forthcoming investigative report would say; rather, we had story approximations of divergent quality. Assumptions had to be made about the thrust of the stories to conceptualize the dependent variables and write questions. The published investigative stories invariably had somewhat different foci than we anticipated. Thus, although the resulting questionnaires were never totally irrelevant to the final investigative reports, the questionnaire focus was sometimes different enough that change in dependent variables in response to exposure to the investigative report could be seen, in retrospect, to be limited.

For example, as noted in chapter 7, the "60 Minutes" story entitled "Missing?" was not so much about the problem of missing children as about international law. The questions framed from a story outline for the segment focused on the problem of "missing children," and no change was observed in the agenda-setting dependent variable. Each of the case studies encountered similar problems; to one degree or another, measurement of effects of investigative reports was affected. Our experience may serve as a lesson to those who contemplate such "real world" investigations.

Another factor that may have contributed to null findings in some of the case studies was the sensitivity of the scales used in measuring the dependent variables. The questionnaires featured Likert-type items with four scale points (e.g., "very important," "somewhat important," "somewhat unimportant," "not important at all"). Pretest mean scores for items like this in some of the case studies were near the top of the four-point scale. Thus, a "ceiling effect" may have attenuated the change in some dependent variables from pretest to posttest.

Though limited knowledge of the final form of the investigative reports and lack of sensitivity in the measurement of change may have contributed to null findings in some of the case studies, the major methodological factor differentiating the measurement of effects of the investigative reports appears to be request to view. None of the case studies following the "Home Health" investigation employed this technique for exposure manipulation, and none turned up public-level effects of the magnitude found in that study. This is not to say that requested viewing was the only, or even the main, reason for the strength of the "Home Health" effects, but of the methodological factors we have considered, it appears to offer the strongest alternative explanation.

ASSESSMENT OF IMPACT ON ELITES

Each case study involved some measurement of the reaction of policy-making elites to the investigative report. In the first five case studies (chapters 3–7), the impact of the reports was gauged through pretest and posttest interviews. Samples of 30 to 50 elites were interviewed with questionnaires much like those used for the general public samples except that, in addition to their own rating of issue importance, the elites were asked to estimate the importance of issues to the public as well. The last case study gleaned elite responses from qualitative interviews with elites after publication of the investigative series.

Elites in these studies included policy makers (legislators and personnel in government agencies) and members of interest groups. The first case study compared responses of the two types of elites (see tables 3.2–3.4); the other studies examined the elite group as a whole, if quantitative analyses were performed (tables 4.2, 5.2, and 6.2).

Depending on whether elites reported exposure to the investigative report, we labeled them as fitting into the "treatment" and "control" groups, like the general public samples in the case studies of chapters 4–8. The percentage of "exposed" and "nonexposed" elites varied considerably from study to study, ranging from an approximately equal split in the "Home Health" investigation to all elites reporting exposure in the "Rape" study.

In the "Home Health" study—the only one to compare "interest group" and "governmental" elites—the governmental elites showed more change from pretest to posttest in both their personal views and their views of the public's perceptions. The other case studies showed less overall impact of the investigative reports and more concentration of impact in the personal views of elites rather than in their views of public perceptions.

SUMMARY

We have reviewed study design, data collection, and analytic approaches in the six case studies presented in this volume. On the whole, the research reflects a good deal of care in trying to isolate the impact of investigative reporting on agenda setting and other dependent variables. We have reviewed the effect of requested viewing and the difference between that type of experimental manipulation and the approach in the other case studies. The lesson is that field experimental research presents a set of difficult tradeoffs and that there is no one "right" way to approach the work.

That there was not one homogeneous approach in these case studies is a reflection of the fact that the investigative reports examined here each had unique qualities and that the researchers involved varied from case study to case study. Although there was a basic design template, the interests of researchers and the external constraints of time and money molded each case study into a unique product.

Finally, though the studies were unique, the accumulation of evidence from them does support a central premise of the book: general public agenda-setting changes are not a necessary condition for investigative reporting to affect public policy. The five "naturalistic" case studies (that did not involve recruitment to view) serve to replicate the overall lack of impact of the investigative reports on the general public. Coupled with public policy analyses that noted governmental response or collusion on the part of journalists and government officials in the process of investigative reporting, these data provide a powerful refutation of the Mobilization Model.

NOTES

1. Donald T. Campbell and Julian C. Stanley, Experimental and Quasi-Experimental Designs for Research (Chicago: Rand McNally, 1963).

2. T. D. Cook and Donald T. Campbell, Quasi-Experimentation: Design and Analysis Issues for Field Settings (Boston: Houghton Mifflin, 1979).

3. Refusal rates for the studies averaged approximately 30 percent.

4. B. C. Cohen, The Press and Foreign Policy (Princeton, NJ: Princeton University Press, 1963).

National Survey of Investigative Reporters and Editors

This appendix isolates the relevant results from the surveys conducted in 1989 with 927 investigative reporters and editors.[1]

1. Are you an investigative reporter, an editor, or do you have some other connection with investigative reporting and editing?

	Number	Percentage
Investigative reporter	471	51.8%
Editor	224	24.6%
Staff writer or beat reporter	109	12.0%
Management	48	5.3%
Other	58	6.3%
Total	910	100.0%

2. How long have you been an investigative reporter or editor?

	Number	Percentage
Less than a year	14	1.5%
1–4 years	298	32.2%
5–9 years	313	33.9%
10–19 years	241	26.0%
20 years or more	59	6.4%
Total	925	100.0%

(median = 6–7 years)

3. In your career as an investigative reporter or editor, have you worked for a newspaper, magazine, or broadcast operation, or in both print and broadcast organizations?

	Number	Percentage
Exclusively newspaper	603	67.2%
Exclusively magazine or periodical	57	6.4%
Exclusively broadcast	120	13.4%
Both print and broadcast	113	12.6%
Other	4	0.4%
Total	897	100.0%

4. What is the size of the market in which you currently work?

	Number	Percentage
Under 10,000	23	2.5%
10,000 to under 100,000	178	19.7%
100,000 to under 500,000	239	26.4%
500,000 to under 1 million	148	16.3%
One million or over	318	35.1%
Total	906	100.0%

5. Thinking about *your* work in the past year, tell us whether each of the following has increased significantly, increased somewhat, decreased somewhat, decreased significantly, or remained the same.

   a. Time *you* spent on investigative projects compared to other forms of journalism.

	Number	Percentage
Increased significantly	138	15.3%
Increased somewhat	280	31.2%
Decreased somewhat	156	17.4%
Decreased significantly	99	11.0%
Remained the same	225	25.1%
Total	898	100.0%

   b. Number of reporters and researchers assigned to work on investigative projects at your news organization.

	Number	Percentage
Increased significantly	65	7.5%
Increased somewhat	254	29.2%
Decreased somewhat	104	11.9%
Decreased significantly	88	10.1%
Remained the same	360	41.3%
Total	871	100.0%

c. Number of investigative projects you worked on that took *longer* than three months to prepare.

	Number	Percentage
Increased significantly	67	7.9%
Increased somewhat	151	17.9%
Decreased somewhat	69	8.2%
Decreased significantly	123	14.6%
Remained the same	433	51.4%
Total	843	100.0%

d. Number of investigative projects you worked on that took *less* than three months to prepare.

	Number	Percentage
Increased significantly	84	9.6%
Increased somewhat	319	36.4%
Decreased somewhat	100	11.4%
Decreased significantly	54	6.1%
Remained the same	320	36.5%
Total	877	100.0%

e. Number of investigative projects you worked on that focused primarily on *governmental* wrongdoing.

	Number	Percentage
Increased significantly	73	8.5%
Increased somewhat	225	26.2%
Decreased somewhat	68	7.9%
Decreased significantly	47	5.5%
Remained the same	446	51.9%
Total	859	100.0%

f. Number of investigative projects you worked on that focused primarily on wrongdoing in the *private* sector.

	Number	Percentage
Increased significantly	57	6.5%
Increased somewhat	222	25.5%
Decreased somewhat	87	10.0%
Decreased significantly	60	6.9%
Remained the same	446	51.1%
Total	872	100.0%

g. Number of investigative projects you worked on that focused equally on both
    governmental and private sectors.

	Number	Percentage
Increased significantly	25	3.1%
Increased somewhat	116	14.2%
Decreased somewhat	45	5.5%
Decreased significantly	36	4.4%
Remained the same	594	72.8%
Total	816	100.0%

h. Number of times that ethical problems arose in the course of an investigative
    project.

	Number	Percentage
Increased significantly	62	7.2%
Increased somewhat	261	30.1%
Decreased somewhat	37	4.3%
Decreased significantly	16	1.8%
Remained the same	491	56.6%
Total	867	100.0%

i. Amount of contact you had with your news organization's attorney.

	Number	Percentage
Increased significantly	128	14.9%
Increased somewhat	239	27.8%
Decreased somewhat	58	6.7%
Decreased significantly	50	5.8%
Remained the same	385	44.8%
Total	860	100.0%

6. Thinking back over the stories you have worked on in the last year or so, how
    often have you contacted government policy makers for each of the following
    reasons?

    a. To get background information for the story.

	Number	Percentage
Very frequently	512	57.7%
Somewhat frequently	284	32.0%
Somewhat infrequently	59	6.6%
Very infrequently	33	3.7%
Total	888	100.0%

b. To get public records that might be useful in preparing the story.

	Number	Percentage
Very frequently	486	54.7%
Somewhat frequently	289	32.6%
Somewhat infrequently	80	9.0%
Very infrequently	33	3.7%
Total	888	100.0%

c. To get authoritative statements or quotes about the problems revealed by the study.

	Number	Percentage
Very frequently	523	59.0%
Somewhat frequently	270	30.5%
Somewhat infrequently	73	8.2%
Very infrequently	20	2.3%
Total	886	100.0%

d. To discuss policy reforms that might result from publication of the story.

	Number	Percentage
Very frequently	207	23.6%
Somewhat frequently	228	26.0%
Somewhat infrequently	185	21.1%
Very infrequently	257	29.3%
Total	877	100.0%

7. Has an investigative piece of yours been submitted for any journalism prizes or awards in the past year?

	Number	Percentage
Yes	529	59.1%
No	366	40.9%
Total	895	100.0%

8. Did you win?

	Number	Percentage
Yes	250	47.4%
No	277	52.6%
Total	527	100.0%

9. In your view, how important is the "impact" of an investigative piece (on public opinion or government policy making) for determining whether it wins one of the major prizes or awards?

	Number	Percentage
Very important	325	42.3%
Somewhat important	334	43.5%
Somewhat unimportant	71	9.3%
Very unimportant	38	4.9%
Total	768	100.0%

10. Rank from 1 to 5 in order of importance to *you* the rewards that sometimes result from doing "successful" investigative pieces.

a. Monetary (bonus or salary increase)

	Number	Percentage
Most important	20	2.6%
Second most important	41	5.2%
Third most important	135	17.4%
Fourth most important	202	26.0%
Least important	380	48.8%
Total	778	100.0%

b. Journalism awards or prizes

	Number	Percentage
Most important	33	4.0%
Second most important	106	12.9%
Third most important	212	25.8%
Fourth most important	267	32.4%
Least important	204	24.9%
Total	822	100.0%

c. Reformer in you satisfied

	Number	Percentage
Most important	481	56.1%
Second most important	190	22.2%
Third most important	84	9.8%
Fourth most important	52	6.1%
Least important	50	5.8%
Total	857	100.0%

d. Increased freedom over time or assignments

	Number	Percentage
Most important	157	19.3%
Second most important	281	34.5%
Third most important	171	21.0%
Fourth most important	97	11.9%
Least important	108	13.3%
Total	814	100.0%

e. Personal recognition

	Number	Percentage
Most important	108	12.9%
Second most important	198	23.7%
Third most important	252	30.2%
Fourth most important	157	18.8%
Least important	120	14.4%
Total	835	100.0%

11. Do you agree strongly, agree somewhat, disagree somewhat, or disagree strongly with each of the following statements?

a. The general public is becoming increasingly antagonistic toward investigative reporting.

	Number	Percentage
Agree strongly	99	11.0%
Agree somewhat	345	38.4%
Disagree somewhat	281	31.3%
Disagree strongly	173	19.3%
Total	898	100.0%

b. The general public is becoming increasingly indifferent toward investigative reporting.

	Number	Percentage
Agree strongly	106	11.9%
Agree somewhat	327	36.6%
Disagree somewhat	286	32.0%
Disagree strongly	174	19.5%
Total	893	100.0%

c. There is more investigative reporting being done today by television stations than newspapers.

	Number	Percentage
Agree strongly	35	4.0%
Agree somewhat	122	13.8%
Disagree somewhat	234	26.4%
Disagree strongly	494	55.8%
Total	882	100.0%

d. The news media's commitment to investigative reporting is as strong today as it was a year or two ago.

	Number	Percentage
Agree strongly	95	10.7%
Agree somewhat	311	34.9%
Disagree somewhat	298	33.5%
Disagree strongly	186	20.9%
Total	890	100.0%

*   *   *

FACT SHEET DATA

	Number	Percentage
Gender		
Male	301	67.5%
Female	145	32.5%
Total	446	100.0%
Race		
Caucasian	439	97.0%
Hispanic	4	0.8%
Native American	3	0.7%
Asian	3	0.7%
Black	4	0.8%
Total	453	100.0%
Age		
Mean	36.9 years	
Low	22 years	
High	68 years	
Total	442	

NOTE

1. These data are based on two waves of mailed survey interviews to members of Investigative Reporters and Editors (IRE), the largest national association of its kind. IRE provided us with mailing labels for 2,741 of its approximately 3,000 members, having excluded virtually all of the nonjournalists from its membership list. In July 1989, we mailed questionnaires to the 2,741 IRE members with a cover letter indicating the support of the IRE Board of Directors for our research project; 623 questionnaires were returned, for a response rate of 22.8 percent. In October 1989, we mailed a second round of questionnaires to IRE members. An additional 304 questionnaires were returned, for a total of 927 questionnaires or a response rate of 33.6 percent. The surveys included optional questions about personal background information, which explains the lower response rate for those questions. The surveys did not require IRE members to identify themselves by name or news organization. However, many did, providing the quotes used in chapter 10.

References

Abrams, F. (1981). "The Pentagon Papers: A Decade Later." *New York Times Magazine*.

Adler, R. (1986). *Reckless Disregard*. New York: Knopf.

Agee, W.K. (1968). *The Press and the Public Interest*. Washington, DC: Public Affairs Press.

Allen, F.L. (1931). *Only Yesterday*. New York: Harper & Row.

Altschull, H. (1977). "The Journalist and Instant History: An Example of the Jackal Syndrome." *Journalism Quarterly* 54:389–396.

American Society of Newspaper Editors. (1985). *Newspaper Credibility: Building Reader Trust*. Washington, D.C.: ASNE.

Anderson, D., and P. Benjaminson. (1976). *Investigative Reporting*. Bloomington: University of Indiana Press.

Anderson, J., and J. Boyd. (1979). *Confessions of a Muckraker*. New York: Random House.

Bagdikian, B.H. (1974). *The Effete Conspiracy*. New York: Harper & Row.

Bagdikian, B.H. (1983). *The Media Monopoly*. Boston: Beacon Press.

Banfield, E.C. (1961). *Political Influence*. New York: Free Press.

Barrett, J.R. "Introduction." In U. Sinclair. (1988). *The Jungle*. Urbana and Champaign: University of Illinois Press.

Bart, P., and P.H. O'Brien. (1985). *Stopping Rape: Successful Survival Strategies*. Elmsford, NY: Pergamon Press.

Bayley, E.R. (1981). *Joe McCarthy and the Press*. Madison: University of Wisconsin Press.

Berger, P., and T. Luckmann. (1967). *The Social Construction of Reality*. Garden City, NY: Anchor/Doubleday.

Bernstein, C., and B. Woodward. (1974). *All the President's Men*. New York: Warner Books.

Bezanson, R.P., G. Cranberg, and J. Soloski. (1987). *Libel Law and the Press: Myth and Reality*. New York: Free Press.

Blanchard, M.A. "Filling the Void: Speech and Press in State Courts Prior to *Gitlow*." In C.J. Brown and B.F. Chamberlin. (1982). *The First Amendment Reconsidered: New Perspectives on the Meaning of Freedom of Speech and the Press*. New York: Longman.

281

Bogart, L. (1989). *Press and Public.* Hillsdale, NJ: Lawrence Erlbaum.

Bok, S. (1978). *Lying: Moral Choice in Public and Private Life.* New York: Vintage Books.

Bok, S. (1984). *Secrets: On the Ethics of Concealment and Revelation.* New York: Pantheon.

Braestrup, P. (1977). *Big Story* (2 vols.). Boulder: Westview.

Broder, D. (1972). *The Party's Over.* New York: Harper & Row.

Burgess, A.W., and L.L. Holmstrom. (1974). *Rape: Victims of Crisis.* Bowie, MD: Brady.

Campbell, D.T., and J.C. Stanley. (1963). *Experimental and Quasi-Experimental Designs for Research.* Chicago: Rand McNally.

Christians, C.G. (1985–86). "Enforcing Media Codes." *Journal of Mass Media Ethics* 1:14.

Christians, C.P., K.B. Rotzoll, and M. Fackler (eds.). (1987). *Media Ethics.* New York: Longman.

Clark, P.B. (1974). "The Opinion Machine." In H.M. Clor. *The Mass Media and Modern Democracy.* Chicago: Rand McNally.

Cobb, R.W., and C.D. Elder. (1972). *Participation in American Politics: The Dynamics of Agenda-Building.* Baltimore: Johns Hopkins Press.

Cobb, R.W., and C.D. Elder. (1981). "Communications and Public Policy." In D. Nimmo and K. Sanders (eds.). *Handbook of Political Communications.* Beverly Hills: Sage.

Cobb, R.W., J.K. Ross, and M.H. Ross. (1976). "Agenda-building as a Comparative Political Process." *American Political Science Review* 70:127.

Cohen, B.C. (1963). *The Press and Foreign Policy.* Princeton, NJ: Princeton University Press.

Cohen, M., J. March, and J. Olsen. (1972). "A Garbage Can Model of Organizational Choice." *Administrative Science Quarterly* 17:1–25.

Cook, F.J. (1972). *The Muckrakers.* Garden City, NY: Doubleday.

Cook, F.L. (1981). "Crime and the Elderly: The Emergence of a Policy Issue." In D.A. Lewis (ed.). *Reactions to Crime.* Beverly Hills: Sage.

Cook, F.L., and W.G. Skogan. (1991). "Agenda-setting: Convergent and Divergent Voice Models and the Rise and Fall of Policy Issues." In M.E. McCombs and D.L. Protess (eds.). *Setting the Agenda: Readings on Media, Public Opinion, and Policymaking.* Hillsdale, NJ: Lawrence Erlbaum.

Cook, F.L., T. R. Tyler, E.G. Goetz, M.T. Gordon, D. L. Protess, and H.L. Molotch. (1983). "Media and Agenda-setting: Effects on the Public, Interest Group Leaders, Policy Makers and Policy." *Public Opinion Quarterly* 47:16–35.

Cook, T.D., and D.T. Campbell. (1979). *Quasi-Experimentation: Design and Analysis Issues for Field Settings.* Boston: Houghton Mifflin.

Crouse, T. (1976). *The Boys on the Bus.* New York: Ballantine.

Current, R.N., F. Freidel, and T.H. Williams. (1964). *American History.* New York: Knopf.

Dahl, R.A. (1956). *A Preface to Democratic Theory.* Chicago: University of Chicago Press.

de Sola Pool, I. (1973). "Newsmen and Statesmen: Adversaries or Cronies?" In M.J. Nyhan and W.L. Rivers. *Aspen Notebook on Government and the Media*. New York: Praeger.

Downie, L. (1976). *The New Muckrakers*. Washington, DC: New Republic Books.

Downs, A. (1957). *An Economic Theory of Democracy*. New York: Harper & Row.

Downs, A. (1972). "Up and Down with Ecology: The Issue Attention Cycle." *Public Interest* 28:38–50.

Editor and Publisher. (1984). "Is Investigative Reporting Dead?"

Elder, C.D., and R.W. Cobb. (1984). "Agenda-building and the Politics of Aging." *Policy Studies Journal* 13:115–129.

Emery, E., and M. Emery. (1984). *The Press and America: An Interpretative History of the Mass Media*. Englewood Cliffs, NJ: Prentice-Hall.

Entman, R.M. (1989). *Democracy without Citizens*. New York: Oxford.

Epstein, E. (1973). *News from Nowhere*. New York: Random House.

Ettema, J.S. (1988). *The Craft of the Investigative Journalist*. Evanston, IL: Institute for Modern Communications Research Monograph.

Ettema, J.S., and T.L. Glasser. (1988). "Narrative Form and Moral Force: The Realization of Innocence and Guilt through Investigative Journalism." *Journal of Communication* 38:8–26.

Ettema, J.S., D.L. Protess, D.R. Leff, P.V. Miller, J. Doppelt, and F.L. Cook. (1991). "Agenda-setting as Politics: A Case Study of the Press–Public-policy Connection." *Communication* 12:1–24.

Fedler, F. (1989). *Reporting for the Print Media*. New York: Harcourt, Brace, Jovanovich.

Fishman, M. (1978). "Crime Waves as Ideology." *Social Problems* 25:531–543.

Fishman, M. (1980). *Manufacturing the News*. Austin: University of Texas Press.

Gallup Organization. (1986). Times Mirror Investigation of Public Attitudes Toward the News Media. The People and the Press.

Gandy, O.H. (1982). *Beyond Agenda-Setting: Information Subsidies and Public Policy*. Norwood, NJ: Ablex.

Gans, H.J. (1979). *Deciding What's News*. New York: Pantheon.

Ginsberg, B. (1976). "Elections and Public Policy." *American Political Science Review* 70:41–49.

Ginsberg, B. (1986). *The Captive Public*. New York: Basic Books.

Gitlin, T. (1980). *The Whole World Is Watching*. Berkeley: University of California Press.

Glasser, T.L., and J.S. Ettema. (1989). "Investigative Journalism and the Moral Order." *Critical Studies in Mass Communication* 6:1–20.

Goldstein, T. (1985). *The News at Any Cost*. New York: Simon & Schuster.

Gordon, M.T., and S. Riger. (1989). *The Female Fear*. New York: Free Press.

Graber, D.A. (1984). *Mass Media and American Politics*. Washington, DC: Congressional Quarterly Press.

Greene, R.N. (1983). "Foreword." In Investigative Reporters and Editors. *The Reporter's Handbook*. New York: St. Martin's Press.

Greer, S. (1969). *The Logic of Social Inquiry*. Chicago: Aldine.

Grossman, M.B., and M.J. Kumar. (1981). *Portraying the President: The White House and the News Media*. Baltimore: Johns Hopkins Press.

Hallett, J.J. (1984). Issues Management Letter. Washington, DC: *Conference on Issues and Media*.

Herman, E.S., and N. Chomsky. (1988). *Manufacturing Consent: The Political Economy of the Mass Media*. New York: Pantheon.

Hewitt, D. (1985). *Minute by Minute . . .* New York: Random House.

Hofstadter, R. (1955). *The Age of Reform*. New York: Knopf.

Hofstadter, R. (1963). *The Progressive Movement*. Englewood Cliffs, NJ: Prentice-Hall.

Hohenberg, J. (1978). *The Professional Journalist*. New York: Holt, Rhinehart & Winston.

Hume, B. (1974). *Inside Story*. Garden City, NY: Doubleday.

Isaacs, N. E. (1986) *Untended Gates. The Mismanaged Press*. New York: Columbia University Press.

Joseph, J. (1974). *Political Corruption*. New York: Pocket Books.

Key, V.O., Jr. (1964). *Public Opinion and American Democracy*. New York: Knopf.

Kingdon, J.W. (1981). *Congressmen's Voting Decisions*. New York: Harper & Row.

Kingdon, J.W. (1984). *Agendas, Alternatives, and Public Policies*. Boston: Little, Brown.

Kreig, A. (1987). *Spiked*. Old Saybrook, CT: Peregrine Press.

Kutler, S. I. (1990). *The Wars of Watergate*. New York: Knopf.

Lang, G.E., and K. Lang. (1983). *The Battle for Public Opinion*. New York: Columbia University Press.

Lang, K., and G.E. Lang. (1973). "Televised Hearings: The Impact out There." *Columbia Journalism Review* 12:52–57.

Lasswell, H.A. (1941). *Democracy through Public Opinion*. Menasha, WI: Banta.

Lawler, P.F. (1984). *The Alternative Influence: The Impact of Investigative Reporting Groups on America's Media*. Lanham, MD: University Press of America.

Lee, A.M. (1973). *The Daily Newspaper in America*. New York: Octagon Books.

Leff, D.R., S.C. Brooks, and D.L. Protess. (1986). "Changing Public Attitudes and Policymaking Agendas: The Variable Effects of Crusading Journalism." *Public Opinion Quarterly* 50:300–314.

Leonard, T.C. (1986). *The Power of the Press: The Birth of American Political Reporting*. New York: Oxford University Press.

Lewis, A.H. (1905). "A Trust in Agricultural Implements." *Cosmopolitan*.

Linsky, M. (1983). *Television and the Presidential Elections*. Lexington, MA: Lexington Books.

Linsky, M. (1986). *Impact: How the Press Affects Federal Policymaking*. New York: W.W. Norton.

Lippmann, W. (1922). *Public Opinion*. New York: Harcourt Brace.

Lippmann, W. (1925). *The Phantom Public*. New York: Harcourt Brace.

Lipset, S.M., and W. Schneider. (1983). *The Confidence Gap: Business, Labor, and Government in the Public Mind*. New York: Free Press.

Lowi, T.J. (1976). "Gosnell's Chicago Revisited via Lindsay's New York." In S.M.

David and P.E. Peterson (eds.). *Urban Politics and Public Policy: The City in Crisis*. New York: Praeger.

Lyons, M. (1981). Testimony on home health care fraud and abuse, hearings before the Permanent Subcommittee on Investigations, Committee on Governmental Affairs, U.S. Senate. Washington, DC: Government Printing Office.

MacDougall, C.D. (1982). *Interpretative Reporting*. New York: Macmillan.

Malcolm, J. (1990). *The Journalist and the Murderer*. New York: Knopf.

Marimow, W.K. (1985). "Who Silenced the I-Team?" *Philadelphia Inquirer Magazine* April 14, pp. 22–30.

McClure, R.D., and T.E. Patterson. (1976). *The Unseeing Eye: The Myth of Television Power in National Elections*. New York: Putnam.

McCombs, M.E., and D.L. Shaw. (1972). "The Agenda-setting Function of the Mass Media." *Public Opinion Quarterly* 36:176–87.

McConnell, G. (1967). *Private Power and American Democracy*. New York: Knopf.

McGill, L. (1987). "Priorities in News Coverage and the Role of Beats in the Careers of U.S. Newspaper Editors." Unpublished doctoral dissertation, Northwestern University, Evanston.

Mencher, M. (1987). *News Reporting and Writing*. Dubuque, IA: William C. Brown.

Meyer, P. (1973). *Precision Journalism*. Bloomington: Indiana University Press.

Meyer, P. (1987). *Ethical Journalism*. New York: Longman.

Mitford, J. (1963). *The American Way of Death*. New York: Simon & Schuster.

Mitford, J. (1988). *Poison Penmanship: The Gentle Art of Muckraking*. New York: Noonday Press.

Mollenhoff, C.R. (1968). "Life Line of Democracy." In W.K. Agee (ed.). *The Press and the Public Interest*. Washington, DC: Public Affairs Press.

Mollenhoff, C.R. (1981). *Investigative Reporting*. New York: Macmillan.

Molotch, H., D.L. Protess, and M.T. Gordon. (1987). "The Media-Policy Connection: Ecologies of News." In D.L. Paletz (ed.). *Political Communication: Theories, Cases and Assessments*. Norwood, NJ: Ablex.

Mowry, G.E. (1958). *The Era of Theodore Roosevelt*. New York: Harper & Row.

Nelson, B.J. (1984). *Making an Issue of Child Abuse*. Chicago: University of Chicago Press.

Nimmo, D., and K. Sanders (eds.). (1981). *Handbook of Political Communication*. Beverly Hills: Sage Publications.

Noggle, B. (1962). *Teapot Dome*. New York: W.W. Norton.

O'Neill, M. (1963). "The Ebbing of the 'Great Investigative Wave.' " *ASNE Bulletin*.

O'Neill, M.J. (1983). *The Adversary Press*. St. Petersburg, FL: Modern Media Institute.

Page, B.I., and R.Y. Shapiro. (1983). "Effects of Public Opinion and Policy." *American Political Science Review* 77:175–190.

Paletz, D.L. (1987). *Political Communication: Theories, Cases and Assessments*. Norwood, NJ: Ablex.

Patner, A. (1988). *I.F. Stone: A Portrait*. New York: Anchor.

Patterson, T.E. (1980). *The Mass Media Election*. New York: Praeger.

Peck, A. (1985). *Uncovering the Sixties*. New York: Pantheon.

Persico, J.E. (1988). *Edward R. Murrow: An American Original*. New York: Dell.

Protess, D.L. (1984, Spring). "How Investigative Reporters See Themselves." *The IRE Journal*.

Protess, D.L. (1985). "Uncovering Rape: The Watchdog Press and the Limits of Agenda-setting." *Public Opinion Quarterly* 49:19–37.

Protess, D.L. (1986, Winter). "Investigative Reporters: Endangered Species?" *The IRE Journal*.

Protess, D.L., F.L. Cook, T.R. Curtin, M.T. Gordon, D.R. Leff, M.E. McCombs, and P. Miller. (1987). "The Impact of Investigative Reporting on Public Opinion and Policymaking: Targeting Toxic Waste." *Public Opinion Quarterly* 51:166–185.

Regier, C.C. (1931). *Era of the Muckrakers*. Chapel Hill: University of North Carolina Press.

Roberts, D.F., and C.M. Bachen. (1981). "Mass Communication Effects." *Annual Review of Psychology*. 32:307–356.

Rogers, E., and J. Dearing. (1988). "Agenda-setting Research: Where Has It Been, Where Is It Going?" In J. Anderson (ed.). *Communication Yearbook 11*. Newbury Park, CA: Sage.

Roshco, B. (1975). *Newsmaking*. Chicago: University of Chicago Press.

Salisbury, H. (1980). *Without Fear or Favor*. New York: Times Books.

Schattschneider, E.E. (1960). *The Semi-Sovereign People*. New York: Holt, Rinehart & Winston.

Schiller, D. (1981). *Objectivity and the News*. Philadelphia: University of Pennsylvania Press.

Schlesinger, A., Jr. (1957–60). *The Age of Roosevelt*. Boston: Houghton Mifflin.

Schudson, M. (1978). *Discovering the News*. New York: Basic Books.

Schumpeter, J.A. (1950). *Capitalism, Socialism, and Democracy*. New York: Harper & Row.

Schwarzlose, R.A. (1989). "The Marketplace of Ideas: A Measure of Free Expression." *Journalism Monographs* 118:20–27.

Siebert, F., T. Peterson, and W. Schramm. (1956). *Four Theories of the Press*. Urbana and Champaign: University of Illinois Press.

Sinclair, B.D. (1977). "Party Realignment and the Transformation of the Political Agenda." *American Political Science Review* 71:940–953.

Sinclair, U. (1906). "What Life Means to Me." *Cosmopolitan*.

Sinclair, U. (1946). *The Jungle*. Cambridge, MA: Robert Bentley.

Skogan, W.G., and A.C. Gordon. (1983). "Detective Division Reporting Practices: A Review of the Chicago Police Crime Classification Audit." *Crime in Illinois*, pp. 166–182.

Skogan, W.G., and M.G. Maxfield. (1981). *Coping with Crime: Victimization, Fear and Reactions to Crime in Three American Cities*. Beverly Hills: Sage Publications.

Smith, H. (1988). *The Power Game*. New York: Random House.

Smith, Z., and P. Zekman. (1979). *The Mirage*. New York: Random House.

Steffens, L. (1931). *The Autobiography of Lincoln Steffens*. New York: Harcourt, Brace.

Stone, I. F., and A. Miller. (1987). *The Haunted Fifties: Nineteen Fifty-Three to Sixty-Three*. New York: Little, Brown.

Tarbell, I.M. (1902). "History of the Standard Oil Company." *McClure's*.

Tarbell, I.M. (1910). "The Mysteries and Cruelties of the Tariff." *American Magazine* 70:735–743.

Tavoulareas, W.P. (1985). *Fighting Back*. New York: Simon & Schuster.

Tuchman, G. (1978). *Making News*. New York: Free Press.

Turow, J. (1985). "Cultural Augmentation through the Mass Media: A Framework for Organizational Research." *Communication* 8:139–164.

Ullmann, J. H. (1983). *The Reporter's Handbook: An Investigator's Guide to Documents and Techniques*. New York: St. Martin's Press.

United States Census Bureau. (1976). *Historical Statistics of the United States, Colonial Times to 1970*. Washington, DC: Government Printing Office.

Weinberg, A., and L. Weinberg. (1961). *The Muckrakers*. New York: Simon & Schuster.

Weinberg, S. (1981). *Trade Secrets of Washington Journalists*. Washington, D.C.: Acropolis Books.

White, G.J. (1979). *FDR and the Press*. Chicago: University of Chicago Press.

Whitehead, R. (1983, July/August). "Toe-to-toe in the Windy City." *Columbia Journalism Review*.

Wicker, T. (1978). *On Press*. New York: Viking Press.

Williams, P.N. (1978). *Investigative Reporting and Editing*. Englewood Cliffs, NJ: Prentice-Hall.

Winter, J.P., and C.H. Eyal. (1981). "Agenda-setting for the Civil Rights Issue." *Public Opinion Quarterly* 45:376–383.

Wolf, L. (1984). "Accuracy in Media Rewrites News and History." *Covert Action Information Bulletin*.

INDEXES

Name Index

Subject Index

Adversary journalism, 20–21
Advocacy journalism, 248–249
Agenda building, 4, 200, 231–254
  actors influencing, 241
  conditions for, 242
  convergent voice model of, 241
  definition, 6
  investigative
    conceptualization stage, 205, 211
    initiation stage, 205–207
    investigation stage, 205, 214–222
    investigative influence, 205
    presentation stage, 205, 223–227
  Kingdon's theory of, 241
  pace of, 239
  particularity of, 239
  priority of, 239
  and public policy, 238–249
Agenda setting, 6, 25, 165, 248
American Society of Newspaper Editors, 13–15, 20
  public survey on media obligations, 14–15
  statement of principles, 13–14

B

"Beating Justice," 212, 224, 237, 240, 245, 247
  awards received, 132
  conclusion, 132–133
  genesis of the probe, 119–123
  investigative influence, 126–132
  Mobilization Model, 133
  preparing the investigative report, 123–126
  WMAQ-TV investigative report on, 118–133

C

Coalition building, 163, 220–222
Coalition Journalism, 115, 185, 246

D

Democracy and the press, watchdog role of media, 29
"Dialysis: The Profit Machine," 208, 240, 247
  awards received, 199
  genesis of the probe, 179–182
  investigative influence, 191–200
  investigative process, 182–186
  Philadelphia Inquirer series, 176–200
  preparing the investigative report, 186–191

E

Economic Opportunity Act of 1964, 47
Exposés, 3–20
  1960s and 70s, 3
  characters in, 10–11
  journalist-generated, 206

297